1990

W9-ACQ-225

Doll Values

ANTIQUE TO MODERN

THIRD
EDITION

PATSY MOYER

COLLECTOR BOOKS
A Division of Schroeder Publishing Co., Inc.

The current values in this book should be used only as a guide. They are not intended to set prices, which vary from one section of the country to another. Auction prices, as well as dealer prices, vary greatly and are affected by availability, condition, and demand. Neither the Author nor the Publisher assumes responsibility for any losses that might be incurred as a result of consulting this guide.

Searching for a Publisher?

We are always looking for knowledgeable people considered experts within their fields. If you feel that there is a real need for a book on your collectible subject and have a large comprehensive collection, contact Collector Books.

On the Cover:

Top left: 16" all-cloth Kathe Kruse I, wide hips, all original, circa 1910, $3,500.00. Courtesy Sherryl Shirran.

Center left: 21½" Dornheim, Koch & Fischer Parian-type untinted bisque, elaborate blonde hairdo, floral decorations, painted eyes, molded necklace, nicely dressed, circa 1870s, $2,700.00. Courtesy Elizabeth Surber.

Bottom left: 14" composition Arranbee (R&B) Debu' Teen in original ski outfit with wooden skis and poles, hang tag, circa 1940, $475.00. Courtesy Peggy Millhouse.

Right: 22" pressed bisque, marked Jumeau with marked Jumeau body, original costume, including marked shoes, earmarks of both early Portraits and E.J.s, circa 1880s, $12,000.00. Courtesy Barbara DeFeo.

Cover by Beth Summers
Book design by Holly C. Long
Printed in the U.S.A. by Image Graphics, Inc., Paducah KY

Collector Books
P.O. Box 3009
Paducah, KY 42002-3009

Copyright ©1999 by Patsy Moyer

Credits

June Algeier, Cleveland Atkinson, Bonnie Baskins, Lee Ann Beaumont, Elaine Beling, Carol Bennett, Micki Beston, Dorothy Bohlin, Lilian Booth, Sue Ann Blott, Millie Busch, Teddy Callens, Rose Capriccio, Barbara Carol, Millie Carol, Dee Cermak, Cathie Clark, Carol Coffey, Martha Cramer, Patricia Christlieb, Debbie Crume, Helga Cunha, Diane Godfrey Daily, Debby L. Davis, Barbara DeFeo, Sally DeSmit, Marie Emmerson, Fran Fabian, Carol Fairchild, Darleen Foote, Jane Foster, Betty Jane Fronefield, Faye Newberry Gallagher, Sondra Gast, Cherie Gervais, Evelyn Gibson, Angie Gonzales, Mary Evelyn Graf, Odis Gregg, Irene Grundtvig, Debbie Hamilton, Amanda Hash, Georgia Henry, Janet Hill, Barbara Hilliker, Linda Holton, Jane Horst, Penny Hustler, Jennine Jacobs, Maxine Jackson, Diana Jenness, Chantal Jeschien, Delores L. Jesurun, Iva Mae Jones, Jeff Jones, Waneta Jost, Sue Kinkade, Rae Klenke, Karen Koch, Sharon Kolibaba, Nancy Laurenovics, Nancy Lazenby, Hazel Lester, Marguerite Long, C.K. Maher, Connie Lee Martin, Christine McWilliams, Jan Mealer, Ursula Mertz, Peggy Millhouse, Bev Mitchell, Arthur Mock, Marcie Montgomery, Joanne Morgan, Donna Nance, Margaret Obert, Dorisanne Osborn, Joyce Peters, Terry Peters, Marian Pettygrove, Penny Pittsley, Marilyn Ramsey, Nancy Rich, Marie Rodgers, Lori Rose, Jill Sanders, Evelyn Sears, Nelda Shelton, Sherryl Shirran, Catherine Shupe, Gay Smedes, Kathy & Roy Smith, Virginia Smith, Zelia Still, Elizabeth Surber, Linda Lee Sutton, Ruth Swalwell, Leslie Tannenbaum, Jean Thompson, Mia Tognacci, Ann Van Arnum, Kim Vitale, Paula Van Overloeke Voris, Jennifer Warren, Sheryl Wetenkamp, Louise Williams, Patricia Wright, Bette Yadon, and a very special thanks to Shari McMasters of McMasters Doll Auctions.

How to Use this Book

Welcome to the world of doll collecting. This book is designed to give you an overview of doll collecting, the doll market, and groups associated with it. You are encouraged to seek more knowledge to help you understand more about dolls so you can make wise decisions as you acquire your collection.

This book is divided into two sections, ANTIQUE and MODERN as general ways to separate dolls made of older materials like bisque, wax, cloth, and wood, and dolls made of newer materials such as composition, hard plastic, and vinyl. This immediately becomes confusing to the novice, because some of the composition modern dolls are as old as the bisque dolls in the antique section. We do this only to help the reader who can save time looking for older dolls in the front antique section and newer dolls in the back modern section. A new classification is emerging that refers to dolls made in the last 30 years as "collectible." In this book, collectible dolls are grouped with modern.

Many published references have been used for descriptions and marks. Every effort was made to check early advertising, where possible, but the main references are Johanna Anderton; John Axe; Dorothy, Jane, and Ann Coleman; Jurgen and Marianne Cieslik; Jan Foulke; Judith Izen; Pam and Polly Judd; and Patricia N. Schoonmaker. My thanks to these respected authorities and others who have contributed so much in research to collectors. A helpful bibliography is listed at the back of the book.

The dolls in each section are listed alphabetically by manufacturer or type, including a brief history, marks, description, and prices. Dolls are identified by the type of material used on the head — for example; if the head is hard plastic, the doll is referred to as hard plastic, even though the body may be of another material. They may be further classified as a category, such as Oriental, black, or souvenir dolls. Most black and brown dolls are grouped in the category Black. Souvenir dolls are dolls from special occasions, functions, or events, such as a special doll convention that may have a souvenir doll that all who attend receive. We have tried to use the general categories set forth in prior issues of this book, but have taken the liberty to add new categories or delete some of them. Your suggestions will be considered if enough data is available to research. We will continue to refine categories, descriptions, and data.

In addition to separating dolls generally into antique and modern sections, we have also **grouped them by manufacturer or type.** Modern manufacturers might be Alexander, Mattel, and Remco. Types are another way dolls can be grouped. Although Barbie is a Mattel doll, she has such a following that she has her own category. Another modern type category is artist dolls; this category is for dolls of any medium created for sale to the public, whether they are one-of-a-kind works of art or numbered limited editions. They reflect dolls that are not mass produced, but may be produced in numbers.

Where practical, we have also **classified dolls by material,** such as bisque, cloth, composition, hard plastic, porcelain, and vinyl. Look for all-cloth dolls except Lenci, Kathe Kruse, and Steiff under the category Cloth. For the novice collector, decide what material the head of your doll is, remembering that antique dolls are generally made of bisque, china, cloth, papier-mache, wax, or wood. Modern dolls may be made of composition, porcelain, hard plastic, vinyl, or some other material. Look for little known manufacturers in broad categories such as bisque, German, hard plastic, or vinyl.

Some of the things to consider in evaluating a doll are **quality, condition, rarity, originality, and desirability.** These can vary considerably as any two collectors may rate one or more of these attributes differently or two identical dolls can differ greatly with those same factors. All of these things are desirable factors to keep in mind. Since doll collectors mostly have limited budgets, it is smart buyers who familiarize themselves with as much knowledge about the subject as is available. This guide is a good starting place and is written with the novice as well as the more experienced collector in mind.

All dolls were not born equal. Dolls from the same mold can vary because of the conditions at the time of their manufacture. Successful production techniques developed over time; some of which arose only with the passage of time. Bisque dolls could be made with different grades of porcelain giving a range from fine to poor quality. Humidity and temperature could affect the production techniques of composition made up of various formulas of glue, wood pulp, sawdust, and other ingredients, causing their finish to later crack or peel. The formula used for some rubber and early plastic dolls caused them to turn darker colors or become sticky. The durability of the material did not show up immediately — only after the passage of time.

It is important for the collector to become aware of the many different factors that influence the manufacture, durability, popularity, and availability of a doll. Many influences can affect your decision to choose a particular doll to add to your collection. It takes time and effort before you can know the particular subtle differences in the exact same model of one doll, much less the endless variations and levels of differences that can exist in a particular era, category, or type of doll. This guide will serve as the starting point for your search for knowledge in the areas you choose to pursue.

Quality is an important consideration when purchasing a doll. Buy the best doll you can afford. Look at enough dolls so that you can tell the difference in a poorly finished or painted doll and one that has been artistically done. The head is the most important part of the doll. Signs of quality include good coloring; original clothing, wig, and body; and a pleasing appearance.

The condition of the doll is a very important factor in pricing a doll. A beautiful doll re-dressed, dirty, and missing a wig should not be priced as high as a beautiful doll with original clothing, a well-done wig, and clean and unrepaired body. Only consider composition dolls that have cracks, peeling paint, or lifting of paint *if* they have added incentives, such as wonderful coloring, original clothes, boxes, and tags. Try to find composition dolls without severe crazing, cracks, lifting, or peeling. Look for a smooth finish with rosy cheek color on the face as well as bright crisp clothing.

Originality is also important. Original clothing is an advantage on any doll, but especially if the clothing is in good condition. Also important is the correct body with the correct head and original wig on the doll. Patricia Schoonmaker once told me that we are only caretakers of our dolls for awhile — they then are passed on to someone else to care for. As some older dolls come on the market, they may be found on different bodies as they were acquired before the importance of originality became known and the ability to identify the correct body became available.

Rarity is another consideration in dolls. Many dolls were made by the thousands. Some dolls were not made in such quantity. If a doll was a quality, beautiful doll and not many were made, it may be more desirable and higher priced. Age can play a factor in pricing dolls, but not age alone. Modern dolls such as Shirley Temple dolls or Barbie dolls can out price some older antique dolls.

Desirability is another factor in choosing a doll. Some dolls may be rare, in original clothing, and still just not appeal to others. Beauty can be in the eye of the beholder; but some dolls are just not as appealing as others because they were poorly made or unattractive from the start. A well-made doll of quality is generally the one sought after, even in dirty, not original condition. A poorly made doll of inferior quality will always be a poorly made doll whether it is in top condition or cracked and damaged.

The pricing in this book is based on a number of factors including information from informed collectors, doll shows and sales, auctions, and doll-related publications. These factors have led us to build a database of actual sales. This database consists of records of over 12,000 dolls. You will see what actually is happening in the auction market place. Although any one auction's prices may vary widely; tracking the results over a period of time does reveal some consistency. The rarity and desirability of the same doll will fluctuate from area to area and with time. When a limited number of a certain doll are in the database, I have added the notation, "Too few in database for reliable range." I have arbitrarily set this figure at less than five dolls and the figure may change.

Demand sets the price. If a prosperous buyer has just won the lottery or has their own gold mine, the average buyer cannot compete with them. The good news is that these buyers usually cannot cover every collector, shop, or show that may have dolls for sale. The limited few that do have big bucks, cannot be everywhere at once. So the prudent may wish to back off, when the "high rollers" appear. Persons who have the ready cash have the right to spend it wherever they wish. If they want a particular doll and have the means to acquire it, more power to them. Many of these collectors share their dolls via museums, lectures, and exhibits, and that is wonderful. Extraordinary dolls may command higher prices because of all of the above factors.

So what price is too much to pay for a doll? That is a personal decision left entirely up to you and your bank account. The one great thing about collecting is that you are free to make your own choices of what you can afford and what you want to spend. You owe no explanation to others. You may, however, wish to arm yourself with knowledge if your funds are limited, so you can get the most for your money. In these days of fluctuating investment returns, many are turning to transportable assets in which to stash their cash. Dolls are one example.

Doll collecting need not be a short term intense pursuit. More often it becomes a long-term hobby of gathering things to love around you and good values as well. And after some years of loving enjoyment, one might look around and, in the process of collecting dolls, realize they have accumulated a solid investment as well — much as collecting fine art. A wise collector will document their collection so their estate will show the gains from their love and endeavors.

This guide makes no attempt to set price standards and should not be considered the final authority. It is simply meant to report prices realized in areas that can be tracked and reported. Every effort has been made to present an unbiased and impartial viewpoint to the collector of the results found in the areas researched. But remember, this is a compilation of data, and can only represent input from the various sources used. The goals are to bring together information from many sources to give the collector an additional viewpoint so that he/she can make his/her own personal choice. The collector has the final decision in buying or selling a doll; it is his/her decision alone.

The number of categories is immense and no one can be familiar with all of the changing and different areas. For this reason, I have consulted with a broad group of knowledgeable collectors who keep up to date with the sales market in their particular fields. Some of these collectors have agreed to provide their name and address as references in certain areas. These can be found in the Collectors' Network section at the back of the book. If you would like to become part of this network and are willing to share your knowledge with others in your particular field, please send your name, address, field of specialty, and references to the address listed. Please also include your e-mail or web site address, if you have one.

The more collectors share, the more we all gain from the experience. If you have questions, you may write the individual collectors listed. It is common courtesy to send a self-addressed stamped envelope if you wish to receive a reply to your question. If you would like to see other categories added to this guide, please drop us a line and tell us what your interests are. If possible, we will add categories when there is enough interest and data is available. We would like to hear from you.

The collector needs to be well informed to make proper judgment when spending his/her hard earned money in buying a doll. The more information he/she accumulates, the better able to make that judgment. Collectors can turn to a national organization whose goals are education, research, preservation, and enjoyment of dolls. The United Federation of Doll Clubs can tell you if a doll club in your area is accepting members or tell you how to become a member-at-large. You may write for more information at:

United Federation of Doll Clubs, Inc.
10920 North Ambassador Drive, Suite 130
Kansas City, MO 64153
UFDC has a web site: http://www.ufdc.org/

There are also many smaller groups that focus on particular dolls or on some aspect of doll collecting. A list of some of those groups and their interests is located in the Collectors' Network at the back of the book. You gain more knowledge, and the collecting experience is more enjoyable when you participate more with others.

Happy collecting!

Antique and Older Dolls

 21" felt Lenci Surprise Eye girl in Becassine-type costume, circa 1920 – 1930s, $2,400.00. *Courtesy Barbara DeFeo.*

 18" bisque Bebe Jumeau, closed mouth, paperweight eyes, pierced ears, marked "E 7 D" with spiral spring to attach head, tete face, produced by Emile Douiller director of Jumeau factory circa 1890, $4,500.00. *Courtesy Barbara DeFeo.*

19" poured bisque Jumeau socket head, paperweight eyes, pierced ears mohair wig, closed mouth, marked Tete Jumeau Paris on head, marked Jumeau, jointed composition body with straight wrists, nicely dressed, circa 1885+, $4,600.00. *Courtesy Elizabeth Surber.*

1888 – 1892, Paris. Bisque head, paperweight eyes, closed mouth with a white space between the lips, fat cheeks, and early French bodies with straight wrists.

First price indicates doll in good condition, but with flaws or nude; second price indicates doll in excellent condition, in original clothes, or appropriately dressed.

Marks:

16"	$4,200.00	$5,500.00
19"	$4,950.00	$6,500.00
21"	$5,300.00	$7,100.00

BEBE PHENIX

Alexandre was succeeded by Tourrel in 1892, in 1895, the Bebe Phenix trademark was used by Jules Steiner, who in 1899 was succeeded by Jules Mattais. Bisque head, closed mouth, paperweight eyes, pierced ears, composition body.

Child, closed mouth
Mold numbers:

81	10"	$1,375.00	$1,800.00
85	14"	$2,175.00	$2,900.00
88	17"	$2,925.00	$3,900.00
90	18"	$3,375.00	$4,500.00
91	20"	$3,900.00	$5,200.00
93	22"	$4,125.00	$5,500.00
95	24"	$4,275.00	$5,700.00

Child, open mouth

	17"	$1,350.00	$1,800.00
	19"	$1,575.00	$2,100.00
	22"	$1,800.00	$2,400.00
	25"	$2,000.00	$2,700.00

All-Bisque, French

Jointed neck, shoulders, hips; more delicate body with slender arms and legs, glass eyes, molded shoes or boots and stockings. Many all-bisque once thought to be of French manufacture are now believed to have been made in Germany expressly for the French market.

First price indicates doll in good condition, with some flaws, undressed; second price is for doll in excellent condition, with original or appropriate clothing. Allow more for original clothes and tags, less for chips or repairs.

Glass eyes, swivel head, molded shoes or boots

	4"	$450.00	$600.00
	6"	$525.00	$700.00
	8"	$825.00	$1,100.00

Bare feet

	4"	$1,000.00	$1,250.00
	6"	$1,500.00	$2,000.00
	9"	$3,375.00	$4,700.00

Too few in database for reliable range.

3½" all-bisque girl closed mouth, glass eyes, in pink and black lace dress, molded boots, long mohair wig, $275.00. Courtesy Marguerite Long.

Five-strap boots, glass eyes, swivel neck

6"	$1,500.00	$2,100.00

Painted eyes, swivel neck, blue boots, ethnic costumes

2½"	$125.00	$175.00
4"	$250.00	$350.00

Jointed elbows

6"	$2,000.00	$2,700.00

Jointed elbows and knees

5"	$2,250.00	$3,000.00

Too few in database for reliable range.

Marked E.D., F.G., or similar French makers

7"	$1,875.00	$2,500.00+

Marked S.F.B.J., Unis, or similar French makers

6"	$475.00	$625.00

All-Bisque, German

Many German firms made all-bisque dolls in smaller sizes from 1860 until 1930. Some were made by well-known firms such as Amberg; Alt, Beck & Gottschalck; Bahr & Proschild; Hertel Schwab & Co.; Kammer & Rheinhart; J.D. Kestner; Kling; Limbach; Bruno Schmidt; and Simon & Halbig, and may have corresponding mold marks. Some are only marked "Made in Germany" and/or may have a paper label. They are often marked inside arms and legs with matching mold numbers.

3½" all-bisque German dolls with molded painted shoes and socks, wire joints, mohair wigs, glass eyes, all original, circa 1890s, $300.00 each. Courtesy Debbie Crume.

First price indicates doll in good condition, with some flaws or nude; second price is for doll in excellent condition, original clothes, or well dressed. More for labels, less for chips and repairs.

For All-Bisque, Black or Brown, See Black or Brown Section.

BABIES, CA. 1900+

Rigid neck (molded to torso), jointed shoulders and hips only, bent limbs, painted hair

Glass eyes

5"	$250.00	$350.00
7"	$325.00	$425.00

Painted eyes

4"	$65.00	$85.00
6"	$150.00	$200.00

Swivel necks (socket neck), jointed shoulders and hips, wigs or painted hair

Glass eyes

4"	$150.00	$275.00
6"	$275.00	$450.00
8"	$425.00	$575.00

Four all-bisque, from left: 4" Bye-Lo, designed by Grace S. Putnam, circa 1923+, $275.00; 7" Bonnie Babe, $475.00; 6" Bonnie Babe, $800.00; and 6" Bonnie Babe, designed by Geor-gene Averill for Borgfeldt, circa 1926+. $575.00. Courtesy Connie Lee Martin.

Painted eyes

4"	$125.00	$175.00
6"	$225.00	$300.00
8"	$175.00	$350.00

Babies with Character Face, ca. 1910+

Jointed shoulders and hips, molded hair

Glass eyes

5"	$325.00	$450.00
7"	$400.00	$525.00

Painted eyes

5"	$165.00	$225.00
7"	$225.00	$300.00

Swivel neck, glass eyes

5"	$375.00	$500.00
9"	$750.00	$1,000.00

Swivel neck, painted eyes

5"	$250.00	$325.00
7"	$350.00	$450.00
9"	$550.00	$750.00

Mold 830, 833, and others

7"	$375.00	$500.00
9"	$750.00	$1,000.00

Baby Bo Kaye, mold 1394

Designed by Kallus, distributed by Borgfeldt

5"	$850.00	$1,125.00
7"	$1,050.00	$1,425.00

Baby Bud, glass eyes, wig

6 – 7"	$975.00	$1,300.00

Baby Darling, mold 497, Kestner, 178
One-piece body, painted eyes

6"	$400.00	$500.00
8"	$475.00	$625.00
10"	$635.00	$825.00

Swivel neck, glass eyes, more for toddler body

6"	$450.00	$600.00
8"	$625.00	$825.00

Baby Peggy Montgomery
Made by Louis Amberg, paper label, pink bisque with molded hair, painted brown eyes, closed mouth, jointed at shoulder and hips, molded and painted shoes/socks

3½"	$225.00	$400.00
5½"	$450.00	$600.00

Bonnie Babe, 1926+, designed by Georgene Averill
Glass eyes, swivel neck, wig, jointed arms and legs

4½"	$500.00	$650.00
8"	$750.00	$1,000.00

Molded-on clothes, dome head, swivel neck, jointed arms and legs

5"	$400.00	$600.00
6"	$600.00	$775.00

Immobiles, one-piece, in various poses

3"	$175.00	$350.00

Mildred (The Prize Baby), mold 880, ca. 1914+
Made for Borgfeldt; molded, short painted hair; glass eyes; closed mouth; jointed at neck, shoulders, and hips; round paper label on chest; molded and painted footwear

5"	$950.00	$1,250.00
7"	$900.00	$1,800.00

Tynie Baby, made for E.I. Horsman
Glass eyes

5"	$525.00	$725.00
8"	$950.00	$1,250.00

Painted eyes

5"	$350.00	$475.00

Pink Bisque Candy Baby, ca. 1920+
May be German or Japanese, lesser quality paint finish, given away with purchase of candy

3½"	$25.00	$35.00
6"	$35.00	$45.00

Mold 231 (A.M.), toddler, swivel neck, with glass eyes

9"	$1,025.00	$1,400.00

Mold 369, 372

7"	$545.00	$725.00
9"	$875.00	$1,100.00
11"	$1050.00	$1,400.00+

CHILDREN

All-Bisque Child, Rigid Neck, Glass Eyes, 1890+
Head molded to torso, sometimes legs also, excellent bisque, open/closed mouth, sleep or set eyes, good wig, nicely dressed, molded one-strap shoes.

Allow more for unusual footwear such as yellow multi-strap boots.

3"	$135.00	$250.00
5"	$165.00	$285.00
7"	$250.00	$400.00
9"	$475.00	$650.00

Bent knees

| 6" | $145.00 | $285.00 |

Mold 100, 125, 150, 225 (preceded by 83/)

Rigid neck, fat tummy, jointed shoulders and hips, glass sleep eyes, open/closed mouth, molded black one-strap shoes with tan soles, white molded stockings with blue band. Similarly molded dolls, imported in 1950s by Kimport, have synthetic hair, lesser quality bisque. Add more for original clothing.

Mold number appears as a fraction, with the following size numbers under 83; Mold "83/100," "83/125," "83/150," or "83/225." One marked "83/100" has a green label on torso reading, "Princess//Made in Germany."

100	5¾"	$225.00	$325.00
125	6¾"	$275.00	$350.00
150	7½"	$325.00	$425.00
225	8¼"	$350.00	$475.00

6" all-bisque Kestner #103, glass eyes, closed mouth, mohair wig, wearing yellow boots, circa 1890s, $400.00. Courtesy Terry Peters.

Mold 130, 150, 168, 184, 257, 602, 790 (Bonn or Kestner)

Painted blue or pink stockings, one-strap black shoes

4"	$150.00	$295.00
6"	$200.00	$385.00
7"	$215.00	$425.00
8"	$250.00	$500.00
9"	$300.00	$675.00
10"	$375.00	$750.00
11"	$450.00	$900.00

Mold 155, 156 (smile)

| 6" | $225.00 | $450.00 |

Swivel neck

| 5½" | $300.00 | $600.00 |
| 7" | $165.00 | $325.00 |

All-Bisque Child, Glass Eyes, Swivel Neck, ca. 1880+

Pegged or wired joints, open or closed mouth, molded-on shoes or boots and stockings. Allow more for unusual footwear such as yellow or multi-strap boots.

3"	$175.00	$300.00
4"	$200.00	$350.00
5½"	$350.00	$525.00
7"	$375.00	$675.00
8"	$600.00	$800.00

10½" all-bisque Kestner mold 150, open mouth dolly face, stiff neck, sleep eyes, mohair wig, painted and molded stocking and shoes, circa 1897, $875.00. Courtesy McMasters Doll Auctions.

6" all-bisque Kestner Wrestler-type, painted eyes, wearing black booties, circa 1890s, $400.00. Courtesy Terry Peters.

7½" all-bisque child, stiff neck, painted blue eyes, closed mouth, molded and painted blonde hair, molded clothing, socks and shoes, jointed at shoulders and hips, circa 1890+, $100.00. Courtesy McMasters Doll Auctions.

9"	$675.00	$900.00
10"	$975.00	$1,300.00

Mold 130, 150, 160, 208, 602 (Kestner)

4"	$250.00	$500.00
6"	$300.00	$600.00
8"	$450.00	$900.00
10"	$650.00	$1,300.00

Mold 184 (Kestner)

4 – 5"	$350.00	$700.00
8"	$800.00	$1,600.00

Simon & Halbig or Kestner types

Closed mouth, excellent quality

5"	$400.00	$775.00
6"	$600.00	$1,150.00
8"	$975.00	$1,900.00

Jointed knees

6"	$1,500.00	$3,000.00

Original factory box with clothes/accessories

5"	$1,750.00	$3,500.00

Bare feet

5"	$1,350.00	$1,800.00
7½"	$1,950.00	$2,600.00

Early round face

6"	$525.00	$900.00
8"	$900.00	$1,300.00

Mold 881, 886, 890 (Simon & Halbig)

Painted high-top boots with four or five straps

4½"	$600.00	$800.00
7½"	$1,200.00	$1,600.00
9½"	$1,500.00	$2,100.00

Long stockings, above knees

4½"	$325.00	$650.00
6"	$450.00	$900.00

Mold 102, Wrestler (so called)

Fat thighs, arm bent at elbow, open mouth (can have two rows of teeth) or closed mouth, stocky body, glass eyes, socket head, individual fingers or molded fist

6"	$900.00	$1,250.00
8"	$1,250.00	$1,650.00
9"	$1,600.00	$2,150.00

All-Bisque Child with Molded Clothes, ca. 1890+

Jointed at shoulders only or at shoulders and hips, painted eyes, molded hair, molded shoes or bare feet, excellent workmanship, no breaks, chips, or rubs

4½"	$75.00	$150.00
6"	$150.00	$300.00

Lesser quality

3"	$45.00	$85.00
4"	$50.00	$100.00
6"	$70.00	$140.00

Molded on hat or bonnet
In perfect condition

5 – 6½"	$190.00	$365.00+
8 – 9"	$250.00	$500.00+

Stone (porous) Bisque

4 – 5"	$70.00	$135.00
6 – 7"	$85.00	$165.00

All-Bisque Child with Painted Eyes, ca. 1880+

Head molded to torso, molded hair or wig, open or closed mouth, painted-on shoes and socks, dressed or undressed, all in good condition. Allow more for unusual footwear such as yellow boots.

2"	$45.00	$85.00
4½"	$100.00	$185.00
6½"	$125.00	$250.00
8"	$175.00	$350.00

Black stockings, tan slippers

6"	$275.00	$400.00

Ribbed hose

4½"	$150.00	$200.00
6"	$275.00	$375.00
8"	$425.00	$575.00

Molded hair

4"	$90.00	$175.00
6½"	$175.00	$350.00

Early very round face

7"	$1,200.00	$2,300.00

Mold 130, 150, 160, 168, 184, 208, 602 (Kestner)

5"	$115.00	$225.00
6"	$150.00	$275.00
7"	$170.00	$325.00
8"	$200.00	$400.00
9"	$275.00	$550.00
10½"	$415.00	$825.00
12"	$600.00	$1,200.00

All-Bisque with Slender Bodies, ca. 1880+

Slender dolls with head molded to torso, usual wire or peg-jointed shoulders and hips. Allow much more for original clothes. May be in regional costumes. Add more for unusual color boots, such as gold, yellow, or orange, all in good condition.

Glass eyes, open or closed mouth

4"	$200.00	$285.00
5 – 6"	$250.00	$350.00

Swivel neck, closed mouth

4"	$275.00	$375.00
5 – 6"	$350.00	$500.00
8½"	$600.00	$900.00
10"	$900.00	$1,300.00

4" Gebruder Heubach all-bisque, painted eyes, blue slippers, white socks with blue trim, circa 1910+, $450.00. Courtesy Amanda Hash.

8½" all-bisque Gebruder Kuhnlenz, orange boots, black tassels, kid-lined joints, $600.00. Courtesy McMasters Doll Auctions.

4½" all-bisque action baby (immobiles, no joints) with painted molded features and molded shoes, circa 1920s – 1930s, $125.00. Courtesy Marguerite Long.

4½" all-bisque Amberg Mibs, painted blue eyes, closed mouth, painted molded hair, all pink bisque body, jointed at shoulders, painted molded socks and shoes, original green dress, circa 1921, $300.00. Courtesy McMasters Doll Auctions.

Bent at knees

6"	$100.00	$200.00

Jointed knees and/or elbows with swivel waist

6"	$1,000.00	$1,950.00
8"	$1,600.00	$3,200.00

Swivel waist only

6"	$1,000.00	$2,000.00

Painted eyes, swivel neck, open or closed mouth, painted one-strap shoes

4"	$100.00	$200.00
6"	$175.00	$350.00
8"	$250.00	$475.00
10"	$350.00	$675.00

All-Bisque Child with Character Face, ca. 1910+

Campbell Kids, molded clothes, Dutch bob

5"	$125.00	$245.00

Chin-chin

Gebruder Heubach, ca. 1919, jointed arms only, triangular label on chest

4"	$225.00	$300.00

Jeanne Orsini

Designed by Orsini for Borgfelt, produced by Alt, Beck & Gottschalck; Chi Chi, Didi, Fifi, Mimi, Vivi, ca. 1919+

Glass eyes

5"	$975.00	$1,300.00

Painted eyes

5"	$675.00	$925.00

Mibs, all-bisque, ca. 1921

Molded blonde hair, molded/painted socks and shoes, pink bisque, jointed at shoulders, legs molded to body

Mark: "C./ L.A. & S. 1921/GERMANY"

3"	$185.00	$250.00
5"	$375.00	$425.00

All-Bisque Child with Flapper Body, ca. 1920+

One-piece body and head with thin limbs, fired-in fine bisque, wig, painted eyes, painted-on long stockings, one-strap painted shoes

5"	$225.00	$300.00
7"	$325.00	$450.00

Molded hair

6"	$250.00	$350.00
8"	$325.00	$450.00

Pink Bisque

Wire joints, molded hair, painted eyes

4"	$40.00	$75.00

Molded hat

4"	$185.00	$250.00

All-bisque German Nodders. Left to right: 3¾" Moon Mullins, $235.00; 3¼" Auntie Blossom, $175.00; Solhess 3¾" Rudy Hebb, $225.00; 3¾" Fanny Hebb, $185.00; circa 1920s. Courtesy Nancy Laurenovics.

Aviatrix			
	5"	$175.00	$250.00
Swivel waist			
	4½"	$300.00	$400.00
Molded cap with rabbit ears			
	4½"	$275.00	$400.00

ALL-BISQUE IMMOBILES, figures with no joints

Child	3"	$25.00	$50.00
Adults	5"	$75.00	$165.00
Santa	4"	$70.00	$140.00
Child with animal on string			
	4"	$75.00	$165.00

ALL-BISQUE NODDERS, CA. 1920

When their heads are touched, they "nod," molded clothes, made both in Germany and Japan, decoration not fired in so wears off easily, all in good condition.

Animals, cat, dog, rabbit			
	3 – 5"	$35.00	$75.00
Child/Adult, made in Germany			
	4 – 6"	$35.00	$150.00
Child/Adult with molded-on clothes			
	4"	$65.00	$135.00
Child/Adult comic characters			
	3 – 5"	$65.00	$250.00
Child/Adult, sitting position			
	5"	$70.00	$140.00
Santa Claus or Indian			
	6"	$145.00	$180.00
Teddy Bear			
	5"	$85.00	$170.00
Japan/Nippon			
	3½"	$10.00	$25.00
	4½"	$20.00	$45.00

ALL-BISQUE FIGURES, PAINTED

Top layer of paint not fired on and the color can be washed off, usually one-piece figurines with molded hair, painted features, including clothes, shoes, and socks. Some have molded hats.

First price indicates with paint chips, second price is good condition with no paint chips, can be German or Japanese.

Baby, German

3½"	$35.00	$50.00
5"	$40.00	$60.00

Baby, Japanese

3"	$9.00	$15.00
5"	$15.00	$25.00

Child, German

3"	$20.00	$30.00
5"	$45.00	$65.00

Child, Japanese

3"	$7.50	$15.00
5"	$15.00	$25.00

All-Bisque, Japanese

Made by various Japanese companies. Quality varies greatly. They are jointed at shoulders and may also be jointed at hips. Good quality bisque is well painted with no chips or breaks.

The first price indicates poorer quality, flaking paint, flaws; second price indicates good quality, nicely finished.

BABY, WITH BENT LIMBS

May or may not be jointed at hips and shoulders, very nice quality

3"	$20.00	$30.00
5"	$35.00	$70.00

Bye-Lo Baby-type, fine quality

3½"	$45.00	$85.00
5"	$70.00	$140.00

Medium to poor quality

2½"	$4.00	$7.50
6"	$23.00	$50.00

Betty Boop

Bobbed hair style, large eyes painted to side, head molded to torso

4"	$20.00	$45.00
6"	$35.00	$65.00

CHILDREN

Child with molded clothes

4½"	$23.00	$35.00
6"	$35.00	$50.00

5" painted all-bisque Indian pair, marked "Made in Japan" circa 1920s, few flakes of paint missing, $45.00 each. Courtesy Marguerite Long.

Child, ca. 1920s – 1930s

Pink or painted bisque with painted features, jointed at shoulders and hips, has molded hair or wig, excellent condition

3"	$7.50	$15.00
4"	$15.00	$35.00

Skippy

6"	$55.00	$135.00

Snow White

5"	$55.00	$110.00

Boxed with Dwarfs

	$325.00	$650.00

Three Bears/Goldilocks, boxed set

	$165.00	$325.00+

Nippon mark

3½"	$18.00	$30.00
5"	$28.00	$50.00

Occupied Japan mark

4"	$13.00	$35.00
5"	$18.00	$40.00
7"	$25.00	$55.00

4" Japanese all-bisque Bride and Groom wedding topper from owners' parents' 1930 wedding cake, all original groom wears silk top hat, painted features, molded hair, jointed arms only, $100.00 for pair. Courtesy Sue Ann Blott.

Alt, Beck & Gottschalck

Established as a porcelain factory in 1854 at Nauendorf, Thuringia, Germany, the Ciesliks report the company exported doll heads to the USA by 1882. They made heads in both china and bisque for other companies such as Bergmann, using Wagner and Zetzsche kid bodies. The Colemans report mold numbers from 639 to 1288.

Mark:

1352

First price indicates doll in good condition, with some flaws, or nude; second price is for doll in excellent condition, original clothes or appropriately dressed.

BABIES, CA. 1920+

Open mouth, some have pierced nostrils, bent-leg baby body, wigs, more for toddler body or flirty eyes

11"	$275.00	$365.00
15"	$350.00	$475.00
20"	$575.00	$775.00
24"	$850.00	$1,150.00

Character Baby, ca. 1910+

Socket head on jointed composition body, glass or painted eyes, open mouth, nicely dressed with good wig or molded hair

Mold 1322, 1342, 1346, 1352, 1361

12"	$325.00	$425.00
16"	$425.00	$600.00
19"	$500.00	$675.00
24"	$725.00	$975.00

CHILD, ALL-BISQUE: See All-Bisque Section.

21½" Alt Beck & Gottschalck mold 1214, china shoulder head, heavily painted molded hair, cloth body, china lower arms and legs, nicely dressed, circa 1890+, $325.00. Courtesy McMasters Doll Auctions.

CHILD, BISQUE

Mold 630, glass eyes, closed mouth, ca. 1880

22"	$1,800.00	$2,400.00

Open mouth

9"	$575.00	$775 00

Mold 911, swivel head, closed mouth, ca. 1890+

Mold 915, shoulder head, closed mouth, ca. 1890

22"	$1,975.00	$2,650.00

Character Child, ca., 1921+

Mold 1357, solid dome or wigged, painted eyes, open mouth; **Mold 1358,** molded hair, ribbon, flowers, painted eyes, open mouth

15"	$750.00	$975.00
20"	$1,250.00	$1,700.00

Mold 1322, 1342, 1352, 1361, glass eyes

12"	$325.00	$425.00
14"	$375.00	$500.00
18"	$500.00	$650.00

Mold 1362, Sweet Nell, ca. 1912, more for flapper body

16"	$510.00	$675.00
24"	$735.00	$975.00
28"	$900.00	$1,200.00

Mold 1367, 1368, ca. 1914

15"	$355.00	$475.00

SHOULDER HEADS, BISQUE, CA. 1880+

Mold 639, 698, 784, 870, 890, 911, 912, 916, 990, 1000, 1008, 1028, 1032, 1044, 1046, 1064, 1123, 1127, 1142, 1210, 1234, 1235, 1254, 1304, cloth or kid body, bisque lower limbs, molded hair or wig, no damage and nicely dressed. Allow more for molded hat or fancy hairdo.

> *Mark:*
> 1000 # 10

Glass eyes, closed mouth

12"	$600.00	$850.00
16"	$750.00	$1,000.00
18"	$1,125.00	$1,500.00
22"	$1,350.00	$1,800.00

Painted eyes, closed mouth

14"	$300.00	$385.00
20"	$525.00	$700.00

Turned Bisque Shoulder Heads, 1885+

Bald head or plaster pate, kid body, bisque lower arms, all in good condition, nicely dressed. Dolls marked "DEP" or "Germany" after 1888. Some have Wagner & Zetzsche marked on head, paper label inside top of body. Allow more for molded bonnet or elaborate hairdo.

19½" bisque Alt, Beck & Gottschalck lady, mold 698, set blue eyes, closed mouth, original mohair wig, cloth body, well defined waist, kid lower arms, stitched fingers, circa 1880, $335.00. Courtesy McMasters Doll Auctions.

Glass eyes, closed mouth

15"	$600.00	$800.00
18"	$750.00	$1,000.00

Painted eyes, closed mouth

15"	$300.00	$400.00
18"	$375.00	$500.00
22"	$490.00	$650.00

SHOULDER HEADS, CHINA, CA. 1880+

Mold 784, 786, 880, 882, 1000, 1003, 1008, 1028, 1046, 1112, 1142, 1144, 1210, 1214, blonde- or black-haired china heads, cloth body, china limbs, nicely dressed, all in good condition.

15"	$275.00	$365.00
19"	$318.00	$425.00
23"	$395.00	$525.00
28"	$475.00	$625.00

Amberg, Louis & Sons

Ca. 1878 – 1930, Cincinnati, Ohio; from 1898 on, New York City. Used other name before 1907. Imported dolls made by other firms. First company to manufacture all American-made dolls of composition.

BISQUE

Baby Peggy, ca. 1924

Bisque socket head, sleep eyes, closed mouth, original wig with bangs, dimples, composition or kid body with bisque lower arms

Mold 972 (solemn socket head), Mold 973 (smiling socket head)

17"	$1,725.00	$2,300.00
22"	$1,995.00	$2,650.00

Mold 982 (solemn shoulder head), Mold 983 (smiling shoulder head)

17"	$1,800.00	$2,400.00
22"	$2,100.00	$2,800.00

BABY PEGGY, ALL-BISQUE, see All-Bisque section.
MIBS, ALL-BISQUE, 1921, see All-Bisque section.

Newborn Babe, ca. 1914, reissued 1924

Bisque head with cloth body; either celluloid, composition, or rubber hands; lightly painted hair; sleep eyes; closed mouth with protruding upper lip

8"	$275.00	$365.00
11"	$325.00	$425.00
14"	$375.00	$500.00
18"	$655.00	$825.00

Open mouth, marked *"L.A.& S. 371"*

10"	$300.00	$400.00
15"	$340.00	$450.00

Baby Peggy Mark:
"19 ©. 24//LA & S NY// GERMANY"

Newborn Babe Marks:
"L.A.&S. 1914/G45520 GERMANY, L. AMBERG AND SON/7886" or "COPYRIGHT By LOUIS AMBERG"

Body Twist Tag attached to clothes reads: "AN AMBERG DOLL/ BODY TWIST/PAT. PEND. #32018."

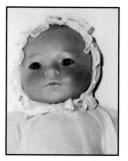

12" bisque Louis Amberg & Sons baby with solid dome head, cloth body, celluloid hands, original dress, ca. 1914, $425.00. Courtesy Gay Smedes.

13½" composition Amberg Edwina marked "Amberg/ /Pat. Pend.//LA&S C. 1928," in old dress, painted molded hair, swivel waist, painted eyes, circa 1928, $375.00. Courtesy Dorothy Bohlin.

Vanta Baby, ca. 1927 – 1930

Bisque head, sleep eyes, crier, bent-limb body, in sizes from 10" to 25", distributed by Sears with advertising promotion for Vanta baby garments

Glass eyes, open mouth

18"	$825.00	$1,100.00
24"	$1,275.00	$1,700.00

Closed mouth

18"	$1,050.00	$1,400.00
24"	$1,500.00	$2,000.00

COMPOSITION

First price is for doll in good condition, but with flaws, crazing, or nude; second price is for doll in excellent condition, may have light crazing, original or appropriate clothing.

Baby Peggy, ca. 1923

Portrait doll of child actress, Peggy Jean Montgomery; composition head, arms, and legs; cloth body; molded brown bobbed hair; painted eyes with molded lower eyelids; closed mouth. More for boxed, mint.

15"	$85.00	$365.00
18"	$125.00	$500.00
20"	$200.00	$775.00

Body Twists (Teenie Weenies, Tiny Tots), ca. 1929

All-composition with swivel waist made with ball attached to torso, boy or girl with molded hair and painted features

7½" – 8½"	$50.00	$200.00

Charlie Chaplin, ca. 1915

Composition portrait head, painted features, composition hands, cloth body and legs

14"	$175.00	$650.00

Edwina (Sue or It), ca. 1928

All-composition with painted features, molded hair with side part and swirl bang across forehead, body twist (waist swivels on ball attached to torso)

14"	$125.00	$475.00

Happinus, 1918+

Coquette-type, all-composition with head and body molded in one-piece, jointed shoulders and hips, painted molded brown hair, molded ribbon, closed mouth, painted features, unmarked, well modeled torso, original clothes

10"	$75.00	$300.00

Mibs, ca. 1921

Composition turned shoulder head designed by Hazel Drukker, painted molded hair, painted eyes,

Charlie Chaplin Mark:
Black suit, white suit, cloth label on sleeve or inside seam of coat that reads: CHARLIE CHAPLIN DOLL// World's Greatest Comedian// Made exclusively by Louis Amberg//&Son, NY//by Special Arrangement with//Essamay Film Co.

Edwina Sue Mark:
AMBERG
PAT. PEN.
L.A. & S.

Mibs Mark:
Original dress has ribbon label that reads:
"L.A.&S.//Amberg Dolls//The World Standard//Created by//Hazel Drukker//Please Love Me//I'm MIBS."

Sunny Orange Maid Mark on head:
"A.//L.A. & S.//1924."
Label on dress reads:
"SUNNY ORANGE MAID."

closed mouth. Two different body styles: cork-stuffed cloth, composition arms and legs with molded shoes, painted socks; and a barefoot swing-leg mama-type cloth body with crier.

| 16" | $225.00 | $900.00 |

Sunny Orange Maid, 1924

For a photo of Sunny Orange Maid, see 1997 edition.

Composition shoulder plate, cloth body, composition arms and legs, molded orange cap

| 14½" | $400.00 | $1,200.00 |

Vanta Baby, ca. 1927 – 1930

Composition head, sleep eyes, crier, bent-limb body, in sizes from 10" to 25", distributed by Sears with advertising promotion for Vanta baby garments

| 18" | $75.00 | $275.00 |
| 23" | $100.00 | $400.00 |

Arnold, Max Oscar

Ca. 1878 – 1925, Neustadt, Thuringia. Made jointed dressed dolls and mechanical dolls including phonograph dolls.

BABY, BISQUE HEAD

12"	$125.00	$165.00
16"	$215.00	$285.00
19"	$375.00	$500.00

CHILD, MOLD 150, 200, OR JUST "M.O.A."

Excellent bisque

12"	$190.00	$250.00
15"	$265.00	$350.00
21"	$450.00	$600.00
32"	$1,150.00*	

Poor to medium quality bisque

15"	$125.00	$165.00
20"	$200.00	$300.00
24"	$340.00	$450.00

Mark:

30" bisque Max Oscar Arnold girl child, dolly face, open mouth, glass eyes, mohair wig, wood and composition body, circa 1920, $1,000.00. Private collection.

Automatons

Various manufacturers used many different mediums including bisque, wood, wax, cloth, and others to make dolls that performed some action. More complicated models performing more or complex actions bring higher prices. The unusual one-of-a-kind dolls in this category make it difficult to provide a good range. *All these auction prices are for mechanicals in good working order.

Autoperipatetikos, circa 1860 – 1870s

Bisque by American Enoch Rice Morrison, key wound mechanism

| 12" | $1,000.00* |

* at auction

10" bisque Unis France mechanical child seated on a rocking chair. When wound, chair rocks, circa 1916 – 1930, $700.00. Courtesy McMasters Doll Auctions.

Babies with phone, circa 1845 – 1926
Germany, bisque baby in each of two rooms, move head, lift receiver to talk, multiple movements, by Zinner, Gottlieb & Sohne
12" $2,400.00*

Fruitseller, circa 1862 – 1900
Paris, papier-mache figure, multiple intricate movements, by Vichy
26" $21,500.00*

Girl with fan and flowers, circa 1894+
Bisque, Simon & Halbig mold 1159, costume dusty, frail, plays tune, multiple movements, by Leopold Lambert
18" $3,800.00*

Girl with basket of flowers, circa 1885+
Bisque, marked Tete Jumeau, multiple movements, by Leopold Lambert
17" $5,250.00*

Girl with watch and handkerchief, circa 1885+
Bisque, Tete Jumeau, turns head looks at watch, raises handkerchief to face, by Leopold Lambert
18" $4,250.00*

Lady with fan and watch, circa 1890s
Bisque, Simon and Halbig head, replaced costume of vintage fabric, multiple movements, by Leopold Lambert
22" $4,000.00*

Lyre player, circa 1862 – 1900
Paris, papier-mache figure, intricate multiple movements, eyelids keep time to music, Vichy
25" $11,000.00*

Piglet with harp, circa 1865 – 1930
Paris, multiple movements, kid over papier-mache, by Roullet & Decamps
14" $4,200.00*

Seated lady with mandolin, 1880 – 1900
Bisque, Jumeau, damage to arms, costume part original, multiple movements, by Leopold Lambert
21" $7,000.00*

Waltzing lady, ca. 1880 – 1920
French bisque, marked *"Marche des Volontaire"* two tunes, multiple movements, packing box.
21" $6,000.00*

Averill, Georgene

Ca. 1915+ New York City, New York. Georgene Averill made composition and cloth dolls operating as Madame Georgene Dolls, Averill Mfg. Co., Georgene Novelties, and Madame Hendren. The first line included dressed felt dolls, Lyf-

Lyk, the patented Mama Doll in 1918, and the Wonder line. She designed dolls for Borgfeldt, including Bonnie Babe.

First price indicates doll in good condition, some flaws; second price doll in excellent condition, original clothes, or appropriately dressed.

BISQUE

Bonnie Babe, ca. 1926 – 1930+

Designed by Georgene Averill, distributed by Borgfeldt. Bisque head, open mouth, two lower teeth, composition arms (sometimes celluloid) and legs on cloth body

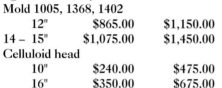

Mold 1005, 1368, 1402

12"	$865.00	$1,150.00
14 – 15"	$1,075.00	$1,450.00

Celluloid head

10"	$240.00	$475.00
16"	$350.00	$675.00

18" bisque Georgene Averill Bonnie Babe flange head, open mouth, two lower teeth, painted and molded hair, cloth body, composition arms and leg, original tagged dress, circa 1929, $1,100.00. Courtesy McMasters Doll Auctions.

ALL-BISQUE BONNIE BABE, see All-Bisque section.

CLOTH DOLLS, 1930+

Mask face with painted features, yarn hair, cloth body

12"	$40.00	$125.00
15"	$70.00	$150.00
22"	$85.00	$295.00
24"	$115.00	$335.00

Characters designed by Maud Tousey Fangel, ca. 1938, Peggy-Ann, Snooks, and Sweets

13"	$350.00	$675.00
17"	$450.00	$875.00
22"	$900.00	$1,150.00

Animals, ca. 1930s

B'rer Rabbit, Fuzzy Wuzzy, Nurse Jane, Uncle Wiggily, etc.

18"	$150.00	$600.00+

Krazy Kat, 1916, felt, not jointed

14"	$90.00	$350.00
18"	$125.00	$500.00

Brownies and Girl Scouts

14"	$80.00	$250.00

Comic Characters

Alvin, Little Lulu, Nancy, Sluggo, Tubby Tom, 1944 – 1961, with mask faces and painted features

14½"	$500.00+

Little Lulu, in cowgirl outfit

16½"	$585.00

Tag on original outfit reads: "BONNIE BABE COPY-RIGHTED BY GEORGENE AVERILL MADE BY K AND K TOY CO."

Mark:
COPR
GEORGENE AVERILL
1005/3652
GERMANY

Original tag reads: "I WHIS-TLE WHEN YOU DANCE ME ON ONE FOOT AND THEN THE OTHER//PATENTED FEB. 1926//GENUINE MADAME HENDREN DOLL."

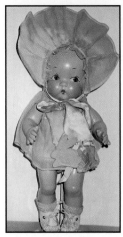

16" composition Georgene Averill Little Cherub designed and marked Harriet C. Flanders, in original box, hinged lid, two extra dresses, towel, two wash cloths, pillow, socks, wears pink organdy dress and bonnet, circa 1937, $750.00. Courtesy Dee Cermak.

Becassine, 1950s, French cartoon character

13"	$500.00	$750.00

Dolly Dingle, 1923+, designed by Grace Drayton

12"	$115.00	$450.00

Tear Drop Baby, one tear painted on cheek

16"	$60.00	$335.00

COMPOSITION

First price is for doll in good condition but with flaws; second price is for doll in excellent condition with original clothes or appropriately dressed. Add more for boxed with tags or exceptional dolls.

Patsy-type, 1928

All-composition, with jointed arms and legs, molded or wigged hair, painted or sleep eyes, open or closed mouth, all in good condition, original clothing

14"	$250.00	$300.00
17"	$325.00	$350.00

Baby Georgene or Baby Hendren

Composition head, arms, and lower legs; cloth body with crier; and marked with name on head

16"	$85.00	$275.00
20"	$95.00	$335.00
26"	$200.00	$600.00

Character or Ethnic

Composition head, cloth or composition body, character face, painted features, composition arms and legs. Whistlers, such as Whistling Dan, Sailor, Indian, Dutch Boy had bellows inside body. When pushed down on feet bellows created a whistling sound. Clothes often felt.

12"	$40.00	$150.00
16"	$75.00	$300.00
Black		
14"	$125.00	$450.00

Dolly Dingle (for Grace Drayton)

14"	$115.00	$450.00

Dolly Record, 1922 – 1928

Composition head, arms, and legs; human hair wig; sleep eyes; open mouth and teeth; record player in torso

26"	$250.00	$650.00

Mama Doll, 1918+

Composition shoulder head and arms, cloth torso with crier, composition swing legs, molded hair or mohair wig, painted or sleep eyes, good condition, original clothes

15 – 18"	$200.00	$300.00
20 – 22"	$400.00	$500.00

Snookums, 1927

Child star of Universal-Stern Bros. movie comedies, has laughing mouth, two rows of teeth, pants attached to shirt with safety pin

14"	$100.00	$375.00

Ca. 1871 – 1930+, Ohrdruf, Thuringia, Germany. This porcelain factory made china, bisque, and celluloid dolls, as well as doll parts and Snow Babies. They made dolls for Kley & Hahn, Bruno Schmidt, Wiesenthal, Schindel & Kallenberg.

BABY, CHARACTER FACE, 1909+

Bisque socket head, solid dome or wigged, bent leg, sleep eyes, open mouth

Mold 585, 586, 587, 602, 604, 619, 624, 630, 641, 678

13"	$355.00	$475.00
17"	$500.00	$675.00
22"	$650.00	$875.00

Toddler body
10"	$475.00	$625.00
18"	$750.00	$1,000.00
26"	$1,950.00	$2,600.00

Mold 526, other series 500, and 2023, 2072, or marked BP baby body, open closed mouth
14"	$2,100.00	$2,800.00
18"	$2,625.00	$3,500.00

23½" bisque Bahr & Proschild girl, blue sleep eyes, open mouth, pierced ears, replaced synthetic wig, jointed wood and composition body, antique lace dress, replaced shoes, circa 1890s, $475.00. Courtesy McMasters Doll Auctions.

CHILD

Belton-type or Dome head

Mold in 200 and 300 series, with small holes, socket head or shoulder plate, composition or kid body

12"	$1,150.00	$1,500.00
16"	$1,450.00	$1,900.00
24"	$2,250.00	$3,000.00

Child, open or closed mouth

Mold 200 and 300 series, full cheeks, jointed composition German body, French-type, or kid body

Mold Numbers 204, 224, 239, 246, 252, 273, 274, 275, 277, 286, 289, 293, 297, 309, 325, 332, 340, 379, 394

9"	$1,450.00* Mold 204	
14"	$510.00	$675.00
17"	$565.00	$750.00
23"	$750.00	$1,000.00

Mold 224, open mouth, dimpled cheeks
15"	$715.00	$950.00
23"	$1,050.00	$1,400.00

Child, kid body, open mouth
16"	$300.00	$400.00
18"	$415.00	$550.00
24"	$510.00	$675.00

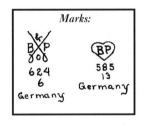

Marks:
B&P 308 624 6 Germany

(BP) 585 13 Germany

Barrois, E.

Ca. 1844 – 1877, Paris, France. Dolls marked "E.B." are attributed to this early manufacturing firm that used bisque and china heads with that mark. It is not known who made the heads for them. Bisque shoulder head with glass or painted eyes, closed mouth, kid body, may have wooden and bisque arms, good

Barrois, E. (cont.)

Marks:
E 3 B
E. 8 DEPOSE **B.**

condition. China head has painted eyes and painted, molded hair. Exceptional dolls may be more.

12"	$1,500.00	$2,000.00
14"	$2,500.00	$3,000.00
21"	$3,750.00	$5,000.00+

Fashion Type
Pressed bisque head, glass eyes, cloth or kid body

14"	$2,500.00	$3,300.00
17"	$3,400.00	$4,500.00

Bathing Dolls

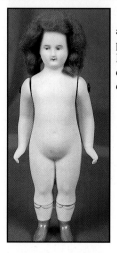

Bathing Beauties, ca. 1920. All-bisque figures, usually one piece, in various poses, were made by most porcelain factories in Germany and the U.S. in the 1920s. Beautifully detailed features, undressed or molded-on clothing or dressed in bathing costumes. All in excellent condition, no chips or damage.

Painted eyes			
	3"	$190.00	$250.00
	6"	$300.00	$400.00
Glass eyes			
	5"	$300.00	$400.00
	6"	$490.00	$650.00
Swivel neck			
	5"	$510.00	$675.00
	6"	$545.00	$725.00
With animal			
	5½"	$1,125.00	$1,500.00
Two modeled together			
	4½ – 5½"	$1,600.00+	
Action figures			
	5"	$340.00	$450.00+
	7½"	$490.00	$650.00
Wigged action figure			
	7"	$450.00	$600.00
Marked Japan			
	3"	$50.00	$75.00
	5 – 6"	$65.00	$100.00
	9"	$125.00	$175.00
Nude Chinese lady with seashell			
	6"	$375.00*	

7½" all-bisque doll, stiff neck, mohair wig, all-bisque body jointed at shoulders only, stiff legs with painted glazed lavender boots, glazed stockings with lavender garters, circa 1890s, $175.00. Courtesy McMasters Doll Auctions.

Belton Type

Ca. 1870+. No dolls marked "Belton" found; only mold numbers. Belton-type refers to small holes found in tops of solid bisque head dolls; holes were used for stringing. Used by various German firms such as Bahr & Proschild, Limbach, and Simon & Halbig. Socket head, paperweight eyes, wood and

Marks: None, or may have Mold 100, 116, 117, 120, 125, 127, 137, 154, 183, 185, 190 or others.

* at auction

composition jointed French type body with straight wrists, appropriately dressed in good condition.

Bru-type face

14"	$1,800.00	$2,400.00
18"	$2,200.00	$2,925.00

French-type face, Mold 125, 137

9"	$900.00	$1,200.00
12"	$1,500.00	$2,000.00
16"	$1,750.00	$2,325.00
20"	$2,250.00	$3,050.00
24"	$2,725.00	$3,650.00

German-type face

9"	$800.00	$1,100.00
12"	$900.00	$1,250.00
18"	$1,450.00	$1,950.00
23"	$2,050.00	$2,750.00
25"	$2,250.00	$3,000.00

15½" bisque Belton-type child, flat on top with three holes, set brown eyes, closed mouth, pierced ears, antique blonde wig, jointed wood and composition body, wooden upper arms and legs, circa 1870+, $1,500.00. Courtesy McMasters Doll Auctions.

Bergman, C.M.

Ca. 1889 – 1930+, Thuringia, Germany. Made dolls, but also used heads made by Alt, Beck & Gottschalck, Armand Marseille, and Simon & Halbig.

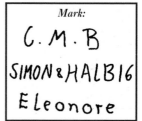

Mark:

C.M.B
SIMON & HALBIG
Eleonore

Baby

Mold 612, open/closed mouth

14"	$1,125.00	$1,500.00
17"	$1,500.00	$2,000.00

Character Baby, open mouth, socket head, five-piece bent-leg body

14"	$245.00	$325.00
18"	$435.00	$575.00
21"	$525.00	$700.00

Child

Head by A.M., or unknown maker, open mouth, wig, jointed composition body

10"	$245.00	$325.00
15"	$285.00	$375.00
20"	$300.00	$400.00
23"	$425.00	$535.00
30"	$900.00*	
34"	$1,000.00	$1,400.00
42"	$1,550.00	$2,050.00

Mold 1916 and other heads by Simon & Halbig

14"	$300.00	$400.00
19"	$355.00	$485.00
23"	$475.00	$650.00
28"	$675.00	$900.00
33"	$800.00	$1,100.00

30" C. M. Bergmann Simon & Halbig girl, blue sleep eyes, open mouth with two upper teeth, pierced ears, replaced wig, jointed wood and composition body, small hair line, circa 1900+, $625.00. Courtesy McMasters Doll Auctions.

* at auction

Eleonore

18"	$490.00	$650.00
25"	$640.00	$850.00

Lady, flapper-style body with thin arms and legs

12"	$470.00	$625.00
16"	$1,125.00	$1,500.00

Bisque, Unknown or Little Known Maker

32½" bisque Limoges Favorite girl, blue sleep eyes, open mouth, six teeth, synthetic wig, jointed wood and composition body, teal two-piece outfit, black bonnet, circa 1890 – 1910, $350.00. Courtesy McMasters Doll Auctions.

ENGLISH

Diamond Tile Co. Ltd., 1933 – 1943, Stoke-on-Trent, Staffordshire, England
Head only $125.00
Too few in database for reliable range.

FRENCH

Ca. 1870+. A number of French doll makers produced unmarked dolls with only a size number, Paris or France. Many are also being attributed to German makers who produced for the French trade. Also included here are little known companies that produced wonderful rarely seen dolls. Unmarked, pressed bisque socket head, closed or open/closed mouth, paperweight eyes, pierced ears, excellent quality bisque and finely painted features, on French wood and composition body with straight wrists. No damage, appropriately dressed.

Unknown Maker

Early desirable very French-style face. Marks such as "J.D." (possible J. DuSerre) "J.M. Paris," and "H. G." (possibly Henri & Granfe-Guimonneau).

17"	$12,750.00	$17,000.00+
21"	$15,750.00	$21,000.00+
27"	$20,250.00	$27,000.00+

Jumeau or Bru style face, may be marked "W. D." or "R. R."

14"	$1,890.00	$2,550.00
19"	$2,400.00	$3,175.00
24"	$3,775.00	$5,050.00
27"	$4,000.00	$5,350.00

Closed mouth, Marks: "F.1," "F.2," "J," "137," "136," or others

21" bisque shoulder head with painted eyes, closed mouth, kid body, anchor mark, possibly by J. Verlingue, re-dressed, circa 1915 – 1920, $1,400.00. Courtesy Debbie Crume.

Excellent quality, unusual face

10"	$1,250.00	$1,700.00
15"	$3,000.00	$4,000.00
18"	$3,600.00	$4,750.00
23"	$4,500.00	$6,000.00
27"	$5,250.00	$7,000.00

Standard quality, excellent bisque

13"	$1,825.00	$2,450.00
18"	$2,600.00	$3,450.00
23"	$3,375.00	$4,500.00

Lesser quality, may have poor painting and/or blotches on cheeks

15"	$900.00	$1,200.00
21"	$1,350.00	$1,800.00
26"	$1,725.00	$2,300.00

Open mouth

Excellent quality, ca. 1890+, French body

15"	$1,125.00	$1,500.00
18"	$1,725.00	$2,300.00
21"	$1,800.00	$2,400.00
24"	$2,325.00	$3,100.00

High cheek color, ca. 1920s, may have five-piece papier-mache body

15"	$475.00	$625.00
19"	$600.00	$800.00
23"	$725.00	$950.00

Known Makers

CSFJ, Chambre Syndicale des Fabricants de Jouets et Jeux et Engrins Sportif, 1886 – 1928+, Paris, France. Trade organization composed of French toy makers. Numbers refer to numbered list of manufacturers. First price is for doll in good condition, but with flaws; second price indicates doll in excellent condition with original or appropriate clothing.

Child, closed mouth, excellent quality bisque

12"	$700.00	$925.00
16"	$975.00	$1,300.00

Danel & Cie, 1889 – 1895, Paris. Danel, once director of Jumeau factory, was sued by Jumeau for copying Bebes Jumeau.

Paris Bebe

Bisque socket head, appropriate wig, pierced ears, paperweight eyes, closed mouth, nicely dressed in good condition

First price is for doll in good condition, but with flaws; second price indicates doll in excellent condition with original or appropriate clothing.

19"	$4,500.00	$6,000.00
21"	$4,725.00	$6,500.00
27"	$4,900.00*	

Delcrois, Henri, ca. 1865 – 1867

Bisque socket head, closed mouth, pierced ears, paperweight eyes, wig, marked *"PAN"* with size mark that varies with size of doll, wood and composition jointed French body

13"	$2,100.00	$3,000.00*

Too few in database for reliable range.

23" bisque K & K, marked "K & K//88//Thuringia" with open mouth, two upper teeth, cloth body, composition arms and legs, human hair wig, nicely dressed, circa 1915 – 1925, $500.00. Private collection.

Marks:

*E. (Size number) D. on head.
Eiffel Tower "PARIS BEBE" on body; shoes with "PARIS BEBE" in star.*

22" bisque Dressel & Koch, marked D&K dep 10, dark brown eyes, open mouth, human hair wig, crude composition body, circa 1893 – 1897, $300.00. Courtesy McMasters Doll Auctions.

Halopeau, A, ca. 1880

Marked "H," pressed bisque, open/closed or closed mouth, glass paperweight eyes, pierced ears, cork pate, French wood/composition body with straight wrists

21½"	$36,340.00*
22½"	$52,693.00*

Too few in database for reliable range.

Marks:
On head:
MASCOTTE
On body:
Bebe Mascotte/
Paris
Child marked:
Mascotte on head

Mascotte, 1882 – 1901

Trademark of May Freres Cie, using sizes similar to Bebes Jumeau. Became part of Jules Steiner in 1898. Bisque socket head, wig over cork pate, closed mouth, paperweight eyes, pierced ears, jointed composition French style body.

23"	$7,500.00*

Too few in database for reliable range.

Mothereau, ca. 1880 – 1895

Bebe Mothereau was made by Alexandre C. T. Mothereau who patented a joint for doll bodies. Upper arms and legs of wood, lower arms and legs have rounded joint and metal bracket for stringing. Pressed bisque socket head, glass eyes, closed mouth, pierced ears, cork pate, jointed composition body.

Bebe	12"	$12,000.00*

Too few in database for reliable range.

Marque, Albert, ca. 1915

Mark:

MARQUE DEPOSÉE
ARTICLE
FRANÇAIS
N°84

Marked "a Marque," molded bisque character, closed pouty mouth, glass paperweight eyes, pierced ears

21¾"	$92,746.00*
22"	$113,602.00*

Too few in database for reliable range.

Pannier, ca. 1875

Marked "C 8 P," pressed bisque head, closed mouth, glass paperweight eyes

20"	$57,986.00*

P.D., Frederic Petit & Andre Dumontier, 1878 – 1890, Paris

Made dolls with bisque heads from Francois Gaultier factory. Pressed bisque socket head, rounded face, glass eyes, closed mouth, pierced ears, wig over cork pate, French composition and wood jointed body

Mark:
P 3 D

19"	$10,000.00	$13,000.00
25"	$11,450.00	$15,250.00

Radiguet & Cordonnier, ca. 1880

Marked "R C Depose" on breast plate, bisque head, shoulder plate with molded bosom, closed mouth, glass eyes, bent bisque arm, molded shoes

17"	$9,993.00*

Too few in database for reliable range.

Rochard, Antoine Edmond, ca. 1868

Pressed bisque swivel head, open mouth to hold kaleidoscope, glass eyes, used Stanhope lenses, multicolored with scenes as jewel decor

6¾" head only	$24,530.00*	

Too few in database for reliable range.

Rostal, Henri, 1914, Paris

Made a bisque socket head, open mouth, glass eyes, wood and composition jointed body.
Mark: "Mon Tresor"

31"	$1,500.00*

GERMAN, CA. 1860+

Unknown or little-known German factories
Marks: May be unmarked or only a mold or size number or Germany.

Baby – Newborn

Cloth body

Bisque head, molded/painted hair, composition or celluloid hands, glass eyes, good condition, appropriately dressed

11"	$225.00	$300.00
14"	$345.00	$450.00
17"	$450.00	$600.00

Baby

25" bisque turned German shoulder head with shoulder crease marks on her shoulder plate, glass eyes, no marks, mohair wig, kid body, circa 1890s, $1,200.00. Courtesy Debbie Crume.

Composition body

Solid dome or wigged, five-piece baby body, open mouth, good condition, appropriately dressed

Glass eyes

10"	$185.00	$250.00
15"	$375.00	$510.00
20"	$525.00	$700.00

Painted eyes

11"	$150.00	$200.00
16"	$210.00	$315.00
18"	$340.00	$450.00

Allow more for closed, or open/closed mouth, unusual face, or toddler body.

Child

Character face, 1910+

Glass eyes, closed or open/closed mouth. Unidentified, may have wig or solid dome, excellent quality bisque, good condition, appropriately dressed

15"	$2,800.00	$3,800.00
19"	$3,400.00	$4,600.00

Mold 111, glass eyes

22"	$16,500.00	$22,000.00+

Too few in database for realiable range.

Mold 128

18"	$6,250.00	$8,950.00+

Too few in database for reliable range.

Mold 163, painted eyes, closed mouth

16"	$900.00	$1,200.00

Too few in database for realiable range.

Child, closed mouth

Excellent bisque, appropriately dressed, jointed composition body

13"	$575.00	$765.00
16"	$800.00	$1,075.00
20"	$1,115.00	$1,350.00
24"	$1,450.00	$1,950.00

16½" bisque unmarked child, pierced ears, mohair wig, composition and wood ball-jointed body with wardrobe of three complete outfits, very nicely made, with accessories, a family doll, circa 1880, $750.00. Courtesy Paula Van Overloeke Voris.

Kid, or cloth body, may have turned head, bisque lower arms

13"	$475.00	$625.00
15"	$650.00	$850.00
19"	$875.00	$1,150.00
23"	$1,000.00	$1,350.00

Child, open mouth, ca. 1880+

Dolly face, excellent pale bisque, glass eyes, jointed composition body

12"	$140.00	$190.00
15"	$220.00	$290.00
20"	$345.00	$455.00
25"	$440.00	$580.00
28"	$480.00	$630.00

Kid body

12"	$110.00	$145.00
15"	$135.00	$180.00
18"	$165.00	$215.00
22"	$200.00	$265.00

Molded hair doll, ca. 1880+

Bisque shoulder head with well modeled hair, often blonde, painted or glass eyes, closed mouth with kid or cloth body, bisque lower arms, good condition, appropriately dressed. Mold 890, 1000, 1008, 1028, 1064, 1142, 1256, 1288 may be made by Alt, Beck & Gottschalck.

American Schoolboy, 1880+

Side-parted painted hair swept across forehead, glass eyes, closed mouth

Jointed composition body

11"	$950.00* original	
15"	$485.00	$650.00

Kid or cloth body

11"	$300.00	$400.00
15"	$385.00	$515.00
20"	$500.00	$665.00

Child or lady, molded hair, closed mouth

Glass eyes

8"	$145.00	$195.00
11"	$185.00	$250.00
15"	$375.00	$500.00
19"	$650.00	$875.00
23"	$1,075.00	$1,450.00

Painted eyes

8"	$85.00	$115.00
15"	$245.00	$325.00
19"	$350.00	$475.00
23"	$575.00	$775.00

21" bisque German American Schoolboy, shoulder head, glass eyes, closed mouth, molded and painted hair, kid body, front shoulder plate break, body wear, circa 1880s, $225.00. Courtesy McMasters Doll Auctions.

Decorated shoulder plate, fancy hairdo

Glass eyes

20"	$2,075.00	$2,750.00+

Painted eyes

22"	$1,800.00*

Smaller unmarked doll

Head of good quality bisque, glass eyes, on five-piece papier-mache or composition body, good condition, appropriately dressed

Open mouth

6"	$140.00	$185.00
8"	$165.00	$225.00
10"	$235.00	$325.00

Jointed body

6"	$170.00	$225.00
8"	$250.00	$335.00
10"	$345.00	$460.00

Poorly painted

6"	$65.00	$85.00
9"	$95.00	$125.00
12"	$135.00	$175.00

Closed mouth

Jointed body

6"	$245.00	$325.00
8"	$300.00	$400.00
11"	$425.00	$575.00

Five-piece body

6"	$170.00	$235.00
9"	$245.00	$335.00
12"	$300.00	$415.00

18" painted bisque Maar toddler marked Emasco, set brown eyes, open mouth, four teeth, painted molded hair in coiled braids, five-piece composition toddler body, red print dress, circa 1920s, $325.00. Courtesy McMasters Doll Auctions.

JAPANESE, CA. 1915 – 1926+

Mark:

Various Japanese firms such as Morimura and Yamato (marked "Nippon" or "J.W.") made dolls for export when supplies were cut off from Germany during World War I. Quality varies greatly.

First price indicates doll in good condition, but with flaws; second price is for doll in excellent condition, appropriately dressed or original clothes. Add more for boxed, tagged, or labeled.

Baby, character face

Good to excellent quality bisque, well painted, nice body and appropriately dressed

9"	$120.00	$155.00
11"	$160.00	$215.00
15"	$225.00	$300.00
19"	$400.00	$525.00
23"	$575.00	$765.00

12" bisque Japanese child marked Nippon and tagged "Gold Medal," original dress, wig, circa 1915 – 1926, $250.00. Courtesy Marguerite Long.

* at auction

Poor quality bisque

11"	$85.00	$115.00
15"	$125.00	$165.00
19"	$185.00	$250.00
23"	$300.00	$400.00

Hilda-type

Excellent quality, glass eyes, open mouth with two upper teeth

14"	$525.00	$700.00
17"	$635.00	$850.00
22"	$355.00	$475.00

Poor quality bisque

14"	$85.00	$115.00
18"	$160.00	$215.00
22"	$235.00	$315.00

Mold 600, marked "Fy"

13"	$285.00	$395.00
17"	$400.00	$535.00

RUSSIAN

Juravlev & Kocheshkova, before the Revolution, ca. 1915+. Bisque socket head, sleep eyes, wig, jointed wood and composition body.

26"	$400.00* with repair to head

Too few in database for reliable range.

Black or Brown Dolls

Black or brown dolls can have fired-in color or be painted bisque, composition, cloth, papier-mache, or other materials. The color can be from very black to a light tan. They can have the typical open mouth dolly faces or ethnic features. The quality of this group of dolls varies greatly and the prices will fluctuate with the quality.

The first price indicates doll in good condition, but with flaws, perhaps nude; the second price indicates doll in excellent condition with original clothes or appropriately dressed. Add more for boxed, labeled, tagged, or exceptional quality.

ALL-BISQUE

Glass eyes, head molded to torso

4 – 5"	$200.00	$385.00+

Swivel neck

5 – 6"	$300.00	$500.00+

Painted eyes, head molded to torso

5"	$125.00	$245.00

Swivel head

5"	$250.00	$500.00

French-type

4"	$300.00	$500.00

All-bisque, marked by known maker such as J.D. Kestner or Simon & Halbig

6 – 7"	$975.00	$1,300.00

Automaton

Bisque standing man, key-wound, smoker

29"	$3,630.00*

Belton-type
   Closed mouth

12"	$1,350.00	$1,800.00
15"	$2,025.00	$2,700.00

BISQUE, FRENCH
Bru (circle dot or Brevete)

13"	$6,000.00*
19"	$50,000.00*

Too few in database for reliable range.

   Bru-Jne

23"	$26,250.00	$35,000.00+

Too few in database for reliable range.

E.D., open mouth

16"	$1,725.00	$2,300.00
22"	$1,950.00	$2,600.00

Fashion-type unmarked
   Bisque shoulder head, kid body, glass eyes

14"	$1,500.00	$2,000.00+

   Swivel neck, articulated body, original

16"	$9,750.00	$12,750.00

   Shoulder head, original

16"	$4,500.00	$6,000.00

F.G., open/closed mouth
   Kid body, swivel neck

14"	$1,800.00	$2,400.00
17"	$2,800.00	$3,800.00

French, unmarked or marked DEP
   Closed mouth

11 – 12"	$1,350.00	$1,800.00+
15"	$2,250.00	$3,000.00
20"	$3,150.00	$4,200.00

   Open mouth

10"	$450.00	$600.00
15"	$825.00	$1,100.00
22"	$1,650.00	$2,200.00

   Jumeau-type
   Closed mouth

12"	$1,950.00	$2,600.00
15"	$2,700.00	$3,600.00
19"	$3,600.00	$4,800.00

   Open mouth

12"	$825.00	$1,100.00
15"	$1,575.00	$2,100.00
19"	$2,400.00	$3,200.00

   Painted bisque
   Closed mouth

15"	$735.00	$975.00
20"	$800.00	$1,200.00

13½" brown bisque Schoeneau & Hoffmeister, mold 1909, socket head, sleep eyes, open mouth, four upper teeth, human hair wig, jointed wood and composition body, repainted body, circa 1909+, $225.00. Courtesy McMasters Doll Auctions.

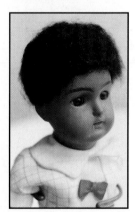

11½" black Kammer and Reinhardt bisque child, open mouth, glass eyes, circa 1890s, $600.00. Courtesy Marguerite Long.

12" black bisque Simon & Halbig girl, mold 1039, set brown eyes, open mouth with four upper teeth, pierced ears, curly wig, jointed wood and composition body, crown breaks repaired, circa 1891, $750.00. Courtesy McMasters Doll Auctions.

17½" black bisque Ernst Heubach, mold 399, solid dome, pupiless eyes, bent-limb baby body, circa 1930, $325.00. Courtesy McMasters Doll Auctions.

Open mouth

15"	$375.00	$500.00
20"	$750.00	$1,000.00

With ethnic features

18"	$3,450.00	$4,600.00+

Jumeau

Tete Jumeau, closed mouth

15"	$3,525.00	$4,700.00
18"	$3,825.00	$5,100.00
23"	$4,575.00	$6,100.00

Open mouth

10"	$1,650.00	$2,200.00
15"	$2,025.00	$2,700.00
18"	$2,250.00	$3,000.00
23"	$2,625.00	$3,500.00

E. J., closed mouth

15"	$6,200.00	$8,200.00+
17"	$7,000.00	$9,300.00+
19"	$31,000.00*	

Paris Bebe

16"	$3,450.00	$4,600.00
19"	$4,125.00	$5,500.00

S.F.B.J.

Mold 226

16"	$2,175.00	$2,900.00

Mold 235, open/closed mouth

15"	$1,950.00	$2,600.00
17"	$2,212.50	$2,950.00

S & Q (Schuetzmeister & Quendt)

Mold 251

9"	$450.00	$600.00
15"	$1,500.00	$2,000.00

Mold 252, baby

20"	$1,250.00	$1,650.00

Child

20"	$1,350.00	$1,800.00

Jules Steiner

A series, closed mouth

18"	$4,425.00	$5,900.00
22"	$4,875.00	$6,500.00

Open mouth

13"	$3,225.00	$4,300.00
16"	$3,600.00	$4,800.00
21"	$5,750.00*	

C series

18"	$4,000.00	$6,000.00
21"	$4,650.00	$6,200.00

* at auction

Unis

Mold 301 or 60, open mouth

14"	$340.00	$450.00
17"	$600.00	$800.00

BISQUE, GERMAN

Unmarked

Closed mouth

10 – 11"	$225.00	$300.00
14"	$300.00	$400.00
17"	$395.00	$525.00
21"	$600.00	$800.00

Open mouth

10"	$375.00	$500.00
13"	$490.00	$650.00
15"	$640.00	$850.00

Painted bisque

Closed mouth

16"	$265.00	$350.00
19"	$375.00	$500.00

Open mouth

14"	$225.00	$300.00
18"	$375.00	$500.00

Ethnic features

15"	$2,250.00	$3,000.00
18"	$2,850.00	$3,800.00

Bahr & Proschild, open mouth, mold 277

12"	$525.00	$700.00
16"	$1,250.00	$1,650.00

Bye-Lo Baby

16"	$2,250.00	$3,000.00

Cameo Doll Company

Kewpie (Hottentot) bisque

4"	$400.00
5"	$565.00
9"	$985.00

Composition

12"	$400.00
15"	$725.00

Papier-mache

8"	$265.00

Scootles, composition, original outfit

13"	$750.00
13"	$1,050.00*

Handwerck, Heinrich, mold 79, 119

Open mouth

12"	$525.00	$700.00
18"	$1,200.00	$1,600.00
22"	$1,425.00	$1,900.00
29"	$1,950.00	$2,600.00

12" mulatto bisque on tinted toddler body, no marks, $600.00. Courtesy Cherie Gervais.

11½" bisque black Kestner, unmarked, open mouth with four teeth, mohair wig, remnants of plaster pate, wood and composition body, circa 1910+, $950.00. Courtesy McMasters Doll Auctions.

* at auction

Composition Leo Moss marks. Courtesy O. Gregg.

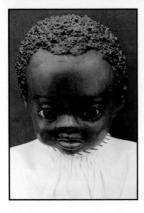

16½" composition Leo Moss shoulder head, incised LM//Dale on back, dark cloth body, papier-mache arms and legs, glass eyes, heavily molded hair, pouty expression, circa 1880+, $3,700.00. Courtesy O. Gregg.

16" composition black baby, by unknown maker, probably not from the U.S.A., glassene eyes, open mouth, painted molded hair, composition baby body, circa 1940s, $400.00. Courtesy Margaret Obert.

Heubach, Gebruder, Sunburst mark
Boy, eyes to side, open/closed mouth

12"	$1,875.00	$2,500.00

Mold 7657, 7658, 7668, 7671

9"	$950.00	$1,250.00
13"	$1,275.00	$1,700.00

Mold 7661, 7686

10"	$900.00	$1,200.00
14"	$1,950.00	$2,600.00
17"	$2,850.00	$3,800.00

Heubach, Ernst (Koppelsdorf)
Mold 320, 339, 350

10"	$325.00	$425.00
13"	$400.00	$535.00
18"	$525.00	$700.00

Mold 399, allow more for toddler

10"	$300.00	$400.00
14"	$415.00	$550.00
17"	$525.00	$700.00

Mold 414

9"	$340.00	$450.00
14"	$525.00	$700.00
17"	$715.00	$950.00

Mold 418 (grin)

9"	$510.00	$675.00
14"	$525.00	$700.00

Mold 444, 451

9"	$300.00	$400.00
14"	$525.00	$700.00

Mold 452, brown

7½"	$285.00	$375.00
10"	$360.00	$475.00
15"	$510.00	$675.00

Mold 458

10"	$350.00	$465.00
15"	$525.00	$700.00

Mold 463

12"	$450.00	$600.00
16"	$715.00	$950.00

Mold 1900

14"	$375.00	$500.00
17"	$450.00	$600.00

Kammer & Reinhardt (K * R)

Child, no mold number

7½"	$340.00	$450.00
14"	$515.00	$675.00
17"	$660.00	$875.00
19"	$2,000.00*	

Mold 100

10"	$525.00	$700.00
14"	$825.00	$1,100.00
17"	$1,200.00	$1,600.00
20"	$1,785.00*	

Mold 101, painted eyes

13"	$7,000.00*	

Mold 101, glass eyes

17"	$3,700.75	$4,925.00

Mold 114

13"	$3,150.00	$4,200.00

Mold 116, 116a

15"	$2,250.00	$3,000.00
19"	$2,800.00	$3,725.00

Mold 126, baby body

12"	$565.00	$750.00
18"	$845.00	$1,125.00

Mold 126, toddler

18"	$1,200.00	$1,600.00

Kestner, J. D.

Baby, no mold number, open mouth, teeth

10"	$1,500.00*	

Hilda, mold 245

10"	$2,500.00*	
14"	$4,125.00	$5,500.00

Child, no mold number

Closed mouth

14"	$475.00	$625.00
17"	$715.00	$950.00

Open mouth

12"	$340.00	$450.00
16"	$490.00	$650.00

Five-piece body

9"	$215.00	$285.00
12"	$265.00	$350.00

Konig & Wernicke (KW/G)

18"	$565.00	$750.00
19"	$1,500.00*	

Ethnic features

17"	$750.00	$1,000.00

Kuhnlenz, Gebruder

Closed mouth

15"	$675.00	$900.00
18"	$1,350.00	$1,800.00

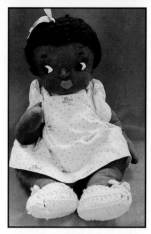

14" black cloth doll made by cottage sewers, sold to department stores, yarn hair, hand-embroidered face, circa 1946, $75.00. Courtesy Patricia Wright.

15½" black unmarked cloth girl with molded mask face, painted side-glancing eyes, tufts of yarn hair, circa 1930s, $130.00. Courtesy Dorothy Bohlin.

16" black Armand Marseille composition toddler, mold 518, molded and lightly painted hair, circa 1938, $195.00. Courtesy McMasters Doll Auctions.

13½" cloth black baby with painted side-glancing eyes, yarn hair, oil cloth body, all original, circa 1940s, $195.00. Courtesy Chantal Jeschien

Open mouth, mold 34.14, 34.16, 34.24, etc.

3"	$725.00* boxed	
3½"	$450.00*	
6"	$700.00*	
12"	$415.00	$550.00

Ethnic features

16"	$3,000.00	$4,000.00

Marseille, Armand

No mold number, ebony

11"	$850.00*	

Mold 341, 351, 352, 562

10"	$275.00	$365.00
16"	$545.00	$825.00
20"	$925.00	$1,200.00

Mold 390, 390n

16"	$415.00	$550.00
19"	$585.00	$775.00
23"	$675.00	$895.00
25"	$2,200.00*	
28"	$825.00	$1,100.00

Mold 451, 458 (Indians)

9"	$265.00	$350.00
12"	$375.00	$500.00

Mold 970, 971, 992, 995 (baby or toddler)

9"	$200.00	$265.00
14"	$415.00	$550.00
18"	$660.00	$875.00

Mold 1894, 1897, 1912, 1914

12"	$400.00	$525.00
14"	$550.00	$750.00
18"	$635.00	$850.00

Recknagel, marked "R.A.," mold 138

16"	$545.00	$725.00
22"	$1,075.00	$1,430.00

Schoenau Hoffmeister (S PB H)

Hanna

8"	$285.00	$375.00
10 – 12"	$415.00	$550.00
15"	$525.00	$700.00
18"	$640.00	$850.00

Mold 1909

16"	$400.00	$525.00
19"	$525.00	$700.00

Simon & Halbig

Mold 639

14"	$5,100.00	$6,800.00
18"	$7,500.00	$10,000.00

Mold 739, open mouth

11"	$1,800.00*	
22"	$2,100.00	$2,800.00+

Closed mouth

13"	$1,500.00*	
17"	$1,950.00	$2,600.00
22"	$2,775.00	$3,700.00

Mold 939, closed mouth

18"	$2,475.00	$3,300.00
21"	$3,375.00	$4,500.00

Open mouth

13"	$2,300.00* original outfit	
17"	$1,050.00	$1,400.00
21"	$1,575.00	$2,100.00

Mold 949, closed mouth

18"	$2,550.00	$3,400.00
21"	$3,000.00	$3,950.00

Open mouth, fat cheeks

18"	$5,500.00	$7,500.00

Too few in database for reliable range.

12½" black, stockinette, molded-faced, cloth African child with mohair wig, shell necklace, circa 1940s – 1950s, $50.00. Courtesy Marguerite Long.

Mold 1009, 1039, 1079, open mouth

8"	$1,550.00*	
12"	$950.00	$1,250.00
16"	$1,250.00	$1,700.00
19"	$1,500.00	$2,000.00

Pull-string sleep eyes

19"	$1,725.00	$2,300.00

Mold 1248, open mouth

15"	$1,125.00	$1,500.00
16"	$4,100.00*	
18"	$1,350.00	$1,800.00

Mold 1302, closed mouth, glass eyes, black character face

18"	$5,250.00	$7,000.00

Indian, sad expression, brown face

18"	$5,500.00	$7,400.00

Mold 1303, Indian, thin face, man or woman

16"	$4,574.00	$6,100.00
21"	$6,000.00	$8,000.00

Mold 1339, 1358, 1368

16"	$4,450.00	$5,900.00
19"	$6,750.00*	
21"	$8,000.00*	

20" all-vinyl child, marked C. 1967//Beatrice Wright, rooted hair, sleep eyes, re-dressed but has original outfit, circa 1967, $65.00. Courtesy Marcie Montgomery.

CELLULOID

The first price indicates doll in good condition, but with flaws, perhaps nude; the second price indicates doll in excellent condition with original clothes or appropriately dressed.

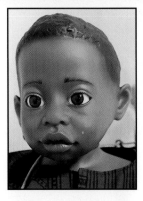

23½" black vinyl Gotz Yoramong by Philip Heath, all original, circa 1990s, $600.00. Courtesy Helga Cunha.

All-celluloid

10"	$150.00	$200.00
15"	$265.00	$350.00
18"	$400.00	$600.00

Celluloid shoulder head, kid body, add more for glass eyes

17"	$265.00	$350.00
21"	$340.00	$450.00

French-type, marked "SNF"

14"	$265.00	$350.00
18"	$400.00	$600.00

Parsons Jackson Baby (Biskoline)

13"	$340.00	$450.00

Toddler

14"	$435.00	$575.00

CLOTH

The first price indicates doll in good condition, but with flaws, perhaps nude; the second price indicates doll in excellent condition with original clothes or appropriately dressed.

Alabama, see Cloth dolls.

Bruckner, see Cloth dolls.

Chase, Martha

24"	$5,500.00	$7,400.00
28"	$6,900.00	$9,200.00

Golliwog, 1895 to present

Character from 1895 book, *The Adventures of Two Dutch Dolls and a Golliwogg,* all cloth, various English makers. See also Cloth, Deans Rag.

1895 – 1920

13"	$375.00	$750.00

1930 – 1950

11"	$150.00	$300.00
15"	$250.00	$400.00

1950 – 1970s

13"	$150.00	$250.00
18"	$200.00	$400.00

13½" vinyl Shindana baby, rooted hair, ethnically correct features, drink and wet doll, rooted hair, first major manufacturer of black dolls, circa 1972, $45.00. Courtesy Marcie Montgomery.

Stockinette, oil-painted features, excellent condition

16"	$1,800.00	$2,400.00
22"	$2,475.00	$3,300.00

COMPOSITION

The first price indicates doll with heavy crazing, perhaps nude; the second price indicates doll in excellent condition, may have very fine crazing, with original clothes. More for boxed, labeled, or exceptional quality.

Unmarked, or unknown company

16"	$200.00	$600.00

Borgfeldt, Geo

   Tony Sarg Mammy with baby

     18" $145.00 $575.00

Effanbee

   Baby Grumpy

     10" $75.00 $300.00

     16" $115.00 $475.00

   Bubbles

   Light crazing, original clothing, very good condition

     17" $110.00 $450.00

     22" $165.00 $700.00

   Candy Kid

   With original shorts, robe, and gloves

     12" $75.00 $300.00

   Skippy, with original outfit

     14" $900.00*

Horsman

     12" $475.00*

Ideal

   Marama, Shirley Temple body, from the movie, *Hurricane*

     13" $800.00*

17" black vinyl Australian doll purchased at the Tjapukai Aboriginal Cultural Park, dressed by Aboriginal people, circa 1997, $30.00. Courtesy Laura Jennine Jacobs.

CHINA

   Frozen Charlie/Charlotte

     3" $100.00 $135.00

     6" $190.00 $250.00

  8 – 9" $265.00 $350.00

   Jointed at shoulder

     3" $150.00 $200.00

     6" $265.00 $350.00

HARD PLASTIC

   Terri Lee, Patty-Jo

     16" $450.00 $600.00+

PAPIER-MACHE

   Leo Moss, late 1880s – early 1900s

   Papier-mache head and lower limbs, molded hair or wig, inset glass eyes, closed mouth, full lips, brown twill body filled with excelsior. May have tear on cheek.

     17" $5,475.00 $7,300.00

     23" $11,025.00*

   Papier-mache with ethnic features

     8" $210.00 $275.00

     17" $625.00 $825.00

VINYL

   Shindana, 1968 – 1983, Operation Bootstrap, Los Angeles, ethnic features

     14" $35.00 $75.00

---

* at auction

Bonnet Head

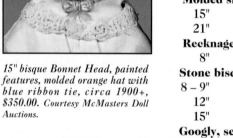

1860 – 1940+. Heads of various materials with painted molded bonnets, hats, or headgear.

ALL BISQUE

German, one-piece body and head, painted or glass eyes

5"	$135.00	$175.00
7"	$175.00	$235.00
8"	$215.00	$285.00
10"	$285.00	$375.00

BISQUE

Molded hair, bisque head, glass eyes, hat or bonnet

Five-piece papier-mache, kid, or cloth body

7"	$140.00	$185.00
12"	$325.00	$425.00
18"	$750.00	$1,000.00

Bisque arms, jointed composition, kid or cloth body

7"	$150.00	$200.00
9"	$265.00	$350.00
12"	$365.00	$485.00
15"	$545.00	$725.00

Alt, Beck & Gottschalck

Glass eyes

18"	$2,907.00*

Painted eyes

18"	$1,430.00*

Handwerck, Max, WWI military figure, painted eyes, marked *"Elite"*

12"	$2,200.00*

Heubach, Gebruder, Baby Stuart

10"	$825.00	$1,100.00
15"	$1,125.00	$1,500.00

Japanese

8 – 9"	$55.00	$85.00
12"	$95.00	$135.00

Molded shirt or top

15"	$625.00	$825.00
21"	$1,015.00	$1,350.00

Recknagel, painted eyes

8"	$425.00*

Stone bisque

8 – 9"	$125.00	$165.00
12"	$170.00	$225.00
15"	$290.00	$385.00

Googly, see that section.

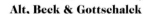

13" bisque Bonnet Head, shoulder head, painted features, bisque limbs, cloth body, circa 1900+, $325.00. Courtesy McMasters Doll Auctions.

15" bisque Bonnet Head, painted features, molded orange hat with blue ribbon tie, circa 1900+, $350.00. Courtesy McMasters Doll Auctions.

Borgfeldt & Co., George

Ca. 1881 – 1930+, New York. Assembled and distributed dolls. Used dolls from many companies and employed designers such as Rose O'Neill, Grace Corry, Grace Storey Putnam, Joseph L. Kallus, Georgene Averill, and others. Konig & Wernicke made dolls for Borgfeldt.

Bisque Baby, 1910+

Five-piece bent-leg baby body, open mouth

10"	$225.00	$300.00
17"	$425.00	$575.00
27"	$675.00	$900.00+

Mold 251, 1915+

Made by Armand Marseille, character baby, closed mouth

17"	$3,100.00*

Baby BoKaye

Designed by Joseph Kallus, made by Alt, Beck & Gottschalk for Borgfelt, bisque molded hair, open mouth, glass eyes, cloth body, composition limbs, Mold 1394

11"	$1,700.00*	
15"	$1,725.00	$2,300.00
18"	$2,025.00	$2,700.00

Babykins, 1931

Made for Borgfeldt by Grace Storey Putnam, round face, glass eyes, pursed lips

14"	$735.00	$980.00
17"	$900.00	$1,190.00+

Bisque Child Mold 325, 327, 329, or marked "G.B.," "My Girlie," "Pansy"

1910 – 1922, bisque head, fully jointed composition body, open mouth, good condition, and appropriately dressed

10"	$255.00	$340.00
13"	$340.00	$450.00
15"	$400.00	$525.00
17"	$450.00	$600.00
20"	$525.00	$700.00
22"	$550.00	$750.00
25"	$640.00	$850.00

Composition

Hug Me, closed mouth, googly eyes

24"	$735.00*

25" bisque George Borgfeldt & Co. My Girlie, brown sleep eyes, open mouth, four teeth, human hair wig in braids over head, jointed wood and composition body, re-dressed, circa 1912, $300.00. Courtesy McMasters Doll Auctions.

```
251
G.B.
Germany
A 1 M
DRMR 2498
```

Boudoir Dolls

Ca. 1915 – 1940. Bed dolls, originally used as decorations to sit on the bed, usually French, with extra long arms and legs, heads of cloth, composition, ceramics, wax, and suede, mohair or silk floss wigs, painted features, some with real lashes, cloth or composition bodies, dressed in fancy period costumes. Other manufacturers were Italian, British, or American.

First price is for doll in good condition, but with minor flaws; second price indicates doll in excellent condition, original clothes. Add more for boxed, labeled, or exceptional quality. Less for nude, flaking, cracked.

* at auction

13" composition boudoir doll, side-glancing eyes, marked German on bottom of shoe, cloth body and legs, circa 1930s, $125.00. Courtesy Mary Evelyn Graf.

Standard quality, dressed

16"	$95.00	$125.00
28"	$135.00	$175.00
32"	$175.00	$235.00

Excellent quality, with glass eyes

15"	$225.00	$300.00
28"	$365.00	$475.00
32"	$75.00	$500.00

Lenci

18 – 26"	$1,500.00	$2,250.00+

Smoker, cloth

16"	$215.00	$285.00
25"	$375.00	$525.00

Composition

25"	$185.00	$245.00
28"	$285.00	$375.00

Black

	$450.00	$600.00+

Bru

Bru Jne. & Cie, ca. 1867 – 1899. Paris and Montreuil-sous-Bous French factories, eventually succeeded by Societe Francaise de Fabrication de Bebe & Jouets (S.F.B.J.) 1899 – 1953. Bebes Bru with kid bodies are one of the most collectible dolls, highly sought after because of the fine quality of bisque, delicate coloring, and fine workmanship.

Identifying characteristics: Brus are made of pressed bisque and have a metal spring stringing mechanism in the neck. Add more for original clothes and rare body styles.

Bebe Brevete, ca. 1879 – 1880

Pressed bisque swivel head, shoulder plate, mohair or human hair wig, cork pate, paperweight eyes, multi-stroke eyebrows, closed mouth with space between lips, full cheeks, pierced ears, kid or wooden articulated bodies.

First price is for doll in good condition, but with some flaws; second price is for doll in excellent condition, appropriately dressed, add more for original clothes and marked shoes.

Baby Brevete Marks:
"Baby Brevete"
Head marked with size number only; kid body may have paper Bebe Brevete label.

Bru Jne Marks:
"BRE JNE," with size number on head, kid over wood body marked with rectangular paper label.

Bre Jne R. Marks:
"BRU. JNE R." with size number on head, body stamped in red, "Bebe Bru," and size number.

14"	$9,775.00	$13,500.00
18"	$13,000.00	$17,250.00
20"	$20,000.00* original dress, labeled body	

Bru Jne, 1880 – 1891

Pressed bisque swivel head, deep shoulder molded breastplate, mohair or human hair wig, cork pate, paperweight eyes, multi-stroke eyebrows, open/closed mouth with painted molded teeth, pierced ears, bisque lower arms, good condition, nicely dressed. Add more for original clothes and marked shoes.

12"	$8,750.00	$11,500.00
14"	$10,250.00	$13,500.00
17"	$12,000.00	$16,000.00
20"	$14,250.00	$19,000.00
23"	$23,500.00*	
27"	$19,250.00	$25,500.00

Bru Jne R, 1891 – 1899

Pressed bisque swivel head, mohair or human hair wig, cork pate, paperweight eyes, multi-stroke eyebrows, open mouth with four or six upper teeth or closed mouth, pierced ears, articulated wood and composition body, good condition, nicely dressed. Add more for original clothes.

22" bisque Bru girl, set blue eyes, open mouth with six upper teeth, replaced human hair wig, jointed wood and composition body, working crier, kissing and walking mechanisms, circa 1892+, $2,500.00. Courtesy McMasters Doll Auctions.

Closed mouth

11"	$1,800.00	$2,400.00
14"	$2,200.00	$2,900.00
17"	$2,750.00	$3,453.00
19"	$2,900.00	$3,850.00
23"	$3,500.00	$4,650.00

Open mouth

12"	$1,000.00	$1,350.00
14"	$1,100.00	$1,500.00
16"	$1,600.00	$2,100.00
20"	$2,250.00	$3,000.00

Circle Dot Bebe, 1879 – 1883

Pressed bisque swivel head, deep shoulder molded breastplate, mohair or human hair wig, cork pate, paperweight eyes, multi-stroke eyebrows, open/closed mouth with painted molded teeth, pierced ears, gusseted kid body, bisque lower arms, good condition, nicely dressed. Add more for original clothes.

Circle Dot Bebe Mark: Head marked dot within a circle or half circle.

Fashion-Type Mark: Marked "A" through "M," "11" to "28," indicating size numbers only.

12"	$8,300.00	$11,100.00
14"	$9,700.00	$12,900.00
18"	$12,450.00	$16,600.00
23"	$16,500.00	$22,000.00
26"	$18,050.00	$24,000.00
31"	$21,700.00	$29,000.00

Fashion-type (poupee), 1867 – 1877+

Swivel head of pressed bisque, bisque shoulder plate, metal spring stringing mechanism in neck, kid body, painted or glass eyes, pierced ears, cork pate, mohair wig. Add more for original clothes.

12"	$2,300.00	$3,050.00
15"	$2,400.00	$3,250.00

14" bisque swivel head, on bisque shoulder plate marked F, paperweight eyes, lower bisque hinged arms, original clothes and shoes, sole marked O, human hair wig, kid body and feet, circa 1890s, $3,000.00. Private collection.

Fashion-type (poupee), Smiler 1873+

Pressed bisque swivel head, shoulder plate, articulated wood with metal spring stringing mechanism in neck, wood and kid or kid gusseted lady body, cork pate, mohair or human hair wig, glass paperweight eyes, pierced ears, closed smiling mouth, nicely dressed. Add more for original clothes.

Cloth body

18"	$2,300.00	$3,100.00

Kid body, kid or bisque arms, allow more for wooden arms

13"	$2,250.00	$3,000.00
15"	$3,500.00*	
21"	$4,100.00	$5,500.00

Wood body

15"	$3,950.00	$5,250.00
18"	$5,500.00*	

Variants

Bebe Automate (breather, talker), 1892+

With key or lever in torso, activates talking and breathing mechanism

19"	$15,000.00
24"	$17,000.00

Bebe Baiser (kiss thrower), 1892

With a simple pull-string mechanism, which allows doll's arm to raise and appear to throw kisses

11"	$4,100.00*

Bebe Gourmand (eater), 1880

Open mouth with tongue to take food, which fell into throat and out through bottom of feet, had shoes with specially designed hinged soles to take out food. Legs bisque from knees; used Brevete version

16"	$25,000.00+

Too few in database for reliable range.

Bebe Marchant (walker), 1892

Clockwork walking mechanism which allows head to move and talk, has articulated body with key in torso

17"	$6,800.00
21"	$7,400.00
25"	$8,200.00

Bebe Modele, 1880

Carved wooden body

19"	$19,000.00+

Too few in database for reliable range.

Bebe Teteur (nursing), 1879

Open mouth to insert bottle, usually with screw type key on back of head to allow the doll to drink

14"	$7,000.00
17"	$9,200.00
20"	$9,600.00

Accessories

Bru shoes (marked)	$500.00 – 800.00+

* at auction

Bye-Lo Baby

1922 – 1952. Designed by Grace Storey Putnam to represent a three-day-old baby, manufactured by various firms, such as Kestner; Alt, Beck & Gottschalck; Hertel & Schwab; and others; body made by K&K, a subsidiary of George Borgfeldt & Co., New York, the sole licensee. Composition Bye-Lo Babies made by Cameo Doll Company, and came in sizes 10", 12", 14", and 16½".

First price is for doll in good condition with some flaws; second price is for doll in excellent condition, nicely dressed, add more for tagged original clothes, labels, and pin-back button.

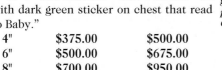

5" all-bisque Bye Lo displays his green sticker, sleep eyes, painted pink shoes, $600.00. Courtesy Cherie Gervais.

ALL-BISQUE

All-bisque versions made by J.D. Kestner were 4" to 8" and marked "G.S. Putnam" on back, with dark green sticker on chest that read "Bye-Lo Baby."

4"	$375.00	$500.00
6"	$500.00	$675.00
8"	$700.00	$950.00
4"	$800.00* with paper label, original gown, and bed	

BISQUE HEAD

Bisque head, painted molded hair, blue sleep eyes, closed mouth, flange neck, cloth baby-shaped ("frog") body, some stamped "Bye-Lo Baby," celluloid hands

10"	$300.00	$400.00
12"	$425.00	$575.00
15"	$550.00	$725.00
18"	$700.00	$925.00
21"	$785.00	$1,050.00

COMPOSITION HEAD

Painted molded hair, sleep or painted eyes, closed mouth, cloth body. First price indicates doll with crazing, flaws; second price is for doll in excellent condition, with good color and original clothes, or appropriately dressed.

12"	$95.00	$375.00
16"	$150.00	$575.00

Mark:

© 1923 by
Grace S. Putnam
MADE IN GERMANY
7372/45

CELLULOID

All-celluloid

4"	$45.00	$165.00
6"	$100.00	$200.00

Celluloid head, cloth body

12"	$175.00	$350.00
15"	$245.00	$465.00

Wax, poured, sold NY boutique, 1925

14½"	$2,100.00*

* at auction

VARIATIONS

Fly-Lo Baby, 1926 – 1930+

Ceramic, bisque, or composition head, glass or metal sleep eyes, painted molded hair, flange type neck, cloth body. Marked *"Copr. by//Grace S. Putnam."* Cloth bodies with celluloid hands, satin wings, in green, gold, or pink.

Bisque, less for ceramic

11"	$2,100.00*	
13"	$3,750.00	$5,000.00

Composition

14"	$300.00	$900.00

VINYL, CA. 1950S

Vinyl head, cloth stuffed limbs, marked *"Grace Storey Putnam"* on head.

16"	$65.00	$225.00

Catterfelder Puppenfabrik

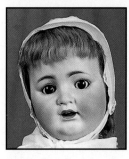

24" bisque Catterfelder Puppenfabrik baby, mold 262, blue sleep eyes, open mouth, two teeth, tongue, original mohair wig, composition bent-limb baby body, circa 1916, $650.00. Courtesy McMasters Doll Auctions.

1894 – 1930+, Catterfeld, Thuringia, Germany. Made dolls using Kestner bisque head on composition bodies.

BABY

1909 and after, wigged, or painted molded hair, bent-leg body, glass or painted eyes. Add more for toddler body

Mold 200 (similar to K*R #100), domed head, painted eyes, open/closed mouth, also black version

Mold 201, domed head, painted eyes, open/closed mouth

Mold 207, character head, painted eyes, closed mouth

Mold 208, character baby or toddler with domed head or wigged, sleep eyes, open mouth, two teeth, movable tongue

Mold 209, character baby, movable tongue

Mold 218, character baby, domed head, sleep eyes, open mouth, movable tongue

Mold 262, character baby, sleep eyes, open mouth, movable tongue, only marked with mold number

Mold 263, character baby

14"	$485.00
20"	$775.00

Too few in database to give reliable range.

CHILD

Open mouth, sleep eyes

18"	$500.00	$675.00

CHILD, CHARACTER FACE

Composition body, open or open/closed mouth

Mold 210, painted eyes, closed mouth

14"	$5,000.00*

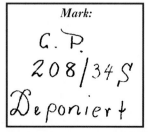

Mark:

C. P.

208/34 S

Deponiert

Mold 212, wide open/closed laughing mouth, painted teeth and eyes

Mold 215, 219, character face, wig, painted eyes

| 215 | 16" | $8,600.00 |
| 219 | 16" | $3,850.00 |

Mark:

1100

Catterfelder Puppenfabrik

2

Mold 220, character doll, sleeping eyes, open/closed mouth with two molded teeth

17" $7,300.00

Mold 264, character face, socket head, sleep eyes, open mouth

27" $550.00*

Mold 270, character face, socket head, open mouth, sleep eyes

Molds 1100, 1200, and 1357 were used for ball-jointed dolls

Celluloid

1869+, celluloid became more durable after 1905 and in 1910, when better production methods were found. Dolls were made in England, France, Japan, Germany, Poland, and the United States. When short hair became faddish, the demand for celluloid hair ornaments decreased and companies produced more dolls.

American manufacturers:
Averill, Bo-Peep (H. J. Brown), Du Pont Viscoloid Co., Horsman, Irwin, Marks Bros., Parsons-Jackson Co. (stork mark), Celluloid Novelty Co.

English manufacturers:
Wilson Doll Co. and Cascelloid Ltd. (Palitoy)

French manufacturers:
Peticolin (profile head of an eagle mark), Widow Chalory, Convert Cie, Parisienne de Cellulosine, Neuman & Marx (Dragon), Societe Industrielle de Celluloid (S.I.C.), Sicoine, Societe Nobel Francaise (S N F in diamond)

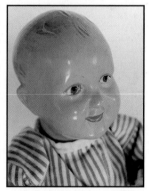

10" celluloid Parsons Jackson bent-leg baby with stork mark, painted eyes, molded hair and boots, original romper, circa 1910 – 1914, $200.00. Private collection.

German manufacturers:
Bahr & Proschild, Buschow & Beck (helmet), Minerva, Catterfelder Puppenfabrik Co., Cuno & Otto Dressel, E. Maar & Sohn (3 M), Emasco, Kammer & Reinhardt, Kestner, Konig & Wernicke, A. Hagedorn & Co., Hermsdorfer Celluloidwarenfabrik (lady bug), Dr. Paul Hunaeus, Kohn & Wengenroth, Rheinsche Gummi und Celluloid Fabrik Co. (turtle mark), Max Rudolph, Bruno Schmidt, Franz Schmidt & Co., Schoberl & Becker (mermaid) Celba, Karl Standfuss, Albert Wacker

Japanese manufacturers:
Various firms may be marked Japan

*18" celluloid Kammer &
Reinhardt toddler, mold 728,
blue flirty eyes, open mouth,
two teeth, original blonde
mohair wig, five-piece composition toddler body, maroon
dress, replaced socks and
shoes, circa 1915, $215.00.
Courtesy McMasters Doll Auctions.*

Polish manufacturers:
Zast ("A.S.K." in triangle)

First price is for doll with some flaws or nude;
second price is for doll in excellent condition. More
for boxed set, labeled, or tagged.

ALL CELLULOID

Baby

Painted eyes

9"	$30.00	$85.00
11"	$35.00	$115.00
13"	$40.00	$165.00
15"	$45.00	$175.00
19"	$70.00	$285.00
25"	$90.00	$365.00

Glass eyes

13"	$45.00	$185.00
15"	$60.00	$250.00
19"	$100.00	$400.00
23"	$115.00	$465.00

Child

Painted eyes, jointed shoulders, hips

5"	$10.00	$37.50
7"	$15.00	$60.00
11"	$30.00	$115.00
14"	$45.00	$185.00
19"	$100.00	$400.00

Jointed shoulders only

6"	$7.50	$30.00
8"	$13.00	$50.00
11"	$25.00	$95.00

Glass eyes

10"	$45.00	$125.00
14"	$60.00	$210.00
17"	$100.00	$400.00

Marked "France"

7"	$30.00	$130.00
9"	$45.00	$180.00
15"	$70.00	$280.00
18"	$140.00	$525.00

Molded-on clothes, jointed shoulders only

3"	$10.00	$40.00
5"	$15.00	$60.00
8"	$30.00	$110.00

Immobiles, no joints

3"	$4.00	$15.00
6"	$10.00	$45.00

Black, all-celluloid: see Black Dolls section.

Carnival Dolls

May have feathers glued to body/head, some have top hats.

8"	$10.00	$40.00
12"	$20.00	$80.00
17"	$45.00	$175.00+

Shoulder head, 1900+

Germany, molded hair or wigged, open or closed mouth, kid or cloth bodies, may have arms of other materials.

Painted eyes

13"	$85.00	$165.00
16"	$110.00	$215.00
18"	$180.00	$365.00

Glass eyes

15"	$110.00	$215.00
17"	$185.00	$375.00
20"	$240.00	$475.00
23"	$275.00	$550.00

5½" celluloid Sun Bonnet Sue A Sunny Twinn Dolly, all original in labeled box, painted features, circa 1920s, $225.00. Courtesy Sue Kinkade.

Bye-Lo Baby: see that section.

Celluloid/Plush, 1910+

Teddy bear body, can have half or full celluloid body with hood half head.

12"	$325.00	$650.00
14"	$400.00	$785.00
17"	$475.00	$925.00

Hitler youth group

8"	$90.00	$175.00

Hermsdorfer Celluloidwarenfabrik, 1923 – 1926, ladybug mark

17"	$90.00* with neck repair

Heubach Koppelsdorf, Mold 399

7"	$8.00	$30.00
9"	$10.00	$40.00
11"	$18.00	$70.00
15"	$40.00	$165.00
18"	$80.00	$330.00

Jumeau, marked on head, jointed body

13"	$245.00	$485.00
16"	$295.00	$585.00

Kammer & Reinhardt (K*R) shoulder head Mold 225, 255, ca. 1920

14"	$185.00	$370.00
17"	$250.00	$485.00

Kammer & Reinhardt (K*R) socket head Mold 406, ca. 1910, glass eyes, open mouth **Mold 700,** child or baby, ca. 1910, painted eyes, open/closed mouth

14"	$250.00	$475.00

10" celluloid child with molded blue ribbon, painted and molded hair, painted eyes, open/closed mouth with teeth, molded black shoes and brown socks, excellent condition, circa 1920s, $125.00. Private collection.

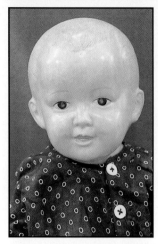

17" celluloid child with molded and painted features, open/closed mouth, jointed body, old costume, small toe damage, circa 1930s, $250.00+. Courtesy Dianne Godfrey-Daily.

Mold 701, ca. 1910, character, painted eyes, closed mouth

14"	$475.00	$950.00

Mold 715, ca. 1912, character, sleep eyes, closed mouth

15"	$300.00	$685.00

Mold 717, ca. 1920, character, sleep eyes, closed mouth

17"	$700.00* flapper body, boxed	
22"	$350.00	$700.00

Mold 728, ca. 1928, character, sleep eyes, open mouth

16"	$250.00	$500.00
20"	$350.00	$700.00

All-celluloid toddler body

18"	$425.00*

Kestner
Mold 203, character baby

12"	$450.00*

Kewpie: see that section.
Konig & Wernicke (K&W)
Toddler

15"	$165.00	$325.00
19"	$250.00	$500.00

Max and Moritz, each

7"	$150.00	$300.00

Parsons-Jackson (stork mark)
Baby

12"	$100.00	$200.00
14"	$150.00	$285.00

Toddler

15"	$200.00	$385.00

Black

14"	$250.00	$485.00

Century Doll Co.

Mark:

CENTURY DOLL C?
Kestner Germany

Chuckles Mark on back:
"CHUCKLES//A CENTURY DOLL"

1909 – 1930, New York City.
Founded by Max Scheuer and sons; used bisque heads on many later dolls. In about 1929, Century merged with Domec to become the Doll Corporation of America. Some heads were made by Kestner, Herm Steiner, and other firms for Century.

First price is for doll in good condition, but with flaws; second price for doll in excellent condition, with original clothes or appropriately dressed. More for boxed, tagged, or labeled exceptional doll.

BISQUE

Baby, ca. 1926, by Kestner

Bisque head, molded painted hair, sleep eyes, open/closed mouth, cloth body

17"	$550.00	$750.00

Mold 275, solid dome, glass eyes, closed mouth, cloth body, composition limbs

14"	$715.00	$950.00

Child

Mold 285, by Kestner, bisque socket head, glass eyes, open mouth, wig, ball jointed body

23"	$545.00	$725.00

COMPOSITION

14" Century Doll Co. composition shoulder head Pudgy Peggy with cloth body, molded loop in hair, circa 1928, $225.00. Courtesy Donna Nance.

Chuckles, 1927 – 1929

Composition shoulder head, arms, and legs, cloth body with crier, open mouth, molded short hair, painted or sleep eyes, two upper teeth, dimples in cheeks. Came as a bent-leg baby or toddler.

16"	$85.00	$325.00

Mama dolls, ca. 1922+

Composition head, tin sleep eyes, cloth body, with crier, swing legs and arms of composition

16"	$70.00	$250.00
23"	$120.00	$475.00

Chase: see Cloth dolls.

China

Ca. 1840+. Most china shoulder head dolls were made in Germany by various firms. Prior to 1880, most china heads were pressed into the mold; later ones poured. Pre-1880, most china heads were sold separately with purchaser buying commercial body or making one at home. Original commercial costumes are rare; most clothing was homemade.

Early unusual features are glass eyes or eyes painted brown. After 1870, pierced ears and blonde hair were found and, after 1880, more child chinas, with shorter hair and shorter necks were popular. Most common in this period were flat tops and low brows and the latter were made until the mid-1900s. Later innovations were china arms and legs with molded boots. Most heads are unmarked or with size or mold number only, usually on the back shoulder plate.

Identification tips: Hair styles, color, complexion tint, and body help date the doll.

First price indicates doll in good condition with some flaws; second price indicates doll in excellent condition with original or appropriate clothes. More for exceptional quality.

CHILD

Swivel neck, shoulder plate, may have china lower limbs

14"	$2,100.00	$2,850.00

14½" pink tint china shoulder plate with black molded headband and swirled blonde hair in back, earrings, china hands, cloth body, nicely dressed, circa 1870s, $500.00. Courtesy Elizabeth Surber.

Child or boy
Short black or blond hairdo, curly with exposed ears

13"	$195.00	$260.00
21"	$275.00	$365.00

French
Glass or painted eyes, open crown, cork pate, wig, kid body, china arms

14"	$2,350.00	$3,150.00
21"	$3,300.00*	

Japanese, ca. 1910 – 1920
Marked or unmarked, black or blond hair

10"	$110.00	$125.00
15"	$140.00	$190.00

K.P.M. (Konigliche Porzellanmanufaktur Berlin), 1840s – 1850s+
Made china doll heads marked KPM inside shoulder plate.

Nymphenburg portrait, circa 1901

16"	$1,500.00*

Pink tint lady w/Latchmann 1874 body

19"	$5,100.00*

Brown hair man, 1869, marked

23"	$7,000.00*

Pink tint Morning Glory," 1860s

24"	$10,250.00*

Brown hair lady with bun, 1860s, marked

24"	$13,500.00*

Kling, marked with bell and number

13"	$265.00	$350.00
16"	$325.00	$435.00
22"	$400.00	$525.00

Man with curls

19"	$1,400.00	$1,850.00

Man or boy, glass eyes

17"	$1,975.00	$2,650.00

Pierced ears, various common hair styles

14"	$365.00	$485.00
18"	$475.00	$635.00

Pierced ears, with elaborate hair style

17"	$1,164.00	$1,550.00+

Queen Victoria, young

16"	$1,195.00	$1,600.00
23"	$1,875.00	$2,500.00

Sophia Smith
Straight sausage curls ending in a ridge around head, rather than curved to head shape

19"	$985.00	$1,325.00+

14" china shoulder head boy with hair painted and molded in soft waves across forehead, paint rubs, cloth body, china hands, molded feet, nicely dressed in sailor suit, circa 1880s, $350.00. Courtesy Elizabeth Surber.

Spill Curls

With or without headband, lots of single curls across forehead, around back to ringlets in back

13"	$325.00	$435.00
20"	$550.00	$750.00
26"	$650.00	$850.00

Swivel neck, flange type

10"	$1,550.00	$2,100.00
13"	$2,025.00	$2,700.00

1840 STYLES

China shoulder head with long neck, painted features, black or brown molded hair, may have exposed ears and pink complexion, with red-orange facial detail, may have bust modeling, cloth, leather, or wood body, nicely dressed, good condition.

16½" china Jenny Lind, so called because of her hair style, with black center part hairdo swirled to back with coiled bun, china arms, molded boots, small crack in shoulder plate, circa 1870s, nicely dressed, $1,200.00. Courtesy Elizabeth Surber.

Bun or coronet

15"	$2,100.00	$2,825.00

Early marked china (Nuremberg, Rudolstadt)

14"	$1,700.00	$2,275.00+
17"	$2,125.00	$2,835.00

Brown hair, bun

16"	$2,650.00	$3,500.00

Boy, pressed china, smiling, side-parted brown hair

21"	$3,450.00	$4,600.00

Too few in database for reliable range.

Covered Wagon

Center part, combed back to form sausage curls

10"	$200.00	$275.00
14"	$300.00	$400.00
17"	$350.00	$475.00
20"	$425.00	$550.00
25"	$525.00	$700.00
31"	$650.00	$900.00+

Wood body

9"	$1,200.00	$1,575.00
13"	$1,600.00	$2,150.00
17"	$2,125.00	$2,850.00+

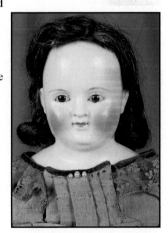

25" china shoulder plate, cobalt blue glass eyes, closed smiling mouth, high cheek color, human hair wig, cloth body, china lower limbs, eye chip, circa 1850s, $1,200.00. Courtesy McMasters Doll Auctions.

1850 STYLES

China shoulder head, painted features, bald with black spot or molded black hair, may have pink complexion, cloth, leather, or wood body, china arms and legs, nicely dressed, good condition.

Alice in Wonderland, snood, headband

12"	$225.00	$300.00
16"	$300.00	$400.00
20"	$375.00	$500.00

20" pink tint china with covered wagon hairdo, china arms, cloth body, molded boots, circa 1840s, $550.00. Courtesy Elizabeth Surber.

Flange neck, Motchmann style body

12"	$1,350.00	$1,800.00
17"	$2,000.00	$2,650.00

Bald head, glazed china with black spot

Formerly called Biedermeir, human hair or mohair wig

12"	$475.00	$650.00
14"	$550.00	$750.00
21"	$800.00	$1,050.00

Bald head, with black spot, glass eyes, wig

14"	$1,250.00	$1,675.00
21"	$1,975.00	$2,650.00

Frozen Charlies or Charlottes: See that section.

Glass eyes, with painted black eyelashes, various hairdos.

13"	$1,850.00	$2,450.00
17"	$2,400.00	$3,200.00
21"	$2,975.00	$4,000.00

1860 STYLES

China shoulder head, center part, smooth black curls, painted features, seldom brushmarks or pink tones, all-cloth bodies or cloth with china arms and legs, may have leather arms. Decorated chinas with fancy hair styles embellished with flowers, ornaments, snoods, bands, ribbons, may have earrings.

Flat top Civil War

Black hair, center part, with flat top, curls on sides and back

10"	$125.00	$165.00
14"	$180.00	$245.00
18"	$225.00	$300.00
22"	$280.00	$365.00
26"	$355.00	$475.00
30"	$415.00	$545.00
34"	$465.00	$625.00

16" china shoulder head, with black curls, china hands, cloth body, molded boots, nicely dressed, circa 1875, $750.00. Courtesy Elizabeth Surber.

Swivel neck

15"	$675.00	$975.00
20"	$975.00	$1,285.00

Molded necklace

21"	$525.00	$700.00+

Too few in database for reliable range.

Highbrow, curls, high forehead, round face

15"	$400.00	$535.00
19"	$525.00	$700.00
22"	$600.00	$800.00+

Grape Lady

With cluster of grape leaves and blue grapes

15"	$1,000.00	$1,325.00
22"	$1,300.00	$1,725.00

Mary Todd Lincoln

Black hair, gold snood, gold luster bows at ears

15"	$475.00	$625.00
21"	$650.00	$850.00

Blonde with snood

21"	$1,300.00	$1,800.00

Too few in database for reliable range.

Morning Glory with flowers behind the ears

21"	$4,200.00	$5,600.00

Too few in database for reliable range.

1870 STYLES

China shoulder head, poured, finely painted, well molded, black or blonde hair, cloth or cloth and leather bodies, now with pink facial details instead of earlier red-orange.

16" china shoulder head with black bangs full cut across forehead, cloth body, china hands, molded boots, nicely dressed, circa 1870s, $400.00. Courtesy Elizabeth Surber.

Adelina Patti

Hair pulled up and away, center part, brush-stroked at temples, partly exposed ears, ringlets across back of head

14"	$195.00	$250.00
20"	$375.00	$500.00
25"	$410.00	$550.00

Bangs, full cut across forehead, sometimes called Highland Mary

Black hair

14"	$225.00	$300.00
19"	$325.00	$425.00
24"	$402.00	$525.00

Blonde hair

14"	$265.00	$325.00
22"	$400.00	$525.00
24"	$415.00	$550.00

Jenny Lind, black hair pulled back into a bun or coronet

15"	$1,150.00	$1,550.00

1880 STYLES

Now may also have many blonde as well as black hair examples, more curls, and overall curls, narrower shoulders, fatter cheeks, irises outlined with black paint, may have bangs. China legs have fat calves and molded boots.

Dolly Madison

Black molded hair, two separate clusters of curls on forehead, molded ribbon and bow across top, ears partially exposed, painted blue eyes, irises and eyes outlined with black, black eyebrows

14"	$260.00	$350.00
18"	$350.00	$475.00
22"	$425.00	$575.00
24"	$475.00	$635.00
28"	$550.00	$725.00

1890 Styles

Shorter fatter arms and legs, may have printed body with alphabet, emblems, flags

Common or low brow

Black or blonde center part wavy hairdo that comes down low on forehead

10"	$85.00	$115.00
14"	$115.00	$155.00
16"	$135.00	$180.00
19"	$150.00	$215.00
23"	$200.00	$300.00
27"	$250.00	$350.00
36"	$355.00	$475.00

With jewel necklace

14"	$175.00	$225.00
20"	$245.00	$325.00

Pet Names, ca. 1899 – 1930+

Agness, Bertha, Daisy, Dorothy, Edith, Esther, Ethel, Florence, Helen, Mabel, Marion, Pauline, and Ruth

Made for Butler Brothers by various German firms. China head and limbs on cloth body. Molded blouse marked in front with name in gold lettering, molded blonde or black allover curls.

9"	$80.00	$110.00
14"	$150.00	$200.00
17"	$185.00	$245.00
21"	$215.00	$290.00

14½" pet name china Agnes with molded blouse and name, black hair, cloth body, molded boots, circa 1899 – 1930s, $200.00. Courtesy Elizabeth Surber.

Cloth

First price is for doll in good condition, but with some wear or soiled; second price is for doll in very good condition and clean with good color. Exceptional doll may be more.

Alabama Indestructible Dolls

Ca. 1900 – 1925, Roanoke, Alabama. Ella Gauntt Smith, made all-cloth dolls with painted features; jointed at shoulders and hips. Head construction may include round "monk's cap" on top of head. Painted feet varied, some with stitched toes, but most had one-button slippers or low boots. Shoes were painted black, brown, pink or blue; came in seven heights, from 12" to 27".

Alabama Indestructible Dolls Marks:
"MRS. S.S. SMITH//
MANUFACTURER
AND DEALER IN//
THE ALABAMA
INDESTRUCTIBLE
DOLL// ROANOKE,
ALA.//
PATENTED//
SEPT. 26, 1905."

Baby

12"	$750.00	$1,500.00
14"	$4,600.00* unplayed with	

Black Baby

20"	$3,200.00	$6,200.00

Barefoot Baby, rare

23"	$1,500.00	$3,000.00

Child

15"	$800.00	$1,600.00
22"	$1,200.00	$2,400.00

Black Child

18"	$3,100.00	$6,200.00
23"	$3,400.00	$6,800.00

ART FABRIC MILLS

1899 – 1910+, New York, New Haven, and London. Lithographed in color, made cloth cut-out dolls

Improved Life Size Doll, with printed underwear

20"	$75.00	$275.00
30"	$100.00	$400.00

Punch and Judy, pair

27"	$200.00	$800.00

BABYLAND RAG

1893 – 1928. Babyland Rag Dolls were made by E. I. Horsman, with oil-painted or lithographed faces.

Lithographed

14½"	$175.00	$335.00
16½"	$200.00	$400.00
24"	$275.00	$550.00

Black

14½"	$240.00	$480.00
16½"	$275.00	$550.00
24"	$400.00	$800.00

Molded painted faces

13"	$350.00	$700.00

Flat painted faces

16½"	$450.00	$900.00
20"	$540.00	$1,080.00
30"	$810.00	$1,620.00

Black

16½"	$490.00	$975.00
20"	$590.00	$1,180.00
30"	$885.00	$1,770.00

> *Art Fabric Mills Marks:*
> *"ART FABRIC MILLS,*
> *NY, PAT. FEB. 13TH,*
> *1900" on shoe or*
> *bottom of foot.*

17" cloth Ella Smith Doll Co. Alabama Baby with body stamp, stitched crown, painted face, limbs, painted blue shoes, circa early 1900s, $2,500.00. Courtesy Barbara DeFeo.

BEECHER, JULIA JONES

Ca. 1893 – 1910, Elmira, New York. Wife of Congregational Church pastor Thomas K., sister-in-law of Harriet Beecher Stowe. Made Missionary Ragbabies, of old silk jersey underwear, with flat hand-painted and needle sculpted features. All proceeds used for missionary work. Sizes 16" to 23" and larger.

Missionary Ragbabies

16"	$1,725.00	$3,450.00
23"	$2,500.00	$5,000.00

Black

16"	$1,750.00	$3,500.00
23"	$2,800.00	$5,600.00

Beecher-type

	20"	$550.00	$2,200.00

BING ART

Bing Werke, Germany, 1921 – 1932. All-cloth, felt or composition head with cloth body, molded face, oil-painted features, wigged or painted hair, pin-jointed cloth body, seams down front of legs, mitt hands.

Painted hair, cloth or felt, unmarked or "Bing" on bottom of foot

	13"	$275.00	$550.00
	15"	$325.00	$650.00

Wigged

	10"	$175.00	$350.00
	16"	$325.00	$650.00

Composition head

	8"	$40.00	$145.00
	12"	$45.00	$175.00
	16"	$60.00	$225.00

18" cloth Arnold Print Works, Improved Foot Cloth Doll printed on underwear, stockings, and shoes, circa 1901+, $200.00. Courtesy Sherryl Shirran.

BLACK, 1830+

Black cloth doll patterns in *American Girls Book*, describe how to make dolls of black silk or crepe, gingham or calico dress, apron, and cap. Beecher, Bruckner, Chad Valley, Chase, and Lenci made black cloth dolls. Horsman advertised black cloth Topsy and Dinah cloth dolls, ca. 1912. Black cloth dolls were made ca. 1921 by Grace Cory for Century Doll Co. Many cloth dolls were homemade and one-of-a-kind. Patterns were available to make mammy doll toaster covers during the 1940s.

Mammy-style, with painted or embroidered features, 1910 – 1920s

	$65.00	$200.00
12"	$65.00	$200.00
16"	$85.00	$285.00

1930s

15"	$55.00	$165.00+

Topsy-Turvy

Cloth dolls with two heads, some with black doll under one skirt, which when turned over reveals white doll under other skirt.

Oil-painted	$200.00	$650.00
Printed	$150.00	$425.00

Bruckner Topsy Turvy

13"	$950.00*

BROWNIES BY PALMER COX

Brownie Mark:
"Copyright 1892
by Palmer Cox"
on right foot.

1892 – 1907. Printed cloth dolls based on copyrighted figures of Palmer Cox; 12 different figures, including Canadian, Chinaman, Dude, German, Highlander, Indian, Irishman, John Bull, Policeman, Sailor, Soldier, and Uncle Sam.

Set of three uncut, one yard length

	7½"	$350.00
	7½"	$100.00

Set of 12 with book		$825.00*

* at auction

BRUCKNER, ALBERT

Ca. 1901 – 1930+, Jersey City. Obtained patent for cloth dolls using printed, molded mask face. Made dolls for Horsman.

14"	$165.00	$325.00
Black		
14"	$215.00	$425.00

CHAD VALLEY

1917 – 1930+, Harbourne, England. Founded by Johnson Bros., made all types of cloth dolls, early ones had stockinette faces, later felt, with velvet body, jointed neck, shoulders, hips, glass or painted eyes, mohair wig. Mabel Lucie Atwell was an early designer.

Bruckner Mark: On shoulder, "Pat'd July 8, 1901."

Chad Valley Marks: Usually on sole of foot, "THE CHAD VALLEY CO. LTD//(BRITISH ROYAL COAT OF ARMS)//TOY-MAKER TO//H.M." or "HYGIENIC TOYS//MADE IN ENGLAND BY//CHAD VALLEY CO. LTD."

Animals

Cat

12"	$75.00	$215.00+

Bonzo, cloth dog with painted eyes, almost closed and smile

4"	$65.00	$210.00
13"	$110.00	$415.00

Bonzo, eyes open

5½"	$80.00	$275.00
14"	$150.00	$575.00

Dog, plush

12"	$65.00	$260.00

Characters

Captain Blye, Fisherman, Long John Silver, Pirate, Policeman, Train Conductor, etc.

Glass eyes

18"	$325.00	$1,000.00
20"	$375.00	$1,300.00

Painted eyes

18"	$225.00	$775.00
20"	$250.00	$875.00

Ghandi/India

13"	$175.00	$675.00

Rahmah-Jah

26"	$225.00	$900.00

Child

Glass eyes

14"	$165.00	$625.00
16"	$200.00	$725.00
18"	$225.00	$775.00

Painted eyes

9 – 10"	$40.00	$150.00
12"	$65.00	$225.00
15"	$115.00	$425.00
18"	$160.00	$625.00

14" felt Chad Valley Grenadier Guard blue glass eyes, red felt jacket, black and gold plaid kilt, black "bearskin" hat with chin strap, marked on foot, "Hygenienic Toys/made in England by /Chad Valley Co. Ltd.," circa 1930s, $900.00. Courtesy Dee Cermak.

13" cloth Chad Valley child, glass eyes, hang tag, original outfit, circa 1920s – 1930s, very good condition, $550.00. Courtesy Sharon Kolibaba

> *Martha Chase Marks: "CHASE STOCKINET DOLL" on left leg or under left arm. Paper label, if there, reads "CHASE//HOSPITAL DOLL// TRADE MARK// PAWTUCKET, RI// MADE IN U.S.A."*

20" oil-painted cloth Martha Chase baby, stamped upper leg, nicely dressed, circa 1900 – 1910, $850.00. Courtesy Marian Pettygrove.

Royal Family, all with glass eyes, 16" – 18"

Princess Alexandra		
	$400.00	$1,500.00
Prince Edward, Duke of Windsor		
	$400.00	$1,500.00
Princess Elizabeth		
	$425.00	$1,700.00
Princess Margaret Rose		
	$400.00	$1,500.00

Story Book Dolls

Dong Dell		
14"	$125.00	$475.00
Dwarfs		
9½"	$165.00	$675.00
My Elizabeth, My Friend		
14"	$165.00	$675.00
Snow White		
17"	$250.00	$1,000.00
Red Riding Hood		
14"	$125.00	$500.00

MARTHA CHASE

Ca. 1889 – 1930+, Pawtucket, Rhode Island. Heads were made from stockinette covered masks reproduced from bisque dolls, heavily painted features including thick lashes, closed mouth, sometimes nostrils, painted textured hair, jointed shoulder, elbows, knees, and hips; later dolls only at shoulders and hips.

First price indicates doll in good condition with some flaws; second price indicates doll in excellent condition with original or appropriate clothes.

Baby

16"	$425.00	$575.00
19"	$495.00	$700.00
24"	$625.00	$875.00
Hospital-type		
20"	$500.00*	
29"	$450.00	$575.00

Child

Molded bobbed hair		
12"	$900.00	$1,200.00
16"	$1,200.00	$1,600.00
22"	$1,650.00	$2,200.00
Solid dome, simple painted hair		
15"	$365.00	$485.00
18"	$475.00	$625.00
Unusual hairdo, molded bun		
15"	$2,200.00*	

* at auction

Characters

Alice in Wonderland, character, circa 1905, set of six dolls, including Alice, Duchess, Tweedledee and Tweedledum, Mad Hatter, and Frog Footman, 12" tall excluding hats, hard pressed muslin, with oil painted features, stitch-jointed limbs, rare to find as a group

12"	$67,000.00* set of six	

Benjamin Franklin

15"	$6,875.00*	

Too few in database to give reliable range.

Later Dolls

Baby

14"	$150.00	$200.00
15"	$190.00	$250.00
19"	$300.00	$400.00

Child

15"	$215.00	$285.00
20"	$300.00	$400.00

20½" cloth Martha Chase boy, painted hair, features, cloth body and painted limbs, jointed elbows and knees, nicely dressed, some paint rubs, circa 1900 – 1920, $1,800.00. Courtesy Elizabeth Surber.

COLUMBIAN DOLL

Emma E. Adams made rag dolls, distributed by Marshall Field & Co., and won awards at the 1893 Chicago World Fair. Succeeded by her sister, Marietta Adams Ruttan. Cloth dolls had hand-painted features, stitched fingers and toes.

14"	$4,600.00*	
15"	$2,225.00	$4,500.00
19"	$2,850.00	$5,700.00

Columbian-type

16"	$650.00	$1,280.00
22"	$1,100.00	$2,200.00

Comic Characters

15"	$150.00	$450.00

Columbian Doll Marks:
"COLUMBIAN DOLL, EMMA E. ADAMS, OSWEGO, NY"

DEANS RAG BOOK CO.

1905+, London. Subsidiary of Dean & Son, Ltd., a printing and publishing firm, used "A1" to signify quality, made Knockabout Toys, Tru-to-life, Evripoze, and others. An early designer was Hilda Cowham.

Front and back views of 13½" cloth Colonial Toy Mfg. Co. Hug Me Tight" doll, designed by G.G. Drayton, circa 1916, $200.00. Courtesy Sherryl Shirran.

12" cloth girl designed by Maud Tousey Fangel, printed features on stuffed cloth body, wear and soil, circa 1930s, $350.00. Courtesy Sharon Kolibaba.

Child

10"	$100.00	$285.00
16"	$185.00	$550.00
17"	$250.00	$750.00

Lithographed face

9"	$30.00	$85.00
15"	$55.00	$165.00
16"	$75.00	$225.00

Mask face, velvet, with cloth body and limbs

12"	$45.00	$125.00
18"	$90.00	$265.00
24"	$125.00	$385.00
30"	$155.00	$475.00
34"	$185.00	$565.00
40"	$225.00	$695.00

Golliwogs (English black character doll)

13"	$85.00	$250.00
15"	$150.00	$450.00

DRAYTON, GRACE

1909 – 1929, Philadelphia, Pennsylvania. An illustrator, her designs were used for cloth and other dolls. Made printed dolls with big eyes, flat faces.

Chocolate Drop, 1923, Averill Mfg. Corp., brown cloth, printed features, three tufts yarn hair

10"	$135.00	$400.00
14"	$185.00	$550.00

Dolly Dingle, 1923, Averill Mfg. Corp., cloth, printed features, marked on torso

11"	$115.00	$385.00
15"	$165.00	$550.00

Double face or topsy turvy

15"	$190.00	$625.00

Hug Me Tight, 1916, Colonial Toy Mfg. Co., printed cloth with boy standing behind girl, one-piece

12"	$75.00	$250.00
16"	$150.00	$435.00

Kitty Puss, all-cloth, cat face, wired posable limbs and tail

15"	$135.00	$400.00

Peek-A-Boo, Horsman, 1913 – 1915, printed features

9"	$55.00	$175.00
12"	$75.00	$225.00
15"	$90.00	$275.00

FANGEL, MAUD TOUSEY

1920 – 1930+. Designed cloth dolls, with flat printed faces, some with mitten hands. Some had three-piece heads and feet.

Baby

13"	$150.00	$425.00
17"	$200.00	$600.00

17" Kamkins oil-painted cloth swivel head with molded features, mohair wig, cloth body, old outfit, some touch-up, circa 1919 – 1928, $800.00. Courtesy McMasters Doll Auctions.

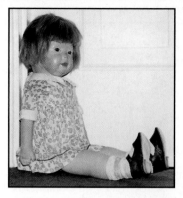

19" cloth Kamkin child, Louise R. Kampes Studio, made by cottage industry workers at home, all-cloth, molded mask face, painted features, swivel head, jointed shoulders, hips, mohair wig, extra wardrobe, circa 1919 – 1928, $2,000.00+. Courtesy Lilian Booth.

Child, Peggy Ann, Rosy, Snooks, Sweets

9"	$100.00	$300.00
12"	$165.00	$500.00
15"	$200.00	$625.00
21"	$250.00	$800.00

FARNELL, J.K. & CO. LTD. 1871 – 1968, LONDON

Baby

15"	$150.00	$475.00
18"	$200.00	$600.00

Child

10"	$85.00	$250.00
15"	$165.00	$500.00

King George VI, "H.M. The King"

15"	$400.00	$1,000.00

Palace Guard, "Beefeater"

15"	$225.00	$700.00

KAMKINS

1919 – 1928. Cloth doll made by Louise R. Kampes Studio, made by cottage industry workers at home. All-cloth, molded mask face, painted features, swivel head, jointed shoulders, hips, mohair wig.

19"	$600.00	$1,600.00

KRUSE, KATHE: See that section.

KRUEGER, RICHARD

1917+. Made many cloth dolls, some of oilcloth or with oilcloth clothing, oil painted mask face, yarn or mohair wig, label.

> *Kamkins Marks:*
> *Heart-shaped sticker:*
> *KAMKINS// A DOLLY*
> *MADE TO LOVE //*
> *PATENTED//FROM// L.R.*
> *KAMPES//STUDIOS//*
> *ATLANTIC CITY//N.J.*
>
> *Kreuger Marks:*
> *"KRUEGER NY//REG. U.S.*
> *PAT. OFF//MADE IN U.S.A."*
> *on body or clothing seam.*

15½" cloth Ronnaug Petterssen boy, pressed felt face, painted features, stitched fingers, in Norwegian Hardanger costume, circa 1940s – 1970s, $500.00. Courtesy Elaine Beling.

Child

12"	$40.00	$135.00
16"	$60.00	$195.00
20"	$80.00	$240.00

Walt Disney and other characters

Dwarf

12½"	$65.00	$200.00

Pinocchio

16"	$125.00	$425.00+

LENCI: See that section.

MOLLY-'ES

1929 – 1930+. Trademark used by Mollye Goldman of International Doll Co. of Philadelphia, PA. Made clothes for cloth dolls with masked faces (and composition dolls), dressed in international costumes.

Child

13"	$90.00	$130.00
17"	$45.00	$150.00
22"	$65.00	$200.00
27"	$85.00	$275.00

Lady, in long dresses or gowns

16"	$55.00	$175.00
21"	$75.00	$250.00

Internationals

13"	$30.00	$90.00
15"	$45.00	$135.00
27"	$100.00	$300.00

Princess, Thief of Bagdad

Blue painted Oriental-style eyes, harem outfit

14"	$100.00	$300.00

PETERSSEN, RONNAUG

1901 – 1980, Norway. Made cloth dolls, pressed felt head, usually painted side-glancing eyes, cloth bodies, intricate costumes, paper tags.

8"	$20.00	$40.00
14½"	$350.00	$700.00

PETZOLD, DORA

Germany, 1919 – 1930+. Made and dressed dolls, molded head, painted features, wig, stockinette body, sawdust filled, short torso, free-formed thumbs, stitched fingers, shaped legs.

18"	$200.00	$600.00
22"	$225.00	$775.00

PHILADELPHIA BABIES, J.B. SHEPPARD & CO.

Ca. 1860 – 1935. Shoulder head, stockinette rag doll with molded eyelids, stitched fingers and toes, painted features, sizes 18" – 22", also known as Sheppard Dolls.

18"	$1,200.00	$3,500.00
22"	$1,320.00	$4,000.00
21"	$4,730.00*	

* at auction

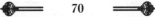

PRINTED CLOTH

Ca. 1876+. Made by various firms such as Arnold Print Works, North Adams, MA (some marked Cocheco Manufacturing Co.), Art Fabric Mills (see above listing), and other lesser or unknown firms who printed fabric for making cutout dolls, to be sewn together and stuffed.

Aunt Jemima

    Set of four dolls $100.00 each

Black Child

        16" $150.00 $425.00

Cream of Wheat, Rastus

        16" $40.00 $125.00

Printed underwear, Dolly Dear, Flaked Rice, Merry Marie, etc.

  Cut and sewn

        7" $35.00 $95.00

        16" $60.00 $175.00

  Uncut

        7" $125.00

        19" $275.00

With printed clothing, ca. 1903

  Cut and sewn

        14" $65.00 $200.00

        19" $115.00 $325.00

  Uncut

  Cocheco Darkey, 17" x 24"

        $250.00*

  Our Soldier Boys, 17" x 24"

        $175.00*

  Red Riding Hood, 18" x 24"

        $300.00*

Santa Claus/St. Nicholas

Marks: "Pat. Dec 18, 1886//Made by E.S.Peck NY"

  Cut and sewn

        15" $100.00 $325.00

  Uncut

        15" $600.00

RALEIGH, JESSIE MCCUTCHEON

Shoebutton Sue, flat face, painted spit curls, mitten hands, sewn on red shoes, shown in 1921 Sears catalog

        15" $1,900.00*

RAYNAL

1922 – 1930+, Paris. Edouard Raynal made dolls of felt, cloth, or with celluloid heads with widely spaced eyebrows. Dressed, some resemble Lenci, except fingers were together or their hands were of celluloid; marked *"Raynal"* on soles of shoes and/or pendant.

        14½" $165.00 $500.00

        17" $225.00 $700.00

Printed Cloth Marks:
Cloth label usually on sole of the foot reads: "MADE IN ENGLAND// BY// NORAH WELLINGS."

Raynal Trademark:
POUPEES RAYNAL.

26" cloth Rollison child, painted molded face, painted features, wigged, open/closed mouth, beautiful coloring, purple stamp on back of body, circa 1916 – 1929, $2,000.00. Courtesy Debbie Crume.

Stamp on back of 26" cloth Rollison child, circa 1916 – 1929. Courtesy Debbie Crume.

ROLLISON, GERTRUDE F. ROLLISON

Ca. 1916 – 1929 Holyoke, Massachusetts. Designed and made cloth dolls with molded faces treated to be washable, painted features. Dolls were produced by Utley Co., distributed by Borgfeldt, L. Wolf and Strobel, and Wilken.

Molded painted hair

20"	$400.00	$1,150.00

Wigged, stamped body

26"	$1,500.00	$2,000.00

RUSSIAN

Ca. 1920+. All-cloth, molded painted stockinette head, hands, in regional costumes

7"	$25.00	$70.00
15"	$50.00	$150.00
18"	$60.00	$180.00

STEIFF: See that section.

WALKER, IZANNAH

Ca. late 1800s, Central Fall, Rhode Island. Made cloth stockinette dolls, with pressed mask face, oil-painted features, applied ears, brush-stroked or corkscrew curls, stitched hands and feet, some with painted boots.

First price indicates very worn; second price for good condition. More for unusual hair style.

16"	$4,500.00	$18,000.00

WELLINGS, NORAH

Victoria Toy Works, 1926 – 1930+, Wellington, Shropshire, England. Chief designer for Chad Valley, she and brother, Leonard, started their own factory. Made cloth dolls of velvet, velveteen, plush, and felt, specializing in sailor souvenir dolls for steamship lines. The line included children, adults, blacks, ethnic, and fantasy dolls.

Baby

Molded face, oil painted features, some papier-mache covered by stockinette, stitched hip and shoulder joints

15"	$200.00	$600.00
22"	$300.00	$900.00

Child, painted eyes

13"	$125.00	$400.00
18"	$200.00	$600.00
22"	$235.00	$700.00
28"	$300.00	$900.00

Glass eyes

15"	$175.00	$550.00
18"	$275.00	$850.00
22"	$425.00	$1,300.00

Characters in uniform, regional dress

Mounties, Policemen, others

13"	$125.00	$385.00
17"	$250.00	$750.00
24"	$350.00	$1,100.00

Black Islander or Scot

9"	$30.00	$90.00
13"	$61.00	$185.00
16"	$75.00	$225.00

Creche

Figures of various materials made especially for religious scenes such as the Christmas manger scene. Usually not jointed, some with elaborate costumes. Some early created figures were gesso over wood head and limbs, fabric covered bodies with wire frames, later figures made of terra-cotta or other materials. Some with inset eyes.

Man, wood shoulder head, glass eyes, wire body
8" $115.00
Lady, carved shoulder head, glass eyes, wire body
10½" $350.00
Lady, gesso over wood, glass eyes, wire frame
14½" $500.00
Too few in database for reliable range.

24" terra cotta Creche woman, glass eyes, painted molded hair, wire armature body, padded, carved wooden hands and feet, $105.00. Courtesy McMasters Doll Auctions.

DEP

The "DEP" mark on the back of bisque heads stands for the French "Depose" or the German "Deponirt," which means registered claim. Some dolls made by Simon & Halbig have the "S&H" mark hidden above the "DEP" under the wig. Bisque head, swivel neck, appropriate wig, paperweight eyes, open or closed mouth, good condition, nicely dressed on French style wood and composition body.

First price is for doll in good condition, but with flaws; second price indicates doll in excellent condition with original or appropriate clothing.

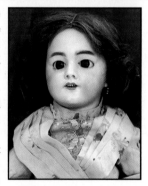

22" oily bisque socket head, marked DEP, pierced ears, human hair wig, composition jointed body, old silk costume, eye chip, circa 1890s – 1900s, $1,200.00. Courtesy Debbie Hamilton.

Closed mouth

15"	$1,600.00	$2,150.00
19"	$1,900.00	$2,550.00
23"	$2,300.00	$3,150.00

Open mouth

13"	$625.00	$825.00
18"	$875.00	$1,200.00
23"	$1,300.00	$1,725.00
28"	$1,900.00	$2,550.00

> *Mark:*
>
> *DEP*
> (Size number)

6" small china with common 1890s hairstyle, china arms, molded boots, cloth body, worn costume, $75.00. Courtesy Carol Coffey.

Small dolls generally under 8" usually dressed as member of a family or in household-related occupations, often sold as a group. Made of any material, but usually bisque head by 1880.

First price is for doll in good condition, but with flaws; second price is for doll in excellent condition with original clothes.

BISQUE

Adult, man or woman, painted eyes, molded hair, wig

6"	$125.00	$225.00

Glass eyes, molded hair

6"	$300.00	$400.00

Glass eyes, wigged

6"	$400.00	$600.00

Black man or woman, molded hair, original clothes

6"	$360.00	$475.00

Chauffeur, molded cap

6"	$200.00	$285.00

Grandparents, or with molded on hats

6"	$200.00	$265.00

Military man, mustache, original clothes

6"	$435.00	$575.00+

With molded on helmet

6"	$525.00	$700.00+

Children, all-bisque

4"	$40.00	$75.00

CHINA

With early hairdo

4"	$225.00	$300.00

With low brow or common hairdo, ca. 1900s+

4"	$115.00	$150.00

COMPOSITION, PAPIER-MACHE, PLASTER, ETC.

5"	$150.00	$225.00

Door of Hope

1901 – 1950, Shanghai, China. Corneilia Bonnell started the Door of Hope Mission in Shanghai, to help poor girls sold by families. As a means to learn sewing skills, the girls dressed carved pearwood heads from Ning-Po. The heads and hands were natural finish, stuffed cloth bodies were then dressed in correct representation for 26 different Chinese classes. Carved wooden head with cloth or wooden arms, original handmade costumes, in very good condition.

First price indicates doll with faded clothing or soiled; second price is for doll in excellent condition with clean, bright clothing. Exceptional dolls could be higher.

ADULT, MAN OR WOMAN

12"	$225.00	$550.00

Bride

11"	$1,050.00* elaborate dress	
12"	$325.00	$650.00

Groom

12"	$325.00	$650.00

Bridal couple in traditional dress

12"	$1,000.00*	

Amah with Baby

	$375.00	$750.00

Manchu Lady or Man

12"	$500.00	$1,000.00

Mourner

	$325.00	$750.00

Policeman

	$325.00	$750.00

SCHOOLCHILD

8"	$300.00	$600.00

11½" wood Door of Hope Manchu Lady with colorful headdress, carved features, nicely dressed in original outfit, circa 1930s, $1,000.00. Courtesy Elizabeth Surber.

Dressel, Cuno & Otto

Ca. 1873 – 1945, Sonnenberg, Thuringia, Germany. The Dressels made wood, wax, wax-over-composition, papier-mache, composition, china, and bisque heads for their dolls which they produced, distributed, and exported. Their bisque heads were made by Simon & Halbig, Armand Marseille, Ernst Heubach, Schoenau & Hoffmeister, and others.

Heubach·Köppelsdorf
Jutta-Baby
Dressel
Germany
1922
10

BISQUE

Baby, 1910+

Marked "C.O.D.," more for toddler body

13"	$185.00	$250.00
15"	$375.00	$475.00
19"	$450.00	$600.00

Child, open mouth, jointed composition body

14"	$225.00	$300.00
18"	$450.00	$475.00
22"	$400.00	$525.00

Child, character face, closed mouth, jointed child or toddler body

Painted eyes

13"	$1,200.00	$1,625.00
14"	$1,850.00	$2,450.00
18"	$2,300.00	$3,000.00

Glass eyes

15"	$2,300.00	$2,500.00
18"	$2,400.00	$3,400.00
23"	$3,100.00*	

18" bisque Cuno Otto Dressel mold 1914 Jutta, blue sleep eyes, open mouth with two upper teeth, mohair wig, bent-leg composition body with jointed wrists, small hairline, circa 1914, $375.00. Courtesy McMasters Doll Auctions.

22" bisque Cuno & Otto Dressel mold 1912 child, blue sleep eyes, open mouth, four upper teeth, synthetic wig, jointed wood and composition body, re-dressed in sailor dress, circa 1912, $325.00. Courtesy McMasters Doll Auctions.

14" bisque Dressel, Otto & Cuno fashion-type lady, mold 1469, blue sleep eyes, composition ball-jointed flapper body, high heels, circa 1920s, $3,800.00. Courtesy Barbara DeFeo.

Flapper

Closed mouth, five-piece composition body with thin legs and high heel feet, painted on hose up entire leg, mold 1469

12"	$2,500.00	$3,300.00
15"	$2,850.00	$3,800.00

Jutta

Baby open mouth, bent-leg body

16"	$400.00	$550.00
21"	$600.00	$800.00
24"	$1,000.00	$1,400.00

Child, 1906 – 1921, open mouth, marked with "Jutta" or "S&H" mold 1914, 1348, 1349, etc.

14"	$300.00	$425.00
17"	$450.00	$625.00
21"	$550.00	$750.00
25"	$700.00	$900.00
29"	$875.00	$1,150.00

Toddler

8"	$400.00	$550.00
15"	$500.00	$675.00
18"	$700.00	$950.00
23"	$925.00	$1,300.00
27"	$1,350.00	$1,850.00

Portrait dolls, 1896+

Bisque head, glass eyes, composition body
Admiral Dewey, Admiral Byrd

8"	$500.00	$700.00
12"	$1,100.00	$1,475.00

Buffalo Bill

10"	$575.00	$765.00

Farmer, Old Rip, Witch

8"	$475.00	$650.00
12"	$600.00	$800.00

Father Christmas

12"	$1,125.00	$1,500.00+

Uncle Sam

8"	$550.00	$735.00
13"	$750.00*	

COMPOSITION

Holz-Masse, 1875+. Composition shoulder head, wigged or molded hair, painted or glass eyes, cloth body, composition limbs, molded on boots

Molded hair

13"	$65.00	$250.00
17"	$100.00	$400.00
24"	$150.00	$565.00

Wigged

16"	$80.00	$325.00
24"	$110.00	$425.00

E.D.

E.D. Bebes marked with *"E.D."* and a size number and the word *"Depose"* were made by Etienne Denamure, ca. 1890s, Paris. Other marked E.D. dolls with no Depose mark were made when Emile Douillet was director of Jumeau and should be priced as Jumeau Tete face dolls. Denamure had no relationship with the Jumeau firm and his dolls do not have the spiral spring used to attach heads used by Jumeau. Denamure bebes have straighter eyebrows, the eyes slightly more recessed, large lips, and lesser quality bisque. Smaller sizes of Denamure E.D. bebes may not have the Depose mark.

First price is for doll in good condition, but with some flaws; second price indicates doll in excellent condition, more for original costumes.

30" bisque E.D. Bebe, marked E. 13. D. Depose on back of head, open mouth, four teeth, circa 1890s, $2,750.00+. Courtesy McMasters Doll Auctions.

Closed mouth

11"	$2,800.00*	
20"	$2,500.00	$3,300.00
25"	$3,000.00	$4,000.00
27"	$3,100.00	$4,250.00

Open mouth

14"	$975.00	$1,300.00
16"	$1,200.00	$1,600.00
21"	$1,575.00	$2,100.00
25"	$2,000.00	$2,600.00

Eden Bebe

1890 – 1899, made by Fleischmann & Bloedel; 1899 – 1953, made by Societe Francaise de Fabrication de Bebes & Jouet (S.F.B.J.). Dolls had bisque heads, jointed composition bodies.

First price indicates doll in good condition, but with some flaws; second price indicates doll in excellent condition, with original clothes or appropriately dressed.

Mark:
EDEN BEBE
PARIS

Closed mouth, pale bisque

15"	$1,725.00	$2,275.00
18"	$2,200.00	$2,700.00
22"	$2,250.00	$3,000.00

Closed mouth, high color, five-piece body

13"	$900.00	$1,200.00
19"	$1,200.00	$1,600.00
22"	$1,450.00	$1,950.00

23" bisque Eden Bebe child, socket head, glass eyes, open mouth, pierced ears, mohair wig, circa 1890s, $1,900.00+. Courtesy McMasters Doll Auctions.

* at auction

Open mouth

15"	$1,125.00	$1,500.00
18"	$1,250.00	$1,800.00
26"	$1,950.00	$2,600.00

Walking, Talking, Kissing

Jointed body, walker mechanism, head turns, arm throws a kiss, heads by Simon & Halbig using mold 1039 and others, bodies assembled by Fleischmann & Bloedel. Price for perfect working doll.

21"	$1,600.00

Too few in database for reliable range.

Fashion Type

French Poupee, 1869+. Glass eyes, doll modeled as an adult lady, with bisque shoulder head, stationary or swivel neck, closed mouth, earrings, kid or kid and cloth body, nicely dressed, good condition. Add more for original clothing, jointed body, black, or exceptional doll.

> COLLECTOR ALERT:
> French fashion types are being reproduced, made to look old. Collectors need to arm themselves with knowledge before purchasing. Quality information is available to members and research is continuing by the United Federation of Doll Clubs (UFDC). See Collectors' Network at back of book.

21" bisque French fashion type, glass eyes, earrings, human hair wig, swivel neck on shoulder plate with gusseted kid body, circa 1870 – 1890, $2,500.00. Courtesy Marguerite Long.

UNMARKED OR WITH SIZE NUMBER ONLY

12"	$1,175.00	$1,575.00
14"	$1,375.00	$1,825.00
16"	$1,525.00	$2,025.00
18"	$1,675.00	$2,275.00
21"	$2,400.00	$3,200.00
27"	$3,500.00	$4,600.00

Painted eyes, kid body

15"	$975.00	$1,300.00

Wooden articulated body, glass eyes

13"	$2,300.00	$2,900.00
15"	$3,100.00	$4,000.00
18"	$3,600.00	$4,700.00

BARROIS (E.B.): See that category.

BLACK: See that section.

BRU: See that category.

F. G.: See Gaultier and Gesland categories.

FORTUNE TELLER DOLLS

Fashion-type head with swivel neck, glass or painted eyes, kid body, skirt made to hold many paper "fortunes." Exceptional doll may be more.

Closed mouth

15"	$3,450.00	$4,100.00+

Open mouth
18" $2,150.00 $3,100.00+
China, glazed finish, 1870 – 1880 hairstyle
15" $1,250.00 $1,700.00
Wood, German, with tuck comb
16" $2,300.00 $3,100.00
GESLAND, marked F.G.: See that category.
HURET: See that category.
JUMEAU: See that category.
ROHMER: See that category.
ACCESSORIES
    Dress $500.00+
    Shoes marked by maker $500.00+
    unmarked $250.00
    Trunk $250.00+
    Wig $250.00+

15" bisque French fashion type with painted blue eyes, closed mouth, kid body with stitched fingers, circa 1890s, $900.00. Courtesy McMasters Doll Auctions.

Frozen Charlie or Charlotte

Ca. 1860 – 1940. Most porcelain factories made all-china dolls in one-piece molds with molded or painted black or blond hair, and usually undressed. Sometimes called Bathing Dolls, they were dubbed "Frozen Charlotte" from a song about a girl who went dancing dressed lightly and froze in the snow. Victorians found them immoral. They range in size from under 1" to over 19". Some were reproduced in Germany in the 1970s. Allow more for pink tint, extra decoration, or hairdo.

All china
    2" $65.00 $85.00
    5" $75.00 $100.00
    7" $150.00 $200.00
    9" $200.00 $275.00
    15" $350.00 $450.00
Black china
    6" $200.00 $275.00
    8" $275.00 $375.00
Black hair, flesh tones head and neck
    12" $300.00 $400.00
    15" $400.00 $550.00
Jointed shoulders
    5" $110.00 $145.00
    7" $165.00 $225.00
Molded boots
    4" $135.00 $185.00
    8" $200.00 $275.00
Molded clothes or hats
    3" $185.00 $250.00
    6" $225.00 $300.00
    8" $325.00 $425.00

16" china one-piece Frozen Charlie with pink flesh tones on head, arm damaged and repaired, 1880s – 1900s, $300.00. Private collection.

Pink tint, hairdo

	3"	$200.00	$225.00
	5"	$300.00	$350.00

Pink tint, bonnet-head

	3"	$350.00	$375.00
	5"	$425.00	$475.00

Stone bisque, molded hair, one piece

	3"	$20.00	$25.00
	6"	$30.00	$40.00

Parian-type, ca. 1860

	5"	$135.00	$185.00
	7"	$200.00	$250.00

Fulper Pottery Co.

14" bisque Fulper baby, blue sleep eyes, open mouth with two teeth, mohair wig, hairline, circa 1918 – 1921, $275.00. Courtesy McMasters Doll Auctions.

Mark:

1918 – 1921, Flemington, NJ. Made dolls with bisque heads and all-bisque dolls. Sold dolls to Amberg, Colonial Toy Mfg. Co., and Horsman. "M.S." monogram stood for Martin Stangl, in charge of production.

First price indicates doll in good condition, with flaws; second price indicates doll in excellent condition with original or appropriate clothes.

Baby, bisque socket head, glass eyes, open mouth, teeth, mohair wig, bent-leg body

14"	$300.00	$500.00
19"	$500.00	$700.00

Toddler, straight-leg body

16"	$700.00*	
19"	$625.00	$825.00+
25"	$750.00	$1,000.00+

Gans & Seyfarth

1908 – 1922, Waltershausen, Germany. Made bisque dolls; had a patent for flirty and googly eyes. Partners separated in 1922, Otto Gans opened his own factory.

Baby, bent-leg baby, original clothes or appropriately dressed

16"	$375.00	$525.00
20"	$465.00	$625.00
25"	$575.00	$775.00

Mark:

Child, open mouth, composition body, original clothes, or appropriately dressed

15"	$375.00	$500.00
21"	$500.00	$675.00
28"	$675.00	$900.00

* at auction

1860 – 1899. After 1899, became part of S.F.B.J., located near Paris, they made bisque doll heads and parts for lady dolls and for bebes and sold to many French makers of dolls. Also made all-bisque dolls marked "F.G."

BEBE (CHILD), "F.G." IN BLOCK LETTERS

Closed mouth, excellent quality bisque socket head, glass eyes, pierced ears, cork pate

Mark:

Compo and wood body with straight wrists

11"	$2,975.00	$3,950.00
13"	$3,100.00	$4,100.00
15"	$3,200.00	$4,250.00
20"	$4,200.00	$5,600.00
28"	$5,000.00	$6,750.00

Kid body, may have bisque forearms

15"	$3,300.00	$4,450.00
17"	$3,800.00	$5,000.00

BEBE (CHILD), "F.G." IN SCROLL LETTERS

Composition body, closed mouth

12"	$1,000.00	$1,325.00
17"	$2,225.00	$2,975.00
23"	$2,825.00	$3,725.00
28"	$3,400.00	$4,500.00

With marked Gesland wood body

22"	$10,450.00*

Composition body, open mouth

11"	$475.00	$650.00
16"	$1,350.00	$1,800.00
24"	$2,000.00	$2,700.00

24" bisque Francois Gaultier bebe, marked FG in scroll, paperweight eyes, open mouth, wood and composition body, some heavy wear on body, $975.00. Courtesy McMasters Doll Auctions.

FASHION-TYPE POUPEE

Marked one-piece shoulder head, glass eyes, kid body

13½"	$1,125.00	$1,500.00
17"	$1,800.00	$2,400.00
21"	$2,000.00	$2,750.00

Painted eyes

11"	$600.00	$800.00
15"	$825.00	$1,100.00
18½"	$1,025.00	$1,350.00

F.G., marked swivel head on bisque shoulder plate, kid body

May have bisque lower arms, glass eyes

12"	$1,200.00	$1,600.00
15"	$1,700.00	$2,250.00
18½"	$2,100.00	$2,775.00
20½"	$2,300.00	$3,100.00

Black

16"	$2,500.00	$3,400.00
20"	$3,500.00	$4,650.00

18" pressed pale bisque Francois Gaultier bebe marked in block letters "F 8 G," composition body, circa 1870s, $5,200.00. Courtesy Ann Van Arnum.

Gesland

1860 – 1928, Paris. Made, repaired, exported, and distributed dolls, patented a doll body, used heads from Francois Gaultier with "F.G." block or scroll mark. Gesland's unusual body had metal articulated armature covered with padding and stockinette, with bisque or wood/composition hands and legs.

Mark:

> **E. GESLAND**
> **B**ᵀᴱ **S. G. D. G.**
> **PARIS**

Bebe (child) on marked Gesland body
Closed mouth

12"	$2,900.00	$3,900.00
17"	$3,375.00	$4,500.00
20"	$3,750.00	$5,000.00

Poupee (fashion-type) Gesland
Stockinette covered metal articulated fashion-type body, bisque lower arms and legs

17"	$4,400.00	$5,800.00
23"	$4,950.00	$6,600.00

Gladdie

1928 – 1930+. Tradename of doll designed by Helen Webster Jensen, made in Germany, body made by K&K, for Borgfeldt. Flange heads made of bisque and biscaloid, an imi-

Mark:

> *Gladdie*
> *Copyriht By*
> *Helen W. Jensen*
> *Germany*

tation bisque and composition that is like a terra-cotta ceramic, with molded hair, glass or painted eyes, open/closed mouth with two upper teeth and laughing expression, composition arms, lower legs, cloth torso, some with crier and upper legs. Mark "copyriht" (misspelled).

17" ceramic Gladdie designed by Helen W. Jensen, made by K & K for Borgfeldt, glass eyes, open/closed mouth with two upper teeth, molded painted short blonde bob, ruddy rose cheeks, red print dress, circa 1928 – 1930, $1,250.00. Courtesy Bette Yadon.

Biscaloid Ceramic head

18"	$875.00	$1,150.00
20"	$1,050.00	$1,400.00

Bisque head, Mold 1410

14"	$2,600.00	$3,450.00
18"	$3,300.00	$4,400.00
21"	$4,150.00	$5,400.00

Goebel, Wm. and F. & W.

1871 – 1930 on, Oeslau, Bavaria. Made porcelain and glazed china dolls, as well as bathing dolls, Kewpie-types, and others. Earlier mark was tri-angle with half moon.

First price indicates doll in good condition, with flaws; second price indicates doll in excellent condition, appropriately dressed or original clothes. Exceptional dolls may be more.

Character Baby, after 1909

Open mouth, sleep eyes, five-piece bent-leg baby body

15"	$365.00	$485.00
18"	$450.00	$600.00

Toddler body

14"	$425.00	$550.00
16"	$750.00*	

Child, 1895

Socket head, open mouth, composition body, sleep or set eyes

12"	$200.00	$275.00
17"	$350.00	$475.00

14" bisque F. & W. Goebel dolly face with jointed compo body, circa 1890, $450.00. Courtesy Odis Gregg.

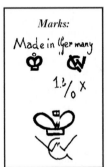

Child, open/closed mouth, shoulder plate, wig, molded teeth, kid body, bisque hands

17"	$625.00	$850.00
20"	$850.00	$1,150.00

Character Child, after 1909

Mold 120, circa 1921 – 1932, sleep eyes, open mouth, wigged

12½"	$300.00	$400.00
18"	$550.00* all original	

Mold 521, circa 1921 – 1932, sleep eyes, open mouth, wigged

19"	$400.00	$525.00

Molded hair

May have flowers or ribbons, painted features, with five-piece papier-mache body

6"	$200.00	$275.00
9"	$325.00	$425.00

Marks:

Made in Germany

Molded on bonnet or hat

Closed mouth, five-piece papier-mache body, painted features

9"	$400.00	$525.00

Googly

(Side-glancing eyes.) Sometimes round, painted, glass, tin, or celluloid, when they move to side they are called flirty eyes. Popular 1900 – 1925, most doll manufacturers made dolls with googly eyes. With painted eyes, they could be painted looking to side or straight ahead; with inserted eyes, the same head can be found with and without flirty eyes. May have closed smiling mouth, composition or papier-mache body, molded hair or wigged.

First price is for doll in good condition with flaws; second price is for doll in excellent condition appropriately dressed or with original clothes. Exceptional dolls can be more.

ALL-BISQUE

Jointed shoulders, hips, molded shoes, socks

Rigid neck, glass eyes

3"	$200.00	$275.00
5"	$365.00	$465.00

5" all-bisque Googly, blue sleep eyes, painted black shoes, marked "0," $750.00. Courtesy Cherie Gervais.

Painted eyes

3"	$150.00	$200.00
5"	$275.00	$350.00

Swivel neck, glass eyes

5"	$425.00	$575.00
7"	$650.00	$875.00

With jointed elbows, knees

5"	$1,725.00	$2,300.00
7"	$2,100.00	$2,750.00

Too few in database for reliable range.

Marked by maker, Mold 189, 292

5"	$675.00	$900.00
7"	$1,050.00	$1,400.00

Mold 217, 330, 501

5"	$435.00	$575.00
7"	$550.00	$725.00

BAHR & PROSCHILD

Marked "B.P."

Mold 401

6"	$350.00	$475.00

Mold 686, Baby

16"	$1,200.00	$1,600.00

Mold 686, Child

13"	$1,850.00	$2,500.00
15"	$2,250.00	$3,000.00

DEMOCOL, MADE FOR DENNIS MALLEY & CO., LONDON

Bisque socket head, closed watermelon mouth, mohair wig, five-piece composition toddler body

10"	$900.00	$1,200.00

HANDWERK, MAX

Marked "Elite," bisque socket head, molded helmet

11"	$1,350.00	$1,800.00

HERTEL SCHWAB & CO.

Mold 163, ca. 1914, solid dome, closed smiling mouth

16"	$6,250.00*

Mold 165, ca. 1914, socket head, closed smiling mouth

11"	$4,100.00*

Mold 172, ca. 1914, solid dome, closed smiling mouth

15"	$4,000.00*

Mold 173, ca. 1914, solid dome, closed smiling mouth

16"	$5,500.00*

Mold 222, Our Fairy, all-bisque, wigged, glass eyes

7"	$800.00	$1,200.00
11"	$1,350.00	$1,800.00

Painted eyes, molded hair

8"	$650.00	$850.00
12"	$1,100.00	$1,500.00

HEUBACH, ERNST

Mold 262, "EH" painted eyes, closed mouth

Mold 264, character

8"	$300.00	$400.00
11"	$375.00	$500.00

Mold 291, "EH" glass eyes, closed mouth

9"	$1,000.00	$1,350.00

Mold 318, "EH" character, closed mouth

11"	$960.00	$1,285.00
14"	$1,500.00	$2,050.00

Mold 319, "EH" character, tearful features

8"	$425.00	$575.00
11"	$850.00	$1,150.00

Mold 322, character, closed smiling mouth

10"	$500.00	$650.00

Mold 417, Mold 419

8"	$400.00	$525.00
13"	$900.00	$1,200.00

HEUBACH, GEBRUDER

9"	$600.00	$800.00
13"	$1,250.00	$1,700.00

9½" bisque Gebruder Heubach mold 9573 Googly with human hair wig, watermelon mouth, composition body, molded painted shoes, circa 1914, $1,350.00. Courtesy Bette Yadon.

Mold 8556

15"	$6,000.00	$8,000.00

Mold 8676

9"	$650.00	$850.00
11"	$775.00	$1,050.00

Mold 8723, 8995, glass eyes

13"	$2,100.00	$2,800.00

Mold 8764, Einco, shoulder head, closed mouth
For Eisenmann & Co.

21"	$3,900.00	$5,250.00

Too few in database for reliable range.

Mold 9056, square, painted eyes closed mouth

8"	$525.00	$700.00

Too few in database for reliable range.

Mold 9573

9"	$675.00	$900.00
11"	$1,050.00	$1,400.00

Mold 9578, Mold 11173, "Tiss Me"

10"	$1,050.00	$1,450.00
14"	$1,200.00	$1,600.00

Mold 9743

Sitting, open/closed mouth, top-knot, star shaped hands

7"	$450.00	$600.00

Winker, one eye painted closed

14"	$1,600.00	$2,200.00

Too few in database for reliable range.

KAMMER & REINHARDT

Mold 131, "S&H//K*R," closed mouth

8½"	$6,500.00*	toddler
13"	$4,150.00	$5,500.00
16"	$5,850.00	$7,800.00

* at auction

14" bisque Kestner mold 221 Googly with mohair wig, oversize Googly glass flirty eyes, watermelon mouth, jointed composition body, circa 1912, $5,000.00. Private collection.

KESTNER

Mold 221, ca. 1913, "JDK ges. gesch"

Character, smiling closed mouth

12"	$3,500.00	$4,730.00
15"	$7,000.00* original	

KLEY & HAHN

Mold 180

"K&H" by Hertel Schwab & Co. for Kley & Hahn, character, laughing open/closed mouth

15"	$2,025.00	$2,700.00
17"	$2,550.00	$3,400.00

LENCI: See Lenci category.

LIMBACH

Marked with crown and cloverleaf, socket head, large round glass eyes, pug nose, closed smiling mouth

8"	$3,600.00*	
10"	$1,050.00	$1,400.00

ARMAND MARSEILLE

Mold 200, "AM 243," character, closed mouth

8"	$925.00	$1,240.00
12"	$1,500.00	$2,000.00

Mold 210, "AM 243," character, solid-dome head, painted eyes, closed mouth

8"	$1,400.00	$1,850.00
12"	$2,000.00	$2,700.00

Mold 223, ca. 1913, character, closed mouth

7"	$550.00	$750.00
11"	$725.00	$950.00

Mold 240, "AM" dome, painted, closed mouth

11"	$1,500.00	$2,000.00
15"	$2,000.00	$2,700.00

Mold 252, "AM 248," ca. 1912

Solid dome, molded tufts, painted eyes, closed mouth

9"	$1,350.00	$1,800.00
12"	$1,800.00	$2,400.00

Mold 253, "AM Nobbikid Reg. U.S. Pat. 066 Germany," ca. 1925

6"	$675.00	$900.00
10"	$2,500.00	$3,400.00

Mold 254, "AM" dome, painted eyes, closed mouth

10"	$600.00	$800.00

Mold 310, "AM //JUST ME" 1929, for Geo. Borgfeldt

9"	$750.00	$950.00
12"	$1,350.00	$1,800.00

6½" bisque Armand Marseille 253 Googly eyes, watermelon mouth, mohair wig, papier-mache body with molded shoes and socks, all original, circa 1925, $1,000.00. Courtesy Karen Koch.

Mold 310, painted bisque, "Just Me"
9"	$525.00	$700.00
12"	$825.00	$1,100.00

Mold 320, "AM 255," ca. 1913, dome, painted eyes
9"	$575.00	$775.00
12"	$700.00	$950.00

Mold 322, "AM," ca. 1914, dome, painted eyes
8"	$500.00	$675.00
11"	$650.00	$875.00

Mold 323, 1914 – 1925, glass eyes, also composition

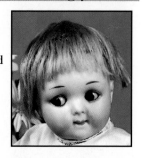

7½"	$750.00	$1,000.00
11"	$985.00	$1,300.00
16"	$1,375.00	$1,800.00

Mold 323, baby body
13"	$700.00	$950.00

Mold 323, painted bisque baby
11"	$350.00	$475.00

Mold 325, ca. 1915, character, closed mouth
9"	$548.00	$725.00
14"	$750.00	$1,000.00

11½" bisque Armand Marseille Googly, mold 243, set brown eyes to side, closed smiling mouth, tip of tongue between lips, original mohair wig, bent-limb composition baby body, circa 1911, $1,250.00. Courtesy McMasters Doll Auctions.

P.M. Pozellanfabrik Mengersgereuth, ca. 1926

"PM" character, closed mouth. Previously thought to be made by Otto Reinecke.

Mold 950
15"	$1,200.00	$1,600.00
18"	$1,400.00	$1,850.00

S.F.B.J.

Mold 245
8"	$975.00	$1,300.00

Fully jointed body
10"	$1,200.00	$1,600.00

Steiner, Herm

Mold 133, "HS" closed mouth, papier-mache body
7"	$500.00	$700.00

Strobel & Wilkin

Mold 208, "SW," closed mouth
7"	$1,000.00*

Mold 405
7"	$1,400.00*

Walter & Sohn

Mold 208, ca. 1920, "W&S" closed mouth

Five-piece papier-mache body, painted socks/shoes
8"	$525.00	$700.00

10" bisque Armand Marseille Googly, mold 240, set dark brown eyes, closed smiling mouth, molded painted hair, five-piece composition toddler body, cupped hands, circa 1914, $800.00. Courtesy McMasters Doll Auctions.

Greiner, Ludwig

30" papier-mache Greiner shoulder plate, '58 paper label, painted molded hair, painted dark blue eyes, exposed ears, repaired cloth body, leather arms, circa 1858+, $1,950.00. Courtesy Marian Pettygrove.

1840 – 1874. Succeeded by sons, 1890 – 1900, Philadelphia, PA. Papier-mache shoulder head dolls, with molded hair, painted/glass eyes, usually made up to be large dolls, 13" – 38".

First price is for doll in good condition with flaws; second price is for doll in excellent condition appropriately dressed or with original clothes.

With "1858" label

17"	$400.00	$550.00
23"	$525.00	$725.00
26"	$600.00	$825.00
30"	$1,600.00*	
35"	$975.00	$1,300.00
38"	$1,350.00	$1,800.00

With "1872" label

18"	$335.00	$450.00
21"	$400.00	$525.00
26"	$475.00	$650.00
30"	$700.00	$975.00

Glass eyes

21"	$1,200.00	$1,600.00
26"	$1,725.00	$2,300.00

Pre Greiner, unmarked, ca. 1850

Papier-mache shoulder head, cloth body, leather, wood, or cloth limbs, painted hair, black glass eyes, no pupils

18"	$900.00	$1,200.00
26"	$1,200.00	$1,600.00
30"	$1,425.00	$1,900.00

Painted eyes

18"	$335.00	$450.00
26"	$475.00	$650.00
30"	$600.00	$825.00

Mark:

GREINER'S PATENT HEADS. No. 0. Pat. March 30th, '58.

Handwerck, Heinrich

1876 – 1930, Gotha, Germany. Made composition dolls' bodies, sent Handwerck molds to Simon & Halbig to make bisque heads. Trademarks included an eight-point star with French or German wording, a shield, and "Bebe Cosmopolite," "Bebe de Reclame," and "Bebe Superior." Sold dolls through Gimbels, Macy's, Montgomery Wards, and others. Bodies marked "Handwerk" in red on lower back torso. Patented a straight wrist body.

First price is for doll in good condition with flaws; second price is for doll in excellent condition appropriately dressed or with original clothes. Exceptional dolls may be more.

Mark:

119 - 13 HANDWERCK 5 Germany

CHILD, NO MOLD NUMBER

Open mouth, sleep or set eyes, ball-jointed body, bisque socket head, pierced ears, appropriate wig, nicely dressed

15"	$350.00	$450.00
18"	$450.00	$575.00
21"	$500.00	$650.00
24"	$550.00	$750.00
28"	$700.00	$950.00
30"	$750.00	$1,000.00
32"	$825.00	$1,200.00
36"	$1,375.00	$1,825.00
40"	$1,975.00	$2,625.00

CHILD WITH MOLD NUMBER, OPEN MOUTH

Molds 69, 79, 89, 99, 109, 119, 139, 199

13"	$350.00	$475.00
15"	$375.00	$500.00
18"	$525.00	$725.00
22"	$550.00	$750.00
25"	$575.00	$775.00
29"	$725.00	$975.00
32"	$1,000.00	$1,325.00
36"	$1,175.00	$1,575.00
40"	$2,350.00	$3,150.00

Kid body, shoulder head, open mouth

14"	$175.00	$235.00
17"	$250.00	$330.00
24"	$350.00	$475.00

Mold 79, 89 closed mouth

15"	$1,275.00	$1,700.00
18"	$1,500.00	$2,000.00

Too few in database for reliable range.

Mold 189, open mouth

15"	$600.00	$800.00
18"	$700.00	$950.00
22"	$900.00	$1,200.00

Mold 421, open mouth, pierced ears

20"	$700.00* all original

18" bisque Heinrich Handwerck Daisy, blonde mohair wig, blue glass eyes, open mouth, wooden composition jointed body, all original in box, circa 1911, $1,500.00. Courtesy Betty Jane Fronfield.

23½" bisque twins made by Simon & Halbig for Heinrich Handwerck, circa 1905, open mouth, glass eyes, mohair wig, jointed composition body, each with wardrobe, one, $1,000.00. One with brown eyes, hairline, $650.00. Private collection.

Handwerck, Max

1899 – 1930, Walthershausen, Germany. Made dolls and doll bodies, registered trademark, "Bebe Elite." Used heads made by Goebel.

CHILD

Bisque socket head, open mouth, sleep or set eyes, jointed composition body

Mold 283, 287, 291, and others

23"	$400.00	$550.00

* at auction

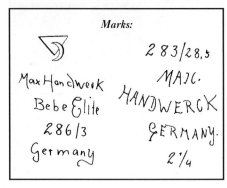

Marks:

Max Handwerck
Bebe Elite
286/3
Germany

283/28.5
MAJC.
HANDWERCK
GERMANY.
2 1/4

BEBE ELITE
Bisque socket head, mohair wig, glass sleep eyes, mohair lashes, open mouth, pierced ears, jointed composition/wood body
Marks: "Max Handwerck Bebe Elite 286 12 Germany" on back of head.

15"	$425.00	$575.00
20"	$600.00	$800.00
27"	$750.00	$975.00

Bebe Elite, flange neck, cloth body

15"	$350.00	$445.00
20"	$475.00	$650.00

GOOGLY: See Googly category.

Hartmann, Carl

Mark:

Globe Baby
DEP
Germany
C 3 H

1889 – 1930, Neustadt, Germany. Made and exported bisque and celluloid dolls, especially small dolls in regional costumes, called Globe Babies. Kammer & Reinhardt made heads for Hartmann.

CHILD
Bisque socket head, open mouth, jointed composition and wood body

22"	$225.00	$375.00

GLOBE BABY
Bisque socket head, glass sleep eyes, open mouth, four teeth, mohair or human hair wig, five-piece papier-mache or composition body with painted shoes and stockings

8"	$315.00	$450.00
9"	$375.00	$500.00

Hartmann, Karl

Marks:

30
K
JK H
J3L

1911 – 1926, Stockheim, Germany. Doll factory, made and exported dolls. Advertised ball-jointed dolls, characters, and papier-mache dolls.

CHILD
Bisque socket head, open mouth, glass eyes, composition body

18"	$350.00	$500.00
22"	$400.00	$600.00
32"	$700.00	$875.00

Hertel Schwab & Co.

1910 – 1930+, Stutzhaus, Germany. Founded by August Hertel and Heinrich Schwab, both designed doll heads, used by Borgfelt, Kley and Hahn, Konig & Wernicke, Louis Wolf, and others. Made china and bisque heads as well as all-porcelain; most with character faces. Molded hair or wig, painted blue or glass eyes (often blue-gray), open mouth with tongue or closed mouth, socket or shoulder heads. Usually marked with mold number and "Made in Germany," or mark of company that owned the mold.

Mark:

Made in Germany 15½

BABY

Bisque head, molded hair or wig, open or open/closed mouth, teeth, sleep or painted eyes, bent-leg baby composition body

Mold 142, 150, 151, 152

9"	$225.00	$300.00
11"	$335.00	$450.00
16"	$475.00	$650.00
22"	$675.00	$900.00
24"	$700.00	$950.00

Toddler body

14"	$375.00	$500.00
20"	$550.00	$750.00

12" bisque Hertel Schwab & Co. baby, brown glass sleep eyes, open mouth, blonde mohair wig, circa 1900s, $500.00. Private collection.

CHILD

Mold 127, ca. 1915, character face, solid dome with molded hair, sleep eyes, open mouth, Patsy-type

15"	$1,000.00	$1,350.00
17"	$1,500.00	$2,000.00

Mold 131, character face, solid dome, painted closed mouth

18"	$1,300.00*

Mold 134, character face, sleep eyes, closed mouth

11"	$3,500.00*

Mold 136, "Made in Germany," character face, open mouth

24"	$900.00	$1,200.00

Mold 140, character, glass eyes, open/closed laughing mouth

12"	$2,550.00	$3,400.00
18"	$4,275.00	$5,700.00

Mold 141, character, painted eyes, open/closed mouth

12"	$2,325.00	$3,100.00

Mold 149, character, glass eyes, closed mouth, ball-jointed body

17"	$9,500.00*

Mold 154, ca. 1912, character, solid dome, molded hair, glass eyes, open mouth

20"	$1,900.00*

Mold 159, ca. 1911, two faces

10"	$850.00*

Mold 167, "K&H" character, ca. 1912, open/closed or closed mouth, made for Kley & Hahn

15"	$2,000.00*

GOOGLY: See Googly category.

24" bisque Hertel, Schwab & Co. baby, mold 152, brown sleep eyes, open/closed mouth, two upper teeth, original mohair wig, composition bent-limb baby body, circa 1912, $950.00. Courtesy McMasters Doll Auctions.

* at auction

Heubach, Ernst

1886 – 1930+, Koppelsdorf, Germany. In 1919, the son of Armand Marseille married the daughter of Ernst Heubach and merged the two factories. Mold numbers range from 250 to 452. They made porcelain heads for Dressel (Jutta), Revalo, and others.

BABY

Open mouth, glass eyes, socket head, wig, five-piece bent-leg composition body, add more for toddler body, flirty eyes

26" bisque Ernst Heubach, mold 342 character baby, flirty eyes, open mouth, two teeth, wobble tongue, composition bent-limb baby body, ca. 1926, $425.00. Courtesy McMasters Doll Auctions.

Mold 267, 300, 320, 321, 342

11"	$180.00	$240.00
14"	$275.00	$375.00
20"	$400.00	$550.00
27"	$725.00	$975.00

Baby, Newborn, ca. 1925+

Solid dome, molded, painted hair, glass eyes, closed mouth, cloth body, composition or celluloid hands

Mark:

Mold 338, 339, 340, 348, 349, 399

12"	$300.00	$425.00
14"	$425.00	$575.00
15"	$525.00	$700.00
17"	$600.00	$800.00

Black, mold 444

12"	$300.00	$400.00

CHILD, 1888+

Mold 1900 with Horseshoe Mark

Open mouth, glass eyes, kid or cloth body

12"	$115.00	$150.00
18"	$210.00	$275.00
22"	$310.00	$415.00
26"	$500.00	$650.00

Painted bisque

12"	$125.00	$175.00
16"	$175.00	$225.00

Mold 250, 251, 275 (shoulder head), 302, open mouth, kid body

9"	$150.00	$200.00
13"	$175.00	$235.00
16"	$225.00	$275.00
19"	$345.00	$450.00
22"	$425.00	$550.00
27"	$525.00	$700.00
32"	$700.00	$950.00
36"	$1,000.00	$1,275.00

Heubach, Gebruder

1820 – 1945, Lichte, Thuringia, Germany. Made bisque heads and all-bisque dolls, characters after 1910, either socket or shoulder head, molded hair or wigs, sleeping or intaglio eyes, in heights from 4" to 26". Mold numbers from 556 to 10633. Sunburst or square marks; more dolls with square marks.

MARKED "HEUBACH," NO MOLD NUMBER

Open/closed mouth, dimples

18"	$3,300.00	$4,450.00
24"	$4,700.00	$6,300.00

Adult, open mouth, glass eyes

14"	$3,350.00	$4,500.00

Smile, painted eyes

15"	$2,700.00	$3,500.00

MARKED HEUBACH Googly: See Googly category.

CHARACTER CHILD, SHOULDER HEAD

Mold 6688, solid dome, molded hair, intaglio eyes, closed mouth

10"	$450.00	$625.00

Mold 6692, sunburst, intaglio eyes, closed mouth

14"	$650.00	$875.00

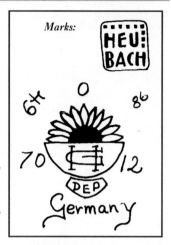

Marks:

Mold 6736, square, painted eyes, laughing mouth

13"	$800.00	$1,100.00
16"	$1,400.00	$1,900.00

Mold 7345, sunburst, pink-tinted closed mouth

17"	$1,150.00	

Too few in database for reliable range.

Mold 7644, sunburst or square mark, painted eyes, open/closed laughing mouth

14"	$650.00	$865.00
17"	$875.00	$1,200.00

Mold 7847, solid dome shoulder head, intaglio eyes, closed smiling mouth, teeth

20"	$2,100.00*	

Too few in database for reliable range.

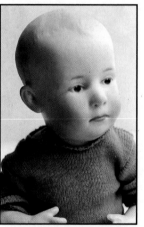

Mold 7850, "Coquette," open/closed mouth

11"	$550.00	$750.00
15"	$800.00	$1,100.00

10" bisque Gebruder Heubach closed mouth baby, molded hair, intaglio eyes, bent-leg composition body, old clothes, circa 1912, $600.00. Courtesy Marguerite Long.

Mold 7925, 7926, shoulder head, glass eyes, smiling open mouth, lady

15"	$1,500.00	$2,000.00
20"	$3,700.00, mold 7925*	

Too few in database for reliable range.

Mold 7972, intaglio eyes, closed mouth

20"	$1,500.00	$2,000.00

Too few in database for reliable range.

Mold 8221, square, dome, intaglio eyes, open/closed mouth

14"	$500.00	$675.00

Too few in database for reliable range.

Mold 9355, square mark, glass eyes, open mouth

13"	$650.00	$850.00
19"	$925.00	$1,250.00

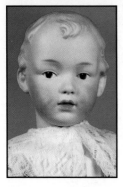

16" bisque Gebruder Heubach, mold 7622, blue intaglio eyes, closed mouth, molded hair, five-piece body, antique white shirt with lace collar, blue velvet pants, replaced socks and boots, circa 1910+, $425.00. Courtesy McMasters Doll Auctions.

14½" bisque Gebruder Heubach character child mold 5636, sunburst mark, open mouth with two lower teeth and molded tongue, some repairs, circa 1912, $1,100.00. Courtesy McMasters Doll Auctions.

CHARACTER BABY OR CHILD, SOCKET HEAD

Mold 5636, glass eyes, open/closed laughing mouth, teeth

13"	$1,500.00	$2,000.00
15"	$1,800.00	$2,400.00

Mold 5689, sunburst mark, open mouth

14"	$1,350.00	$1,800.00
17"	$1,700.00	$2,250.00
22"	$2,200.00	$2,900.00

Mold 5730, "Santa," sunburst mark, made for Hamburger & Co.

16"	$1,250.00	$1,700.00
19"	$1,900.00	$2,500.00
26"	$2,100.00	$2,800.00

Mold 5777, "Dolly Dimple," open mouth, for Hamburger & Co.

14"	$1,725.00	$2,300.00
16"	$1,900.00	$2,500.00
24"	$2,600.00	$3,450.00

Mold 6894, 7759, baby, sunburst or square mark, intaglio eyes, closed mouth, molded hair

7"	$275.00	$375.00
9"	$375.00	$500.00
12"	$525.00	$700.00

Mold 6969, socket head, square mark, glass eyes, closed mouth

12"	$1,475.00	$°1,850.00
16"	$1,800.00	$2,400.00
19"	$2,400.00	$3,300.00

Mold 6970, sunburst, glass eyes, closed mouth

10"	$1,300.00	$1,800.00
13"	$1,700.00	$2,300.00
16"	$2,350.00	$3,000.00

Mold 6971, intaglio eyes, closed smiling mouth in original costume box

11"	$1,200.00*

Mold 7246, 7247, 7248, sunburst or square mark, closed mouth

9"	$1,200.00	$1,700.00
15"	$2,100.00	$2,900.00

Mold 7268, square, glass eyes, closed mouth

12"	$5,000.00*

Mold 7602, 7603, molded hair tufts, intaglio eyes

18"	$2,400.00*

Mold 7604, open/closed mouth, intaglio eyes

14"	$625.00	$850.00

Baby
15"　　$525.00　　$700.00
Mold 7622, 7623, intaglio eyes, closed or open/closed mouth
　16"　　$800.00　　$1,200.00
　18"　　$1,000.00　　$1,400.00
Mold 7681, dome, intaglio eyes, closed mouth
　10"　　$650.00*
Mold 7711, glass eyes, open mouth, flapper body
　10"　　$525.00　　$700.00
　13"　　$650.00　　$900.00
Mold 7759, dome, painted eyes, closed mouth
　14"　　$750.00*
Mold 7911, intaglio eyes, laughing open/closed mouth
　9"　　$525.00　　$700.00
　15"　　$900.00　　$1,200.00
Mold 7975, "Baby Stuart," glass eyes, removable molded bisque bonnet
　13"　　$1,425.00　　$1,900.00
Mold 7977, "Baby Stuart," molded bonnet, closed mouth, painted eyes
　8"　　$600.00　　$800.00
　14"　　$1,300.00　　$1,700.00
Mold 8191, "Crooked Smile," square mark, intaglio eyes, laughing mouth
　9"　　$500.00*
　14"　　$375.00　　$500.00
Mold 8192, sunburst or square mark, sleep eyes, open mouth
　13"　　$675.00　　$900.00
　15"　　$775.00　　$1,050.00
Mold 8316, "Grinning Boy," wig, open/closed mouth, eight teeth, glass eyes
　16"　　$2,500.00　　$3,400.00
　19"　　$3,600.00　　$4,800.00
Mold 8381, "Princess Juliana," molded hair, ribbon, painted eyes, closed mouth
　14"　　$5,000.00　　$6,600.00+
Mold 8413, wig, sleep eyes, open/closed mouth, molded tongue, upper teeth
　19"　　$2,400.00+
Too few in database for reliable range.
Mold 8420, square mark, glass eyes, closed mouth
　15"　　$2,100.00　　$2,800.00
Too few in database for reliable range.
Mold 8429, square mark, closed mouth
　15"　　$2,500.00*
Too few in database for reliable range.

15½" bisque Gebruder Heubach character mold 5636, sunburst mark, blue sleep eyes, laughing open mouth with two teeth, deep dimples, mohair wig, circa 1912, $2,100.00. Courtesy McMasters Doll Auctions.

16½" bisque Gebruder Heubach character mold 6969, blue sleep eyes, closed pouty mouth, human hair wig, jointed composition body, circa 1912, $2,800.00. Courtesy McMasters Doll Auctions.

* at auction

11½" bisque Baby Stuart by Gebruder Heubach mold 7877, blue intaglio eyes, molded bonnet with painted pink roses and leaves, bent-leg composition baby body, circa 1912, $900.00. Courtesy McMasters Doll Auctions.

15" bisque Gebruder Heubach character baby with Sunburst and 8420 mark, bent-leg baby body, glass eyes, closed pouty mouth, circa 1914, $2,800.00. Courtesy Marguerite Long.

12½" bisque Gebruder Heubach walking doll, mold 7969, set blue eyes, open/closed mouth, mohair wig in braids, key wind walking body, cardboard torso, bisque lower arms, composition lower legs, circa 1912, $1,000.00. Courtesy McMasters Doll Auctions.

Mold 8686, glass eyes, open/closed mouth

14"	$3,200.00*

Too few in database for reliable range.

Mold 8774, "Whistling Jim" smoker or whistler, square mark, flange neck, intaglio eyes, molded hair, cloth body, bellows

13"	$900.00	$1,200.00

Too few in database for reliable range.

Mold 8819, square, intaglio eyes, open/closed mouth

9"	$1,050.00*

Too few in database for reliable range.

Mold 9027, dome, intaglio eyes, closed mouth

13"	$900.00	$1,200.00

Too few in database for reliable range.

Mold 9055, intaglio eyes, closed mouth

11"	$275.00	$375.00

Too few in database for reliable range.

Mold 9457, square mark, dome, intaglio eyes, closed mouth, Eskimo

15"	$1,875.00	$2,500.00
18"	$3,000.00	$4,000.00

Mold 9746, square, painted eyes, closed mouth

7½"	$600.00	$800.00

Too few in database for reliable range.

Mold 10532, square mark, open mouth

13½"	$450.00	$600.00
25"	$1,125.00	$1,500.00

Mold 11010, "Revalo," sleep eyes, open mouth, for Gebr. Ohlhaver

19"	$525.00	$700.00
24"	$650.00	$850.00

Mold 11173, "Tiss Me," socket head, wig

8"	$1,500.00	$2,000.00

Too few in database for reliable range.

FIGURINES

Square or Sunburst mark, all at auction

Seated Baby, dog	4½"	$525.00	
Dutch pair	6"	$750.00	
Coquette	16"	$1,900.00	

Piano Baby, Mold 7287, 9693, and others

5"	$400.00	$525.00
9"	$525.00	$700.00
13"	$1,000.00*	

Hulss, Adolph

1915 – 1930+, Waltershausen, Germany. Made dolls with bisque heads, jointed composition bodies. Trademark: "Nesthakchen," "h" in mold mark often resembles a "b." Made babies, toddlers, and child dolls with ball joints.

BABY

Bisque socket head, sleep eyes, open mouth, teeth, wig, bent-leg baby, composition body, add more for flirty eyes.

Mold 156

14"	$425.00	$575.00
19"	$850.00	$1,125.00

Mark:

Toddler

16"	$625.00	$800.00
20"	$775.00	$1,000.00

CHILD

Bisque socket head, wig, sleep eyes, open mouth, teeth, tongue, jointed composition body

Mold 176

15"	$575.00	$750.00
22"	$925.00	$1,250.00

Huret, Maison

1812 – 1930+, France. May have pressed, molded bisque, or china heads, painted or glass eyes, closed mouths, bodies of cloth, composition, gutta-percha, kid, or wood, sometimes metal hands. Used fur or mohair for wigs, had fashion type body with defined waist.

What to look for: Dolls with beautiful painting on eyes and face; painted eyes are more common than glass, but the beauty of the painted features and/or wooden bodies increases the price.

Bisque shoulder head, kid body with bisque lower arms, glass eyes

14"	$4,400.00	$5,800.00
19"	$5,900.00	$7,900.00

Round face, painted blue eyes

Coth body	16"	$8,722.00*
Wood body	17"	$21,000.00*

Too few in database for reliable range.

China shoulder head, kid body, china lower arms

14"	$3,000.00	$4,500.00
Metal hands	18"	$7,875.00*

Huret, Maison (cont.)

Swivel neck, glass eyes
15" $10,550.00* (presumed Huret)
Too few in database for reliable range.
Pressed bisque with wood body, shoulder plate, painted eyes, labeled body
17" $21,000.00*
Too few in database for reliable range.
Gutta-percha, stamped body
9" $1,817.00*
Pressed bisque, doll, marked articulated body, with provenance
18" $62,000.00*
Too few in database for reliable range.
Painted eyes, marked kid body
17" $16,500.00*
Too few in database for reliable range.
Painted eyes, open/closed mouth, fashion body
* Only one reported, extremely rare

Juillen

1827 – 1904, Paris, Conflans, St. Leonard. Had a porcelain factory, won some awards, purchased bisque heads from Francois Gaultier.

CHILD
Bisque socket head, wig, glass eyes, pierced ears, open mouth with teeth or closed mouth, on jointed composition body

Closed mouth
19"	$2,850.00	$3,800.00
24"	$3,175.00	$4,250.00

Open mouth
18"	$1,150.00	$1,500.00

Jumeau

1842 – 1899, Paris and Monttreuil-sous-Bois; succeeded by S.F.B.J. through 1958. Founder Pierre Francois Jumeau made fashion dolls with kid or wood bodies; head marked with size number; bodies stamped *"JUMEAU/ /MEDAILLE D'OR/ /PARIS."* Early Jumeau heads were pressed pre-1890. By 1878, son Emile Jumeau was head of the company and made Bebe Jumeau, marked on back of head, on chemise, band on arm of dress. Tete Jumeaus have poured heads. Bebe Protige and Bebe Jumeau registered trademarks in 1886; Bee Mark in 1891; Bebe Marcheur in 1895, Bebe Francaise in 1896.

Mold numbers of marked EJs and Tetes approximate the following heights: 1 – 10", 2 – 11", 3 – 12", 4 – 13", 5 – 14", 6 – 16", 7 – 17", 8 – 18", 9 – 20", 10 – 21", 11 – 24", 12 – 26", 13 – 30".

First price is for doll in good condition, but with some flaws; second price is for doll in excellent condition, nicely wigged, and with appropriate clothing. Exceptional doll may be much more.

Fashion-type Jumeau
Marked with size number on swivel head, closed mouth, paperweight eyes, pierced ears, stamped kid body, add more for original clothes.

11"	$1,800.00	$2,350.00
17"	$3,050.00	$3,800.00
20"	$3,675.00	$4,900.00

Wood body, bisque lower arms

16"	$3,800.00	$5,100.00

Jumeau Portrait

18"	$4,250.00	$5,650.00
22"	$4,850.00	$6,450.00
28"	$6,300.00	$8,400.00

Wood body

15"	$4,300.00	$5,750.00
18"	$6,600.00	$8,800.00

Almond eye

13½"	$6,000.00	$8,000.00+
17"	$6,750.00	$9,000.00+
20"	$12,500.00	$15,000.00+

20½" bisque Jumeau Portrait fashion-type, unmarked, set blue eyes, closed mouth, pierced ears, original mohair wig, kid fashion-type body, gussets at elbows, hips, and knees, stitched fingers, circa 1872, $3,700.00. Courtesy McMasters Doll Auctions.

E.J. BEBE, 1881 – 1886

Earliest "EJ" mark above with number over initials, pressed bisque socket head, wig, paperweight eyes, pierced ears, closed mouth jointed body with straight wrists

17"	$7,200.00	$10,250.00
20"	$9,000.00	$12,000.00
24"	$15,000.00*	

EJ/A marked Bebe

17"	$20,000.00+

Only this size has been reported; too few in database for reliable range.

Mid "EJ" mark has size number centered between E and J (E 8 J)

9 – 10"	$4,375.00	$5,800.00
15"	$4,600.00	$6,100.00
17"	$4,900.00	$6,600.00
20"	$5,400.00	$7,200.00
23"	$5,800.00	$7,700.00
26"	$6,500.00	$8,700.00

Later "EJ" mark is preceded by DEPOSE (DEPOSE/E 8 J)

14"	$3,350.00	$4,500.00
19"	$4,300.00	$5,850.00
22"	$5,000.00	$6,600.00
26"	$5,850.00	$7,800.00

26" bisque Portrait Jumeau on marked Jumeau body, closed mouth, paperweight eyes, pierced ears, replaced human hair wig, kid fashion-type body, nicely dressed, 1877 – 1883, $3,900.00. Courtesy McMasters Doll Auctions.

DEPOSE JUMEAU, CA. 1886 – 1889

Poured bisque head marked, "Depose Jumeau," and size number, pierced ears, closed mouth, paperweight eyes, composition and wood body with straight wrists marked "Medaille d'Or Paris"

14"	$3,750.00	$5,000.00
18"	$4,400.00	$5,900.00
23"	$5,200.00	$6,900.00

* at auction

20" bisque Jumeau French bebe, marked E. 6 J., paperweight eyes, closed mouth, straight legs and wrists, circa 1880s, $4,200.00. Courtesy Barbara DeFeo.

Mark:
E.J. Bebe
1881 – 86
6
E.J.

12" bisque Jumeau bebe, paperweight blue eyes, blonde mohair wig, marked "Depose E 4 J," chunky French composition Jumeau body, circa 1882, $6,000.00. Private collection.

LONG FACE TRISTE BEBE, 1879 – 1886

Head marked with number only, pierced applied ears, closed mouth, paperweight eyes, straight wrists on Jumeau marked body

19"	$14,000.00	$18,500.00+
27"	$22,500.00	$27,000.00+

Too few in database for reliable range.

TETE JUMEAU, CA. 1885+

Poured bisque socket head, red stamp on head, stamp or sticker on body, wig, glass eyes, pierced ears, closed mouth, jointed composition body with straight wrists. May also be marked E.D. with size number when Douillet ran factory, uses tete face.

Bebe (Child), closed mouth

10"	$4,500.00	$6,000.00
12"	$2,700.00	$3,500.00
17"	$3,000.00	$4,100.00
19"	$3,500.00	$4,650.00
23"	$3,650.00	$4,900.00
26"	$3,875.00	$5,150.00
30"	$4,550.00	$6,100.00
32"	$4,700.00	$6,250.00

Trouseau/provenance

19"	$13,500.00*

Open mouth

10"	$2,350.00	$3,150.00
17"	$1,750.00	$2,350.00
21"	$2,050.00	$2,725.00
25"	$2,450.00	$3,250.00
28"	$2,650.00	$3,550.00
32"	$3,050.00	$4,050.00

Adult body, closed mouth

20"	$4,500.00	$6,000.00
25"	$4,875.00	$6,500.00

Rare pressed brown bisque swivel head, "Madagascar"

24½"	$89,270.00*

Open mouth

14"	$1,650.00	$2,200.00
19"	$2,175.00	$2,900.00
22"	$2,475.00	$3,300.00
28"	$3,000.00	$4,000.00

"1907," MARKED JUMEAU

Some with Tete Jumeau stamp, sleep or set eyes, open mouth, jointed French body

14"	$975.00	$1,850.00
17"	$1,800.00	$2,450.00
20"	$2,150.00	$2,900.00
23"	$2,350.00	$3,200.00

26"	$2,650.00	$3,600.00
29"	$2,950.00	$3,900.00
32"	$3,100.00	$4,150.00

B. L. Bebe, ca. 1880s

Marked "B. L." for the Louver department store, socket head, wig, pierced ears, paperweight eyes, closed mouth, jointed composition body.

20" $7,035.00*

Too few in database for reliable range.

R. Bebe, ca 1880s

Wig, pierced ears, paperweight eyes, closed mouth, jointed composition body with straight wrists

22" $3,825.00 $5,100.00

Too few in database for reliable range.

Character Child

200 series, marked with mold number and Jumeau

15" $36,000.00+

21" $58,000.00+

Too few in database for reliable range.

Mold 230, open mouth

16" $1,080.00 $1,450.00

20" $1,350.00 $1,800.00

Too few in database for reliable range.

Two-Faced Jumeau

18" $10,500.00*

Too few in database for reliable range.

Phonograph Jumeau

Bisque head, open mouth, phonograph in torso, working condition

20" $7,800.00

27" $11,400.00

Too few in database for reliable range.

Princess Elizabeth

Made after Jumeau joined SFBJ and adopted Unis label, mark will be *"71 Unis//France 149//306//Jumeau//1938//Paris."* Bisque socket head with high color, closed mouth, flirty eyes, jointed composition body.

Mold 306

18" $1,600.00 $2,100.00

30" $2,900.00 $3,900.00

Too few in database for reliable range.

Accessories

Marked shoes

5 – 6" $225.00 $300.00

7 – 10" $450.00 $600.00

9" bisque Tete Jumeau with trunk trousseau, wood and composition jointed body with jointed wrists, glass eyes, human hair wig, circa 1885+, $7,500.00. Courtesy Marguerite Long.

> **Mark:**
> Mid EJ mark has size number centered between E and J
> (E 8 J)

17" bisque Jumeau mold 1907 socket head, red stamp, red human hair wig, with glass paperweight eyes, open mouth, teeth, composition jointed body, circa 1907, $2,300.00. Private collection.

Marks:

Germany
1126 - 21

1886 – 1930+, Waltershausen, Germany. Registered trademark K*R, Majestic Doll, Mein Leibling, Die Kokette, Charakterpuppen (character dolls). Designed doll heads, most bisque were made by Simon & Halbig; in 1918, Schuetzmeister & Quendt also supplied heads; Rheinische Gummi und Celluloid Fabrik Co. made celluloid heads for Kammer & Reinhardt. Kammer & Reinhardt dolls were distributed by Bing, Borgfeldt, B. Illfelder, L. Rees & Co., Strobel & Wilken, and Louis Wolf & Co. Also made heads of wood and composition, later cloth and rubber dolls.

Mold numbers identify heads starting with 1) bisque socket heads; 2) shoulder heads, as well as socket heads of black or mulatto babies; 3) bisque socket heads or celluloid shoulder heads; 4) heads having eyelashes; 5) googlies, black heads, pincushion heads; 6) mulatto heads; 7) celluloid heads, bisque head walking dolls; 8) rubber heads; 9) composition heads, some rubber heads. Other letters refer to style or material of wig or clothing.

First price indicates doll in good condition, but with some flaws. Second price indicates doll in excellent condition well dressed. Exceptional dolls may be more.

CHILD, DOLLY FACE

5" bisque Kammer & Reinhardt, closed mouth girl, sleep eyes, mohair wig, papier-mache/composition body with molded brown two-strap shoes, circa 1900, $500.00. Courtesy Jan Mealer.

Mold 191, open mouth, sleep eyes, jointed child body

17"	$650.00	$865.00
30"	$900.00	$1,200.00

Mold 192, open mouth, sleep eyes, jointed child's body

9"	$750.00	$1,000.00
18"	$750.00	$1,000.00
22"	$800.00	$1,200.00

With trunk
9"	$1,800.00*

Closed mouth
18"	$3,100.00*

No mold numbers, or marked only "K*R" or size number in centimeters, or mold 401, 402, 403, socket head, glass eyes, open mouth

6½"	$1,400.00* trunk, wardrobe	
19"	$550.00	$750.00
25"	$825.00	$1,100.00

Closed mouth, flapper body
14"	$2,400.00*

CHARACTERS
Mold 100

Once called Kaiser Baby, but no connection has been found. Character baby, with dome head, jointed bent-leg body, intaglio eyes, open/closed mouth, appropriate dress, good condition

11"	$475.00	$650.00
15"	$600.00	$800.00
20"	$1,050.00	$1,400.00

Mold 101, Peter or Marie, painted eyes, closed mouth

7 – 8"	$1,200.00	$1,600.00
12"	$2,125.00	$2,800.00
15"	$2,250.00	$3,000.00+
18"	$3,700.00	$4,900.00+
19"	$8,725.00*	

Glass eyes

18"	$8,000.00*

Too few in database for reliable range.

Mold 102, Elsa or Walter, painted eyes, molded hair, closed mouth, very rare

14"	$32,000.00

Too few in database for reliable range.

11¾" bisque Kammer & Reinhardt mold 101, "Marie," painted blue eyes, closed pouty mouth, blond mohair in coiled braids, circa 1909, $1,800.00. Courtesy McMasters Doll Auctions.

Mold 103, painted eyes, closed mouth

19"	$60,000.00

Too few in database for reliable range.

Mold 104, painted eyes, laughing closed mouth, very rare

18"	$58,000.00+

Too few in database for reliable range.

Mold 105, painted eyes, open/closed mouth, very rare

21"	$170,956.00*

Too few in database to give reliable range.

Mold 106, painted intaglio eyes to side, closed mouth, very rare

22"	$144,886.00* w/wrong body

Too few in database for reliable range.

Mold 107, Carl, painted intaglio eyes, closed mouth

21"	$46,000.00*

Too few in database for reliable range.

Mold 108, only one example reported

	$275,000.00+*

Mold 109, Elise, painted eyes, closed mouth

12"	$5,500.00*
24"	$20,000.00*

Too few in database for reliable range.

Mold 112, painted open/closed mouth

14"	$7,200.00	$9,700.00

Glass eyes

10½"	$8,000.00*

Too few in database for reliable range.

23" bisque Kammer & Reinhardt, mold 115A character toddler, child, sleep eyes, closed mouth, original wig, composition body with diagonal hip joints, jointed knees and elbows, but not wrists, circa 1911, $6,000.00. Courtesy Ann Van Arnum.

Mold 114, Hans or Gretchen, painted eyes, closed mouth

9"	$1,500.00*	
13"	$2,450.00	$3,275.00
18"	$4,200.00	$5,700.00
24"	$6,150.00	$8,200.00

15" bisque Kammer & Reinhardt mold 116A baby, blue sleep eyes, open/closed mouth with two upper teeth, dimples, original mohair wig, bent-limb composition body, circa 1911, $1,050.00. Courtesy McMasters Doll Auctions.

16" bisque Kammer & Reinhardt character child Gretel, mold 114, intaglio eyes, closed mouth, composition body, circa 1909, $4,500.00. Courtesy Barbara DeFeo.

Glass eyes

9"	$5,900.00*	
15"	$9,250.00*	

Mold 115, solid dome, painted hair, sleeping eyes, closed mouth

15"	$3,750.00	$5,000.00

Mold 115A, sleep eyes, closed mouth, wig

Baby, bent-leg body

12"	$1,650.00	$2,220.00
19"	$5,000.00*	

Toddler, composition, jointed body

15 – 16"	$3,750.00	$5,000.00
18"	$4,000.00	$5,300.00+

Mold 116, dome head, sleep eyes, open/closed mouth, bent-leg baby body

17"	$3,200.00*	

Mold 116A, sleep eyes, open/closed mouth or open mouth, wigged, bent-leg baby body

15"	$2,100.00	$2,800.00

Toddler body

16"	$2,400.00	$3,200.00

Mold 117 Mein Leibling (My Darling), glass eyes, closed mouth

15"	$3,325.00	$4,400.00
18"	$4,100.00	$5,400.00
23"	$5,100.00	$6,850.00

Mold 117A, glass eyes, closed mouth

18"	$3,400.00	$4,600.00
24"	$6,250.00	$8,300.00
28"	$6,500.00	$8,500.00

Flapper body

8"	$3,500.00*	

Mold 117N, Mein Neuer Liebling (My new Darling), flirty eyes, open mouth

17"	$1,100.00	$1,500.00
20"	$1,350.00	$1,800.00
28"	$2,400.00	$3,100.00

Mold 117X, socket head, sleep eyes, open mouth

14"	$3,700.00*	

Mold 118, 118A, sleep eyes, open mouth, baby body

15"	$1,125.00	$1,500.00
18"	$1,700.00	$2,275.00

Mold 119, sleep eyes, open/closed mouth, marked *"Baby,"* five-piece baby body

25"	$16,000.00*	

---

* at auction

Mold 121, sleep eyes, open mouth, baby body

16"	$700.00	$900.00
20"	$800.00	$1,100.00
24"	$950.00	$1,300.00

Toddler body

14"	$750.00	$1,100.00
18"	$1,850.00*	

Mold 122, sleep eyes, bent-leg baby body

11"	$525.00	$700.00
16"	$635.00	$850.00
20"	$825.00	$1,100.00

Original wicker layette basket and accessories

22"	$2,800.00*

Toddler body

13"	$825.00	$1,100.00
19"	$975.00	$1,300.00
22"	$1,125.00	$1,500.00

13½" bisque Kammer & Reinhardt mold 117X with flirty eyes, mohair wig, composition and wood jointed body, open mouth, circa 1911, $3,000.00+. Courtesy Marguerite Long.

Mold 123 Max and Mold 124 Moritz, sleep, flirty eyes, laughing/closed mouth

16" Max	$14,500.00*
16" Moritz	$23,000.00*

Mold 126 Mein Liebling Baby (My Darling Baby)

Sleep or flirty eyes, bent-leg baby, 1914 – 1930s

14"	$550.00	$750.00
18"	$800.00	$1,200.00
22"	$1,125.00	$1,500.00

Toddler body

6"	$400.00	$500.00
8"	$1,000.00	$1,450.00
17"	$750.00	$1,000.00
22"	$1,050.00	$1,400.00
24"	$1,425.00	$1,900.00

Child body

22"	$750.00	$1,000.00
32"	$1,300.00	$1,725.00

16" bisque Kammer & Reinhardt Max, mold 123, character from German comics, original black flax wig and red and white jumpsuit, circa 1913, $14,500.00. Courtesy McMasters Doll Auctions.

Mold 127, 127N, domed head-like mold 126, bent-leg baby body, add more for flirty eyes

14"	$800.00	$1,200.00
18"	$1,200.00	$1,600.00

Toddler body

20"	$1,650.00	$2,200.00
26"	$1,950.00	$2,600.00

Mold 128, sleep eyes, open mouth, baby body

18"	$1,100.00	$1,450.00

8½" bisque Kammer & Reinhardt #126 Mein Liebling Baby (My Darling Baby), character with sleep eyes, toddler composition body, starfish hands, marked "K*R//Germany//126-21," circa 1914, $1,000.00+. Courtesy Ann Van Arnum.

Original clothes, with layette in wicker basket
> 10" $1,600.00*

Mold 131: See Googly category.

Mold 135, sleep eyes, open mouth, baby body
> 13" $625.00 $850.00

Toddler body
> 18" $1,050.00 $1,450.00

Mold 171 Klein Mammi (Little Mammy), dome, open mouth
> 18" $1,500.00*

Too few in database for reliable range.

Mold 214, shoulder head, painted eyes, closed mouth
Similar to mold 114, muslin stitch-jointed body
> 12" $2,600.00*

Too few in database for reliable range.

Kestner, J.D.

Marks:

20" bisque Kestner Baby Jean marked "JDK/ /Made in Germany," solid dome head, blue sleep eyes, open mouth with two teeth, spring tongue, molded brush-stroked hair, fat cheeks, circa 1900+, $1,050.00. Courtesy McMasters Doll Auctions.

1805 – 1930+, Waltershausen, Germany. Kestner was one of the first firms to make dressed dolls. Supplied bisque heads to Catterfelder Puppenfabrik. Borgfeldt, Butler Bros., Century Doll Co., Horsman, R.H. Macy, Sears, Siegel Cooper, F.A.O. Schwarz, and others were distributors for Kestner. Besides wooden dolls, papier-mache, wax over composition, and Frozen Charlottes, Kestner made bisque dolls with leather or composition bodies, chinas, and all-bisque dolls. Early bisque heads with closed mouths marked X or XI, turned shoulder head, and swivel heads on shoulder plates are thought to be Kestners. After 1892, dolls were marked *"made in Germany"* with mold numbers.

Bisque heads with early mold numbers are stamped *"Excelsior DRP No. 70 685"*; heads of 100 number series are marked *"dep."* Some early characters are unmarked or only marked with the mold number. After "211" on, it is believed all dolls were marked *JDK* or *JDK, Jr.* Registered the "Crown Doll" (Kronen Puppe) in 1915, used crown on label on bodies and dolls.

The Kestner Alphabet is registered in 1897 as a design patent. It is possible to identify the sizes of doll heads by this key. Letter and number always go together: B/6, C/7, D/8, E/9, F/10, G/11, H/12, H¾/12¾, J13, J¾/13¾, K/14, K½/14½, L/15, L½/15½, M/16, N/17. It is believed all dolls with plaster pates were made by Kestner.

First price is for doll in good condition with some flaws; second price is for doll in excellent condition with original clothes or appropriately dressed. Exceptional dolls may be more.

EARLY BABY

Unmarked, or only "JDK," "made in Germany" or with size number, solid dome bisque socket head, glass sleep eyes, molded and/or painted hair, composition bent-leg baby body. Add more for body with crown label and /or original clothes.

Open mouth

14"	$700.00	$950.00
17"	$750.00	$1,000.00

Closed mouth

15"	$1,050.00	$1,400.00
20"	$1,350.00	$1,800.00

15" bisque Kestner marked with only a 9 on her head, closed pouty mouth, brown sleep eyes mohair wig, jointed composition body, straight wrists, well dressed, circa 1890s, $3,100.00. Courtesy McMasters Doll Auctions.

EARLY CHILD

Bisque shoulder head

Closed or open/closed mouth, plaster pate, may be marked with size numbers only, glass eyes, may sleep, kid body, bisque lower arms, appropriate wig and dress, in good condition, more for original clothes.

15"	$525.00	$700.00
17"	$600.00	$800.00
19"	$1,050.00*	

Open mouth, Mold 145, 147, 148, 154, 166, 195

20"	$250.00	$350.00
24"	$300.00	$400.00
28"	$450.00	$600.00

Mold 154, all original, unplayed-with condition

22"	$950.00*	

Turned shoulder head, closed mouth, size number only

16"	$525.00	$700.00
18"	$600.00	$800.00
22"	$650.00	$850.00
25"	$750.00	$1,000.00
28"	$2,700.00*	

21" bisque Kestner, turned shoulder head, closed mouth, glass sleep eyes, mohair wig, leather body, bisque forearms, dressed, circa 1890s, $2,000.00. Private collection.

Bisque socket head

Open mouth, glass eyes, Kestner ball-jointed body, add more for square cut teeth on body marked only with number and letter.

Mold 142, 144, 146, 164, 167, 171

8"	$450.00	$600.00
18"	$700.00	$950.00
25"	$1,075.00	$1,450.00
42"	$4,100.00*	

24" bisque Kestner, long face with open mouth, leather body, marked only "11" on back of head, human hair wig, sleep eyes, $1,500.00. Private collection.

12" bisque Kestner, mold 167, socket head, glass eyes, open mouth with upper teeth, dolly face, mohair wig, circa 1898+, $750.00. Courtesy Zelia Still.

Mold 171, 18" size only called "Daisy"

18"	$750.00	$1,000.00

A.T. type, closed mouth, glass eyes, mohair wig over plaster pate, early composition and wood ball-jointed body with straight wrists. Marked only with size number such as 15 for 24".

24"	$19,000.00*

Mold XI, 103 pouty closed mouth

16"	$3,500.00*	
20"	$1,950.00	$2,600.00
23"	$2,625.00	$3,500.00

Mold 128, 169, pouty closed mouth, glass eyes, composition and wood ball-jointed body, wigged

9"	$2,500.00*	original costume
14"	$1,425.00	$1,900.00
26"	$2,700.00	$3,400.00

Mold 129, 130, 149, 155, 160, 161, 168, 173, 174, 196, 214, open mouth, glass eyes, composition wood jointed body, add more for fur eyebrows

12"	$400.00	$550.00
15"	$450.00	$625.00
19"	$650.00	$875.00
23"	$750.00	$1,000.00
28"	$1,100.00	$1,400.00
33"	$1,700.00*	

Mold 143, open mouth, glass eyes, jointed body

8"	$450.00	$600.00
9"	$625.00	$850.00
13"	$750.00	$1,000.00
18"	$825.00	$1,100.00

Mold 155, open mouth, glass eyes, five-piece or fully jointed body

7½"	$700.00	$925.00

CHARACTER BABY, 1910+

Socket head with wig or solid dome with painted hair, glass eyes, open mouth with bent-leg baby body. More for toddler body.

Mold 211, 226, 236, 260, 262, 263

8"	$650.00	$800.00
12"	$600.00	$775.00
16"	$675.00	$900.00
18"	$750.00	$1,000.00
24"	$1,050.00	$1,450.00+
26"	$1,250.00	$1,650.00

Mold 210, Mold 234, 235, shoulder head, solid dome, sleep eyes, open/closed mouth or open mouth

12"	$400.00	$550.00
15"	$500.00	$700.00

Too few in database for reliable range.

Mold 220, sleep eyes, open/closed mouth

14"	$3,225.00	$4,300.00

Toddler

19"	$4,650.00	$6,200.00
26½"	$10,000.00*	

Mold 237, 245, (Mold 1070, bald solid dome), Hilda, sleep eyes, open mouth

13"	$1,800.00	$2,400.00
15"	$2,400.00	$3,200.00
17"	$2,500.00	$3,350.00
25"	$5,795.00*	

Mold 243, Oriental baby, sleep eyes, open mouth

13"	$3,000.00	$4,000.00
15"	$3,900.00	$5,400.00
19"	$4,950.00	$6,600.00

Mold 247, socket head, open mouth, sleep eyes

15"	$1,425.00	$1,900.00

Mold 249, socket head, open mouth, sleep eyes

14"	$1,300.00*

Too few in database for reliable range.

Mold 255, marked *"O.I.C. made in Germany,"* solid dome flange neck, glass eyes, large open/closed screamer mouth, cloth body

10½"	$750.00* nude

Too few in database for reliable range.

Mold 257, socket head, sleep eyes, open mouth

10"	$450.00	$625.00
14"	$675.00	$900.00
17"	$775.00	$1,025.00
23"	$1,050.00	$1,400.00
25"	$1,800.00	$2,400.00

Toddler body

16"	$700.00	$950.00
24"	$1,350.00	$1,800.00

CHARACTER CHILD, CA. 1910+

Socket head, wig, closed mouth, glass eyes, composition and wood jointed body; add more for painted eyes.

Mold 175, 176, 177, 178, 179, 180, 181, 182, 184, 185, 187, 188, 189, 190

15"	$3,000.00	$4,000.00
20"	$3,750.00	$5,000.00

18" bisque Kestner mold 168, open mouth, blue glass sleep eyes, mohair wig, composition and wood body, circa 1898, $650.00. Private collection.

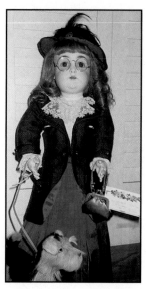

23" bisque Kestner mold 146, open mouth, dolly face, jointed composition body, circa 1897, $1,200.00. Courtesy Rose Capricio.

6½" bisque Kestner mold 260, with open mouth, glass eyes, original in Kestner marked box, circa 1916, $875.00. Courtesy Jan Mealer.

21" bisque Kestner character child, mold 211, open/closed mouth, two teeth, composition body, in old felt outfit, copy of an original, circa 1912, $2,100.00. Courtesy Georgia Henry.

Mold 206, fat cheeks, closed mouth, glass eyes child or toddler

15"	$6,700.00	$8,900.00

Too few in database for reliable range.

Mold 208, glass eyes, for all-bisque, see that category

16"	$6,750.00	$9,000.00

Too few in database for reliable range.

Mold 208, painted eyes

12"	$2,500.00	$3,300.00
20"	$7,000.00	$9,300.00

Mold 239, socket head, open mouth, sleep eyes Toddler, also comes as baby

16"	$2,325.00	$3,100.00

Too few in database for reliable range.

Mold 241, socket head, open mouth, sleep eyes

18"	$3,900.00	$5,200.00

Too few in database for reliable range.

ADULT

Mold 162, bisque, open mouth, glass eyes, composition body, slender waists and molded breasts

18"	$1,150.00	$1,525.00
22"	$1,800.00	$2,400.00

Mold 172, Gibson Girl, shoulder head, closed mouth, glass eyes, kid body, bisque forearms

10"	$625.00	$825.00
18"	$1,500.00	$2,600.00
20"	$2,125.00	$2,900.00

WUNDERKIND

Set includes doll body with four interchangeable heads, some with extra apparel, one set includes heads with mold numbers 174, 178, 184, and 185.

11"	$7,500.00	$10,000.00
15"	$9,375.00	$12,500.00

21" bisque Kestner mold 245 Hilda, character baby with original wig, sleep eyes, open mouth, nicely dressed, circa 1914, $4,800.00. Courtesy Iva Mae Jones.

1912+, designed by Rose O'Neill. Manufactured by Borgfeldt, later Joseph Kallus, and then Jesco in 1984, and various companies with special license, as well as unlicensed companies. They were made of all-bisque, celluloid, cloth, composition, rubber, vinyl, zylonite, and other materials. Kewpie figurines (action Kewpies) have mold numbers 4843 through 4883. Kewpies were also marked with a round paper sticker on back, *"KEWPIES DES. PAT. III, R. 1913; Germany; REG. US. PAT. OFF."* On the front, was a heart-shaped sticker marked *"KEWPIE//REG. US. // PAT. OFF."* May also be incised on the soles of the feet, *"O'Neill."*

Mark:

First price indicates doll in good condition, with some flaws; second price indicates doll in excellent condition with no chips. Add more for label, accessories, original box or exceptional doll.

ALL-BISQUE

Immobiles

Standing, legs together, immobile, no joints, blue wings, molded painted hair, painted side-glancing eyes

2"	$55.00	$110.00
2½"	$70.00	$135.00
4½"	$75.00	$150.00
5"	$90.00	$175.00
6"	$150.00	$275.00

Jointed shoulders

2"	$50.00	$95.00
4½"	$65.00	$130.00
6"	$100.00	$195.00
8½"	$200.00	$400.00
10"	$350.00	$625.00

10" bisque Kestner Kewpie Googly, painted molded hair, smiling closed mouth, circa 1920s, $6,400.00. Courtesy McMasters Doll Auctions.

Carnival chalk Kewpie with jointed shoulders

13"	$50.00	$165.00

Jointed shoulders with any article of molded clothing

2½"	$100.00	$200.00
4½"	$2,600.00* pirate	
6"	$115.00	$330.00
8"	$190.00	$375.00

With Mary Jane shoes

6½"	$250.00	$500.00

Jointed hips and shoulders

5"	$275.00	$550.00
7"	$375.00	$750.00
10"	$500.00	$1,000.00
12½"	$650.00	$1,300.00

4" all-bisque, circa 1912+, Kewpie Traveler, $125.00; 3¼" bisque seated Kewpie with cat, $835.00. Courtesy McMasters Doll Auctions.

* at auction

3½" all-bisque Kewpie action figure unjointed with side-painted eyes and open/closed mouth, marked O'Neill on bottom, holds a fly or bug (missing) in its hand, circa 1912+, $350.00. Courtesy McMasters Doll Auctions.

6½" all-bisque Kewpie, painted eyes to side, molded and painted tufts of hair, stiff neck, jointed at arms, starfish hands, legs molded together, circa 1912+, $95.00. Courtesy McMasters Doll Auctions.

BISQUE ACTION FIGURES

Arms folded
6"	$300.00	$600.00

Aviator
8½"	$425.00	$850.00

Back, laying down, kicking one foot
4"	$100.00	$200.00

Basket and ladybug, Kewpie seated
4"	$900.00	$1,800.00

Bear holding Kewpie
3½"	$110.00	$220.00

"Blunderboo," Kewpie falling down
1¾"	$240.00	$465.00

Bottle, green beverage, Kewpie standing, kicking out
2½"	$330.00	$660.00

Bottle stopper
2"	$75.00	$150.00

Box, heart shaped, with Kewpie kicker atop
4"	$440.00	$880.00

Bride and Groom
3½"	$175.00	$350.00

Boutonniére
1½"	$55.00	$110.00
2"	$70.00	$135.00

Candy container
4"	$250.00	$500.00

Card holder
2"	$250.00	$500.00

With label
2¼"	$330.00	$660.00

Carpenter, wearing tool apron
8½"	$550.00	$1,100.00

Cat, black with Kewpie
2¼"	$150.00	$300.00

Cat, gray on lap of seated Kewpie
2¼"	$850.00*

Cat, gray with Kewpie on back
3"	$275.00	$525.00

Cat, tan with Kewpie
3"	$150.00	$300.00

Cat, white with Kewpie
3"	$220.00	$440.00

Chick with seated Kewpie
2"	$300.00	$600.00

Cowboy
10"	$400.00	$800.00

Dog, with Kewpie on stomach
3"	$3,400.00*

4½" unmarked bisque Kew-pie Bride and Groom, $330.00; bisque Kewpie Hug-gers marked O'Neill on bot-tom of foot, circa 1912+. $305.00. Courtesy McMasters Doll Auctions.

Dog, with Red Cross Kewpie

4"	$300.00	

Doodle Dog alone

1½"	$350.00	$700.00
3"	$625.00	$1,350.00

Doodle Dog with Kewpie

2½"	$125.00	$250.00

Drum on brown stool, with Kewpie

3½"	$1,200.00	$2,400.00

Farmer

6½"	$300.00	$600.00

Flowers, Kewpie with bouquet in right hand

5"	$475.00	$935.00

Fly on foot of Kewpie

3"	$300.00	$600.00

Governor

2½"	$150.00	$275.00
3¼"	$250.00	$500.00

Hottentot, black Kewpie

3½"	$225.00	$425.00
5"	$300.00	$575.00
9"	$450.00	$950.00
12"	$4,500.00+	

Huggers

2½"	$65.00	$125.00
3½"	$75.00	$150.00
4½"	$100.00	$200.00

Inkwell, with writer Kewpie

4½"	$250.00	$500.00

Jack-O-Lantern between legs of Kewpie

2"	$250.00	$500.00

Jester, with white hat on head

4½"	$300.00	$575.00

Kneeling

4"	$375.00	$750.00

3" china German Kewpie perfume holders with stopper, one-piece immobiles, with painted features, one with hands down is marked "Germany/794"; with reddish forelock, hands behind body, stamped "Germany," no chips, 1920s, $600.00 each. Courtesy Patricia Wright.

Mandolin, green basket and seated Kewpie

2"	$150.00	$275.00

Mandolin held by seated Kewpie in blue chair

4"	$475.00	$925.00

Mandolin, with Kewpie seated on moon swing

2½"	$4,400.00*

Mayor, seated Kewpie in green wicker chair

4½"	$475.00	$950.00

Minister

5"	$125.00	$250.00

Nursing bottle, with Kewpie

3½"	$300.00	$600.00

Reader Kewpie seated with book

2"	$125.00	$250.00
3½"	$165.00	$325.00
4"	$250.00	$500.00

Sack held by Kewpie with both hands

4½"	$1,430.00*

Salt Shaker

2"	$165.00

Seated in fancy chair

4"	$200.00	$400.00

Soldier bursting out of egg

4"	$6,900.00*

Soldier, Confederate

4"	$200.00	$400.00

Soldier in egg

3½"	$6,600.00*

Soldier taking aim with rifle

3½"	$500.00	$990.00

Soldier vase

6½"	$330.00	$660.00

Soldier with black hat, sword, and rifle

4½"	$200.00	$385.00

Soldier with helmet

2¾"	$300.00	$400.00
4½"	$300.00	$600.00

Soldier with red hat, sword, and rifle

3½"	$150.00	$300.00
5¼"	$415.00	$825.00

Stomach, Kewpie laying flat, arms and legs out

4"	$225.00	$450.00

Thinker

4 – 5"	$150.00	$275.00

* at auction

Traveler with dog and umbrella
 3½" $1,300.00*

Traveler with umbrella and bag
 4" $175.00 $350.00
 5" $300.00 $600.00

Vase with card holder and Kewpie
 2½" $165.00 $330.00

Vase with farmer Kewpie
 6½" $1,045.00*

Vase with huggers
 3¾" $325.00 $650.00

Writer, seated Kewpie with pen in hand
 2" $255.00 $475.00
 4" $265.00 $550.00

BISQUE SHOULDER HEAD
 Cloth, or stockinette body
 7" $285.00 $565.00
 Head only
 3" $165.00+

CELLULOID
 Bride and Groom
 4" $15.00 $40.00
 Jointed arms, heart label on chest
 12" $175.00 $325.00

CHINA
 Perfume holder, one piece with opening at back of head
 4½" $550.00 $1,100.00
 Salt Shaker
 1¼" $85.00 $165.00
 Dishes
 Service for 4 $650.00 $900.00
 Service for 6 $975.00 $1,200.00

HEAD AND BODY
 "Cuddle Kewpie," silk screened face, satin body, tagged
 12" $825.00
 Plush, with stockinette face, tagged
 8" $115.00 $225.00

COMPOSITION
 Hottentot, all-composition, heart decal to chest, jointed arms, red winks, ca. 1946
 11" $300.00 $575.00
 All-composition, jointed body, blue wings
 11" $125.00 $375.00
 13" $200.00 $450.00
 Composition head, cloth body, flange neck, composition forearms tagged floral dress
 11" $250.00 $875.00
 Talcum container
 One-piece composition talcum shaker with heart label on chest
 7" $35.00 $65.00

21½" Japanese celluloid Kewpie with painted side-glancing eyes, damage on foot and wing, circa 1930s, $225.00. Courtesy Patrica Christlieb.

Kewpie (cont.)

HARD PLASTIC

Original box, ca. 1950, Kewpie design

8½"	$200.00	$385.00

Sleep eyes, five-piece body with starfish hands

14"	$150.00	$300.00

METAL

Figurine, cast steel on square base, excellent condition

5½"	$30.00	$55.00

SOAP

Kewpie soap figure with cotton batting

Colored label with rhyme, marked *"R.O. Wilson, 1917"*

4"	$55.00	$110.00

Kley & Hahn

Marks:

525
6
Germany

꒓K & H꒠

1902 – 1930+, Ohrdruf, Thuringia, Germany. Bisque heads, jointed composition or leather bodies, exporter; bought heads from Kestner (Walkure) and Hertel Schwab & Co. Also made composition and celluloid head dolls.

First price indicates doll in good condition, but with some flaw; second price indicates doll in excellent condition, with original clothes, or appropriately dressed.

CHARACTER BABY

Mold 133, 135, 138, 158, 160, 161, 167, and 571

Mold 133 (made by Hertel Schwab & Co.), solid-dome, painted eyes, closed mouth

Mold 135 (made by Hertel Schwab & Co.), solid-dome, painted eyes, open/closed mouth

Mold 138 (made by Hertel Schwab & Co.), solid-dome, painted eyes, open/closed mouth

Mold 158 (made by Hertel Schwab & Co.), painted eyes, open mouth

Mold 160 (made by Hertel Schwab & Co.), sleep eyes, open/closed mouth

Mold 161 (made by Hertel Schwab & Co.), character face, sleep eyes, open/closed mouth

Mold 167 (made by Hertel Schwab & Co.), sleep eyes, open/closed or open mouth

Mold 571, "K&H" (made by Bahr & Proschild) character, solid-dome, glass eyes, open/closed mouth, laughing, giant baby

16" bisque Kley & Hahn child, mold 526, painted brown eyes, closed mouth, wig, jointed composition body, circa 1912, $3,500.00. Courtesy Barbara DeFeo.

13"	$450.00	$575.00
16"	$500.00	$675.00
19"	$600.00	$800.00
22"	$750.00	$1,025.00
Toddler body		
21"	$1,050.00	$1,400.00
26"	$1,300.00	$1,750.00

Mold 567 (made by Bahr & Proschild) character multi-face, laughing face, glass eyes, open mouth; crying face, painted eyes, open/closed mouth

15"	$1,475.00	$1,950.00
17"	$1,875.00	$2,500.00
19"	$2,550.00	$3,400.00

Mold 680 "K & CO K&H" with "266 K&H," made by Kestner, character, sleep eyes, open mouth

17"	$700.00	$925.00

Toddler

19"	$975.00	$1,300.00

CHILD

Mold 250, 282, or Walkure, circa 1920 (made by J.D. Kestner, Jr.), dolly face, sleep eyes, open mouth

21"	$475.00	$625.00
28"	$700.00	$925.00
33"	$900.00	$1,200.00

18" bisque Kley & Hahn boy child, mold 566, painted hair, closed mouth, glass eyes, composition body, circa 1910+, $4,000.00. Courtesy Barbara DeFeo.

Mold 325, "Dollar Princess," open mouth

25"	$325.00	$500.00

CHARACTER CHILD

Mold numbers 154, 166, 169

Mold 154, 166 (made by Hertel Schwab & Co.), solid-dome, glass eyes, closed mouth

Mold 169 (made by Hertel Schwab & Co.), sleep eyes, closed or open/closed mouth

17"	$2,000.00	$2,600.00
19"	$2,175.00	$2,900.00
27"	$2,600.00	$3,500.00

Baby body with bent legs

12"	$1,785.00*

Mold 162 (made by Hertel Schwab & Co.), open mouth, voice cut out

17"	$1,100.00	$1,500.00

Too few in database for reliable range.

25" bisque Kley & Hahn Dollar Princess socket head, sleep eyes, open mouth, human hair wig, jointed wood and composition body, nicely dressed, circa 1920s, $325.00. Courtesy McMasters Doll Auctions.

Mold 178 (made by Hertel Schwab & Co.), dome, molded hair, googly, open mouth

Mold 180 (made by Hertel Schwab & Co.), googly, open/closed mouth

17"	$2,550.00	$3,400.00

Too few in database for reliable range.

Mold 292, 520, 525, 526, 531, character face

Mold 292 "KH 1930" (made by J. D. Kestner, Jr.), character face

Mold 520 "K&H" (made by Bahr & Proschild), painted eyes, closed mouth

Mold 525 "K & H" (by Bahr & Proschild), dome, painted eyes, open/ closed mouth

Mold 526 "K&H" (made by Bahr & Proschild), painted eyes, closed mouth

Mold 531 "K&H" (made by Bahr & Proschild), solid dome, painted eyes, open/closed mouth

Baby bent-leg body

9½"	$250.00	$325.00

Child

14"	$3,700.00*Mold 520	
17"	$2,200.00*Mold 531	
21"	$2,250.00	$3,000.00

Mold 546, 549, character face

Mold 546 "K&H" (made by Bahr & Proschild), glass eyes, closed mouth, child body

Mold 549 "K&H" (made by Bahr & Proschild), painted eyes, closed mouth, also in celluloid

16"	$3,150.00	$4,200.00
18"	$3,375.00	$4,500.00

Mold 554, 568, character face

Mold 554 "K&H" (made by Bahr & Proschild), glass eyes, open/closed mouth

Mold 568 (made by Bahr & Proschild), solid dome, sleep eyes, smiling

17"	$635.00	$850.00+

Too few in database for reliable range.

Kling, C.F. & Co.

1836 – 1930+ Ohrdruf, Thuringia, Germany. Porcelain factory that made chinas, bisque dolls, all-bisque, and snow babies. Often mold number marks are followed by size number.

Mark:

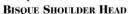

First price indicates doll in good condition, but with some flaws; second price indicates doll in excellent condition, with original clothes, or appropriately dressed, more for exceptional doll with elaborate molded hair or bodice.

BISQUE SHOULDER HEAD

Painted eyes, wig or molded hair, cloth or kid body

15"	$300.00	$400.00
19"	$465.00	$625.00
21"	$475.00	$650.00

Glass eyes

13"	$400.00	$525.00

Mold 123, 124, incised with bell mark, glass eyes, closed mouth, shoulder head

15"	$650.00	$850.00

Mold 131, 167, 178, 182, 189

Mold 131, incised bell, shoulder head, glass eyes, closed mouth

Mold 167, incised bell, solid dome, with wig, closed mouth

Mold 178, shoulder head, molded hair, glass eyes, closed mouth

Mold 182, shoulder head, molded hair, painted eyes, closed mouth

Mold 189, shoulder head, molded hair, painted eyes, closed mouth

15"	$800.00	$1,075.00

* at auction

Mold 135, molded bodice, flower in molded hair

20"	$1,300.00*	

Mold 370, 372, 373, 377, sleep eyes, open mouth

15"	$375.00	$500.00
21"	$525.00	$700.00

Bisque socket head, open mouth, jointed body

13"	$300.00	$400.00
17"	$425.00	$550.00
21"	$550.00	$725.00

15" bisque C.F. Kling girl, pale blue glass eyes, closed mouth, replaced wig, kid body, bussets at elbows, hips, and knees, stitched fingers, plum silk and velvet dress, high button boots, circa 1880, $800.00. Courtesy McMasters Doll Auctions.

CHINA SHOULDER HEAD

Mold numbers 131, 188, 189, 202

Cloth or kid body, china limbs, blonde or black molded hair

Mold 131, painted eyes, closed mouth

Mold 188, molded hair, glass eyes, closed mouth

Mold 189, molded hair, painted eyes, closed mouth

Mold 202, molded hair, painted eyes, closed mouth

13"	$200.00	$275.00
18"	$335.00	$450.00
21"	$375.00	$500.00

Knoch, Gebruder

1887 – 1918+, Neustad, Thuringia, Germany. Made bisque doll heads and doll joints, with cloth or kid body. Succeeded in 1918 by Max Oscar Arnold.

SHOULDER HEAD

Mold 203, 205

Mold 203, character face, painted eyes, closed mouth, stuffed cloth body

Mold 205, "GKN" character face, painted eyes, open/closed mouth, molded tongue

12"	$600.00	$800.00
14"	$750.00	$1,000.00

Too few in database for reliable range.

Mold 223, "GKN GES. NO. GESCH"

Character face, solid-dome or shoulder head, painted eyes, molded tears, closed mouth

Too few in database for reliable range.

Mark:

Made in Germany
Ges N° 216 Gesch
15/0

SOCKET HEAD

Mold 179, 181, 190, 192, 193, 201

(Mold 201 also came as black), dolly face, glass eyes, open mouth

13"	$185.00	$250.00
17"	$300.00	$425.00

Mold 204, character face

15"	$865.00	$1,150.00

  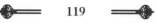

Mold 206, "DRGM" solid dome, intaglio eyes, open/closed mouth
    11" $750.00*

Mold 216, "GKN" solid dome, intaglio eyes, laughing, open/closed mouth
    12" $315.00*

Too few in database for reliable range.

229: See All-Bisque category.

230, molded bonnet, character shoulder head, painted eyes, open/closed mouth laughing

232, molded bonnet, character shoulder head, laughing

13"	$675.00	$900.00
15"	$1,200.00	$1,600.00

Koenig & Wernicke

24" Koenig & Wernicke bisque socket head with toddler composition body, character face, open mouth, sleep eyes, human hair wig, nicely dressed, circa 1912, $2,000.00. Private collection.

1912 – 1930+, Waltershausen, Germany. Had doll factory, made bisque or celluloid dolls with composition bodies, later dolls with hard rubber heads.

Mark:
K&W
HARTGUMMI
555 ○
GERMANY

BISQUE BABY

Mold 98, 99, "made in Germany" (made by Hertel Schwab & Co.) character, socket head, sleep eyes, open mouth, teeth, tremble tongue, wigged, composition bent-leg baby body

18"	$500.00	$675.00
22"	$600.00	$800.00
27"	$900.00	$1,200.00

Mold 1070, ca. 1915, socket head, open mouth, bent-leg baby body

12"	$400.00	$550.00
16"	$500.00	$650.00
Toddler		
17"	$1,000.00	$1,400.00
19"	$1,150.00	$1,575.00

COMPOSITION CHILD

Composition head on five-piece or fully-jointed body, open mouth, sleep eyes, add more for flirty eyes.

14"	$225.00	$300.00
16"	$350.00	$450.00

Kruse, Kathe

1910 – 1980 on, Prussia, after W.W.II, Bavaria. Made dolls of waterproof muslin, wool, and stockinette with heads, hair, and hands oil painted. The skeleton frame was rigid with movable parts; early dolls are stuffed with deer hair. Early thumbs are part of the hand; after 1914 are attached separately, later again, part of the hand. Marked on the bottom of the left foot with number and name "Kathe Kruse," in black, red, or purple ink. After 1929, dolls had wigs, but some still had painted hair. Original doll modeled after Dutch bust sculpture "Fiammingo," by Francois Duquesnois.

CLOTH

Doll I Series, 1910 – 1929

All-cloth, jointed shoulders, wide hips, painted eyes and hair

Three vertical seams in back of head, marked on left foot

Mark:

17"	$1,700.00	$4,700.00

Ball-jointed knees, 1911 variant produced by Kammer & Reinhardt

17"	$5,000.00+

Too few in database for reliable range.

Doll I Series, later model, 1929+, now with slim hips

17"	$1,500.00	$2,900.00

Doll IH Series, wigged version, 1929+

17"	$1,600.00	$3,000.00

Bambino, a doll for a doll, circa 1915 – 1925

8"	$500.00+

Too few in database for reliable range.

Doll II Series, "Schlenkerchen," circa 1922 – 1936

Smiling baby, open/closed mouth, stockinette covered body and limbs, one seam head

13"	$10,400.00*

Too few in database for reliable range.

Doll V, VI, Sandbabies Series, 1920s+

"Traumerchen" (closed eyes) and "Du Mein" (open eyes) were cloth dolls with painted hair, weighted with sand or unweighted, with or without belly buttons, in 19⅝" and 23⅝" sizes. One- or three-seam heads, or cloth over cardboard. Later heads were made in the 1930s from a heavy composition called magnesit.

19⅝"	$1,900.00	$3,700.00

Magnesit head, circa 1930s+

20"	$325.00	$1,350.00
40"	$2,650.00	$3,500.00

Doll VII Series, circa 1927 – 1952

Two versions were offered.

A smaller 14" Du Mein open eye baby, painted hair or wigged, three seam head, wide hips, sewn on thumbs, 1927 – 1930

14"	$3,000.00

Too few in database for reliable range.

A smaller Doll I version, with wide hips, separately sewn on thumbs, painted hair or wigged, after 1930 – 1950s slimmer hips with thumbs formed with hand

14"	$1,000.00	$2,000.00

17" cloth Kathe Kruse Series I, with wide hips, applied thumbs, circa 1910 – 1929, $4,700.00. Courtesy Ann Van Arnum.

40" magnesite Kathe Kruse store mannequin with cloth stockinette body over wire armature, circa 1930s, $3,500.00. Courtesy Barbara DeFeo.

Doll VIII Series, Deutsche Kind, the "German child," 1929+
Modeled after Kruse's son, Friedebald, hollow head, swivels, one verticle seam in back of head, wigged, disk-jointed legs, later made in plastic during the 1950s

20"	$1,200.00	$2,400.00

Doll IX Series, "The Little German Child," 1929+
Wigged, one seam head, a smaller version of Doll VIII

14"	$1,000.00	$1,900.00

Doll X Series, 1935+
Smaller Doll I with turning one seam head

14"	$1,200.00	$2,400.00

Doll XII Series, 1930s
Hampelchen with loose legs, three vertical seams on back of head, painted hair, button and band on back to make legs stand.
The 14" variation has head of Doll I; the 16" variation also has the head of Doll I, and is known after 1940s as Hempelschatz, Doll XIIB.

14"	$800.00	$1,200.00
16"	$900.00	$1,500.00
18"	$1,000.00	$2,000.00

XIIH, wigged version

18"	$1,200.0	$2,200.00

XII/I, 1951+, legs have disc joints

18"	$300.00	$650.00

U.S. Zone, after World War II, circa 1946+
Cloth

14"	$200.00	$500.00

Magnesit (heavy composition)

14"	$400.00	$800.00

HARD PLASTIC, 1952 – 1975 (CELLULOID AND OTHER SYNTHETICS)
Turtle Dolls, 1955 – 1961, synthetic bodies

14"	$100.00	$300.00
16"	$150.00	$400.00
18"	$200.00	$500.00

Glued on wigs, sleep or painted eyes, pink muslin body

18"	$200.00	$600.00
21"	$250.00	$750.00

1975 to date, marked with size number in centimeters, B for baby, H for hair, and G for painted hair

14"	$350.00
18"	$465.00

Kuhnlenz, Gebruder

Mark:

1884 – 1930, Kronach, Bavaria. Made dolls, doll heads, movable children, and swimmers. Butler Bros. and Marshall Field distributed their dolls.

Mold 32, bisque socket head, closed mouth, glass eyes, pierced ears, wig, wood and composition jointed body

19"	$1,800.00	$2,400.00
23"	$2,175.00	$2,900.00

Mold 34, Bru type, paperweight eyes, closed mouth, pierced ears, composition jointed body

12½"	$1,650.00	$2,200.00

Mold 38, solid dome turned shoulder head, closed mouth, pierced ears, kid body

20"	$900.00	$1,200.00

Mold 41, solid dome socket head, open mouth, glass eyes

16"	$900.00	$1,125.00

Mold 44, small dolls marked Gbr. K in sunburst, socket head, glass eyes, open mouth, five-piece composition body, molded painted socks and shoes

6"	$1,600.00*	with trunk and

wardrobe, at auction

7"	$250.00	$325.00

Mold 165, socket head, sleep eyes, open mouth, teeth

22"	$350.00	$450.00
33"	$525.00	$650.00

19½" bisque Gebruder Kuhnlenz mold 165, blue sleep eyes, open mouth, mohair wig, jointed wood and composition body, new arms, hands don't match, circa 1900, $175.00. Courtesy McMasters Doll Auctions.

Lanternier, A. & Cie.

1915 – 1924, Limoges, France. Porcelain factory, made dolls and heads, including heads marked *"Caprice," "Cherie," "Favorite," "La Georgienne," "Lorraine,"* and *"Toto."* Lady dolls were dressed in French provincial costumes, bodies by Ortyz; dolls were produced for Association to Aid War Widows.

ADULT, CA. 1915

Marked *"Caprice," "Cherie," "Favorite," "La Georgienne," "Lorraine,"* or *"Toto,"* bisque socket head, open/closed mouth with teeth, composition adult body

17"	$975.00	$1,300.00
22"	$1,000.00*	

Painted eyes

12½"	$1,975.00*

CHILD

Bisque socket head, open mouth with teeth, wig, composition jointed body

17"	$525.00	$725.00
23"	$700.00	$950.00

Leather

Leather was an available resource for Native Americans to use for making doll heads, bodies, or entire dolls. Some examples of Gussie Decker's dolls were advertised as "impossible for child to hurt itself" and leather was fine for teething babies.

12"	$275.00

Too few in database for reliable range.

25"	$325.00

Too few in database for reliable range.

---

* at auction

1918 – 80+, Turine, Italy. Trademark and name of firm started by Enrico and Elenadi Scavini, that made felt dolls with pressed faces, also made composition head dolls, wooden dolls, and porcelain figurines and dolls. Early Lenci dolls have tiny metal button, hang tags with *"Lenci//Torino//Made in Italy."* Ribbon strips marked *"Lenci//Made in Italy"* were found in the clothes ca. 1925 – 1950. Some, but not all dolls have Lenci marked in purple or black ink on the sole of the foot. Some with original paper tags may be marked with a model number in pencil.

14" felt Lenci girl, painted features, all original in felt and organdy, excellent condition, circa 1930s, $900.00. Courtesy Nancy Lazenby.

Dolls have felt swivel heads, oil-painted features, often side-glancing eyes, jointed shoulders and hips, sewn together third and fourth fingers, sewn-on double felt ears, often dressed in felt and organdy original clothes, excellent condition. May have scalloped socks.

The most sought after are the well-constructed early dolls from the 1920s and 1930s, when Madame Lenci had control of the design and they were more elaborate with fanciful well-made accessories. They carried animals of wood or felt, baskets, felt vegetables, purses, or bouquets of felt flowers. This era of dolls had eye shadow, dots in corner of eye, two-tone lips, with lower lip highlighted and, depending on condition, will command higher prices.

The later dolls of the 1940s and 1950s have hard cardboard-like felt faces, with less intricate details, like less elaborate appliqués, fewer accessories, and other types of fabrics such as taffeta, cotton, and rayon, all showing a decline in quality and should not be priced as earlier dolls. The later dolls may have fabric covered cardboard torsos. Model numbers changed over the years, so what was a certain model number early, later became another letter or number.

Mark:

Identification Tips:

Lenci characteristics include double layer ears, scalloped cotton socks. Early dolls may have rooted mohair wig, 1930s dolls may have "frizzed" played-with wigs. Later dolls are less elaborate with hard cardboard-type felt faces.

First price indicates doll in poor condition, perhaps worn, soiled, or faded, price in this condition should reflect 25 percent value of doll in excellent condition; second price indicates doll in excellent condition, clean, with colors still bright. Deduct for dolls of the 1940s and 1950s or later. Add more for tags, boxes, or accessories. Exceptional dolls and rare examples may go much higher.

BABY

13"	$375.00	$1,500.00
16"	$1,700.00*	
22"	$2,000.00	$3,200.00

* at auction

7½" felt Lenci Twins, all original, circa 1930s, $1,200.00 as twins; separately, $400.00 each. Courtesy Nancy Lazenby.

CHILD, 1920s – 1930s, softer face, more elaborate costume

13"	$500.00	$1,750.00
17"	$650.00	$2,500.00
21"	$750.00	$2,750.00

1940s – 1950s+, hard face, less intricate costume

13"	$75.00	$400.00
15"	$100.00	$500.00
17"	$125.00	$600.00

SMALL DOLLS
Miniatures, 9"

Child	$125.00	$400.00
Tyrol Boy	$100.00	$375.00
Young Flower Merchant		
	$1,300.00*	
10 – 11"	$125.00	$500.00

Mascottes, 8½", have swing legs like Mama dolls, may have loop on neck

8½"	$80.00	$325.00

In rare outfit, carrying accessories

8½"	$115.00	$450.00

LADY
With adult face, flapper or boudoir body with long slim limbs

17"	$265.00	$1,050.00
32"	$650.00	$2,600.00
48"	$1,250.00	$5,000.00

CELEBRITIES
Bach

17"	$715.00	$2,850.00

Jack Dempsey

18"	$875.00	$3,500.00

Tom Mix

18"	$875.00	$3,500.00

Mendel

22"	$925.00	$3,700.00

* at auction

16" felt Lenci Baby with series 149 face, painted features, side-glancing eyes, original costume, circa 1920s – 1930s, $1,700.00. Courtesy Nancy Lazenby.

14½" cloth Lenci mountain climber smoker, with cigarette in mouth, painted side-glancing brown eyes, hang tag, all original, with walking stick, circa 1920s, $895.00. Courtesy Bette Yadon.

Mozart
14"	$3,000.00*	

Pastorelle
14"	$3,000.00*	

CHARACTERS

Aladdin
14"	$1,925.00	$7,750.00

Athlete, Golfer, ca. 1930
17"	$2,700.00 *a few moth holes	

Aviator, girl with felt helmet
18"	$800.00	$3,200.00

Bernadetta
19"	$260.00	$1,050.00

Clown
19"	$450.00	$1,800.00

Court Gentleman
18"	$400.00	$1,600.00

Cupid
17"	$1,300.00	$5,200.00

Devil
9"	$1,500.00*	

Fascist Boy, rare
14"	$750.00	$1,500.00
17"	$1,800.00*	

Flower Girl, ca. 1930
20"	$250.00	$1,000.00

Henriette
26"	$625.00	$2,500.00

Indian
17"	$900.00	$3,600.00

* at auction

Squaw with papoose
17" $1,050.00 $4,200.00

Li Tia Guai
17" $7,000.00*

Londrio
18" $200.00 $800.00

Lucia 48, ca. 1930
14" $200.00 $800.00

Merry Widow
20" $350.00 $1,450.00

Pan, hooved feet
8" $1,000.00*

Riomaggio
20" $3,000.00*

Sailor
17" $360.00 $1,450.00

Salome, ca. 1920, brown felt, ball at waist allows doll to swivel
17" $850.00 $3,500.00

Series 300 Children
Eastern European boy
17" $275.00 $1,100.00

Turkish boy
17" $375.00 $1,500.00

Smoker
Painted eyes
28" $600.00 $2,400.00

Glass eyes
24" $975.00 $3,900.00

Val Gardena
19" $225.00 $900.00

Winking Bellhop with Love Letter
11" $200.00 $750.00

ETHNIC OR REGIONAL COSTUME
Bali dancer
15" $375.00 $1,500.00

Eugenia
25" $275.00 $1,100.00

Oriental child
17" $900.00 $3,600.00

Chinese man, ca. 1925
15" $600.00 $2,400.00

Hu Sun
22" $575.00 $2,300.00

Japanese boy
17" $3,780.00*

Japanese lady
21" $5,800.00*

14" cloth Lenci girl with jump rope, all original, painted blue eyes, mohair wig, cloth torso, felt arms and legs, green jumper, white organdy blouse, circa 1920s – 1930s, $500.00. Courtesy McMasters Doll Auctions.

Madame Butterfly, ca. 1926

17"	$800.00	$3,200.00
25"	$1,200.00	$4,800.00

Marenka, Russian girl, ca. 1930

14"	$1,100.00*

Scottish girl, ca. 1930

14"	$175.00	$700.00

Spanish girl, ca. 1930

14"	$200.00	$800.00
17"	$250.00	$1,000.00

Tyrol boy or girl, ca. 1935

14"	$200.00	$800.00

EYE VARIATIONS

Glass eyes

16"	$400.00	$1,600.00
22"	$750.00	$3,000.00

Flirty glass eyes

15"	$550.00	$2,200.00
20"	$700.00	$2,800.00

Surprise eye, "O" shaped eyes and mouth

16"	$400.00	$1,200.00+

ACCESSORIES

Lenci Catalogs	$900.00 – 1,200.00
Lenci Dog	$100.00 – 150.00

Lenci-Type

1920 – 1950. These were made by many English, French, or Italian firms from felt or cloth with painted features, mohair wig, original clothes.

These must be in very good condition, tagged or unmarked. Usually Lenci-types have single felt ears or no ears.

CHILD

15"	$35.00	$145.00
19"	$200.00* worn	

Regional costume

19"	$115.00	$450.00

16" felt Lenci-type Dutch Boy by Eros, painted features, mohair wig, all original with lovely facial color, pipe, circa 1930s, $400.00. Courtesy Nancy Lazenby.

Limbach

1772 – 1927+, Alsbach, Thuringia, Germany. This porcelain factory made bisque head dolls, china dolls, bathing dolls, and all-bisque dolls. Usually marked with three leaf clover.

ALL-BISQUE

Child, small doll, molded hair or wigged, painted eyes, molded painted shoes and socks, may have mark "*8661*," and cloverleaf. More for exceptional dolls.

6"	$100.00	$175.00
8"	$185.00	$275.00

Glass eyes

6"	$200.00	$275.00

Mark:

BABY

Mold 8682, character face, bisque socket head, glass eyes, clover mark, bent-leg baby body, wig, open/closed mouth

8½"	$450.00*

CHILD

May have name above mold mark, such as Norma or Rita, bisque socket head, glass eyes, clover mark, wig, open mouth

20"	$700.00	$950.00

24" bisque Limbach girl, with crown/clover mark, brown sleep eyes, open mouth, four teeth, synthetic wig, jointed wood and composition body, blue dress with ruffle trim, ecru satin blouse, circa 1919+, $300.00. Courtesy McMasters Doll Auctions.

Marottes

Ca. 1860 on and earlier. Doll's head on wooden or ivory stick, sometimes with whistle; when twirled some play music. Bisque head on stick made by various French and German companies. Add more for marked head.

Bisque, open mouth

14"	$625.00	$1,025.00

Marseille, Armand, Mold 3200, open mouth

13"	$1,000.00	$1,300.00

Mold 600, closed mouth, squeaker mechanism

13"	$900.00	$1,200.00

Schoenau & Hoffmeister, mold 4700, circa 1905

15"	$800.00* pristine

Celluloid

11"	$190.00	$250.00

See 1997 DOLL VALUES for photo.

Marseille, Armand

1885 – 1930+, Sonneberg, Koppelsdorf, Thuringia, Germany. One of the largest suppliers of bisque doll heads, ca. 1900 – 1930, to such companies as Amberg, Arranbee, Bergmann, Borgfeldt, Butler Bros., Dressel, Montgomery Ward, Sears, Steiner, Wiegand, Louis Wolf, and others. Made some doll heads with no mold numbers, but names, such as Alma, Baby Betty, Baby Gloria, Baby Florence, Baby Phyllis, Beauty, Columbia, Duchess, Ella, Floradora, Jubilee, Mabel, Majestic, Melitta, My Playmate, Nobbi Kid, Our Pet, Princess, Queen Louise, Rosebud, Superb, Sunshine, and Tiny Tot. Some Indian dolls had no mold numbers. Often used Superb kid bodies, with bisque hands.

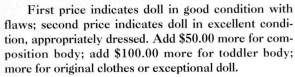

Marks:

Armand Marseille
Germany
390
A. 4. M.

Made in Germany

Florodora

A 5 M

Queen Louise
Germany
7.

First price indicates doll in good condition with flaws; second price indicates doll in excellent condition, appropriately dressed. Add $50.00 more for composition body; add $100.00 more for toddler body; more for original clothes or exceptional doll.

BABY

Newborn, bisque solid-dome socket head or flange neck, may have wig, glass eyes, closed mouth, cloth body with celluloid or composition hands

Mold 341, My Dream Baby, 351, Rock-A-Bye Baby, marked *"AM"* in original basket with layette

9" twins	$650.00*	
10"	$185.00	$250.00
12"	$225.00	$300.00
15"	$350.00	$450.00

Mold 345, Kiddiejoy, ca. 1926, 352, bisque solid-dome socket head or flange neck, may have wig, glass eyes, closed mouth, cloth body with celluloid or composition hands

8"	$150.00	$225.00
11"	$200.00	$275.00
16"	$350.00	$515.00

With toddler body

28"	$900.00	$1,200.00

Mold 372 Kiddiejoy, ca. 1925, shoulder head, molded hair, painted eyes, open/closed mouth, two upper teeth, kid body

12"	$300.00	$400.00
18"	$500.00	$650.00
21"	$775.00	$1,025.00

Character face

Baby Betty, usually found on child composition body, some on bent-leg baby body

16"	$500.00*

Baby Gloria, solid dome, open mouth, painted hair

15"	$575.00*

Baby Phyllis, painted hair, closed mouth

13"	$285.00	$500.00
17"	$475.00	$625.00
21"	$850.00	$1,150.00

Fany, mold 230, 231, can be child, toddler, or baby, more for molded hair

#231

16"	$6,300.00*	
17"	$3,150.00	$4,200.00

Mold 256, 259, 326, 327, 328, 329, 360a, 750, 790, 900, 927, 970, 971, 975, 980, 984, 985, 990, 991, 992 Our Pet, 995, 996, bisque

17" bisque Armand Marseille My Dream Baby, socket head, glass eyes, open mouth, two teeth, composition bent-leg baby body, large hairline on solid dome, beautifully dressed, circa 1926, $200.00. Courtesy C.K. Maher.

solid-dome or wigged socket head, open mouth, glass eyes, composition bent-leg baby body, add more for toddler body or flirty eyes or exceptional doll

12"	$225.00	$300.00
15"	$335.00	$450.00
17"	$425.00	$575.00
21"	$585.00	$800.00
24"	$625.00	$850.00

CHILD

No mold number, or just marked *"A.M.,"* bisque socket head, open mouth, glass eyes, wig, composition jointed body

17"	$300.00	$400.00
32"	$700.00	$925.00
42"	$1,500.00	$2,000.00

18" bisque Armand Marseille mold 231 Fany character, toddler body, $5,750.00. Courtesy Cherie Gervais.

Mold 1890, 1892, 1893 (made for Cuno & Otto Dressel), 1894, 1897, 1898 (made for Cuno & Otto Dressel), 1899, 1900, 1901, 1902, 1903, 1909, and 3200, kid body, bisque shoulder or socket head, glass eyes, open mouth with teeth, wig. Add more for original clothes, labels.

12"	$150.00	$200.00
16"	$140.00	$250.00
19"	$210.00	$280.00
22"	$255.00	$340.00
26"	$330.00	$445.00

Composition body

8"	$245.00	$325.00
10"	$200.00	$275.00
16"	$550.00* original	
18"	$350.00	$450.00
21"	$375.00	$500.00
24"	$465.00	$624.00

Mold 370, 390, Duchess, Floradora, Lilly, Mabel, My Playmate, open mouth, glass eyes

Kid body

12"	$125.00	$165.00
15"	$190.00	$255.00
18"	$245.00	$325.00
22"	$525.00	$700.00

Composition body

10"	$375.00* original costume	
13"	$200.00	$270.00
18"	$285.00	$375.00
21"	$375.00	$500.00
24"	$425.00	$575.00
27"	$550.00	$750.00
31"	$750.00	$1,025.00

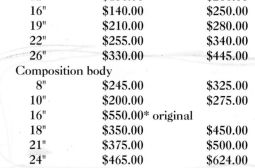

13" bisque Armand Marseille mold 971 character baby, open mouth, sleep eyes, mohair wig, bent-leg baby composition body, circa 1913, $400.00. Courtesy Hazel Lester.

* at auction

13" bisque Armand Marseille character with glass eyes, closed mouth, mohair wig, stick legs on composition and wood jointed body, circa 1911+, $1,500.00. Courtesy Dorothy Bohlin.

10" bisque Armand Marseille mold 1894 socket head with blonde pigtail mohair wig, glass eyes, open mouth with teeth, papier-mache body, with molded and painted shoes, pink dress, circa 1894, $325.00. Courtesy Sheryl Wetenkamp.

Alma, Beauty, Columbia, Melitta, My Companion, Princess, Queen Louise, Rosebud

Kid body

17"	$300.00	$400.00
24"	$400.00	$550.00

Composition body

13"	$205.00	$275.00
17"	$285.00	$375.00
22"	$425.00	$565.00
28"	$475.00	$650.00
31"	$775.00	$1,075.00

Character Face

Mold 225, bisque socket head, glass eyes, open mouth, two rows of teeth, composition jointed body

14"	$2,700.00	$3,600.00
19"	$3,500.00	$4,650.00

Mold 250

9"	$400.00*	
15"	$450.00	$600.00
18"	$750.00	$1,000.00

Mold 251, socket head, open/closed mouth

13"	$1,100.00	$1,450.00
17"	$1,400.00	$1,900.00

Open mouth

14"	$600.00	$800.00

Mold 253: See Googly.

Mold 310, Just Me, bisque socket head, wig, flirty eyes, closed mouth, composition body

7½"	$750.00	$1,000.00
9"	$900.00	$1,300.00
11"	$1,200.00	$1,600.00
13"	$1,500.00	$2,000.00

Painted bisque, with Vogue labeled outfits

8"	$625.00	$850.00
10"	$750.00	$1,000.00

Mold 340

14"	$2,100.00	$2,800.00

Too few in database for reliable range.

Mold 350, glass eyes, closed mouth

16"	$1,650.00	$2,250.00
20"	$2,100.00	$2,850.00

Mold 360a

12"	$300.00	$400.00

Too few in database for reliable range.

Mold 400, 401, glass eyes, closed mouth

13"	$1,000.00	$1,300.00

Flapper body, thin limbs
16"	$1,700.00	$2,250.00

Mold 449, painted eyes, closed mouth
13"	$475.00	$635.00
18"	$900.00	$1,200.00

Painted bisque
11"	$250.00	$350.00
15"	$575.00	$765.00

Mold 450, glass eyes, closed mouth
14"	$550.00	$725.00

Mold 500, 620, 630, domed shoulder head, molded/painted hair, painted intaglio eyes, closed mouth
16"	$750.00	$1,000.00

Mold 520, domed head, glass eyes, open mouth
Composition body
12"	$575.00	$775.00
19"	$1,625.00	$2,175.00

Kid body
16"	$700.00	$1,000.00
20"	$1,125.00	$1,500.00

Mold 550, domed, glass eyes, closed mouth
14"	$1,400.00*

Too few in database for reliable range.

Mold 560, character, domed, painted eyes, open/closed mouth or **560A,** wigged, glass eyes, open mouth
14"	$600.00	$800.00

Mold 570, domed, closed mouth
12"	$1,400.00	$1,850.00

Mold 590, sleep eyes, open/closed mouth
9"	$375.00	$500.00
16"	$1,050.00*	

Mold 600 (dome), #640, character, painted eyes, closed mouth
10"	$625.00	$850.00
17"	$1,350.00	$1,800.00

Mold 700, closed mouth
Painted eyes
12½"	$1,500.00	$1,870.00

Glass eyes
14"	$4,200.00*

Too few in database for reliable range.

Mold 701, 711, socket or shoulder head, sleep eyes, closed mouth
16"	$1,835.00	$2,450.00

Too few in database to give reliable range.

Mold 800, socket head, 840 shoulder head
18"	$1,800.00	$2,400.00

Too few in database for reliable range.

24" bisque Armand Marseille mold #400 character, sleep eyes, closed mouth, composition body, legs jointed above knees, circa 1926, $4,000.00. Courtesy Ann Van Arnum.

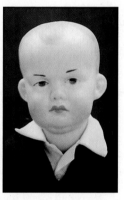

12" solid-dome Armand Marseille mold 570 socket head, with painted features, pouty character, composition jointed body, nicely dressed in brown suit, circa 1910, $1,400.00. Courtesy Debbie Crume.

Metal Heads

◄ 18" metal Minerva shoulder plate marked with letters MINERVA and a helmet symbol, with glass sleep eyes, open mouth and teeth, wigged, cloth body, circa 1920s – 1930s, $215.00. Courtesy Martha Cramer.

▶

18" American metal head Giebeler Falk, marked G in star, tin sleep eyes, open/closed mouth, four painted teeth, wig, jointed wood/composition body, metal hands, flat wooden feet, circa 1918 – 1921, $205.00. Courtesy McMasters Doll Auctions.

Ca. 1850 – 1930+. Often called Minerva, because of a style of metal shoulder head widely distributed in the United States. Dolls with metal heads were made by various manufactures, including Buschow & Beck, Alfred Heller, who made Diana metal heads, and Karl Standfuss who made Juno metal heads. In the United States, Art Metal Works made metal head dolls. Various metals used were aluminum, brass, and others, and they might be marked with just a size and country of origin or unmarked.

Metal shoulder head, cloth or kid body, molded painted hair, glass or painted eyes

16"	$160.00	$215.00
18"	$215.00	$290.00
21"	$250.00	$335.00

Painted eyes

14"	$100.00	$140.00
20"	$185.00	$250.00

Child, all metal or with composition body, metal limbs

15"	$335.00	$445.00
20"	$475.00	$625.00

Swiss all metal jointed dolls, ca. 1921 – 1940, metal ball joints

7"	$100.00	$145.00
10"	$140.00	$190.00

Multi-Face, Multi-Head Dolls

1866 – 1930+. Various firms made dolls with two or more faces, or more than one head

BISQUE

French

Bru, Surprise poupee, awake/asleep faces
12" $9,500.00
Too few in database for reliable range.

Jumeau, crying, laughing faces, cap hides knob
18" $15,950.00*
Too few in database for reliable range.

* at auction

German

Bergner, Carl, bisque socket head, three faces, sleeping, laughing, crying, molded tears, glass eyes, on composition jointed body may have molded bonnet or hood, marked *"C.B."* or *"Designed by Carl Bergner"*

12"	$900.00	$1,200.00
15"	$1050.00	$1,400.00

Kestner, J. D., ca. 1900+, Wunderkind, bisque doll with set of several different mold number heads that could be attached to body. Set of one doll and body with additional three heads and wardrobe

With heads 174, 178, 184 & 185
11" $10,000.00*
With heads, 171, 179, 182 & 183
14½" $12,650.00*

Kley & Hahn, solid-dome bisque socket head, painted hair, smiling baby and frowning baby, closed mouth, tongue, glass eyes, baby body
13" $1,100.00*

Simon & Halbig, smiling, sleeping, crying, turn ring at top of head to change faces, glass/painted eyes, closed mouth
14½" $935.00*

14" composition Three in One Doll Corp. Trudy, with sleepy, weepy and smiley faces, head turns by knob at top of head, re-dressed, good condition, ca. 1946, $100.00. Courtesy Christine McWilliams.

Cloth

Topsy-Turvy: one black, one white head. See Cloth section.

Composition

Berwick Doll Co., Famlee Dolls, ca. 1926+, composition head and limbs, cloth body with crier, neck with screw joint, allowing different heads to be screwed into the body, painted features, mohair wigs and/or painted molded hair. Came in sets of two to 12 heads, with different costumes for each head.

Seven-head set including baby, girl in fancy dress, girl in sports dress, Indian, and clown
16" $600.00 $800.00+

Effanbee, Johnny Tu Face
16" $275.00
Too few in database for reliable range.

Ideal, 1923, Soozie Smiles, composition, sleep or painted eyes on happy face, two faces, smiling, crying, cloth body, composition hands, cloth legs, original romper and hat
15½" $300.00 $400.00

Three in One Doll Corp., 1946+, Trudy, composition head with turning knob on top, cloth body and limbs, three faces, "Sleepy, Weepy, Smiley," dressed in felt or fleece snowsuit, or sheer dresses, more for exceptional doll
15½" $85.00 $300.00

Papier Mache

Smiling/crying faces, glass eyes, cloth body, composition lower limbs
19" $550.00 $700.00

Multi-Face, Multi-Head Dolls (cont.)

WAX

Smiling/crying faces, glass eyes, carton body, crier

15"	$400.00	$600.00

Munich Art Dolls

1908 – 1920s. Marion Kaulitz hand painted heads designed by Marc-Schnur, Vogelsanger, and Wackerle, dressed in German or French regional costumes. Usually composition heads and bodies distributed by Cuno & Otto Dressell and Arnoldt Doll Co.

Composition, painted features, wig, composition body, unmarked

19"	$2,100.00*

Ohlhaver, Gebruder

<table>
<tr><td>

Mark:

.Revalo.
Germany

</td><td>

1913 – 1930, Sonneberg, Germany. Had Revalo (Ohlhaver spelled backwards omitting the two H's) line; made bisque socket and shoulder head and composition dolls. Ernst Heubach supplied some heads to Ohlhaver.

Baby or Toddler, character face, bisque socket head, glass eyes, open mouth, teeth, wig, composition and wood ball-jointed body (bent-leg for baby)

</td></tr>
</table>

Baby

16"	$425.00	$575.00
20"	$525.00	$700.00

Toddler

14"	$525.00	$700.00

Child

Bisque socket head, open mouth, sleep eyes, composition body

16"	$425.00	$575.00

Coquette-type

Bisque solid dome with molded painted hair, ribbon, eyes, composition and wood body

13"	$500.00	$675.00

Oriental Dolls

ALL-BISQUE
Kestner

6"	$1,050.00	$1,400.00
8"	$1,200.00	$1,600.00

Schmidt, Bruno, marked "BSW"

6"	$600.00	$800.00

Simon & Halbig

6"	$965.00	$1,275.00
9"	$1,400.00	$1,850.00

Unmarked or unknown maker, presumed German or French

6"	$400.00	$550.00

EUROPEAN BISQUE

Bisque head, jointed body

Amusco, mold 1006

17"	$900.00	$1,200.00

* at auction

Belton-type, mold 193, 206

10"	$1,550.00	$2,075.00
14"	$2,000.00	$2,700.00
17"	$2,800.00	$3,775.00

Bru, pressed bisque swivel head, glass eyes, closed mouth

20"	$26,000.00*

Too few in database for reliable range.

Kestner, J. D. 1899 – 1930+, mold 243, bisque socket head, open mouth, wig, bent-leg baby body, add more for original clothing

14"	$3,400.00	$4,550.00
16"	$6,600.00*	

Solid dome, painted hair

15"	$3,750.00	$5,000.00

13" bisque Kestner 243 Oriental baby, in original romper, tunic, head piece, circa 1914+, $4,700.00. Courtesy McMasters Doll Auctions.

Armand Marseille, ca. 1925

   Mold 353, solid-dome bisque socket head, glass eyes, closed mouth

   Baby body

7½"	$900.00	$1,200.00
14"	$925.00	$1,225.00
16"	$1,050.00	$1,400.00

   Toddler

16"	$975.00	$1,300.00

   Painted bisque

7"	$350.00*

Schmidt, Bruno, marked "BSW"

   Mold 500, glass eyes, open mouth

14"	$1,600.00	$2,100.00
18"	$2,200.00*	

Schoenau & Hoffmeister

   Mold 4900, bisque socket head, glass eyes, open mouth, tinted composition wood jointed body

10"	$350.00	$475.00

Simon & Halbig

   Mold 1099, bisque socket head, glass eyes, open mouth, pierced ears

16"	$9,000.00*

18½" bisque Bruno Schmidt Oriental girl mold 500, brown sleep eyes, open mouth with four teeth, pierced ears, original mohair wig, wood and composition jointed body, circa 1905, $2,200.00. Courtesy McMasters Doll Auctions.

   Mold 1129, 1159, 1199, 1329, bisque socket head, glass eyes, open mouth, pierced ears, composition wood jointed body

13"	$1,350.00	$1,800.00
30"	$1,875.00	$2,500.00

Unknown maker, socket head, jointed body, closed mouth

14"	$975.00	$1,300.00
20"	$2,200.00	$2,800.00

JAPANESE BISQUE

   Various makers including Morimura, Yamato, marked *"FY,"* and others marked *"Nippon"* or *"J.W."* made dolls when doll production was halted in Europe during World War I.

14" bisque Simon & Halbig mold 1329 Oriental socket head, glass eyes, black mohair wig, pierced ears, nicely dressed, circa 1910, $2,250.00. Courtesy Sharon Kolibaba.

10½" bisque S.F.B.J. Oriental swivel head on shoulder plate, marked Paris with painted eyes, closed mouth, cloth body, composition forearms, nicely dressed, circa 1920s, $450.00. Courtesy Evelyn Sears.

Baby, marked *"Japan"* or *"Nippon"* or by other maker

11"	$135.00	$180.00
13"	$180.00	$245.00
15"	$225.00	$300.00
19"	$400.00	$525.00
24"	$585.00	$785.00

Child, marked *"Nippon"* or *"Japan"* or other maker

14"	$195.00	$250.00
17"	$250.00	$330.00
22"	$415.00	$550.00

COMPOSITION

Effanbee

Butin-nose, in basket with wardrobe, painted Oriental features including black bobbed hair, bangs, side-glancing eyes, excellent color and condition

8"	$125.00	$500.00

Patsy, painted Oriental features, including black bangs, straight across the forehead, brown side-glancing eyes, dressed in silk Chinese pajamas and matching shoes, excellent condition

14"	$200.00	$750.00+

Horsman

Baby Butterfly, ca. 1911 – 1913, composition head, hands, cloth body, painted hair, features

13"	$175.00	$650.00

Quan-Quan Co., California

Ming Ming Baby, all-composition jointed baby, painted features, original costume, yarn que, painted shoes

11"	$50.00	$200.00

TRADITIONAL CHINESE

Man or woman, composition type head, cloth-wound bodies, may have carved arms and feet, in traditional costume

11"	$115.00	$350.00
14"	$175.00	$525.00

TRADITIONAL JAPANESE

Papier-mache swivel head, shoulder plate, cloth midsection, upper arms, and legs. Limbs and torso are papier-mache, glass eyes, pierced nostrils. Early dolls have jointed wrists and ankles. Original dress. Many of the later dolls imported by Kimport.

Traditional, early fine quality, ca. 1890s,

16"	$200.00	$400.00
19"	$275.00	$545.00
25"	$550.00	$1,100.00

16" composition Oriental child with cloth body, composition hands, original outfit, $195.00. Courtesy June Algeier.

11" all-cloth Chinese child with embroidered features, made by Lutheran World Service Crafts, tagged, five extra pieces of delightfully made wardrobe complete with scrolls and accessories, in wicker basket, circa 1970s, $175.00. Courtesy Joanne Morgan.

Traditional, early boy, painted hair

15"	$280.00	$560.00
20"	$425.00	$950.00
24"	$650.00	$1,300.00

Traditional boy, 1930s

14"	$80.00	$155.00
19"	$150.00	$300.00

Traditional boy, 1940s

15"	$50.00	$100.00

Traditional Lady, 1920s

14"	$135.00	$270.00
16"	$165.00	$325.00

Traditional Lady, 1940s – 1950s

14"	$50.00	$95.00
16"	$70.00	$135.00

Emperor or Empress, seated, ca. 1890s

8"	$285.00	$575.00

Ca. 1920s

6"	$90.00	$180.00
8"	$115.00	$225.00

Warrior, 1880 – 1890s

16"	$500.00	$650.00

Too few in database for reliable range.

On horse

15"	$1,100.00+

Too few in database for reliable range.

Warrior, 1920s

15"	$400.00

Too few in database for reliable range.

On horse

13"	$850.00+

Japanese baby, ca. 1920s, bisque head, sleep eyes, closed mouth, papier-mache body

8"	$50.00	$70.00
14"	$65.00	$90.00

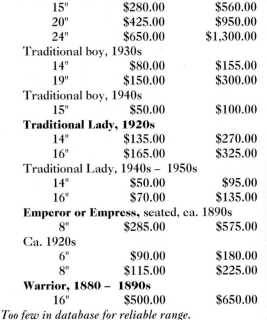

8½" composition Japanese Warrior by unknown maker, glass eyes, original costume, rides 10" papier-mache horse with glass eyes, post World War II, $700.00. Courtesy Marie Emmerson.

Glass eyes

8"	$95.00	$125.00
14"	$200.00	$265.00

Japanese baby, crushed oyster-shell head, painted flesh color, papier-mache body, glass eyes and original clothes

8"	$25.00	$50.00
14"	$45.00	$95.00
18"	$95.00	$185.00

WOOD

Door of Hope: See that section.
Schoenhut: See that section.

Papier-mache

Pre-1600 on. Varying types of composition made from paper or paper pulp could be mass produced in molds for heads after 1810. It reached heights of popularity by mid-1850s and was also used for bodies. Papier-mache shoulder head, glass or painted eyes, molded and painted hair, sometimes in fancy hairdos. Usually no marks.

First price indicates doll in good condition with flaws, less if poorly repainted; second price is for doll in excellent condition, nicely dressed. More for exceptional examples.

14" diameter French papier-mache shoulder head with glass eyes, open mouth with teeth, pierced ears, black painted hair with brush-marks, red dots inner eyes, and nostrils, $2,500.00. Courtesy Sharon Kolibaba.

EARLY TYPE, CA. 1840s – 1860s

Cloth body, wooden limbs, with topknots, buns, puff curls or braids, dressed in original clothing or excellent copy, may have some wear. More for painted pate.

Painted eyes

9"	$225.00	$450.00
12"	$340.00	$675.00
18"	$525.00	$1,050.00
21"	$575.00	$1,150.00
26"	$1,200.00	$2,400.00
32"	$985.00	$1,975.00

Glass eyes

24"	$1,100.00	$2,200.00
28"	$1,500.00	$3,025.00

Long curls

12"	$325.00	$650.00
14"	$375.00	$750.00
16"	$775.00	$1,550.00

Covered Wagon or Flat Top hair style

10"	$175.00	$325.00
14"	$250.00	$500.00
16"	$300.00	$600.00

MILLINER'S MODELS TYPE, CA. 1820 – 1860s

Many collectors may use this term "Milliner's models" to describe dolls with a shapely waist, kid body, and wooden limbs

Apollo top knot (beehive), side curls

10"	$400.00	$800.00
14"	$2,200.00*	
16"	$1,050.00	$2,125.00

Braided bun, side curls

10"	$500.00	$1,000.00
15"	$800.00	$1,600.00

Center part, molded bun

9"	$325.00	$650.00
13"	$500.00	$1,000.00

Center part, sausage curls

14"	$275.00	$575.00
21"	$450.00	$950.00

Coiled braids over ears, braided bun

15"	$795.00	$1,590.00
21"	$1,150.00	$2,300.00

Molded bonnet, kid body, wood limbs, bonnet painted to tie under chin, very rare

15"	$1,700.00

Too few in database for reliable range.

Molded comb, side curls, braided coronet

16"	$1,650.00	$3,300.00

Too few in database for reliable range.

5½" papier-mache shoulder head, molded black hair, painted features, original kid body, wooden arms and legs, original clothes, circa 1845 – 1860s, $275.00. Courtesy Elizabeth Surber.

FRENCH-TYPE, CA. 1835 – 1850

Painted black hair, brush marks, solid-dome, some have nailed on wigs, open mouth, bamboo teeth, kid or leather body, appropriately dressed

Glass eyes

16"	$900.00	$1,750.00
21"	$1,150.00	$2,300.00
24"	$1,300.00	$2,600.00
33"	$1,450.00	$2,900.00

Painted eyes

12"	$375.00	$750.00
16"	$500.00	$1,000.00

Wooden jointed body

8"	$385.00	$765.00

GERMAN TYPE

1844 – 1892

"M & S Superior," Muller & Strasburger, Sonneberg, Germany, shoulder head, with blonde or molded hair, painted blue or brown eyes, cloth body, with kid or leather arms and boots. Mold numbers on stickers reported are

14½" papier-mache milliner's model with painted blue eyes, closed mouth, painted hair, unjointed kid body with wooden lower arms and legs with painted shoes, 1840s – 1860s, $475.00. Courtesy McMasters Doll Auctions.

Mold 1020, 2020, 2015, and 4515

17"	$225.00	$425.00
22"	$365.00	$725.00
27"	$425.00	$850.00

* at auction

17" German papier-mache shoulder head with glass eyes, mohair wig, cloth body, leather lower arms, circa 1860s – 1880s, $750.00. Courtesy McMasters Doll Auctions.

19½" papier-mache M & S Superior shoulder head, cloth body, kid arms possible, original dress, light crazing, painted rubs, normal wear, circa 1880+ $250.00. Courtesy McMasters Doll Auctions.

Glass eyes

12"	$400.00	$600.00
16"	$600.00	$800.00

Wigged

13"	$675.00	$900.00

1879 – 1900s

Molded blonde or black hair styles, closed mouth

Painted eyes

15"	$125.00	$250.00
19"	$200.00	$400.00
22"	$225.00	$450.00
28"	$350.00	$700.00

Glass eyes

15"	$275.00	$550.00
18"	$400.00	$800.00

Turned shoulder head, solid dome, glass eyes, closed mouth, cloth body, composition forearms

16"	$350.00	$700.00
22"	$465.00	$925.00

Character heads, molded like the bisque ones, glass eyes, closed mouth, on fully-jointed body

15"	$515.00	$1,025.00
21"	$815.00	$1,625.00

PAPIER-MACHE, 1920+

Head has brighter coloring, wigged, child often in ethnic costume, stuffed cloth body and limbs, or papier-mache arms

French

9"	$65.00	$125.00
13"	$100.00	$200.00
15"	$150.00	$300.00

German

10"	$40.00	$80.00
15"	$90.00	$165.00

Unknown maker

8"	$30.00	$60.00
12"	$60.00	$115.00
16"	$90.00	$175.00

Clowns, papier-mache head, with painted clown features, open or closed mouth, molded hair or wigged, cloth body, composition or papier-mache arms, or five-piece jointed body

8"	$120.00	$235.00
14"	$245.00	$485.00
20"	$395.00	$785.00
26"	$460.00	$925.00

Eden Clown, socket head, open mouth, blue glass eyes, blond mohair wig, five-piece jointed body, all original with labeled box

16"	$4,000.00*

Ca. 1850 – 1900+, Germany. Refers to very white color of untinted bisque dolls, often with molded blonde hair, some with fancy hair arrangements and ornaments or bonnets; can have glass or painted eyes, pierced ears, may have molded jewelry or clothing. Occasionally solid dome with wig. Cloth body, nicely dressed in good condition.

First price indicates doll in good condition, but with flaws; second price indicates doll in excellent condition, appropriately dressed. Exceptional examples may be much higher.

16" Parian-type untinted bisque, simple hairdo, blonde, center part, glass eyes, untinted bisque arms and black molded boots, old dress, circa 1860 – 1870s, $1,000.00. Courtesy Elizabeth Surber.

LADY

Common hair style

Undecorated, simple molded hair

10"	$125.00	$165.00
15"	$225.00	$300.00
21"	$325.00	$425.00
25"	$400.00	$525.00

Wigged, solid dome, circa 1850s

16"	$625.00	$850.00
18"	$700.00	$950.00
21"	$1,025.00	$1,350.00

Fancy hair style

With molded combs, ribbons, flowers, bands, or snoods, cloth body, untinted bisque limbs, more for very elaborate hairstyle

Painted eyes, pierced ears

16"	$685.00	$900.00
22"	$1,300.00	$1,700.00

Painted eyes, ears not pierced

13"	$550.00	$700.00

Glass eyes, pierced ears

15"	$1,200.00	$1,600.00
20"	$2,100.00	$2,700.00

Swivel neck, glass eyes

15"	$1,950.00	$2,625.00

Mark: Seldom any mark; may have number inside shoulder plate.

Countess Dagmar, no mark, head band, cluster curls on forehead

25"	$700.00	$900.00

Molded bodice

Irish Queen, Limbach, clover mark, #8552

14"	$350.00	$575.00

Empress Eugenie, unmarked, painted eyes

25"	$500.00	$750.00

Molded hat, blonde or black painted hair

Painted eyes

16"	$1,700.00	$2,300.00
19"	$2,150.00	$2,900.00

Glass eyes

14"	$1,850.00	$2,400.00
17"	$2,250.00	$3,000.00

Front and back view of 21½" Dornheim, Koch & Fischer Parian type untinted bisque, elaborate blonde hairdo, floral decorations, painted eyes, molded necklace, nicely dressed, circa 1870s, $2,500.00. Courtesy Elizabeth Surber.

Molded headband or comb, Alice in Wonderland

13"	$325.00	$450.00
16"	$475.00	$625.00
19"	$550.00	$750.00

Necklace, jewels, or standing ruffles

17"	$9,700.00+

Too few in database for reliable range.

MEN OR BOYS

Center or side-part hair style, cloth body, decorated shirt and tie
Painted eyes

13"	$575.00	$775.00
17"	$750.00	$1,000.00

Glass eyes

16"	$2,100.00	$2,825.00

Piano Babies

13" unmarked German bisque Piano Baby unjointed body, $435.00. Courtesy McMasters Doll Auctions.

Ca. 1880 – 1930+, Germany. These all-bisque figurines were made by Gebruder Heubach, Kestner, Dressel, Limbach, and others. May have molded on clothes; came in a variety of poses. Some were reproduced during the 1960s and 1970s and the skin tones are paler than the others.

First price indicates figurine in good condition with flaws; second price indicates figurine in excellent condition.

Excellent quality or marked Heubach, fine details

4"	$235.00	$300.00
6"	$350.00	$475.00
7½"	$600.00* with sunburst mark	
9"	$525.00	$700.00
16"	$850.00	$1,125.00

Black

5"	$300.00	$425.00
9"	$375.00	$500.00
14"	$675.00	$900.00

With animal, pot, flowers, chair, or other items

5"	$195.00	$260.00
8"	$315.00	$425.00
10"	$400.00	$525.00
15"	$750.00	$1,000.00

Medium quality, unmarked, may not have painted finish on back

4"	$75.00	$100.00
8"	$150.00	$200.00
12"	$225.00	$300.00

Pincushion or Half Dolls

Ca. 1900 – 1930s, Germany, Japan. Half dolls can be made of bisque, china, composition, or papier-mache, and were used not only for pincushions but on top of jewelry or cosmetic boxes, brushes, and lamps. The hardest to find have arms molded away from the body as they were easier to break with the limbs in this position and thus fewer survived.

First price is for doll in good condition, with flaws; second price is for doll in excellent condition; add more for extra attributes. Rare examples may bring more.

5" china half doll marked 4630, with painted features, coiled blonde braids, both arms away, one extended, one close back to body, circa 1910+, $500.00. Courtesy Jan Mealer.

ARMS AWAY

China or bisque figure, bald head with wig

4"	$105.00	$140.00
6"	$155.00	$210.00

Goebel mark, dome head, wig

5"	$195.00*

Holding items, such as letter, flower

4"	$135.00	$185.00
6"	$200.00	$275.00

Marked by maker or mold number

4"	$150.00	$200.00
6"	$225.00	$300.00
8"	$300.00	$400.00
12"	$675.00	$900.00

ARMS IN

Close to figure, bald head with wig

4"	$55.00	$80.00
6"	$80.00	$115.00

Hands attached

3"	$20.00	$35.00
5"	$30.00	$45.00
7"	$45.00	$70.00

3½" German china half doll with molded Art Deco type hat, painted features, arms in, hands under chin, circa 1920s, $200.00. Courtesy Patricia Wright.

4" bisque German half doll marked 3803, with painted features, blonde mohair wig, jointed arms, circa 1915 – 1920, $500.00. Courtesy Patricia Wright.

Decorated bodice, necklace, fancy hair or holding article

3"	$85.00	$125.00
5"	$105.00	$145.00

Marked by maker or mold number

5"	$80.00	$135.00
6"	$110.00	$155.00

With legs, dressed, fancy decorations

5"	$225.00	$300.00
7"	$300.00	$400.00

Papier-mache or composition

4"	$25.00	$35.00
6"	$60.00	$80.00

JOINTED SHOULDERS

China or bisque, molded hair

5"	$110.00	$145.00
7"	$150.00	$200.00

Solid dome, mohair wig

4"	$165.00	$220.00
5¾"	$685.00*	
6"	$330.00	$400.00

MAN OR CHILD

4"	$90.00	$120.00
6"	$120.00	$160.00

MARKED GERMANY

4"	$150.00	$200.00
6"	$375.00	$500.00

MARKED JAPAN

3"	$10.00	$15.00
6"	$38.00	$50.00

OTHER ITEMS

Brush, with porcelain figurine for handle, molded hair, may be holding something

9"	$55.00	$75.00

Dresser box, unmarked, with figurine on lid

7"	$265.00	$350.00
9"	$345.00	$450.00

Dresser box, marked with mold number, country, or manufacturer

5"	$210.00	$285.00
6"	$275.00	$350.00

Perfume bottle, stopper is half doll, skirt is bottle

6½"	$165.00*

Rabery & Delphieu

1856 – 1930 and later, Paris. Became S.F.B.J. in 1899. Some heads pressed (pre-1890) and some poured, purchased heads from Francois Gaultier.

Mark:

R.3. D

* at auction

First price indicates doll in good condition, but with some flaws; second price indicates doll in excellent condition, appropriately dressed. Exceptional dolls may be more.

CHILD

Closed mouth, bisque socket head, paperweight eyes, pierced ears, mohair wig, cork pate, French composition and wood jointed body

11"	$3,000.00	$4,500.00
17"	$3,800.00*	
23"	$4,200.00	$5,600.00

Open mouth, row of upper teeth

18"	$975.00	$1,300.00
24"	$1,200.00	$1,600.00
26"	$1,600.00	$2,200.00

16½" bisque Rabery & Delphieu bebe with glass eyes, closed mouth, heavy eyebrows, human hair wig, composition and wood ball-jointed body, circa 1880s+, $3,300.00. Courtesy Bette Yadon.

Recknagel

1886 – 1930+, Thuringia, Germany. Made bisque heads of varying quality, incised or raised mark, wigged or molded hair, glass or painted eyes, open or closed mouth, flange neck or socket head.

Mark:

BABY

Bent-limb baby body, painted intaglio eyes, open/closed mouth with teeth

6½"	$225.00	$300.00
8"	$250.00	$375.00

Bonnet head baby, painted eyes, open/closed mouth, teeth

Mold 22, 28, 44, molded white boy's cap, bent-leg baby body

8"	$425.00*	
9"	$400.00	$550.00
11"	$600.00	$800.00

Oriental baby, solid-dome bisque socket head

Sleep eyes, closed mouth five-piece yellow tinted body

11"	$2,300.00*

Newborn, flange neck, sleep eyes, closed mouth, mold 137, cloth body, boxed

13"	$545.00*

8½" bisque Recknagel child marked "R," glass eyes, closed mouth, composition body with molded on shoes and socks, circa 1890s – 1910, $175.00. Courtesy Jill Sanders.

CHILD

Dolly face, 1890s – 1914

Mold 1907, 1909, 1914, open mouth, glass eyes

7"	$85.00	$110.00
12"	$150.00	$200.00
15"	$250.00	$325.00
21"	$400.00	$525.00

Character face, ca. 1910+, may have crossed hammer mark

Painted eyes, open/closed mouth, some with molded hat or ribbon

9"	$550.00	$750.00
12"	$675.00	$900.00

Boy, solid-dome bisque socket head, painted brush-stroked hair, intaglio eyes, closed mouth, composition and wood fully jointed body

18"	$1,700.00*

Rohmer

1857 – 1880, Paris. Mme. Rohmer held patents for doll bodies, made dolls of various materials.

First price is for doll in good condition, but with flaws; second price is for doll in excellent condition, appropriately dressed; may be much more for exceptional dolls.

FASHION-TYPE

Bisque or china glazed shoulder or swivel head on shoulder plate, closed mouth, kid body with green oval stamp, bisque or wood lower arms

Mark:

Glass eyes

14"	$3,400.00*	
17"	$7,200.00	$9,500.00

Painted eyes

14"	$4,200.00	$5,600.00
18"	$5,400.00* pink tint	

Untinted bisque swivel head, lined shoulder plate, cobalt glass eyes, kid over wood arms, kid gusseted body, original costume

16"	$7,400.00*

China head, painted eyes

17"	$2,800.00	$3,700.00

Schmidt, Bruno

1900 – 1930+, Waltershausen, Germany. Made bisque, composition, and wooden head dolls, after 1913 also celluloid. Acquired Bahr & Proschild in 1918. Often used a heart-shaped tag.

BABY

Marked *"BSW"* in heart, may have no mold number, bisque socket head, glass eyes, open mouth, wig, composition bent-leg baby body, add more for flirty eyes and toddler body.

Mold 2095, 2097, or unmarked

11"	$375.00	$500.00
15"	$400.00	$550.00
19"	$625.00	$850.00

---

* at auction

Mold 2097, toddler

15"	$500.00	$675.00
21"	$750.00	$1,000.00

CHILD

Bisque socket head, jointed body, sleep eyes, open mouth, add $50.00 more for flirty eyes.

14"	$335.00	$450.00
18"	$475.00	$625.00
23"	$625.00	$850.00

CHARACTER

Child, Oriental, mold 500, yellow tint bisque socket head, glass eyes, open mouth, teeth, pierced ears, wig, yellow tint composition jointed body

11"	$1,100.00	$1,450.00
18"	$1,450.00	$1,900.00

Mold 529, 539, 2023, solid dome, closed mouth, painted eyes

24"	$2,250.00	$3,000.00

Mold 2025, solid dome or with wig, painted eyes, closed mouth

15"	$2,625.00	$3,500.00
21"	$3,500.00	$4,750.00

Mold 537, 2033, sleep eyes, closed mouth

13½"	$14,000.00*

Too few in database for reliable range.

Mold 2048, 2094, 2096, solid dome, molded painted hair or wig, sleep eyes, open or closed mouth, composition jointed body

Open mouth

12"	$650.00	$900.00
15"	$950.00	$1,250.00
30"	$1,400.00	$2,000.00

Closed mouth

16"	$1,560.00	$2,050.00

Mold 2072, sleep eyes, open or closed mouth

Closed mouth

16"	$2,550.00*

Too few in database for reliable range.

Mark:

5

13½" bisque Bruno Schmidt Wendy, mold 2033, bisque socket head, closed mouth, human hair wig, made by Bahr & Proschild for Bruno Schmidt, circa 1912, $14,000.00. Courtesy, McMasters Doll Auctions.

Schmidt, Franz

1890 – 1930+, Georgenthal, Germany. Made, produced, and exported dolls with bisque, composition, wood, and celluloid heads. Used some heads made by Simon Halbig.

Heads marked "S & C," mold 269, 293, 927, 1180, 1310

Heads marked "F.S. & C," mold 1250, 1253, 1259, 1262, 1263, 1266, 1267, 1270, 1271, 1272, 1274, 1293, 1295, 1296, 1297, 1298, 1310

Walkers: mold 1071, 1310

Schmidt, Franz (cont.)

BABY

Bisque head, solid dome or cut out for wig, bent-leg body, sleep or set eyes, open mouth, some pierced nostrils. Add more for flirty eyes.

Mark box:
> *Marks:*
>
> **1310**
> **F.S.& C**
> or
> S & C
> ANVIL MARK

Mold 1271, 1272, 1295, 1296, 1297, 1310

10"	$300.00	$375.00
13"	$350.00	$475.00
18"	$475.00	$625.00
21"	$850.00	$1,100.00

Toddler

12"	$625.00	$825.00
18"	$900.00	$1,200.00
23"	$1,100.00	$1,475.00
25"	$1,325.00	$1,800.00

CHARACTER FACE

Mold 1267, dome, painted eyes, closed mouth

14"	$2,050.00	$2,750.00
19"	$2,800.00	$3,700.00

Mold 1270, solid dome, painted eyes, open/closed mouth

9"	$475.00	$650.00
13"	$1,350.00	$1,800.00

With two faces

16"	$1,075.00	$1,450.00

CHILD

Dolly face, open mouth, glass eyes

14"	$335.00	$450.00
19"	$500.00	$650.00
23"	$625.00	$850.00
27"	$800.00	$1,050.00

Marked "S &C," glass eyes, open mouth

6½"	$900.00*
32"	$2,420.00*

Mold 1262, 1263, painted eyes, closed mouth

14"	$4,350.00	$5,800.00

Too few in database for reliable range.

Mold 1272, solid dome or wig, sleep eyes, pierced nostrils, open mouth

9½"	$700.00	$950.00

Too few in database for a reliable range.

Mold 1071, 1310, walker, papier-mache, composition body, walker mechanism of rollers on feet, open mouth, sleep eyes, working mechanism

16"	$540.00	$725.00
22"	$725.00	$950.00

Too few in database for reliable range.

Schmitt & Fils

1854 – 1891, Paris. Made bisque and wax-over-bisque, or wax-over-composition dolls. Heads were pressed. Used neck socket like on later composition Patsy dolls.

---

* at auction

First price is for doll in good condition, but with flaws; second price is for doll in excellent condition, appropriately dressed; more for exceptional doll with wardrobe or other attributes.

Mark:

Shield on head, "SCH" in shield on bottom of flat cut derriere.

CHILD

Pressed bisque head, closed mouth, glass eyes, pierced ears, mohair or human hair wig, French composition and wood eight ball-jointed body with straight wrists.

23" bisque Schmitt & Fils socket head, marked "SCH" crossed hammers in a shield, open/closed mouth, composition and wood ball-jointed body, circa 1870s – 1890, $18,000.00+. Courtesy McMasters Doll Auctions.

Early round face

12"	$7,875.00	$10,500.00
13"	$12,000.00* trousseau, box	
19"	$10,175.00	$13,566.00
24"	$12,850.00	$17,125.00

Long face modeling

19"	$8,000.00	$11,970.00
24"	$11,400.00	$15,250.00

Wax over papier-mache, swivel head, cup and saucer type neck, glass eyes, closed mouth, eight ball-jointed body

16"	$1,125.00	$1,500.00
22"	$1,300.00	$1,700.00

Schmitt body only, eight ball joints, straight wrists, separated fingers, marked "*SCH*" in shield

15"	$1,400.00*

Schoenau & Hoffmeister

1901 – 1953, Sonneberg, and Burggrub, Bavaria. Had a porcelain factory, produced bisque heads for dolls, also supplied other manufacturers, including Bruckner, Dressel, E. Knoch, and others.

First price is for doll in good condition with flaws; second price is for doll in excellent condition, appropriately dressed. More for exceptional dolls.

BABY

Bisque solid-dome or wigged socket head, sleep eyes, teeth, composition bent-leg body, closed mouth, newborn, solid dome, painted hair, cloth body, may have celluloid hands, add more for original outfit.

Mark:

9" pair	$950.00* pair	
13"	$625.00	$825.00
15"	$700.00	$950.00
Toddler		
15"	$600.00	$800.00
21"	$1,100.00	$1,500.00

27" bisque Schoenau & Hoffmeister child, blue sleep eyes, open mouth, four teeth, replaced synthetic wig, jointed wood and composition body, circa 1906, $325.00. Courtesy McMasters Doll Auctions.

Mold 169, open mouth, composition bent-leg body, wigged

23"	$385.00	$500.00
25"	$425.00	$575.00

Mold 170, open mouth, composition five-piece toddler body

19"	$350.00	$475.00

Hanna, sleep eyes, open/closed mouth, bent-leg baby body

13"	$345.00	$460.00
18"	$600.00	$800.00
22"	$1,000.00	$1,350.00

Princess Elizabeth, socket head, sleep eyes Smiling open mouth, chubby leg toddler body

16"	$1,450.00	$1,950.00
22"	$1,925.00	$2,550.00

CHILD

Dolly face, bisque socket head, open mouth with teeth, sleep eyes, composition ball-jointed body

Mold 1906, 1909, 4000, 4600, 4700, 5500, 5700, 5800

14"	$225.00	$300.00
18"	$325.00	$425.00
26"	$600.00	$800.00
34"	$1,100.00	$1,500.00

Mold 914, ca. 1925, character

30"	$625.00*

Mold 4900, Oriental doll face

10"	$350.00	$475.00

Schoenhut, A., & Co.

1872 – 1930+, Philadelphia, PA. Made all-wood dolls, using spring joints, had holes in bottoms of feet to fit into stands. Later made elastic strung with cloth bodies. Carved or molded painted hair or wigged, intaglio or sleep eyes, open or closed mouth. Later made composition dolls.

Mark:

First price is for doll in good condition, but with some flaws, perhaps touch-up; second price is for doll in excellent condition, appropriately dressed; more for exceptional doll.

INFANT

Graziano Infants, circa May 1911 – 1912

Schnickel – Fritz, carved hair, open/closed grinning mouth, four teeth, large ears, toddler

15"	$2,250.00	$3,000.00

Tootsie Wootsie, carved hair, open/closed mouth, two upper teeth, large ears on child body

15"	$2,600.00	$3,400.00

Too few in database for reliable range.

* at auction

Model 107, 107W (walker)

Baby, nature (bent) limb, 1913 – 1926
13" $375.00 $550.00
Toddler, 1917 – 1926
11" $500.00 $650.00
Toddler, 1913 – 1926
14" $575.00 $750.00
Toddler, elastic strung, 1924 – 1926
14" $575.00 $750.00
Toddler, cloth body with crier
14" $475.00 $600.00

Model 108, 108W (walker)

Baby, nature (bent) limb, 1913 – 1926
15" $425.00 $575.00
Toddler, 1917 – 1926
17" $650.00 $850.00
Toddler, elastic strung, 1924 – 1926
17" $475.00 $725.00
Toddler, cloth body, crier, 1924 – 1928
17" $425.00 $550.00

Model 109 W, 1921 – 1923

Baby, nature (bent) limb, sleep eye, open mouth
13" $350.00 $500.00
Toddler, sleep eye
14" $575.00 $800.00

Too few in database for reliable range.

Model 110 W, 1921 – 1923

Baby, nature (bent) limb, sleep eye, open mouth
15" $450.00 $600.00
Toddler
17" $675.00 $900.00

Too few in database for reliable range.

Bye-Lo Baby, "Grace S. Putnam" stamp, cloth body, closed mouth, sleep eyes,
13" $2,400.00*

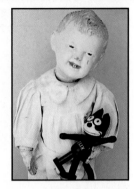

15" wood Schoenhut Schnickel-Fritz 15/76, termed an infant in the 1911 company catalog, has a grinning face with narrow eyes, open/closed mouth with teeth, molded painted hair, original romper, circa 1911 – 1912, $3,000.00. Courtesy Sherryl Shirran.

CHILD

Graziano Period, 1911 – 1912, dolls may have heavily carved hair or wigs, painted intaglio eyes, outlined iris. All with wooden spring-jointed bodies and are 16" tall, designated with 16 before the model number, like "16/100."

Model 100, girl, carved hair, solemn face
Model 101, girl, carved hair, grinning, squinting eyes
Model 102, girl, carved hair, bun on top
Model 103, girl, carved hair, loose ringlets
Model 200, boy, carved hair, short curls
Model 201, boy, carved hair, based on K*R 114
Model 202, boy, carved hair, forelock

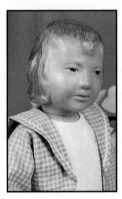

6" wooden Schoenhut 16/103, a very early carved hair doll made during the Graziano period, about the first six months of production, repainted, circa 1911, $2,100.00. Courtesy McMasters Doll Auctions.

14" wood Schoenhut toddler, 14/107, painted eyes, brown human hair wig, old dress, wooden jointed body, circa 1913 – 1926, $550.00. Courtesy Sharon Kolibaba.

14" wood Schoenhut 14/312 girl with spring-jointed body, decal mark, blue intaglio eyes, blonde mohair wig, original cotton knit union suit, pink stockings, white Schoenhut shoes, holes in sole, old dress circa 1912 – 1913, $1,500.00+. Courtesy Dee Cermak.

Model 203, boy, carved hair, grinning, some with comb marks

Carved hair dolls of this early period; add more if excellent condition, original clothes

16" $2,200.00 $3,000.00+

Too few in database for reliable range.

Model 300, girl, long curl wig, face of 102

Model 301, girl, bobbed wig with bangs, face of 300

Model 302, girl, wig, bases on K*R 101

Model 303, girl, short bob, no bangs, grinning girl, squinting eyes

Model 304, girl, wig in braids, ears stick out

Model 305, girl, snail braids, grinning girl, face of 303

Model 306, girl, wig, long curls, face of 304

Model 307, girl, short bob, no bangs, "dolly-type" smooth eye

Model 400, boy, short bob, K*R 101 face

Model 401, boy, side part bob, face of 300/301

Model 402, boy, side part bob, grin of 303

Model 403, boy, long curls, face of 304/306

Wigged dolls, with intaglio eyes, outlined iris of this period, more if original costume and paint.

16" $750.00 $1,500.00

Transition Period, 1911 – 1912, designs by Graziano and Leslie, dolls may no longer have outlined iris, some models have changed, still measure 16", now have a groove above knee for stockings.

Model 100, girl, same, no iris outline

Model 101, girl, short carved hair, bob/bow, round eyes/smile

Model 102, girl, braids carved around head

Model 103, girl, heavy carved hair in front/fine braids inb ack

Model 104, girl, fine carved hair in front/fine braids in back

Model 200, boy, carved hair, same, no iris outline

Model 201, boy, carved hair, same, iris outline, stocking groove

Model 202, boy, carved hair, same, smoother

Model 203, boy, smiling boy, round eyes, no iris outline

Model 204, boy, carved hair brushed forward, serious face

Carved hair is smoother, may no longer have outlined iris, some with stocking groove; more for excellent condition and original costume.

| 16" | 1,800.00 | $2,400.00 |

Model 300, girl, long curl wig, dimple in chin
Model 301, girl, bob wig, face of 102
Model 302, girl, wig, same like K*R 101
Model 303, girl, wig, similar to 303G, smiling, short bob, no bangs
Model 304, girl, wig, braids, based on K*R
Model 305, girl, wig, braids, face of 303
Model 306, girl, long curl wig, same face as 304
Model 307, girl, smooth eyeball
Model 400, boy, same (like K*R 101)
Model 401, boy, like K*R 114 (304)
Model 402, boy, smiling, round eyes
Model 403, boy, same as 300 with side part bob
Model 404, boy, same as 301, side part bob

Wigged boy or girl, similar to earlier models with some refinements; more for excellent condition, original costume.

| 16" | $1,000.00 | $1,500.00 |

9" wood Schoenhut Theodore Roosevelt, painted features, painted molded boots, has spring-jointed knees to kneel to shoot rifle, tan safari costume (missing hat and rifle) part of Teddy's Adventures in Africa, circa 1909, $800.00. Courtesy Evelyn Gibson.

Classic Period, 1912 – 1923

Some models discontinued, some sizes added, those marked with* were reissued in 1930

Model 101, girl, short carved hair bob, no iris outline
1912 – 1923*

| 14" | $1, 600.00 | $2,200.00 |

1911 – 1916

| 16" | $1,800.00 | $2,400.00 |

Model 102, girl, heavy carved hair in front, fine braids in back
1912 – 1923*

| 14" | $1,300.00 | $1,900.00 |

1911 – 1923*

| 16" | $1,400.00 | $2,000.00 |

1912 – 1916

| 19 – 21" | $1,500.00 | $2,100.00 |

Model 105, girl, short carved hair bob, carved ribbon around head
1912 – 1923*

| 14 – 16" | $1,100.00 | $1,900.00 |

1912 – 1916

| 19 – 21" | $1,300.00 | $2,100.00 |

Model 106, girl, carved molded bonnet on short hair, 1912 – 1916

14"	$1,500.00	$2,200.00
16"	$1,950.00	$2,600.00
19"	$2,100.00	$2,800.00

Model 203, 16" boy, same as transition
Model 204, 16" boy, same as transition*
Model 205, carved hair boy, covered ears

1912 – 1923
14" – 16"	$1,800.00	$2,400.00

1912 – 1916
19 – 21"	$2,000.00	$2,600.00

Model 206, carved hair boy, covered ears, 1912 – 1916
19"	$2,000.00	$2,600.00

Model 207, carved short curly hair boy, 1912 – 1916
14"	$1,800.00	$2,400.00

Model 300, 16" wigged girl, same as transition period, 1911 – 1923

Model 301, 16" wigged girl, same as transition, 1911 – 1924

Model 303, 16" wigged girl, same as transition 305, 1911 – 1916

Model 307, long curl wigged girl, smooth eye, 1911 – 1916
16"	$625.00	$850.00

Model 308, girl, braided wig, 1912 – 1916
14"	$575.00	$800.00

Bobbed hair, 1912 – 1924
19"	$650.00	$900.00

Bob or curls, 1917 – 1924
19 – 21"	$650.00	$900.00

Model 309, wigged girl, two teeth, long curls, bobbed hair, 1912 – 1913
16"	$650.00	$825.00

1912 – 1916
19 – 21"	$675.00	$875.00

Model 310, wigged girl, same as 105 face, long curls, 1912 – 1916
14 – 16"	$625.00	$775.00
19 – 21"	$675.00	$825.00

Model 311, wigged girl, heart shape 106 face, bobbed wig, no bangs, 1912 – 1916
14 – 16"	$650.00	$825.00

1912 – 1913
19"	$675.00	$850.00

Model 312, wigged girl, bobbed, 1912 – 1924; bobbed wig or curls, 1917 – 1924
14"	$625.00	$775.00

Model 313, wigged girl, long curls, smooth eyeball, receding chin, 1912 – 1916
14 – 16"	$650.00	$800.00
19 – 21"	$675.00	$825.00

Model 314, wigged girl, long curls, wide face, smooth eyeball, 1912 – 1916
19"	$575.00	$725.00

Model 315, wigged girl, long curls, four teeth, triangular mouth, 1912 – 1916
21"	$675.00	$825.00

Model 403, 16" wigged boy, same as transition, bobbed hair, bangs, 1911 – 1924

Model 404, 16" wigged boy, same as transition, 1911 – 1916

Model 405, boy, face of 308, bobbed wig, 1912 – 1924
14"	$450.00	$650.00
19"	$850.00*	

Model 407, wigged boy, face of 310 girl, 1912 – 1916
19 – 21"	$625.00	$825.00

MISS DOLLY

Model 316, open mouth, teeth, wigged girl, curls or bobbed wig, painted or decal eyes, all sizes, four sizes, circa 1915 – 1925
15 – 21"	$500.00	$675.00

* at auction

Model 317, sleep eyes, open mouth, teeth, wigged girl, long curls or bob, sleep eyes four sizes, 1921 – 1928

15 – 21"	$525.00	$700.00

Manikin

Model 175, man with slim body, ball-jointed waist, circa 1914 – 1918

19"	$2,400.00*

VARIATIONS

Circus performers, rare figures may be much higher

Bisque head, Bareback Lady Rider or Ringmaster

9"	$650.00*, all original

Clowns

8"	$150.00 – $300.00
32"	$4,500.00* store display

Lion Tamer

8½"	$300.00 – $450.00

Ringmaster

8"	$225.00 – $325.00

Animals*some rare animals may be much higher

	$100.00 – $500.00

Humpty Dumpty Circus Set, with tent, figures, and animals

$2,600.00*

Bandwagon

$7,000.00*

Seven Bandsmen

$14,000.00*

Cartoon Characters

Maggie and Jiggs, from cartoon strip "Bringing up Father"

7 – 9"	$525.00 each

Max and Moritz, carved figures, painted hair, carved shoes

8"	$625.00 each

Pinn Family, all wood, egg-shaped head, original costumes

Mother, and four children

$667.00*

Baby

5"	$133.00*

Rolly-Dolly figures

9 – 12"	$350.00	$850.00

Teddy Roosevelt

8"	$800.00	$1,600.00

Schuetzmeister & Quendt

1889 – 1930+, Boilstadt, Gotha, Thuringia. A porcelain factory that made and exported bisque doll heads, all-bisque dolls, and Nankeen dolls. Used initials "S & Q," mold 301 was sometimes incised "Jeannette."

BABY

Character face, bisque socket head, sleep eyes, open mouth, bent-leg body

Mold 201, 204, 300, 301

14"	$335.00	$450.00
19"	$450.00	$600.00

Mark:

201

ⓈⓆ

Germany

Mold 252, character face, black baby
15" $575.00
Too few in database for reliable range.

CHILD

Mold 101,102, dolly face

17"	$350.00	$400.00
22"	$375.00	$500.00

Mold 1376, character face
19" $550.00
Too few in database for reliable range.

S.F.B.J.

Mark:

23

S.F.B.✔
236

PARIS

4

Societe Francaise de Fabrication de Bebes & Jouets, 1899 – 1930+, Paris and Montreuil-sous-Bois. Competition with German manufacturers forced many French companies to join together including Bouchet, Fleischmann & Bloedel, Gaultier, Rabery & Delphieu, Bru, Jumeau, Pintel & Godchaux, Remignard and Wertheimer, and others. This alliance lasted until the 1950s. Fleischman owned controlling interest.

First price indicates doll in good condition, but may have flaws; second price indicates doll in excellent condition, appropriately dressed; more for exceptional dolls.

CHILD

Bisque head, glass eyes, open mouth, pierced ears, wig, composition jointed French body

26" bisque S.F.B.J. mold 236 socket head, with open/closed mouth, two painted teeth, mohair wig, glass eyes, wood and composition ball-jointed body, circa 1920s, $2,400.00. Courtesy Elizabeth Surber.

Bleuette, 1905 – 1960, a bisque head doll with various markings, made for a weekly children's periodical, *La Semaine De Suzette* (The Week of Suzette) that also had a pattern for her. Bleuette was first given as a premium with a year subscription. She usually had blue set glass eyes, open mouth, four teeth, wig, pierced ears, and a jointed composition body, 10½" tall.

Many variations of Bleuette were made over the years, including mold 60 and 301 and a later variation marked "71 Unis/France 149//301//1 1/2." After 1919, sleep eyes were added. Some later tagged dolls were 12" and 14" tall. Her clothing reflected the changing fads and fashions. This group has a larger variation in quality; lesser quality dolls will be less.

Bleuette, mold 60, 301, and 71 Unis/France 149//301

10½"	$635.00	$850.00
12"	$725.00	$975.00
14"	$850.00	$1,125.00

Mold 301

6"	$225.00	$300.00
16"	$625.00	$850.00
24"	$850.00	$1,150.00

Mold 301, Kiss Thrower

24"	$1,650.00*

Lady body

22"	$1,350.00	$1,800.00

Jumeau type, no mold number, open mouth

13"	$675.00	$900.00
20"	$1,200.00	$1,600.00
24"	$1,500.00	$2,050.00
28"	$1,875.00	$2,700.00

14½" bisque S.F.B.J. mold 226 solid dome character with painted hair, open/closed mouth, glass eyes, composition body with jointed wrists, black velvet suit, circa 1910+, $1,950.00. Courtesy Odis Gregg.

CHARACTER FACES

Bisque socket head, wigged or molded hair, set or sleep eyes, composition body, some with bent baby limb, toddler or child body. Mold number 227, 235 and 236 may have flocked hair. Add $100.00 for toddler body.

Mold 226, glass eyes, closed mouth

20"	$1,800.00	$2,400.00

Mold 227, open mouth, teeth, glass eyes

14"	$1,125.00	$1,500.00
17"	$1,425.00	$1,900.00
21"	$1,750.00	$2,350.00

Mold 230, glass eyes, open mouth, teeth

12"	$800.00	$1,050.00
22"	$1,500.00	$2,000.00

Mold 233, crying mouth, glass eyes

13"	$2,000.00	$2,600.00
16"	$2,400.00	$3,200.00
21"	$2,600.00	$3,400.00

Mold 234

18"	$2,400.00	$3,250.00

Too few in database for reliable range.

Mold 235, glass eyes, open/closed mouth

18"	$1,350.00	$1,800.00
21"	$2,300.00*	

Mold 236, glass eyes, open/closed mouth

13"	$875.00	$1,150.00
15"	$1,000.00	$1,350.00

Mold 237, glass eyes, open/closed mouth

16"	$1,200.00	$1,600.00

Mold 242, nursing baby

15"	$3,000.00

Too few in database for reliable range.

Mold 247, glass eyes, open/closed mouth

13"	$1,050.00	$1,400.00
16"	$1,300.00	$1,800.00

18" bisque SFBJ mold 252 socket head, cork pate, original sailor costume, toddler body, original auburn human hair wig, glass eyes, circa 1920s+, $6,000.00. Private collection.

Mold 250, open mouth with teeth
    12" $3,300.00* trousseau box
Mold 251, open/closed mouth, teeth, tongue
    15" $1,125.00 $1,500.00
Mold 252, closed mouth, glass eyes
    15" $3,000.00 $4,000.00
    20" $6,000.00*

22" bisque S.F.B.J. walking, kiss-throwing girl, brown flirty eyes, open mouth, four teeth, pierced ears, original human hair wig, jointed wood and composition body, circa 1900 – 1920, $950.00. Courtesy McMasters Doll Auctions.

Simon & Halbig

Marks:

1079
HALBIG
S&H
Germany

SxH. 1249
DEP
Germany
SANTA

Germany
S H 13-1010 DEP.

5½" bisque Simon & Halbig with mohair wig, open mouth, glass set eyes, ball-jointed wood and composition body, circa 1900s, $550.00. Courtesy Virginia Smith.

1869 – 1930+, Hildburghausen and Grafenhain, German. Porcelain factory, made heads for Jumeau (200 series); bathing dolls (300 series); porcelain figures (400 series); perhaps doll house or small dolls (500 – 600 series); bisque head dolls (700 series); bathing and small dolls (800 series); more bisque head dolls (900 – 1000 series). The earliest models of a series had the last digit of their model number ending with an 8; socket heads ended with 9; shoulder heads ended with 0; and models using a shoulder plate for swivel heads ended in 1.

First price indicates doll in good condition, with flaws; second price indicates doll in excellent condition, appropriately dressed. Original or exceptional dolls may be more.

BABY, CHARACTER FACE, 1910+

Molded hair or wig, painted or glass eyes, open or closed mouth, bent-leg baby body. Add more for flirty eyes or toddler body.

Mold 1294, glass eyes, open mouth
    16" $600.00 $800.00
    19" $750.00 $1,000.00
Mold 1294, clockwork mechanism moves eyes
    26" $1,575.00*
Mold 1428, glass eyes, closed mouth
    11" $1,000.00 $1,300.00
Toddler
    12" $1,000.00 $1,350.00

* at auction

8" Simon & Halbig, mold 1000, bisque pair, in original outfits, circa 1887, $650.00 pair. Courtesy June Algeier.

12" bisque Simon & Halbig Mold 905, solid dome, swivel shoulder plate, human hair wig, threaded eyes, circa 1888, $3,000.00. Courtesy Amanda Hash.

Mold 1488, glass eyes, open/closed or open mouth

20"	$3,375.00	$4,500.00

Mold 1489, "Baby Erika," glass eyes, open mouth, tongue

20"	$4,200.00*

Mold 1498, solid dome, painted or sleep eyes, open/closed mouth

20"	$3,750.00	$5,000.00

CHILD
Shoulder head, 1870s
Molded hair, marked "S&H," no mold number

19"	$1,275.00	$1,700.00

Too few in database for reliable range.

Dolly face, 1890+
Mold 530, 540, 550, 570, Baby Blanche

19"	$500.00	$685.00
22"	$550.00	$750.00

Oily bisque

22"	$1,100.00*

Mold 719, sleep eyes, open mouth, pierced ears, composition wood jointed body; add more for closed mouth/square cut teeth

13"	$975.00	$1,300.00
20"	$1,725.00	$2,300.00
23"	$4,800.00* Edison phonograph mechanism in torso	

Mold 739, open or closed mouth, glass eyes, pierced ears, composition/wood jointed body, add more for closed mouth

15"	$1,575.00	$2,100.00

Mold 758, 759, 769, 979

20"	$1,575.00	$2,100.00
36"	$3,300.00*	

Mold 905, ca. 1888, closed mouth; **908, ca. 1888,** open or closed mouth

Closed mouth

17"	$1,800.00*

Open mouth

18"	$1,350.00	$1,800.00
22"	$1,025.00	$2,200.00

25" bisque Simon & Halbig mold 1009, blue sleep eyes, open mouth, mohair wig, jointed wood and composition body, hairline front neck to cheek, circa 1889, $325.00. Courtesy McMasters Doll Auctions.

Mold 1009, sleep eyes, open mouth, teeth, pierced ears, wig, add more for closed mouth
Kid body

19"	$325.00	$425.00

Jointed body

15"	$575.00	$750.00
25"	$1,000.00	$1,300.00

Mold 1010, 1040, 1170, 1080 (shoulder heads), 1029 (socket head)

18"	$425.00	$575.00
25"	$600.00	$800.00
28"	$675.00	$900.00

Mold 1039, 1049, 1059, 1069, 1078, 1079, 1099 (Oriental), bisque socket or swivel head with bisque shoulder plate, pierced ears, open mouth, glass eyes, composition/wood or papier-mache body; less for shoulder plate with kid or cloth body, more for walkers or original outfit

9"	$375.00	$500.00
17"	$550.00	$725.00
23"	$750.00	$1,000.00
34"	$1,300.00	$1,700.00
44"	$4,200.00*	

Pull-string eyes

18"	$1,000.00+

Mold 1079, Asian child, yellow tint bisque

8"	$1,900.00*

Mold 1079, Ondine, swimming doll

16"	$1,600.00*

Mold 1109, open mouth, glass eyes, dolly face

16"	$575.00	$775.00
23"	$750.00	$1,000.00

Mold 1159, circa 1894, glass eyes, open mouth, Gibson Girl

20"	$2,200.00	$2,950.00

Mold 1248, 1249 "Santa," open mouth, glass eyes

6"	$500.00	$650.00
10½"	$525.00	$700.00
18"	$900.00	$1,200.00
24"	$1,200.00	$1,600.00

Mold 1250, 1260, open mouth, glass eyes, shoulder head, kid body

16"	$525.00	$725.00
19"	$600.00	$800.00
23"	$800.00	$1,075.00

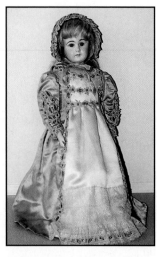

20" bisque Simon & Halbig mold 1010 with closed mouth, marked 1041 breastplate, kid fashion type body, bisque arms and hands, circa 1891, $3,000.00. Private collection.

Mold 1269, 1279, sleep eyes, open mouth

14"	$1,050.00	$1,400.00
16"	$3,500.00* MIB	
25"	$2,550.00	

CHARACTER FACE, 1910+

Mold 150, intaglio eyes, closed mouth

16½"	$12,000.00*

Too few in database for reliable range.

Mold 151, painted eyes, closed laughing mouth

15"	$3,750.00	$5,000.00

Too few in database for reliable range.

Mold 153, molded hair, painted eyes, closed mouth

15"	$19,500.00	$26,000.00

Too few in database for reliable range.

Mold 600, ca. 1912, sleep eyes, open mouth

12"	$850.00*

Too few in database for reliable range.

Mold 720, dome shoulder head, glass eyes, closed mouth, wig, bisque lower arms, kid body

16"	$1,025.00	$2,450.00

16" bisque Simon & Halbig 1039, open mouth, flirty glass eyes, human hair wig, Roullet & Decamps Mechanical Walker, moves eyes from side to side, composition & wood body, steel shoes with three wheels, original dress, $7,500.00. Private collection.

Mold 729, laughing face, glass eyes, open/closed mouth

16"	$1,900.00	$2,550.00

Mold 740, dome shoulder head, glass eyes, closed mouth, cloth or kid body

11"	$1,700.00*	
18"	$1,200.00	$1,600.00

Mold 749, socket head, glass eyes, pierced ears
Closed mouth

21"	$2,325.00	$3,100.00

Open mouth

9"	$700.00	$950.00
9"	$1,700.00* in presentation cabinet	

Mold 919, ca. 1888, glass eyes, closed mouth

15"	$5,700.00	$7,600.00
19"	$6,400.00	$8,550.00

Too few in database for reliable range.

Mold 929, glass eyes, open/closed or closed mouth

14"	$1,725.00	$2,300.00
23"	$2,850.00	$3,800.00
25"	$6,600.00*	

18" bisque Simon & Halbig mold 949 socket head, glass eyes, open mouth with two square teeth above, one tooth below, original blonde mohair wig, original clothing, circa 1888+, $1,600.00. Private collection.

Mold 939, bisque socket head, pierced ears, glass eyes

---

* at auction

20" bisque Simon & Halbig mold 1159, open mouth Gibson Girl, circa 1894, $2,200.00. Courtesy Rose Capricio.

24" bisque Simon & Halbig mold 1159 lady, brown sleep eyes, open mouth, four teeth, pierced ears, original human hair wig, jointed wood and composition lady body, small waist, molded bosom, circa 1894, $3,200.00. Courtesy McMasters Doll Auctions.

Open mouth

11"	$700.00	$925.00
16"	$1,300.00	$1,800.00

Closed mouth

18"	$2,000.00	$2,650.00
21"	$2,500.00	$3,300.00
41"	$3,100.00*	

Mold 940, 950, socket or shoulder head, open or closed mouth, glass eyes

Kid body

14"	$485.00	$650.00
18"	$1,200.00	$1,575.00

Jointed body

8"	$415.00	$550.00
15"	$985.00	$1,300.00
21"	$1,700.00	$2,300.00

Mold 949, glass eyes, open or closed mouth

Closed mouth

10"	$2,000.00*	
16"	$1,750.00	$2,350.00
21"	$2,000.00	$2,700.00
31"	$3,200.00	$4,250.00

Open mouth

15"	$1,000.00	$1,325.00
19"	$1,300.00	$1,700.00
24"	$1,650.00	$2,200.00

Mold 969, glass eyes, open smiling mouth

19"	$5,700.00	$7,600.00

Too few in database for reliable range.

Mold 1019, laughing, open mouth

14"	$4,275.00	$5,700.00

Too few in database for reliable range.

Mold 1148, open/closed smiling mouth, teeth, dimples, glass eyes

18"	$5,500.00	$7,300.00

Too few in database for reliable range.

Mold 1246, bisque socket head, sleep eyes, open mouth

18"	$2,400.00*	

Mold 1299, marked "FS & Co" or "S&H" for Franz Schmidt & Co.

13"	$1,200.00	$1,600.00

Mold 1304, glass eyes, closed mouth

14"	$4,500.00	$6,000.00

Too few in database for reliable range.

Mold 1448, bisque socket head, sleep eyes, closed mouth, pierced ears, composition, wood ball-jointed body

16"	$17,500.00*	

Too few in database for reliable range.

Mold 1478, glass eyes, closed mouth
    15" $6,750.00 $9,000.00
Too few in database for reliable range.
    Mold 1488, bisque socket head, glass eyes, wig, open/closed or open mouth
        20" $3,375.00 $4,500.00
        24" $4,500.00 $6,000.00

ADULTS

    Mold 1303, lady face, glass eyes, closed mouth
        16" $5,400.00 $7,250.00
Too few in database for reliable range.
    Mold 1305, old woman, glass eyes, open/closed laughing mouth
        16" $12,700.00 $17,000.00
Too few in database for reliable range.
    Mold 1308, old man, molded mustache/dirty face, may be solid dome
        18" $4,200.00 $5,600.00
Too few in database for reliable range.

23½" bisque Simon & Halbig, mold 939, open mouth, six teeth, glass eyes, human hair wig, wood and composition ball-jointed body, dress repaired, circa 1888, $2,500.00. Private collection.

    Mold 1388, glass eyes, closed smiling mouth, teeth, wig
        20" $24,000.00*
    Mold 1469, flapper, glass eyes, closed mouth
        15" $2,625.00 $3,500.00

MECHANICALS

    Walker, mold #1039, bisque, glass eyes, open mouth, wig, composition walking body
        13" $1,500.00 $2,000.00+
    Walker, mold #1078, glass eyes, open mouth, pierced ears, clockwork mechanism in torso
        23" $2,200.00 $2,900.00

SMALL DOLLS — DOLLS UNDER 9" TALL

    Mold 749, glass sleep eyes, open mouth, teeth, pierced ears, wig, composition/wood jointed body
        5½" $375.00 $550.00
        9" $700.00 $950.00
    Mold 852, all-bisque, Oriental, swivel head, yellow tint bisque, glass eyes, closed mouth, wig, painted shoes and socks
        5½" $825.00 $1,100.00
    Mold 886, all-bisque swivel head, glass eyes, open mouth, square cut teeth, wig, peg jointed, painted shoes and socks
        7" $1,600.00* in presentation box
        8" $600.00 $800.00
    Mold 950, shoulder head, closed mouth
        8" $375.00 $500.00

---

* at auction

Mold 1078, glass eyes, open mouth, teeth, mohair wig, five-piece body, painted shoes and socks

8"	$400.00	$550.00

Mold 1078, pair Marquis and Marquise, original costume

8½"	$650.00 each*

Flapper body

9"	$400.00	$600.00

Mold 1079, open mouth, glass eyes, five-piece body

8"	$400.00	$600.00

Yellow tinted bisque, glass eyes, open mouth, teeth, five-piece papier-mache body

8"	$1,900.00*

Mold 1160, Little Women, shoulder head, glass eyes, closed mouth

7"	$265.00	$350.00

Snow Babies

½" all-bisque Snow Baby with top hat, $40.00; and 3½" all-bisque Snow Baby laying down with arms out, $200.00. Circa 1900 – 1930s. Courtesy Marguerite Long.

1901 – 1930+. All-bisque dolls covered with ground porcelain slip to resemble snow, made by Bahr & Proschild, Hertwig, C.F. Kling, Kley & Hahn, and others, Germany. Mostly unjointed, some jointed at shoulders and hips. The Eskimos named Peary's daughter Marie, born in 1893, Snow Baby and her mother published a book in which she called her daughter Snow Baby and showed a picture of a little girl in white snowsuit. These little figures have painted features, various poses.

First price indicates figure in good condition, but with flaws or lessor quality; second price is for figure in excellent condition. More for exceptional figures.

SINGLE SNOW BABY

1½"	$40.00	$55.00
3"	$130.00	$175.00
On bear		
	$225.00	$300.00
On sled		
2"	$150.00	$200.00
Pulled by dogs		
3"	$275.00	$375.00
With reindeer		
2½"	$225.00	$300.00

Jointed hips, shoulders

4"	$215.00	$290.00
5"	$275.00	$375.00

With Broom

4½"	$400.00	$550.00

Two Snow Babies, molded together

1½"	$100.00	$125.00
3"	$185.00	$250.00

On sled

2½"	$200.00	$275.00

Mold 3200, Armand Marseille, candy container, two Snow Babies on sled

11"	$3,100.00*

Three Snow Babies, molded together

3"	$190.00	$350.00

On sled

2½"	$190.00	$350.00

Six Snow Babies, band with instruments

2"	$275.00*

New Snow Babies

Today's commercial reproductions are by Dept. 56 and are larger and the coloring is more like cream. Dept. 56 Snow Babies and their Village Collections are collectible on the secondary market. Individual craftsmen are also making and painting reproductions that look more like the old ones. As with all newer collectibles, items must be mint to command higher prices.

First price for Dept 56 Snow Babies is issue price; second price will be upper market price. Secondary market prices are extremely volatile; some markets may not bring upper prices. Usually offered in limited production, prices may rise when production is closed.

Dept 56	Issue Price	Current Price
1986		
Catch a Falling Star, water globe	$18.00	$660.00
Climbing on Snowball, w/candle	$14.00	$118.00
Give Me a Push	$12.00	$75.00
1987		
Climbing on Tree, set 2	$25.00	$880.00
Don't Fall Off	$12.50	$125.00
1988		
Frosty Frolic	$35.00	$990.00
Pony Express	$22.00	$90.00
1989		
All Fall Down, set 4	$36.00	$85.00
Finding Falling Stars	$32.50	$200.00
Penquin Parade	$25.00	$70.00
1990		
A Special Delivery	$15.00	$50.00
Twinkle Twinkle Little Star, set 2	$37.50	$65.00
Who Are You?	$32.50	$140.00
Reproduction crafted Snow Babies, set of ten in various poses		
1 – 1½"	$25.00	

Sonnenberg, Taufling

(Motschmann-type) 1851 – 1900+, Sonneberg, Germany. Various companies made an infant doll with special separated body with bellows and voice mechanism. Motschmann is erroneously credited with the body style; but he did patent the voice mechanism. Some bodies stamped "Motschmann" refer to the voice mechanism. The Sonneberg Taufling is a wax-over-papier-mache head with wood body with twill cloth covered bellows, "floating" twill covered upper joints with lower joints of wood or china.

They have glass eyes, closed mouth, painted hair, or wigged. Other variations include papier-mache or wax over composition. The body may be stamped.

BISQUE: See also Steiner, Jules.

CHINA

China solid dome, shoulder plate, lower torso, arms, feet, padded twill body separates china portion, bellows crier

9½"	$2,750.00*	

Too few in database for reliable range.

PAPIER-MACHE

Brown swivel head, flock-painted hair, black glass eyes, closed mouth, papier-mache shoulder plate, muslin body, working squeak crier, original outfit

5½"	$2,600.00*	

Too few in database for reliable range.

WAX OVER PAPIER-MACHE

Solid dome wax over papier-mache, closed mouth, papier-mache torso, wood arms and legs, original outfit

20"	$2,400.00	$3,200.00

WOOD

Carved wooden socket head, closed mouth, twill and wood torso, nude

17"	$1,000.00*

Steiff, Margarete

1877 – 1930+, Giengen, Wurtembur, Germany. Known today for their plush stuffed animals, Steiff made clothes for children, dolls with mask heads in 1889, clown dolls by 1898. Most Steiff dolls of felt, velvet, or plush have seam down the center of the face, but not all. Registered trademark button in ear in 1905. Button type eyes, painted features, sewn-on ears, big feet/shoes enables them to stand alone, all in excellent condition.

Prices are for older dolls, newer dolls are much less. First price is for doll in good condition, but with some flaws (for soiled, ragged, or worn dolls, use 25% or less of this price); second price is for doll in excellent condition.

12" cloth Steiff Otti, all original with paper hang tag with bear motif, circa 1930s, $475.00. Courtesy McMasters Doll Auctions.

ADULTS

14½"	$1,400.00	$2,000.00
18"	$1,875.00	$2,500.00

CHARACTERS

Man with pipe, some moth holes, some soil
17" $1,300.00*
Alphonse & Garton (Mutt & Jeff), circa 1915
13 – 18" $4,700.00* pair
Happy Hooligan, moth holes
15" $2,500.00*

CHILDREN

14" $1,000.00 $1,300.00

MILITARY

Men in uniform and conductors, firemen, etc.
14" $2,500.00 $3,300.00
18" $3,200.00 $4,275.00

MADE IN U.S. GERMANY, glass eyes
12" $575.00 $750.00

Mark:

Button in
ear

Steiner, Hermann

1909 – 1930+, near Coburg, Germany. Porcelain and doll factory. First made plush animals, then made bisque, composition, and celluloid head dolls. Patented the Steiner eye with moving pupils.

BABY

No mold number, entertwined HS mark
12" $1,050.00* pair of toddlers
Mold 240, circa 1925, newborn, solid dome, closed mouth, sleep eyes
16" $450.00 $600.00
Mold 246, circa 1926, character, solid dome, glass eyes, open/closed mouth, laughing baby, teeth, cloth or composition body
15" $475.00 $625.00
Too few in database for reliable range.
Mary Ann & Her Baby Walker
6¾" $200.00*

CHILD

Mold 128, character bisque socket head, sleep eyes, open mouth, teeth, wig, composition/wood jointed body
9" $700.00*
Too few in database for reliable range.
Mold 401, shoulder head, solid dome, painted eyes, open/closed laughing mouth, teeth, molded tongue
15" $350.00 $475.00

Mark:

Made in
Germany
HermSteiner
$\frac{18}{0}$

14" bisque Herm Steiner solid dome flange head, closed mouth, cloth body, composition hands, frog legs, crier, circa 1920s, $175.00. Courtesy McMasters Doll Auctions.

17½" bisque Jules Steiner bebe, marked flre A, open/closed mouth with dimple in chin, paperweight eyes, mohair wig, jointed wood and composition body, circa 1887+, $5,000.00. Courtesy Elizabeth Surber.

23" pressed bisque Steiner socket head, paperweight eyes, open mouth with teeth, human hair wig, papier-mache body, original ribbon and lace dress, circa 1899+, $2,500.00. Private collection.

1855 – 1891+, Paris. Made dolls with pressed heads, wigs, glass eyes, pierced ears on jointed composition bodies. Advertised talking, mechanical jointed dolls and bebes. Some sleep eyes were operated by a wire behind the ear, marked *"J. Steiner."* May also carry the Bourgoin mark.

> Mark:
>
> BÉBÉ "LE PARISIEN"
> Médaille d'Or
> PARIS

First price is for doll in good condition, but with flaws; second price is for doll in excellent condition, appropriately dressed. Add more for original clothes, rare mold numbers.

Bebe with Taufling (Motschmann) type body
Solid dome bisque head, shoulders, hips, lower arms and legs, with twill body in-between, closed mouth, glass eyes, wig

14"	$3,600.00	$4,800.00
19"	$3,000.00*	

Gigoteur, "Kicker"
Crying bebe, key-wound mechanism, solid dome head, glass eyes, open mouth, two rows tiny teeth, pierced ears, mohair wig, papier-mache torso

21"	$1,725.00	$2,300.00

Early unmarked Bebe
Round face, ca. 1870s, pale pressed bisque socket head, rounded face, pierced ears, bulgy paperweight eyes, open mouth, two rows teeth, pierced ears, wig, composition/wood jointed body

18"	$4,000.00	$5,500.00

Closed mouth, round face, dimples in chin

16"	$6,900.00*

Bebe with series marks, ca. 1880s
Bourgoin red ink, Caduceus stamp on body, pressed bisque socket head, cardboard pate, wig, pierced ears, closed mouth, glass paperweight eyes, French composition/wood jointed body with straight wrists. Series C and A more common. Marked with series mark: Sie and letter and number; rare numbers may be valued much higher.

---

* at auction

Series A and C

8"	$4,200.00*	presentation case
14"	$4,500.00	$6,000.00
22"	$6,400.00	$8,500.00
27"	$7,125.00	$9,500.00
33"	$12,000.00*	all original

Series C

34 – 38"	$9,750.00	$13,000.00+

Series C

28"	$31,900.00*

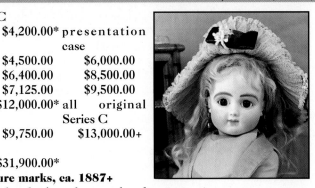

16" bisque Jules Steiner Series C marked bebe with wire lever operated glass eyes, closed mouth, pierced ears, mohair wig, circa 1880s, $4,900.00. Courtesy Barbara DeFeo.

Bebe with figure marks, ca. 1887+

Bisque socket head, pierced ears, closed mouth, glass eyes, wig, composition/wood jointed French body. May use body marked *"Le Petit Parisien."* Marked figure: *"Flre"* and letter and number, usually "A" or "C."

Closed mouth

9"	$4,200.00*	Figure C4 with marked body
13"	$2,625.00	$3,500.00
16"	$3,600.00	$4,800.00
18"	$3,900.00	$5,200.00
23"	$7,750.00*	Figure C with stamped body
24"	$4,500.00	$6,000.00
34"	$8,000.00	$12,000.00

Open/closed mouth, dimple in chin

16"	$3,300.00	$4,400.00
20"	$4,000.00	$5,400.00

Bebe le Parisien, ca. 1895+

Bisque socket head, cardboard pate, wig, paperweight eyes, closed or open mouth, pierced ears, wig, composition jointed body. Head marked with letter, number, and Paris; body stamped in red, *"Le Parisien."*

10"	$2,700.00	$3,600.00
21"	$3,075.00	$4,100.00
27"	$4,000.00	$5,250.00

Swaine & Co.

1910 – 1927, Huttensteinach, Thuringia, Germany. Made porcelain doll heads. Marked *"S & Co.,"* with green stamp. May also be incised *"DIP"* or *"Lori."*

BABY

Baby Lori, marked *"Lori,"* solid dome, open/closed mouth molded hair, sleep eyes

18"	$1,200.00	$1,600.00
23"	$1,870.00	$2,500.00

Mold 232, Lori variation, open mouth

12"	$750.00	$1,000.00
21"	$1,300.00	$1,750.00

Marks:

D
LORI
1

D.I.P.

Swaine & Co. (cont.)

DI, solid dome, intaglio eyes, closed mouth
11"	$575.00	$775.00
16"	$2,100.00* toddler	

DV, solid dome, sleep eyes, closed mouth
15"	$1,125.00	$1,500.00

FP, S&C, socket head, sleep eyes, closed mouth
8"	$550.00*

Too few in database for reliable range.

CHILD

AP, socket head, intaglio eyes, closed mouth
15"	$5,200.00*

BP, socket head, open/closed smiling mouth, teeth, painted eyes
14½"	$3,400.00*

Too few in database for reliable range.

DIP, S&C, socket head, sleep eyes, closed mouth
15"	$1,425.00	$1,900.00

Thuiller, A.

1875 – 1893, Paris. Made bisque head dolls with composition, kid, or wooden bodies. Some of the heads were reported made by Francoise Gaultier.

Mark:

A.14.T

Bisque socket head, or swivel on shoulder plate, glass eyes, closed mouth with white space, pierced ears, cork pate, wig, nicely dressed, in good condition. First price is for doll in good condition, but with flaws; second price is for doll in excellent condition, appropriately dressed. Exceptionally beautiful dolls may run more.

CHILD

Closed mouth
13"	$23,250.00	$31,000.00
17"	$24,000.00*	
26 – 28"	$27,500.00	$36,500.00

**See *1997 Doll Values* for photo of A.Thuiller

Unis

1916 – 1930+. Mark used by S.F.B.J. (Societe Francaise de Fabrication de Bebes & Jouets) is Union Nationale Inter-Syndicale.

CHILD

Mold 60, 301, bisque head, jointed composition/wood body, wig, sleep eyes, open mouth
11½"	$350.00	$475.00
11½"	$1,050.00* trunk, wardrobe	
18"	$475.00	$650.00
21"	$575.00	$750.00

Bleuette, see also S.F.B.J.
10½"	$635.00	$850.00

Composition head and body
12"	$115.00	$150.00
18"	$225.00	$300.00

Mold 251, toddler body

15"	$1,050.00	$1,400.00
27"	$1,650.00	$2,200.00

Wagner & Zetszche

1875 – 1930+, Ilmenau, Thuringia. Made dolls, doll parts, and doll clothes and shoes; used heads by Gebruder Heubach, Armand Marseille, and Simon & Halbig.

CHILD

Bisque head, kid body, bisque lower arms, cloth lower legs

Closed mouth

21"	$675.00	$900.00

Open mouth

14"	$265.00	$350.00

Too few in database for reliable range.

Inge, character, bisque solid dome, closed mouth, kid body

14½"	$1,300.00*

Composition-type swivel head, painted eyes, closed mouth, kid body

16"	$525.00*

Too few in database for reliable range.

Mark:

W.y.Z
y.
Germany

Wax

Ca. 1700 – 1930. Made by English, German, French, and other firms, reaching heights of popularity ca. 1875. Seldom marked, wax dolls were poured, some reinforced with plaster, and less expensive, but more durable with wax over papier-mache or composition. English makers included Montanari, Pierotti, and Peck. German makers included Heinrich Stier.

First price indicates doll in good condition, but with flaws; second price is for doll in excellent condition, original clothes, or appropriately dressed. More for exceptional dolls; much less for dolls in poor condition.

POURED WAX

Baby, shoulder head, painted features, glass eyes, Montanari type, closed mouth, cloth body, wig, or hair inserted into wax

17"	$1,125.00	$1,500.00
25"	$1,700.00	$2,250.00

Infant nurser, slightly turned shoulder head, set glass eyes, open mouth, inserted hair wig, cloth body, wax limbs, nicely dressed

26"	$1,320.00*

21" poured wax baby, inserted human hair, cloth body, wax lower arms and legs, old possibly original outfit, pale coloring, circa 1850s+, $700.00. Courtesy McMasters Doll Auctions.

13½" wax candy container, clothes tagged Marly//238 Rue de Rivoli//Paris, may be made for a department store, painting suggests circa 1920s, $500.00. Courtesy Faye Newberry Gallagher.

24" poured wax lady with wax arms, legs, glass eyes, inserted hair, old costume, $3,500.00. Courtesy Mary Evelyn Graf.

23" wax over papier-mache shoulder head, glass eyes, earrings, heavily modeled blonde hair, wooden carved arms and legs, cloth body, some wear to face, circa 1860s, $400.00. Courtesy Elizabeth Surber.

Child, shoulder head, inserted hair, glass eyes, wax limbs, cloth body

13"	$825.00	$1,100.00
27"	$1,100.00	$1,400.00
24"	$2,600.00* by Lucy Peck	

Lady

8"	$575.00	$770.00
15"	$825.00	$1,100.00

Bride, rose wax shoulder head, blue glass eyes, closed mouth, wig, kid jointed fashion body

15"	$1,650.00*

WAX OVER COMPOSITION OR PAPIER-MACHE

Child, early wax over shoulder head, inserted hair, glass eyes, cloth body

14"	$750.00	$1,000.00

Child, wax over socket head, glass eyes

16"	$1,500.00*

Child, later wax over shoulder head, open or closed mouth, glass eyes, cloth body

11"	$150.00	$200.00
17"	$225.00	$300.00
23"	$400.00	$550.00

Molded hair, wax over composition, shoulder head, glass eyes, cloth body, wooden limbs, molded shoes

15"	$225.00	$300.00
23"	$350.00	$475.00

Alice in Wonderland style, with molded headband

16"	$400.00	$525.00
19"	$475.00	$625.00

* at auction

Slit-head wax, English, ca. 1830 – 1860s, wax over composition shoulder head, glass eyes may use wire closure

14"	$825.00	$1,100.00
18"	$1,100.00	$1,400.00
25"	$1,900.00	$2,500.00

Too few in database for reliable range.

Mechanical Baby, dome over papier-mache, painted hair, glass eyes, open mouth, papier-mache torso with bellows mechanism

18"	$2,000.00*

Two-faced doll, ca. 1880 – 1890s, one laughing, one crying, body stamped "Bartenstein"

15"	$675.00	$900.00

BONNETHEAD

Child, 1860 – 1880, with molded cap

16"	$250.00	$325.00

Lady with poke bonnet

25"	$3,000.00*

Too few in database for reliable range.

Man, turned shoulder head, molded top hat, set eyes, cloth body, wooden arms

17"	$1,000.00*

Too few in database for reliable range.

Wislizenus, Adolf

1850 – 1930+, Walterhausen, Thuringia, Germany. Doll and toy factory that specialized in ball-jointed bodies and used Bahr & Proschild, Simon & Halbig, and Ernst Heubach bisque heads for dolls they made.

Mark:

AW
W
DR 6 M
421481

CHILD

AW, bisque socket head, sleep eyes, open mouth, jointed body

23"	$950.00* original regional costume

AW Special, 101 My Sweetheart, open mouth, sleep eyes

22 – 23"	$375.00	$500.00

Mold #110, socket head, glass eyes, open/closed mouth with teeth

16"	$2,400.00*

Mold #115, solid dome, open/closed mouth, painted eyes

12"	$1,200.00* toddler

Wolf, Louis & Co.

1870 – 1930+, Sonneberg, Germany, Boston, and New York City. They made and distributed dolls, also distributed dolls made for them by other companies such as Hertel Schwab & Co. and Armand Marseille. They made composition as well as bisque dolls and specialized in babies and Red Cross nurses before World War I. May be marked *"L.W. & C."*

Mark:

152
L. W. & C?
12

Wolf, Louis & Co. (cont.)

Baby, open or closed mouth, sleep eyes

12"	$360.00	$475.00

Sunshine Baby, solid dome, cloth body, glass eyes, closed mouth

15"	$1,000.00*

Wooden

4½" wood lady, tiny painted eyes, closed mouth, painted black hair with curls, molded painted tuck comb in hair, wooden peg jointed at shoulders, elbows, hips, knees, silk dress, circa 1810 – 1850s, $365.00. Courtesy McMasters Doll Auctions.

1600s – 1700s+, England, Germany, Switzerland, Russia, United States, and other countries.

ENGLISH

William & Mary Period, 1690s – 1700

Carved wooden head, tiny multi-stroke eyebrow and eyelashes, colored cheeks, human hair or flax wig, wooden body, fork-like carved wooden hands, jointed wooden legs, cloth upper arms, medium to fair condition

19¾"	$36,350.00	$48,500.00
21¾"	$45,500.00	$60,000.00

Too few in database for reliable range.

Queen Anne Period, early 1700s

Dotted eyebrows, eyelashes, painted or glass eyes, no pupils, carved oval-shaped head, flat wooden back and hips, nicely dressed, good condition

14"	$7,500.00	$10,000.00
18"	$11,000.00	$14,900.00
24"	$18,000.00	$24,000.00

Too few in database for reliable range.

Georgian Period, 1750s – 1800

Round wooden head, gesso coated, inset glass eyes, dotted eyelashes and eyebrows, human hair or flax wig, jointed wooden body, pointed torso, medium to fair condition

13"	$2,300.00	$3,000.00
15¾"	$2,750.00	$3,650.00
24"	$3,100.00	$4,200.00

1800 – 1840

Gesso coated wooden head, painted eyes, human hair or flax wig, original clothing comes down below wooden legs

12 – 13"	$900.00	$1,200.00
15"	$1,400.00	$1,875.00
20"	$2,100.00	$2,800.00

GERMAN

1810 – 1850s

Delicately carved painted hair style, spit curls, some with hair decorations, all wooden head and body, pegged or ball-jointed limbs

7"	$475.00	$650.00
12 – 13"	$1,050.00	$1,400.00
28¼"	$16,000.00* peg and disk jointed	

---

* at auction

8" wooden doll forms decoration on pink faille purse. Doll has painted features, pink faille dress with gold metallic lace trim, a novelty item, perhaps French, circa 1920s, $175.00. Courtesy Jan Mealer.

1850s – 1900

All wood with painted plain hair style; may have spit curls

5"	$95.00	$125.00
8"	$150.00	$200.00
14"	$300.00	$400.00

Wooden shoulder head, fancy carved hair style, wood limbs, cloth body

12"	$375.00	$500.00
16"	$1,000.00* man, carved hair	
23"	$650.00	$875.00

1900+

Turned wooden head, carved nose, painted hair, lower legs with black shoes, peg jointed

11"	$60.00	$80.00

Child, all-wood, fully-jointed body, glass eyes, open mouth

15"	$335.00	$450.00
18"	$450.00	$625.00
23"	$600.00	$825.00

GRODNER TAL

1700s – 1930s, originally Austrian town, later Italian

Wooden dolls have been carved in this town for years. The Colemans report 2,000 carvers in the 1870s, plus painters making wooden dolls, jointed and unjointed, in sizes from ½" to 24".

Carved one-piece head and torso, dowel jointed limbs, dressed

5"	$165.00	$220.00
17"	$725.00	$975.00

Carved hair in bun

8½"	$1,050.00*

Peddlar doll

9"	$2,200.00*

Ca. 1810

Molded bosom, painted chemise, dowel pin, eight ball-jointed body

14½"	$2,750.00*

Ca. 1820

Small (up to 5") peg-jointed dolls, period costumes

Set of 7	$4,361.00*

MATRYOSKIA — RUSSIAN NESTING DOLLS, 1900+

Set of wooden canisters that separate in the middle, brightly painted with a glossy finish to represent adults, children, storybook, or fairytale characters and animals. These come in sets usually of five or more related characters, the larger doll opening to reveal a smaller doll nesting inside, and so on.

Set pre 1930s

4"	$70.00	$100.00
7"	$115.00	$150.00
9"	$175.00	$230.00

* at auction

Set new

5"	$20.00	
7"	$30.00	

Political set: Gorbachev, Yeltsin

5"	$35.00	
7"	$60.00	

SWISS, 1900+

Carved wooden dolls with dowel jointed bodies, joined at elbow, hips, knees, some with elaborate hair

8"	$315.00	$425.00
12"	$475.00	$635.00

ELLIS, JOEL

Cooperative Manufacturing Co., 1873 – 74, Springfield, VT. Manufactured wooden dolls patented by Joel Ellis. The head was cut into a cube, steamed until it softened, then compressed in hydraulic press to form features. Metal hands and feet painted black or blue, painted black molded hair sometimes blonde. Similar type Springville wooden dolls were made by Joint Doll Co. and D. M. Smith & Co. have cut out hip joints.

12"	$700.00	$950.00
15"	$975.00	$1,300.00

FORTUNE TELLERS

Wooden half or full doll with folded papers with fortunes printed on them making up the skirt

18"	$2,600.00	$3,500.00

Too few in database for reliable range.

HITTY: See Artist Dolls.

SCHOENHUT: See that section.

21" porcelain artist doll Allexis by Linda Lee Sutton Originals, porcelain limbs, issued in 1995, limited edition of 10, $595.00. Courtesy Linda Lee Sutton.

21" vinyl Madame Alexander Portrait Agatha, #2230 (boxed), blue eyes, closed mouth, dressed in lavender taffeta over pink, closely pleated ruffle at hem, circa 1979 – 1980, $300.00. Courtesy Iva Mae Jones.

14" composition Arranbee (R&B) Nancy Lee with mohair braids, eyeshadow over sleep eyes, red shirt, braided suspenders and trim around neck, replaced white hat, circa 1938 – 1941, $250.00. Courtesy Peggy Millhouse.

17" cloth Comfort Powder Doll, printed on muslin, shown with original fabric directions framed, showing 1915 trademark date, excellent condition, $250.00. Courtesy Marian Pettygrove.

17" vinyl Atlanta Novelty Company 1979 Anniversary Gerber Baby with molded features, flirty eyes, blue checked cloth suit body, vinyl limbs, with rick-rack on sleeves, white eyelet bib and apron, with wear, $20.00. Courtesy Ruth Swalwell.

Bell Telephone "Pioneers of America" Bell

15"	$30.00	$75.00

Buster Brown Shoes

Composition head, cloth body, tag reads *"Buster Brown Shoes"*

26"	$75.00	$300.00+

Capezio Shoes

"Aida, Toe Dancing Ballerina Dolls"

	$40.00	$150.00

Colgate Fab Soap Princess Doll, ca. 1951

5½"	$5.00	$15.00

Gerber Baby, 1936+

An advertising and trademark doll for Gerber Products, a baby food manufacturer located in Fremont, Michigan. First price is for doll flawed, nude, or redressed, second price is for all original with package. More for black or special sets with accessories.

1936, cloth one-piece doll, printed, holds can

8"	$400.00	$500.00

Sun Rubber Company, 1955 – 1958, designed by Bernard Lipfert, vinyl

12"	$50.00	$150.00
18"	$35.00	$100.00

Arrow Rubber & Plastic Co., 1965, vinyl

14"	$40.00	$150.00

Amsco, Milton Bradley, 1972 – 1973, vinyl

10"	$60.00	$100.00
14", 16", 18"	$35.00	$50.00

Atlanta Novelty, 1979 – 1985, vinyl, flirty eyes, cloth body

17"	$25.00	$90.00

Talker

17"	$25.00	$100.00

Collector Doll, christening gown, basket

12"	$25.00	$100.00

Porcelain, limited edition

17"	$75.00	$350.00

Lucky Ltd. 1989 – 1992, vinyl

6"	$5.00	$15.00
11"	$10.00	$40.00
14 – 16"	$10.00	$40.00

Toy Biz, Inc. 1994 – 1996, vinyl

8"	$4.00	$15.00
15"	$7.50	$25.00

Battery operated

12 – 13"	$10.00	$25.00
Talker, 14"	$10.00	$40.00
17"	$10.00	$50.00

Green Giant, Sprout, 1973

10½"	$7.50	$25.00

Highland Mist Scotch Whiskey
Rubber doll in plaid kilt

22"	$40.00	$150.00

Jolly Joan, Portland, Oregan, restaurant

11"	$35.00	$125.00

Kellogg's cereals
Corn Flakes & Pep "Red Riding Hood," cloth

13½"	$40.00	$150.00

Goldilocks & Three Bears, set of four

12 – 15"	$80.00	$225.00

Korn Krisp cereal
"Miss Korn-Krisp," ca. 1900, cloth marked body

24"	$60.00	$225.00

Nabisco cereal "Your Overseas Doll"

8½"	$7.50	$25.00

Texaco Cheerleader
Vinyl, boxed with wardrobe, ca. 1970s

11½"	$20.00	$75.00

Madame Alexander

In 1912, Beatrice and Rose Alexander, known for making doll costumes, began the Alexander Doll Co. They began using the "Madame Alexander" trademark in 1928. Beatrice A. Behrman became a legend in the doll world with her long reign as head of the Alexander Doll Company. Alexander made cloth, composition, and wooden dolls, and eventually made the transition to hard plastic and vinyl. Dolls are listed by subcategories of the material of which the head is made.

First price is for doll in good condition with flaws, may have soiled or worn clothing; second price is for complete beautiful doll in mint condition with original clothes, tag, labels, etc. Unusual dolls with presentation cases or rare costumes may be much more.

11" composition Madame Alexander Butch, all original, blue sleep eyes, painted closed mouth, synthetic wig, cloth body, tagged romper suit outfit, circa 1942 – 1946, $200.00. Courtesy Iva Mae Jones.

CLOTH, CA. 1933 – 1950+

All-cloth head and body, mohair wig, flat or molded mask face, painted side-glancing eyes

Alice in Wonderland

Flat face		$200.00	$875.00
Mask face	16"	$200.00	$675.00
Animals		$70.00	$275.00
Dogs		$75.00	$290.00
Baby			
	13"	$75.00	$300.00
	17"	$125.00	$475.00

13" composition Madame Alexander Betty, blue metal eyes, red mohair wig, original tagged "Betty/ /Madame Alexander/ /New York," blue and white dress, with matching bonnet, teddy, shoes and socks circa 1935, $400.00. Courtesy Dee Cermak.

16" composition Madame Alexander Flora McFlimsey, human hair wig, original tagged dress, gold paper hang tag, circa 1938, $475.00. Courtesy Betty Jane Fronefield.

Bunny Belle

13"	$175.00	$700.00

Dionne Quintuplets

16"	$250.00	$900.00
24"	$450.00	$1,200.00

Clarabell, the Clown

19"	$100.00	$350.00

David Copperfield or other boys

16"	$200.00	$800.00+

Funny

18"	$10.00	$70.00

Little Shaver, 1942, yarn hair

10"	$90.00	$350.00
15"	$150.00	$600.00

Little Women

16"	$125.00	$700.00+

Kamkins-type, hard felt mask face

20"	$250.00	$650.00

Muffin

14"	$25.00	$95.00

So Lite Baby or Toddler

20"	$100.00	$425.00

Suzie Q

	$175.00	$650.00

Teeny Twinkle, disc floating eyes

	$150.00	$525.00

Tiny Tim

	$230.00	$725.00

COMPOSITION, CA. 1930 – 1950

Alice in Wonderland

14"	$125.00	$475.00

Babs Skater, 1948, marked *"ALEX"* on head, clover tag

18"	$400.00	$1,200.00+

Baby Genius, cloth body, sleep eyes, marked *"Alexander"*

22"	$550.00* wrist tag, yellow taffeta tagged gown

Baby Jane

16"	$325.00	$950.00+

Bride and Bridesmaids

15"	$100.00	$400.00
18"	$125.00	$450.00

Carmen Miranda

7"	$325.00* near mint	
14"	$125.00	$450.00

Dionne Quintuplets, ca. 1935 – 1945, all-composition, swivel head, jointed toddler or baby body, molded painted hair or wigged, sleep or painted eyes.

7½" composition Alexander Dionne Quintuplets in original box with extra pink flannel nightgown, matte finish composition, circa 1934+, $1,300.00+. Courtesy Nancy Lazenby.

Outfit colors: Annette, yellow; Cecile, green; Emilie, lavender; Marie, blue; Yvonne, pink. Add more for extra accessories or in layette.

8"	$75.00	$250.00
Set of five		
8"	$475.00	$1,400.00
Set of five		
11"	$550.00	$2,200.00
14"	$575.00	$2,500.00
20"	$850.00	$4,200.00
Set of five with wooden nursery furniture		
8"	$1,750.00*	
Set of five in basket with extra dresses		
8"	$3,800.00*	
11"	$560.00	$2,300.00
Dr. Dafoe		
14"	$525.00	$1,600.00+
Nurse		
13"	$250.00	$900.00+

Fairy Queen, 1939, clover wrist tag, tagged gown

14"	$200.00	$700.00
18"	$225.00	$900.00

Flora McFlimsey, 1938, freckles, marked *"Princess Elizabeth"*

16"	$135.00	$550.00+
22"	$250.00	$985.00

Flower Girl, 1939 – 1947, marked *"Princess Elizabeth"*

20"	$175.00	$650.00+

Happy Birthday, set of 12, side-glancing eyes

7"	$2,700.00* all original

Jane Withers, green sleep eyes, open mouth, brown mohair wig

15"	$425.00	$1,300.00
20"	$800.00	$1,600.00

13" composition Madame Alexander Kate Greenaway, mohair wig, original tagged dress, circa 1938, $600.00. Courtesy Betty Jane Fronefield.

* at auction

13" composition Princess Elizabeth, tagged original dress, circa 1937, $525.00. Courtesy June Algeier.

Jeannie Walker, tagged dress, closed mouth, mohair wig

13"	$1,200.00* in picture box, all original	

Judy, original box, wrist tag, Wendy-Ann face, eyeshadow

21"	$4,000.00* all original	

Karen Ballerina, blue sleep eyes, closed mouth, *"Alexander"* on head

15"	$1,450.00* original	
18"	$325.00	$1,200.00+

Kate Greenaway, yellow wig, marked *"Princess Elizabeth"*

13"	$200.00	$750.00
15"	$225.00	$850.00

Little Betty, 1939 – 1943, side-glancing painted eyes

9"	$75.00	$295.00
9"	$550.00* as "Alice in Wonderland"	

Little Colonel

13"	$175.00	$650.00

Little Genius, blue sleep eyes, cloth body, closed mouth, clover tag

12"	$75.00	$200.00
16"	$100.00	$250.00

Little Women, Meg, Jo, Amy, Beth
Set of four

7"	$450.00	$1,200.00
9"	$475.00	$1,350.00

Madelaine DuBain, 1937 – 1944

14"	$175.00	$525.00
17"	$250.00	$650.00

Marcella, open mouth, wig, sleep eyes

16"	$200.00	$675.00+

Margaret O'Brien, 1946 – 1948

14"	$195.00	$750.00
21"	$300.00	$1,100.00

McGuffey Ana, 1935 – 1937, sleep eyes, open mouth, tagged dress

13"	$175.00	$700.00
15"	$200.00	$650.00
23"	$2,100.00* original	

Marionettes by Tony Sarg

12"	$100.00	$400.00

Military, ca. 1943 – 1944
W.A.A.C. (Army)

14"	$250.00	$1,000.00

13" composition Madame Alexander Snow White, with original dress, wrist tag, sleep eyes, light crazing, circa 1937, $400.00. Courtesy Marie Emmerson.

W.A.A.F. (Air Force)
    14" $250.00 $750.00+

W.A.V.E. (Navy)
    14" $250.00 $1,000.00

Princess Elizabeth, ca. 1937 – 1941

Closed mouth
    13" $185.00 $625.00+

Open mouth
    15" $150.00 $600.00+
    28" $275.00 $1,000.00+

Scarlett, ca. 1937 – 1946, add more for rare costume
    11" $200.00 $750.00
    14" $300.00 $900.00
    18" $400.00 $1,250.00

Snow White, 1939 – 1942, marked *"Princess Elizabeth"*
    13" $125.00 $500.00
    18" $200.00 $750.00

18" Madame Alexander composition Sonja Henie, ca. 1939, excellent condition, original outfit, $995.00. Courtesy June Algeier.

Sonja Henie, 1939 – 1942, open mouth, sleep eyes
    13" $1,000.00* MIB
    15" $200.00 $750.00
    15" $3,200.00* in suitcase with wardrobe
    21" $350.00 $1,200.00

Tiny Betty, 1934 – 1943, side-glancing painted eyes
    7" $75.00 $275.00

Wendy-Ann, 1935 – 1948, more for special outfit
    11" $150.00 $575.00
    13" $2,900.00* pair, swivel waist, original costume
    14" $150.00 $600.00
    19" $250.00 $900.00

HARD PLASTIC, 1948+, AND VINYL

Alexander-kins, 1953+

1953 – 1954

7" – 8" straight-leg non-walker, heavy hard plastic, sleep eyes, closed mouth
Ballgown $250.00 $1,250.00+
Baby, molded hair
        $125.00 $500.00
Nude $75.00 $275.00
Party dress $95.00 $475.00

7" Madame Alexander hard plastic 1954 Alexanderkins tagged Spring Holiday, left and right, Shopping with Auntie, $400.00 each. Courtesy McMasters Doll Auctions.

8" vinyl Madame Alexander Scarlett, Honeymoon in New Orleans trunk with wardrobe, all original, green sleep eyes, black hair, rosebud mouth, fully jointed, 643 on box, circa 1994, $275.00. Courtesy Iva Mae Jones.

13" vinyl Madame Alexander Pussy Cat marked "Alexander," #3225, $50.00. Courtesy Millie Carol.

1955, 8" straight-leg walker

Ballgown	$125.00	$925.00
Basic dress	$60.00	$325.00
Best Man, #461	$990.00*	
Nude	$30.00	$125.00
Party dress	$85.00	$475.00+
Romeo, #474	$200.00	$950.00+

1956 – 1965, bent-knee walker

Ballgown	$175.00	$750.00+
Basic sleeveless dress		
	$60.00	$375.00
Groom	$85.00	$350.00
Nude	$45.00	$225.00
Party dress	$150.00	$725.00+

1965 – 1972, bent-knee non-walker

Party dress	$65.00	$450.00
Nude	$25.00	$85.00

1973 – 1975, marked "*Alex*"

Ballerina or Bride	$35.00	$140.00+
Bent-knee only	$30.00	$120.00
Straight-leg	$15.00	$50.00

1976 – 1994, straight leg non-walker, marked *"Alexander"*

Ballerina or Bride	$20.00	$75.00

BABIES

Baby Angel, #480, tagged tulle gown
    8" $850.00*

Baby Brother or Sister, 1977 – 1982
    14" $20.00 $85.00

Baby Clown, #464, seven-piece walker, leashed dog, Huggy
    8" $300.00 $1,200.00+

Baby Ellen, 1965 – 1972, vinyl, rigid vinyl body, marked *"Alexander 1965"*
    14" $75.00 $250.00

Baby Precious, 1975 only
    14" $25.00 $95.00

Bonnie Toddler, 1954 – 1955, vinyl
    19" $50.00 $165.00

* at auction

Happy, 1970 only, vinyl
20" $60.00 $250.00

Hello Baby, 1962 only
22" $40.00 $175.00

Honeybun, 1951, vinyl
19" $55.00 $200.00

Huggums, Big, 1963 – 1979
25" $25.00 $100.00

Huggums, Lively, 1963
25" $35.00 $150.00

Little Bitsey, 1967 – 1968, all-vinyl
9" $35.00 $150.00

Little Genius, hard plastic, varies with outfit
8" $100.00 $350.00

Littlest Kitten, vinyl
8" $30.00 $155.00

Mary Cassatt, 1969 – 1970
14" $25.00 $85.00
20" $80.00 $250.00

Pinky, composition
23" $100.00 $300.00

Princess Alexandria, composition
24" $95.00 $275.00+

Pussy Cat, vinyl
14" $20.00 $90.00

Pussy Cat, black
14" $35.00 $110.00

Rusty, vinyl
20" $80.00 $330.00

Sweet Tears
9" $20.00 $95.00
With layette $50.00 $175.00

Victoria, 1967 – 1989
20" $20.00 $80.00

Bible Character Dolls, 1954 only
Hard plastic, original box made like Bible
8" $1,500.00 $6,500.00+

18" vinyl Madame Alexander Janie, cloth body, original, circa 1971+, $100.00. Courtesy Millie Carol.

20" vinyl Madame Alexander Victoria #5760, blue sleep eyes, puckered mouth, christening dress and coat with matching bonnet in white eyelet, cloth body, cry box, circa 1966, $75.00. Courtesy Iva Mae Jones.

Cissette, 1957 – 1963

10", hard plastic head, synthetic wig, pierced ears, closed mouth, seven-piece adult body, jointed elbows and knees, high-heeled feet, mold later used for other dolls. Marks: None on body, clothes tagged *"Cissette."*

Ballgown $125.00 $475.00+
Ballerina $125.00 $475.00
Bride $85.00 $275.00
Chemise, boxed $100.00 $350.00
Day Dress $85.00 $275.00

14" vinyl Madame Alexander Sweet Tears, all original mint in box, dark brown sleep eyes, open mouth, nurser, with layette, circa 1965 – 1974, $175.00. Courtesy Iva Mae Jones.

24" hard plastic Alexander Chatterbox, all original with box, talker with button in tummy, circa 1961, $300.00. Courtesy Nancy Lazenby.

FAO Schwarz Travel Trousseau, 1957, exclusive with case

	$200.00	$750.00
Formal	$150.00	$475.00
Gibson Girl	$250.00	$800.00+
Jacqueline	$200.00	$750.00+
Margot	$135.00	$450.00+
Portrette	$125.00	$450.00
Beauty Queen	$90.00	$360.00
Renoir	$135.00	$450.00
Scarlett	$135.00	$450.00
Sleeping Beauty		
	$100.00	$375.00
Tinkerbell	$125.00	$475.00+

Cissy, 1955 – 1959

20" hard plastic, vinyl arms, jointed elbows and knees, high-heeled feet. Clothes are tagged *"Cissy."*

Ballgown	$225.00	$850.00+
Bride	$200.00	$700.00+
Bridesmaid	$350.00	$1,000.00

Flora McFlimsey, vinyl head, inset eyes

15"	$150.00	$600.00
Formal	$400.00	$1,400.00
Formal, #2026, red gown		$2,090.00*
Lady in Red, #1134		$1,800.00+
Lilac layered tulle formal		$4,000.00*
Princess	$275.00	$985.00
Queen	$400.00	$1,200.00
Scarlett	$375.00	$1,350.00
Scarlett, rare white organdy dress		
	$500.00	$2,000.00+
Street dress	$115.00	$385.00
Velvet pants, accessories		
	$250.00	$500.00*

Others

Alice in Wonderland, 1949 – 1952, Margaret and/or Maggie

With trousseau

14"	$700.00	$1,600.00+
20"	$200.00	$800.00+

American Girl, 1962 – 1963, #388, seven-piece walker body, became McGuffey Ana in 1964 – 1965

8"	$100.00	$375.00

Annabelle, Maggie head, ca. 1952

20"	$250.00	$875.00+

Aunt Pitty-Pat, #435, ca. 1957, seven-piece body
    8" $2,035.00*

Babs Skater, 1948 – 1950, hard plastic, Margaret
    15" $250.00 $1,000.00+
    18" $350.00 $1,200.00+

Bill/Billy, ca. 1960, seven-piece walker body
    8" $150.00 $550.00+

Binnie Walker, 1954 – 1955, Cissy
Striped formal, Victoria
    15" $3,420.00*
Ice skating outfit
    15" $1,100.00*
Only in formals
    25" $125.00 $500.00+

Bitsey, ca. 1950, cloth body, molded hair, more for wigged version
    11" $75.00 $275.00

Brenda Starr, 1964 only, 12" hard plastic, vinyl arms, red wig
    Ballgown $75.00 $350.00
    Bride $75.00 $325.00
    Raincoat/hat/dress $65.00 $250.00
    Street Dress $50.00 $225.00
    Caroline, #131, ca. 1961, vinyl
    15" $90.00 $350.00

Cinderella, 1950, Margaret face, 14", hard plastic
Ballgown $225.00 $850.00+
    Pink variation $1,550.00*
Poor Cinderella, gray dress, original broom
        $1,200.00*
Ballgown, #8800, wrist tag, boxed
    18" $2,000.00*
1966, 12", Lissy
Poor outfit $165.00 $650.00
1970 – 1986, 14" vinyl body
Ballgown, pink, blue
        $20.00 $75.00

Cynthia, ca. 1952 only, hard plastic, Margaret
    15" $300.00 $850.00+
    18" $350.00 $950.00+
    23" $400.00 $1,200.00

Davy Crockett, ca. 1955, hard plastic, straight leg walker, coonskin cap
    8" $225.00 $700.00+

Edith, The Lonely Doll, 1958 – 1959, vinyl head, hard plastic body
    8" $250.00 $750.00
    16" $175.00 $375.00

8" hard plastic Madame Alexander Quizkin Peter Pan, tagged inside vest, painted molded hair, sleep eyes, button on back moves head yes or no, circa 1953 – 1954, $500.00. Courtesy Kim Vitale.

15" vinyl Madame Alexander Caroline in party dress, all original, rooted hair, blue sleep eyes, inspired by the daughter of John and Jackie Kennedy and was produced in 1961 – 1962 only, circa 1961 – 1962, $250.00. Courtesy Iva Mae Jones.

36" hard plastic Alexander Joanie with flirty eyes, nurses uniform, less hat, circa 1960 – 1961, $500.00. Courtesy Nancy Lazenby.

Elise, 1957 – 1964, 16", hard plastic body, vinyl arms, jointed ankles/knees

Ballerina	$200.00	$700.00
Ballgown	$225.00	$700.00+
Street clothes	$100.00	$350.00+

Elise, 1963 only, 18", hard plastic, vinyl arms, jointed ankles and knees

Riding Habit	$150.00	$400.00
Bouffant hairstyle	$150.00	$400.00

Elise, 1961 – 1962, 1966+, 17", hard plastic, vinyl arms, jointed ankles and knees

Street dress	$75.00	$250.00
Trousseau/Trunk	$175.00	$650.00+
Formal	$50.00	$200.00
Bride, 1966 – 1987	$40.00	$150.00

Estrella, 1953, Maggie face, walker body, tagged lilac gown, replaced hoop crown, hard plastic body

18"	$3,500.00*	

Fairy Queen, 1948 – 1950, Margaret face

14"	$175.00	$750.00

Fashions of a Century, 1954 – 1955, 14" – 18", Margaret face, hard plastic

Apricot gown

18"	$3,400.00*	

Pink taffeta gown, velvet bodice

18"	$11,000.00*	

First Ladies, 1976 – 1990

Set 1, 1976 – 1978

$150.00 ea.	$1,000.00 set

Set 2, 1979 – 1981

$125.00 ea.	$800.00 set

Set 3, 1982 – 1984

$125.00 ea.	$800.00 set

Set 4, 1985 – 1987

$125.00 ea.	$700.00 set

Set 5, 1988

$125.00 ea.	$700.00 set

Set 6, 1989 – 1990

$125.00 ea.	$700.00 set

Flower Girl, ca. 1954, hard plastic, Margaret

15"	$150.00	$550.00

Glamour Girl Series, 1953 only, hard plastic, Margaret head, auburn wig, straight leg walker

18"	$400.00	$1,400.00+

Godey Bride, Margaret, hard plastic

1950	14"	$250.00	$1,000.00+
1950 – 1951			
	18"	$275.00	$1,100.00

30" hard plastic Alexander Mimi dressed in blue check original dress, made only for one year, multi-jointed body, pierced ears, sleep eyes, closed mouth, 1961, $450.00. Courtesy Carol Bennett.

* at auction

Godey Groom, Margaret, hard plastic
1950, curls over ears
      14" $350.00 $975.00
1950 – 1951
      18" $400.00 $1,200.00
Godey Lady, Margaret, clover wrist tag, hard plastic
1950
      14" $350.00 $950.00
1950 – 1951
      18" $450.00 $1,500.00
Grandma Jane, 1970 – 1972, #1420, Mary Ann, vinyl body
      14" $95.00 $275.00
Groom, 1961 – 1962, Margaret, hard plastic
      14" – 16" $200.00 $750.00+
Groom, 1953, Wendy-Ann, hard plastic
      7" $125.00 $475.00+
Jacqueline, 1961 – 1962, 21", vinyl arms
Exclusive in trunk with wardrobe
            $750.00 $1,800.00+
Riding Habit $275.00 $800.00+
Janie, 1964 – 1966, #1156, toddler, vinyl head, hard plastic body, rooted hair
      12" $75.00 $275.00
Jenny Lind, 1969 – 1970, hard plastic head
      14" $100.00 $375.00
      21" $450.00 $1,400.00
John Robert Powers Model, ca. 1952, with oval beauty box, hard plastic
      14" $475.00 $1,650.00
Kathy, 1949 – 1951, Maggie, has braids
      15" $200.00 $700.00
Kelly, 1958 – 1959, hard plastic
      12" $125.00 $450.00
      15" $75.00 $300.00
Leslie (black Polly), 1965 – 1971, 17", vinyl head, hard plastic body, vinyl limbs, rooted hair
Ballerina $125.00 $375.00
Bride $100.00 $300.00
Lissy, 1956 – 1958, 12", jointed knees and elbows, hard plastic
Ballerina $150.00 $375.00
Bridesmaid $175.00 $450.00+
Cinderella $200.00 $900.00
Poor Cinderella $150.00 $650.00
McGuffey Ana $1,950.00* original box, wrist tag
Southern Belle $325.00 $1,300.00

18" hard plastic Wendy Ann Bride, in tagged costume, beautiful with original hair set, pretty color, circa 1948 – 1950s, $900.00. Courtesy Cleveland Atkinson.

21" hard plastic Madame Alexander Margaret O'Brien, original outfit, circa 1949 – 1951, $1,125.00. Courtesy June Algeier.

18" hard plastic Alexander Maggie Ballerina, circa 1947 – 1950, $500.00. Courtesy Cherie Gervais.

Little Shaver, 1963 – 1965, painted eyes, vinyl body

12"	$75.00	$250.00

Little Women, 1955, Meg, Jo, Amy, Beth, plus Marme, Wendy-Ann, straight-leg walker

8"	$125.00	$375.00
Set	$900.00	$1,800.00

1956 – 1959, Wendy-Ann, bent-knee walker

8"	$100.00	$250.00
Set of five	$400.00	$1,300.00

1974 – 1992, straight leg, #411 – #415

8"	$20.00	$75.00
Set of five	$115.00	$375.00

1959 – 1968, Lissy, one-piece arms and legs

12"	$55.00	$250.00
Set	$500.00	$1,200.00

1957 – 1958, Lissy, jointed elbows and knees

12"	$100.00	$375.00
Set	$800.00	$1,600.00

1947 – 1956, plus Marme, Margaret, and Maggie faces

14 – 15"	$125.00	$450.00
Set of five	$1,000.00	$2,200.00
Set of five	$5,900.00* original box, tags, mint	

Lovey-Dove Ringbearer, 1951, hard plastic, five-piece toddler body, mohair wig, satin top, shorts

12"	$150.00	$600.00+

Maggie Teenager, 1951 – 1953, hard plastic

15" – 18"	$200.00	$650.00+

Maggie Mixup, 1960 – 1961, 8", hard plastic, freckles

Angel	$200.00	$750.00
Overalls	$200.00	$700.00
Riding Habit	$150.00	$550.00
Skater	$200.00	$700.00+

Margaret O'Brien, 1949 – 1951, hard plastic

18"	$175.00	$650.00+

Margot Ballerina, 1953 – 1955, Margaret and Maggie, dressed in various colored outfits

15" – 18"	$200.00	$750.00

Mary Ellen, 1954 only, rigid vinyl walker

31"	$200.00	$600.00+

Mary Ellen Playmate, 1965 only, bendable vinyl body

17"	$125.00	$350.00

Mary Martin, 1948 – 1952, South Pacific character Nell, two-piece sailor outfit, hard plastic

14" – 17"	$350.00	$975.00

Marybel, "The Doll That Gets Well," 1959 – 1965, rigid vinyl, in case

16"	$150.00	$375.00

* at auction

McGuffey Ana, 1948 – 1950, Margaret

14" composition	$300.00	$950.00
17" composition	$250.00	$800.00
21" hard plastic	$2,300.00*	

Melanie, 1955 – 1956, #633, hard plastic, green velvet, Wendy Ann

8"	$400.00	$1,000.00+

"Coco," #2050, rare pink gown, braids around head

21"	$3,900.00*

Melinda, 1962 – 1963, plastic/vinyl, cotton dress

14"	$75.00	$375.00+

Nancy Drew, 1967 only, vinyl body, Literature Series

12"	$1,000.00*

Nina Ballerina, 1949 – 1951, Margaret head, clover wrist tag

14"	$250.00	$550.00+
19"	$300.00	$850.00+
23"	$1,750.00*	

21" vinyl Madame Alexander Southern Belle white tagged costume with green ribbon trim, circa 1967, $495.00. Courtesy Jennifer Warren.

Peter Pan, 1953 – 1954, Margaret head, hard plastic

15"	$300.00	$750.00+

1969, 14" Wendy (Mary Ann head), 12" Peter, Michael (Jamie head), 10" Tinker Bell (Cissette head)

Set of four	$1,100.00

Pink Champagne/Arlene Dahl, hard plastic, red hair, pink lace, rhinestone bodice gown

18"	$950.00	$5,500.00+

Polly, 1965 only, 17"

Ballgown	$100.00	$375.00

Polly Pigtails, 1949 – 1951, Maggie

14"	$175.00	$500.00
17"	$200.00	$625.00

Portraits, 1960+

Marked *"1961,"* Jacqueline, 21", early dolls have jointed elbows, later one-piece. *All portrait prices are for mint condition dolls at auction.

Agatha, 1967 – 1980	$650.00
Coco, 1966	
Formal	$2,200.00
Lissy	$3,000.00
Melanie face	$3,900.00
Renoir	$2,500.00
Scarlett	$3,300.00
Deborah Ballerina	$14,300.00
Gainsborough, 1968 – 1978	$650.00
Godey, 1965 – 1967	$700.00
Madame Alexander	$325.00
Manet, 1982 – 1983	$300.00

8" hard plastic Madame Alexander Marme #781, bent knee, original tagged clothes and wrist tag, circa 1965+, $125.00. Courtesy Millie Carol.

Marie Antoinette, 1987	$425.00	
Mimi, 1971	$500.00	
Toulouse-Lautrec, 1986 – 1987		
	$325.00	
Victorian Bride (Debra)	$5,500.00+	

Prince Charles, 1957 only, #397, hard plastic, blue jacket, cap, shorts

8"	$275.00	$750.00+

Prince Charming, 1948 – 1950, hard plastic, Margaret, brocade jacket, white tights

18"	$300.00	$850.00

Princess Margaret Rose, 1949 – 1953, hard plastic, Margaret

14"	$425.00	$975.00

1953 only, #2020B, hard plastic, Beaux Arts Series, pink taffeta gown with red ribbon, tiara, Margaret

18"	$600.00	$1,700.00

Queen, 1953 only, #2025, hard plastic, Beaux Arts Series, white gown, long velvet cape trimmed with fur, Margaret

18"	$525.00	$1,500.00

Queen, Me and My Shadow Series, 1954 only, hard plastic

8"	$475.00	$1,200.00
18"	$350.00	$975.00

Quiz-Kin, ca. 1953, hard plastic, back buttons, nods yes or no

8"	$225.00	$550.00

Renoir Girl, 1967 – 1968, vinyl body, Portrait Children Series

14"	$90.00	$175.00

Scarlett, 1950s, hard plastic, more for rare costumes
Bent-knee walker

8"	$425.00	$1,250.00+
21"	$475.00	$1,300.00+

Shari Lewis, 1958 – 1959

14"	$1,500.00*	

Sleeping Beauty, ca. 1959, Disneyland Special

9"	$300.00*	
10"	$150.00	$375.00
16"	$200.00	$600.00

Smarty, 1962 – 1963, vinyl body

12"	$90.00	$325.00

Snow White, ca. 1952, gold vest, Walt Disney edition

15"	$250.00	$750.00
18"	$400.00	$1,100.00

Sound of Music, 1965 – 1970, large, 1971 – 1973, small, vinyl

10" Brigitta	$50.00	$175.00
14" Brigitta	$50.00	$150.00
8" Friedrich	$100.00	$250.00
10" Friedrich	$90.00	$225.00

8" Gretl		$50.00	$150.00
10" Gretl		$60.00	$175.00
10" Liesl		$100.00	$250.00
14" Liesl		$50.00	$150.00
10" Louisa		$130.00	$275.00
14" Louisa		$130.00	$275.00
12" Maria		$140.00	$300.00
17" Maria		$140.00	$300.00
8" Marta		$90.00	$225.00
10" Marta		$60.00	$175.00
Set/seven small		$700.00	$1,200.00
Set/seven large		$700.00	$1,200.00

Southern Belle, 1956 – 1963, hard plastic

8"	$300.00	$900.00+
12"	$550.00	$1,300.00

Tommy Bangs, 1952 only, hard plastic, Little Men Series

11"	$200.00	$875.00

Wendy

Ballerina, 1956, *564, tagged tutu

	8"	$935.00*	
	8"	$175.00	$600.00
Bo-Peep	7"	$125.00	$525.00
Bride	8"	$125.00	$475.00
	14"	$150.00	$500.00
	18"	$200.00	$800.00
Bridesmaid	8"	$200.00	$700.00+
Cowgirl	8"	$125.00	$425.00
Ice Skater	8"	$200.00	$700.00+
Nurse/baby	8"	$175.00	$650.00+
Rider	8"	$175.00	$450.00

Sewing basket, FAO Schwarz exclusive

8"	$1,400.00*	
Walker	$150.00	$500.00* more for rare costume

Wendy-Ann, 1948 – 1950, hard plastic Margaret head, straight leg body

	8"	$150.00	$475.00* more for rare costume
	14"	$175.00	$450.00
	18"	$400.00	$875.00
	22"	$425.00	$975.00

Walker body, ca. 1955,*more for unusual costume

8"	$325.00	$1,200.00

Wendy-kin, hard plastic seven-piece body

Ballerina	8"	$100.00	$550.00
Cherry Twin	8"	$400.00	$1,500.00+
Easter Egg	8"	$375.00	$1,400.00+
Nurse	8"	$200.00	$650.00+
Skater	8"	$175.00	$525.00
Walker	8"	$250.00	$1,000.00* more for rare costume

* at auction

Winnie Walker, 1953, Cissy, hard plastic

15"	$75.00	$275.00
25"	$2,000.00*	FAO Schwarz exclusive

SOUVENIR DOLLS, UFDC, LIMITED EDITION

Little Emperor, 1992, limit 400	8"	$500.00
Miss Unity, 1991, limit 310	10"	$400.00
Sailor Boy, limit 260	8"	$750.00
Turn of Century Bathing Beauty, 1992, R9 Conference, limit 300		
	10"	$275.00
Columbia 1893 Sailor, 1993	12"	$250.00

American Character Doll Co.

20" composition American Character Mama doll with tin eyes, mohair wig, cloth body with swing legs, crier, original clothes, circa 1920s, $350.00. Courtesy Joanne Morgan.

1919+, New York City. Made composition dolls; in 1923 began using Petite as a tradename for mama and character dolls; later made cloth, hard plastic, and vinyl dolls.

First price is for dolls in good condition, but with some flaws; second price is for dolls in excellent condition, in original clothes. Exceptional dolls may be more. All vinyl and hard plastic dolls should have original tagged clothes, wrist tags, etc.

CLOTH

Eloise, ca. 1950s, cloth character, orange yarn hair, crooked smile

15"	$75.00	$260.00
Christmas dress	$90.00	$360.00
21"	$100.00	$425.00
Christmas dress	$135.00	$515.00

COMPOSITION

"A. C." or "Petite" marked baby

Composition head, limbs, cloth bodies, original clothes, good condition

14"	$50.00	$185.00
18"	$65.00	$225.00

"A. C." or "Petite" marked mama doll

Composition head, limbs, sleep eyes, mohair or human hair wig, cloth body with crier, swing legs, original clothes

16"	$75.00	$275.00
24"	$100.00	$385.00

Bottletot, 1926

16" hard plastic American Character Tiny Tears, a drink and wet doll, in original romper with vinyl body, circa 1950 – 1962, $125.00. Courtesy Sharon Kolibaba.

Composition head, bent limbs, cloth body with crier, sleep eyes, painted hair, open mouth, composition arm formed to hold bottle, painted hair, original outfit

13"	$75.00	$250.00
18"	$125.00	$325.00

1936 – 1938, rubber drink, wet doll with bottle, original diaper

11"	$35.00	$75.00
15"	$40.00	$95.00

Campbell Kids, 1928
All-composition, jointed neck, shoulders, hips, curl in middle of forehead.
Marks: "A Petite Doll"
Allow more for original dress with label reading *"Campbell Kid."*

12"	$95.00	$350.00

Carol Ann Beery, 1935
All-composition Patsy-type, sleep eyes, closed mouth, braided cornet, celebrity doll, named for daughter of Hollywood actor, Wallace Beery. Originally came with two outfits such as a playsuit and matching dress.
Marks: "Petite Sally" or "Petite"

10½" vinyl American Character Toni in marked original felt outfit, lovely color, sleep eyes, rooted hair, high-heeled doll, circa 1958, $175.00. Courtesy Kathy & Roy Smith.

13"	$100.00	$415.00
16½"	$150.00	$615.00
19½"	$200.00	$785.00

Chuckles, 1930s – 1940s
Composition head, open mouth, sleep eyes, cloth body
Marks: "AM/Character"

20"	$250.00	$350.00

Puggy, 1928
All-composition, jointed neck, shoulders, hip, pug nose, scowling expression, side-glancing painted eyes, painted molded hair. Original costumes include Boy Scout, cowboy, baseball player, and newsboy.
Marks: "A //Petite// Doll;" tag on clothing: "Puggy// A Petite Doll"

13"	$200.00	$500.00

Sally, 1930, a Patsy-look-alike
Composition head, arms, legs, cloth or composition body, crier, painted or sleep eyes
Marks: "Sally//A Petite Doll"

29" vinyl American Character Toodles, blue sleep eyes, open mouth/nurser, rooted saran hair, cry voice, fully jointed, redressed, rare size, circa 1960, $225.00. Courtesy Iva Mae Jones.

12½"	$60.00	$225.00
14"	$100.00	$400.00
16"	$115.00	$450.00
19"	$125.00	$500.00

Sally, 1934, Shirley Temple look-alike
Ringlet curls and bangs, composition shoulder plate, cloth body, sleep eyes, open mouth. Some dressed in Shirley Temple-type costumes.

24"	$100.00	$375.00

20" vinyl American Character Toni, all original high-heeled doll with bag of accessories, $475.00. Courtesy June Algeier.

Sally Joy, 1934
Composition shoulder plate, cloth body, sleep eyes, open mouth, curly wig
Marks: *"Petite; Amer Char. Doll Co."*

24"	$100.00	$400.00

HARD PLASTIC AND VINYL

Baby
Hard plastic head, vinyl body, bottle, boxed

12"	$60.00	$250.00

Vinyl head, marked *"American Character"*

20"	$20.00	$80.00

Tiny Tears, 1950 – 1962, hard plastic and vinyl

8"	$15.00	$50.00
13"	$40.00	$150.00
16"	$50.00	$175.00

Mint-in-box

13"	$300.00+

1963, all-vinyl

9"	$10.00	$40.00
12"	$12.00	$45.00
16"	$15.00	$55.00

Toodles, ca. 1960, box, wardrobe, accessories

11"	$100.00	$385.00
21"	$125.00	$475.00

Toddler, with eight additional pieces of clothing, box #2503

24"	$360.00*

Child or Adult
Annie Oakley, hard plastic walker, embroidered on skirt

14"	$125.00	$400.00

Betsy McCall, 1957: See Betsy McCall category.
Cartwrights, Ben, Hoss, Little Joe, ca. 1966, TV show *Bonanza.*

8"	$40.00	$140.00

Freckles, 1966, face changes

13"	$10.00	$40.00

Hedda-Get-Bedda, 1960

21"	$35.00	$110.00

Little Miss Echo, 1964, talker

30"	$75.00	$300.00

Miss America, 1963

	$15.00	$60.00+

Ricky Jr., 1954 – 1956, *I Love Lucy* TV show, starring Lucille Ball and Desi Arnez, vinyl, baby boy

13"	$15.00	$50.00
20"	$25.00	$100.00

Sally Says, 1965, plastic and vinyl, talker

19"	$20.00	$70.00

Sweet Sue, 1953, hard plastic

Some walkers, some with extra joints at knees, elbows, and/or ankles, some hard plastic and vinyl, excellent condition, good cheek color, original clothes.

Marks: "A.C.," "Amer. Char. Doll," or "American Character" in circle

15"	$75.00	$300.00
17"	$85.00	$350.00

Sweet Sue Sophisticate, vinyl head, tag, earrings

19"	$65.00	$300.00
Bride	$85.00	$350.00
Sunday Best	$100.00	$400.00

Talking Marie, 1963, record player in body, battery operated

18"	$25.00	$90.00

Toni, vinyl head, ca. 1958, rooted hair

10½"	$50.00	$195.00
20"	$300.00* box	

Toodle-Loo, 1961, rooted blonde hair, painted eyes, closed mouth, fully-jointed, "Magic Foam" plastic body

18"	$50.00	$190.00

11½" black unmarked Magic Make Up Face Tressy with bendable leg, with box, circa 1963 – 1966, $300.00+. Courtesy Debby L. Davis.

Tressy, her family and friends, 1963 – 1966, grow hair, 1963 – 1965

Tressy, all-vinyl high heel doll, marked *"American Doll & Toy Corp.//19C.63"* in circle on head

11"	$50.00	$100.00

Black Tressy

11"	$150.00	$300.00+

Pre-teen Tressy, 1963 only, vinyl, marked *"Am.Char.63"* on head

14"	$50.00	$150.00

Cricket, 1964 – 1966, all-vinyl pre-teen sister of Tressy, bendable legs, marked *"Amer Char//1964"* on head

9"	$40.00	$75.00

Mary Make Up, 1965 – 1966, vinyl Tressy's friend, high-heeled doll, no grow hair, not marked

11"	$40.00	$75.00

Magic Make Up, 1965 – 1966, vinyl, bendable legs, grow hair, not marked

11½"	$40.00	$75.00

Whimette/Little People, ca. 1963, Pixie, Swinger, Granny, Jump'n, Go-Go

7½"	$6.00	$30.00

Whimsey, 1960, stuffed vinyl, painted on features, tag reads: *"Whimsey"* with name of doll, Bessie Bride, Dixie, Fanny (angel), Lena the Cleaner, Miss Take, Monk, Polly the Lolly, Raggie, Simon, Strongman, Suzie, Tillie, Wheeler the Dealer, Zack, and Zero (a football player)

Bessie, Bashful Bride, box, tag	$75.00	$250.00
Dixie, the Pixie, box, tag	$75.00	$250.00
Fannie, the Flapper	$75.00	$125.00
Hilda, the Hillbilly, or Devil	$75.00	$125.00

* at auction

1934+, Meredith, NH. Decorative cloth dolls, early labels were white with woven red lettering; then white rayon tags with red embroidered lettering. In about 1969, white satin tags with red lettering were used, after 1976 gauze type cloth was used. Until 1963, the dolls had yarn hair, ca. 1960 – 1963, it was orange or yellow chicken feathers, after 1963, hair was synthetic fur. Collector's Club started in 1983.

First price is issue price, if known; second price for doll in excellent condition on secondary market. Remember secondary market prices are volatile and fluctuate.

Celebrities, 10", all-cloth

Johnny Appleseed		1984	$80.00	$1,000.00
Annie Oakley		1985	$90.00	$700.00
Mark Twain		1986	$117.50	$500.00
Abraham Lincoln		1989	$119.50	$500.00
Christopher Columbus		1991	$119.50	$300.00

Logo Kids, all with collector's club logo

Christmas, with Cookie		1985	$675.00	
Sweetheart		1986	$275.00	
Naughty		1987	$425.00	
Raincoat		1988	$200.00	
Christmas Morning		1989	$150.00	
Clown		1991	$150.00	
Reading		1992	$125.00	
Back to School		1993	$90.00	
Ice Cream		1994	$75.00	
Dress Up Santa		1994	$75.00	
Goin' Fishing		1995	$29.95	$45.00
Little Mae Flower	7"	1996	$29.95	$35.00

Others

Bride & Groom	3"	1987	$38.95	$375.00
Easter Bunny Musical	5"	1983	$29.95	$400.00
Airplane Pilot Mouse	7"	1978	$6.95	$425.00
Angel, paper wings	7"	1966	$400.00	
Baby Angel on Clouds	7"	1962	$2.45	$600.00
Baby in Christmas Bag	7"	1968	$2.95	$350.00
Cheerleader Mouse	7"	1983	$11.95	$450.00
Santa w/oversize bag	7"	1969	$3.95	$350.00
Sheriff Mouse, #92	7"	1991	$49.95	$700.00
Annalee Artist	10"	1982	$295.00	$1,100.00
Bathing Girl	10"	1959	$7.95	$2,800.00
Calypso Dancer	10"	1950	$1,300.00	
Cyrano do Bergerac	10"	1982	$2,200.00	
Woman	10"	1956	$2,800.00	
Woman in Red	10"	1959	$2,200.00	
Santa with bean nose	12"	1955	$1,000.00	
Fireman	14"	1955	$4,700.00	
Americana Couple	18"	1988	$169.95	$700.00
Bell Hop, special order	18"	1974	$1,000.00	

Bob Cratchet, w/ Tim, 7"

18"	1974	$11.95	$425.00

Mr. & Mrs. Fireside Couple

18"	1970	$7.45	$300.00

Holly Hobby

22"	1973	$1,000.00

Bellhop

24"	1963	$13.95	$1,750.00

Woman

26"	1955	$6,500.00

Mr. Santa Mouse with sack

29"	1977	$49.95	$800.00

Mrs. Snow Woman, holder

29"	1972	$19.95	$700.00

Santa in chair, two 18" kids

30"	1984	$169.95	$1,200.00

Boy & Girl Tandem Bike

33"	1959	$4,500.00

Scarecrow

42"	1977	$61.95	$2,050.00

Santa

48"	1978	$49.95	$1,450.00

18" felt Annalee Mobilitee Doll Col, Inc., Man Skater, felt over wire arms and legs for posing, tag on clothes reads "Annalee 93, Code #5476," circa 1993, $50.00. Courtesy Iva Mae Jones.

Arranbee Doll Co.

1922 – 1958, New York. Some of their bisque dolls were made by Armand Marseille and Simon & Halbig. Made composition baby, child, and mama dolls; early dolls have an eight-sided tag. Sold to Vogue Doll Co. which used molds until 1961.

> *Marks:*
> ARRANBEE
> //DOLL Co.
> or R & B

First price is for soiled, faded, or without complete costume dolls; second price is for perfect dolls, with good color, complete costume, more for MIB.

COMPOSITION

Baby, 1930s – 1940s

Cloth body, original clothes or appropriately dressed

16"	$50.00	$150.00

My Dream Baby, 1925

Bisque solid dome heads made by Armand Marseille, painted hair, sleep eyes, open or closed mouth, cloth body, composition hands

Marks: "A.M. 341," "351," or "ARRANBEE"

See Marseille, Armand for prices.

Dream Baby, 1927+, composition, cloth body

14"	$65.00	$250.00
19"	$125.00	$475.00+

Child, 1930s – 1940s, all-composition

Marks: "Arranbee" or "R & B"

9"	$45.00	$125.00
15"	$85.00	$300.00+

18" composition Arranbee Debu'Teen marked R & B on back of head, blonde human hair wig, sleep eyes, eyeshadow, in original brown pinstripe jacket with blocked flannel hat, circa 1939 – 1940s, $425.00. Courtesy Peggy Millhouse.

Debu' Teen, circa late 1930s, 1940

Usually all-composition, some cloth body, mohair or human hair wig, closed mouth, original costumes, unmarked or marked Arranbee. Hang tags or paper label read *"Debu'Teen//R & B Quality Doll."*

14"	$100.00	$375.00
17"	$125.00	$425.00

Kewty, circa 1934 – 1936, all-composition with molded hair, several faces used form the marked Kewty body.

Mark: "KEWTY"

14"	$100.00	$300.00

Nancy, 1930, a Patsy look-alike

Molded hair, or wig, sleep eyes, open mouth

Marks: "ARRANBEE" or "NANCY"

12"	$100.00	$300.00
19"	$150.00	$600.00
21"	$175.00	$750.00

Nancy Lee, 1939+

Sleep eyes, mohair, or human hair wig, original clothes

12"	$75.00	$300.00
17"	$100.00	$400.00

Sonja Skater, 1945, some with Debu' Teen tag

14"	$70.00	$275.00
17"	$100.00	$300.00
21"	$115.00	$425.00

Storybook Dolls, 1930s, Nursery Rhyme Characters

Little Bo-Peep, ca. 1935, with papier-mache lamb

8½"	$100.00	$225.00

Little Boy Blue, ca. 1935, in decorated case, silver horn

8½"	$125.00	$500.00

HARD PLASTIC AND VINYL

Cinderella, ca. 1952, silver/pink dress, silver cords on both wrists

14"	$825.00*	mint, hard to find with cords

Darling Daisy Bride, tagged

18"	$65.00	$325.00

Lil' Imp, 1960, hard plastic, red hair and freckles

10"	$20.00	$75.00

Littlest Angel, 1956+, hard plastic walker, *"R&B"* marked torso and seven-piece body

11"	$65.00	$225.00

Vinyl head, original dress, brochure

11½"	$15.00	$50.00

Red hair/freckles, 1960

10"	$20.00	$70.00

21" composition Arranbee (R&B) Nancy mohair wig, original dress, circa 1940s, $325.00. Courtesy Betty Jane Fronefield.

*10" hard plastic R&B (Arranbee)
Littlest Angel walker, rosy color,
original plaid taffeta dress, box,
hang tag, circa 1956, $200.00. Cour-
tesy Gay Smedes.*

*14" hard plastic Arranbee (R&B)
Nancy Lee with sleep eyes, lashes,
original taffeta gown, hoop petticoat, center snap shoes, $275.00.
Courtesy Micki Beston.*

Miss Coty, ca. 1958, vinyl, *"10 1/2R"* under right arm, high heels

10½"	$210.00* labeled pink box, white and gold formal	

My Angel, 1961, hard plastic and vinyl

17"	$10.00	$45.00
22"	$20.00	$70.00
36"	$45.00	$165.00

Walker, 1957 – 1959

30"	$40.00	$150.00

1959, vinyl head, oilcloth body

22"	$15.00	$60.00

Nancy, 1951 – 1952 vinyl head, arms, hard plastic torso, wigged

14"	$40.00	$150.00
18"	$50.00	$190.00

Walker

24"	$75.00	$285.00

Nancy Lee, 1950 – 1959, hard plastic

14"	$125.00	$475.00
17"	$135.00	$550.00
20"	$900.00* skater, mint-in-box	

Nancy Lee Baby, 1952, painted eyes, crying look

15"	$70.00	$145.00

Nanette, 1949 – 1959, hard plastic, synthetic wig, sleep eyes, closed mouth, original clothes

14"	$100.00	$350.00
15"	$1,300.00* trunk, wardrobe	
17"	$125.00	$400.00

Nannette Walker, 1957 – 1959

17"	$125.00	$450.00
20"	$135.00	$500.00

* at auction

Taffy, 1956, looks like Alexander's Cissy
23" $45.00 $165.00

Artist Dolls

17" felt John Wright Hans Brinker and friend, $1,300.00 each. Courtesy Cherie Gervais.

Original, one-of-a-kind, limited edition, or limited production dolls of any medium (cloth, porcelain, wax, wood, vinyl, or other material) made for sale to the public.

18" felt cloth artist doll by Maggie Iocano, NIADA artist, 1997, $695.00. Courtesy Barb Hilliker.

CLOTH

Barrie, Mirren
Historical children $95.00
Heiser, Dorothy, soft sculpture
Early dolls $400.00+
Queens $1,100.00+
Wright, R. John, cloth
7½" Elfin girl $800.00
Adult characters $1,500.00
Children $900.00 – $1,300.00
Christopher Robin with Winnie the Pooh
     $1,600.00 – $2,500.00
Winnie the Pooh, 1987
    14" $550.00 – $700.00
    18" $1,000.00 – $1,300.00

OTHER MEDIUMS

Blackeley, Halle, high-fired clay lady dolls
     $550.00 – $750.00
Cochran, Dewees, circa 1950s, latex composition
Peter Ponsett
    18" $2,500.00
Commissioned Portraits
    20" $2,500.00
Child
    15–16" $500.00 $900.00

Florian, Gertrude, ceramic/composition dressed ladies $300.00

  Parker, Ann, historical character
        $150.00 – $200.00

  Goodnow, June
  Chocolate Delight, resin, cloth
      14" $920.00
  Indian, Singer Drummer, one-of-a-kind, cernit
      14" $3,000.00
  The Quilter, resin, cloth
      18" $500.00

PORCELAIN AND CHINA

  Armstrong-Hand, Martha, porcelain babies, children $1,200.00+

  Brandon, Elizabeth, porcelain children
        $300.00 – $500.00

  Campbell, Astry, porcelain
  Ricky & Becky, pair $850.00

  Clear, Emma, porcelain, china, shoulder head dolls $350.00 – $500.00

  Susan Dunham, porcelain babies, children/adults $75.00 – $1,000.00+

  Hoskins, Dorothy
  Lilabeth Rose, one-of-a-kind porcelain
        $6,000.00+

  Kane, Maggie Head, porcelain
        $400.00 – $450.00

  Oldenburg, Maryanne, porcelain children
        $200.00 – $250.00

  Redmond, Kathy, porcelain ladies
        $400.00 – $450.00

  Roche, Lynn and Michael, porcelain
  17" children $1,100.00 – $1,500.00

  Sutton, Linda Lee
  Babies, children $400.00 – $1,000.00

  Thompson, Martha, porcelain
  Betsy $900.00
  Little Women, ea. $800.00 – $900.00
  Queen Anne $2,300.00
  Princess Caroline, Prince Charles, Princess Anne   ea. $900.00
  Princess Margaret, Princess Grace
        ea. $1,500.00 – $2,000.00
  Young Victoria $2,300.00

  Thorpe, Ellery, porcelain children
        $300.00 – $500.00

19½" porcelain 1985 UFDC Region 1 souvenir doll Eugenia Lane by Marilyn Stauber, dressed by Delores Smith, $650.00. Photo Don Smith, Courtesy Nancy Lazenby.

14½" latex/composition Dewees Cochran girl, painted brown eyes, closed mouth, blonde saran-type hair, five-piece body, light green dress, embroidery trim, circa 1940 – 1941, $375.00. Courtesy McMasters Doll Auctions.

6" wooden jointed Hitty a literary character from the 1929 children's book, "Hitty, Her First Hundred Years," in wedding dress, hand carved by Janci doll artists, Nancy Elliot and Jill Sanders, circa 1997, $400.00. Courtesy Jill Sanders.

Tuttle, Eunice, miniature porcelain children
$700.00 – $800.00
Angel Baby
$400.00 – $425.00
Walters, Beverly, porcelain miniature fashions
$500.00+
Wick, Faith, porcelain, other materials
$2,500.00+
Wyffels, Berdine, porcelain
Girl, glass eyes   6" $195.00
Zeller, Fawn, porcelain
One-of-a-kind $2,000.00+
Angela $800.00 – $900.00
Polly Piedmont, 1965 $800.00 – $900.00
Holly, U.S. Historical Society $500.00 – $600.00
Polly II, U.S. Historical Society $200.00 – $225.00

VINYL

Good-Krueger, Julie, vinyl
20" – 21" $150.00 $225.00
Hartman, Sonja, 1981+, vinyl and porcelain
Porcelain   20" $300.00
Vinyl
Odette   23" $375.00
Schrott, Rotrout, vinyl
Child $375.00
Spanos, FayZah, vinyl
Baby $250.00

WAX

Gunzel, Hildegard, wax over porcelain
$1,500.00 – $2,000.00
Park, Irma, wax-over-porcelain miniatures
$125.00+

Sorensen, Lewis
Father Christmas	$1,200.00	
Toymaker	$800.00	

Vargas family, wax ethnic figures
10" – 11"	$350.00 – $700.00	

WOOD

Beckett, Bob and June, carved wood children
$300.00 – $450.00

Bringloe, Frances, carved wood
American Pioneer Children $600.00

Bullard, Helen, carved wood
Holly	$125.00
American Family Series (16 dolls)	$250.00 ea.

Hale, Patti, NIADA 1978, hand-carved character dolls, wooden heads, stuffed wired cloth bodies can pose; some all-wood jointed dolls
$200.00+

JANCI, Nancy Elliott, Jill Sanders	$400.00+	
Sandreuter, Regina	$550.00 – $650.00	

Smith, Sherman, simple carved wood
5 – 6"	$65.00	$100.00

With finer details, souvenir dolls, etc.
5 – 6"	$235.00	$300.00

HITTY

Reproduced by modern artists to represent the small 6¼" – 6⅜" wooden doll from the literary character in Rachel Field's 1929 book, *Hitty, Her First 100 Years*. Original doll now resides in Stockbridge Library in Massachusetts.

Judy Brown	$195.00
Ruth Brown	$150.00
Helen Bullard	$350.00
David Greene	$310.00
Patti Hale	$300.00
JANCI	$300.00
Lonnie Lindsay	$205.00
Jeff Scott	$175.00
Larry Tycksen, son-in-law of Sherman Smith	$65.00+

Mary Lee Sundstrom/Sandy Reinke
Hitty, limited edition with jointed legs	$500.00+

Ashton Drake

Niles, IL. Markets via mail order and through distributors, has a stable of talented artists producing porcelain collector dolls. Many of these dolls are available on the volatile secondary markets with prices fluctuating widely. See Gene category for Ashton Drakes' hottest collectible.

Diana, The People's Princess
18"	$150.00	$250.00

Elvis: Legend of a Lifetime, 1991
68 Comeback Special	$75.00

14" porcelain Ashton Drake Peggy Sue, circa 1989, $105.00.
Courtesy Millie Busch.

Fairy Tale Heroines, designed by Diann Effner

Snow White	$65.00

Mother Goose Series, designed by Yolanda Bello

Mary, Mary, Diane Effner	$90.00
Miss Muffet, Yolando Bello	$50.00

Picture Perfect Babies, designed by Yolanda Bello

Jason	$100.00	$475.00
Heather	$50.00	$175.00
Jennifer	$50.00	$175.00
Matthew	$50.00	$125.00
Jessica	$50.00	$75.00
Lisa	$50.00	$75.00
Emily	$50.00	$75.00
Danielle	$50.00	$75.00
Amanda	$50.00	$75.00
Michael	$55.00	$100.00
Sarah	$55.00	$85.00

Precious Memories of Motherhood, designed by Sandra Kuch

Loving Steps	$65.00

Barbie®

Mattel, Inc., 1959+, Hawthorne, CA.

First price indicates mint doll, no box; second price (or one price alone) is for mint never-removed-from-box doll. Doll alone, without box, would be less, and soiled or played-with dolls, much, much less. Even though Barbie is almost 40 years old, she is still considered a newer doll by seasoned collectors.

In pricing newer dolls, the more perfect the doll has to be with mint color, condition, rare pristine outfit, complete with all accessories, retaining all tags, labels, and boxes to command the highest prices. This is not a complete listing of every Barbie doll, her friends, or accessories, but some of the more popular items.

Number One Barbie, 1959

11½", heavy vinyl solid body, faded white skin color, white irises, pointed eyebrows, soft ponytail, brunette or blonde only, black and white striped bathing suit, holes with metal cylinders in balls of feet to fit round-pronged stand, gold hoop earrings

#1 Blonde Ponytail Barbie	$2,750.00	$7,125.00
#1 Brunette Ponytail Barbie	$3,000.00	$7,550.00

> *Marks:*
> *1959 – 1962*
> *BARBIE™*
> *PATS. PEND.*
> *©MCMLVII*
> *BY//MATTEL, INC.*
> *1963 – 1968*
> *MIDGE™©1962*
> *Barbie®/©1958*
> *BY//MATTEL, INC.*
> *1964 – 1966*
> *©1958//MATTEL, IN.*
> *U.S. PATENTED*
> *U.S. PAT. PEND.*
> *1966 – 1969*
> *©1966//MATTEL, INC.*
> *U.S. PATENTED//*
> *U.S. PAT.*
> *PEND//*
> *MADE IN JAPAN*

11½" vinyl Mattel Number One Barbie, #850, brunette soft hair, ringlet bangs, white irises, dark eyeliner, red lips, arched eyebrows, holes in feet, heavy solid body, faded to white, MIB, circa 1959, $7,550.00.   Courtesy McMasters Doll Auctions.

11½" vinyl Mattel Number Two Barbie, #850, brunette soft hair, ringlet bangs, white irises, dark eyeliner, red lips, arched eyebrows, same as No. 1 but no holes in feet, MIB, circa 1959, $6,350.00. Courtesy McMasters Doll Auctions.

#1 Barbie stand	$350.00
#1 Barbie shoes	$20.00
#1 Barbie earrings	$65.00

Number Two Barbie, 1959 – 1960

11½", heavy vinyl solid body, faded white skin color, white irises, pointed eyebrows, but no holes in feet, some with pearl earrings, soft ponytail, brunette or blonde only

#2 Blonde Ponytail Barbie	$2,400.00	$6,600.00
#2 Brunette Ponytail Barbie	$2,300.00	$6,350.00

Number Three Barbie, 1960

11½", heavy vinyl solid body, some fading in skin color, blue irises, curved eyebrows, no holes in feet, soft ponytail, brunette or blonde only

#3 Blonde Ponytail Barbie	$475.00	$1,125.00+
#3 Brunette Ponytail Barbie	$525.00	$1,205.00+

Number Four Barbie, 1960

11½", same as Number Three, but solid body of skin-toned vinyl, soft ponytail, brunette or blonde only

#4 Ponytail Barbie	$245.00	$675.00+

Number Five Barbie, 1961

11½", vinyl head, now less heavy, has hard plastic hollow body, with firmer texture saran ponytail, and now can be redhead, has arm tag

#5 Ponytail Barbie	$200.00	$575.00
#5 Redhead Ponytail Barbie	$250.00	$650.00+

More Basic Barbies

Listed alphabetically, year of issue and value. First price indicates doll in excellent condition, no box; second price indicates mint-in-box doll. Never-removed-from-box (NRFB) dolls would be more; played-with dolls would be less.

Bendable Leg

American Girl, side part	1965	$2,000.00	$4,500.00+
American Girl, 1070	1965	$275.00	$1,300.00+
American Girl, molded	1966	$550.00	$2,000.00

11½" vinyl Mattel Number Three Barbie #850, blonde soft hair, ringlet bangs, blue irises, red lips, curved eyebrows, blue eyeliner, heavy/faded body, circa 1960, if MIB, $1,150.00. Courtesy McMasters Doll Auctions.

11½" vinyl Mattel Number Four Barbie #850, brunette soft hair, ringlet bangs, blue irises, red lips, curved eyebrows, blue eyeliner, heavy body/no fading, circa 1960, if MIB, $675.00. Courtesy McMasters Doll Auctions.

Bubble Cut, 1961 – 1967			
Brown		$350.00	$1,025.00
White Ginger		$250.00	$850.00
Other		$100.00	$445.00
Color Magic			
Bendable leg	1966	$650.00	$2,800.00
Blonde, plastic box	1966	$285.00	$1,700.00
Midnight, plastic box	1966	$1,150.00	$3,000.00
Fashion Queen	1963 – 1964	$100.00	$350.00
Swirl Ponytail	1964 – 1965	$150.00	$625.00
Twist 'N Turn	1967	$125.00	$525.00
Redhead	1967	$350.00	$850.00

Other Barbies

First price is for doll only in excellent condition; second price is for mint-in-box.

Angel Face	1983	$16.00	$45.00
Army	1989	$16.00	$45.00
Astronaut	1986	$30.00	$80.00
Ballerina	1976	$35.00	$95.00
Barbie & the Rockers	1987	$20.00	$60.00
Barbie Baby-sits	1974	$20.00	$60.00
Beautiful Bride, 18"	1978	$95.00	$225.00
Bicyclin'	1994	$15.00	$40.00
Busy Barbie	1972	$75.00	$200.00
Dance Club	1989	$15.00	$40.00
Dance 'n Twirl	1994	$22.50	$65.00
Desert Storm	1993	$12.00	$30.00
Doctor	1988	$22.50	$65.00
Fashion Jeans, black	1982	$16.00	$45.00
Fashion Photo	1978	$25.00	$70.00

Free Moving	1975	$55.00	$150.00
Gift Giving	1989	$15.00	$40.00
Gold Medal	1974	$32.50	$90.00
Growin' Pretty Hair			
	1971	$125.00	$350.00
Hair Fair	1967	$75.00	$200.00
Hair Happenin's			
	1971	$375.00	$1,200.00
Happy Birthday	1981	$17.50	$50.00
Hispanic	1980	$25.00	$70.00
Ice Capades, 50th			
	1990	$14.00	$38.00
Jewel Secrets	1987	$15.00	$35.00
Kellogg Quick Curl			
	1974	$25.00	$65.00
Kissing	1979	$16.00	$45.00
Live Action on Stage			
	1971	$100.00	$265.00
Living Barbie	1970	$65.00	$175.00
Loving You	1983	$25.00	$65.00
Malibu	1971	$18.50	$47.00
My First Barbie	1981	$10.00	$30.00
My Size	1993	$65.00	$175.00
Dream Bride	1994	$60.00	$150.00
Newport	1974	$62.50	$165.00
Peaches 'n Cream			
	1985	$20.00	$50.00
Rappin Rockin'	1992	$22.50	$60.00
Rocker	1986	$20.00	$45.00
Roller Skating	1980	$22.50	$60.00
Sensations	1988	$25.00	$60.00
Skating Star	1988	$27.50	$75.00
Star Dream	1987	$25.00	$60.00
Sun Valley	1974	$32.50	$85.00
Super Size	1977	$95.00	$225.00
Sweet Sixteen	1974	$27.50	$75.00
Talking	1968	$130.00	$365.00
Talking Busy	1972	$125.00	$350.00
Teen Talk – Math Class is Tough			
	1992	$55.00	$160.00
Wedding Fantasy			
	1990	$30.00	75.00
Western	1981	$25.00	$55.00
Western Fun	1990	$22.50	$35.00
Ward's Issue	1972	$275.00	$700.00

Gift Sets

11½" vinyl Mattel Swirl Ponytail Barbie, out of box, near mint, circa 1964, $375.00. Courtesy McMasters Doll Auctions.

11½" vinyl Mattel Bubble Cut Barbie in box, 1964, dark blonde hair, pink lips, pearl earrings, very good condition, $235.00. Courtesy McMasters Doll Auctions.

Mint-in-box prices; add more for NRFB (never removed from box), less for worn or faded.

Air Force Barbie & Ken Thunderbirds	1994	$60.00
Barbie Hostess	1965	$4,000.00
Color Magic Gift Set, Sears	1966	$4,000.00
Fashion Queen Barbie & Friends	1963	$2,250.00
Fashion Queen & Ken Trousseau	1963	$2,600.00
Little Theatre Set	1964	$5,500.00
On Parade	1960	$2,350.00
Party Set	1960	$2,300.00
Pep Rally	1964	$1,400.00
Pink Premier	1969	$1,600.00
Round the Clock	1964	$5,000.00
Sparkling Pink	1964	$2,500.00
Trousseau Set	1960	$2,850.00
Wedding Party	1964	$3,000.00

Custom or Exclusive Barbies

Often the most sought after are the first edition of a series, or exclusive Barbie dolls such as those produced for Disney, FAO Schwarz, WalMart, Target, and others. These types of Barbie dolls usually increase in price because the number made is less than others, so they are not as easily found.

Prices indicate mint-in-box.

Bob Macke Barbies

Gold	1990	$700.00
Starlight Splendor	1991	$675.00
Platinum	1991	$600.00
Neptune Fantasy	1992	$925.00
Empress Bride	1992	$925.00
Masquerade Ball	1993	$425.00
Queen of Hearts	1994	$195.00
Goddess of the Sun	1995	$175.00
Moon Goddess	1996	$150.00

Christmas Happy Holiday Barbies

Red dress, blonde	1988	$750.00
	1989	$245.00
	1990	$165.00
Black	1991	$115.00
	1992	$100.00
	1993	$75.00
	1994	$90.00
	1995	$80.00

Classique Series

Benefit Ball, Carol Spenser	1992	$165.00
City Styles, Janet Goldblatt	1993	$145.00
Opening Night, J. Goldblatt	1994	$95.00
Evening Extravaganza, Perkins	1994	$105.00
Uptown Chic	1994	$90.00

Store Specials or Special Editions

Avon, Spring Blossom	1996	$45.00
Billy Boy, Feeling Groovy	1986	$290.00

Bloomingdales, Savvy Shopper

	1994	$165.00
Disney Fun	1993	$55.00
FAO Schwarz		
Golden Greetings	1989	$225.00
Winter Fantasy	1980	$240.00
Madison Avenue	1991	$245.00
Night Sensation	1991	$200.00
Rockette	1992	$260.00
Silver Screen	1993	$275.00
Jeweled Splendor	1995	$335.00
Hallmark		
Victorian Elegance	1994	$115.00
Holiday Memories	1995	$60.00
Hills		
Party Lace	1989	$45.00
Evening Shade	1990	$45.00
Moonlight Rose	1991	$60.00
Hollywood Legends		
Scarlett O'Hara	1994	$75.00
Dorothy	1995	$60.00
Glinda, Good Witch	1995	$75.00
Home Shopping Club		
Evening Flame	1991	$160.00
J.C. Penney's		
Evening Elegance	1990	$105.00
Evening Enchantment	1991	$105.00
Evening Sensation	1992	$60.00
Happy Holidays w/ornament		
	1995	$105.00
K-Mart		
Peach Pretty	1989	$40.00
Pretty in Purple	1992	$35.00
Mervyns		
Ballerina	1983	$75.00
Fabulous Fur	1986	$70.00
Military		
Army	1989	$45.00
Air Force	1990	$55.00
Desert Storm	1993	$30.00
Navy	1991	$40.00
Marine	1992	$35.00
Prima Ballerina Music Box		
Swan Lake	1991	$250.00
Nutcracker	1992	$285.00
Sears		
Winter Sports	1975	$110.00
Celebration	1986	$100.00

11½" vinyl Mattel Fashion Queen Barbie in box with wigs, near mint, $175.00. Courtesy McMasters Doll Auctions.

11½" vinyl Mattel straight leg Allan #1000, circa 1964, near mint, out of box, $45.00;. mint in box, $145.00. Courtesy McMasters Doll Auctions.

9" vinyl Mattel straight leg Skipper in box #950, near mint, circa 1964, $95.00. Courtesy McMasters Doll Auctions.

Lilac & Lovely	1988	$55.00
Blossom Beautiful	1992	$415.00
Spiegel		
Sterling Wishes	1991	$185.00
Regal Reflections	1992	$500.00
Royal Invitation	1993	$115.00
Target		
Gold 'n Lace	1989	$45.00
Party Pretty	1990	$40.00
Cute 'n Cool	1991	$40.00
Golden Evening	1991	$50.00
Dazzlin' Date	1992	$35.00
Pretty 'n Plaid	1992	$40.00
Toys R Us		
Pepsi Spirit	1989	$80.00
Vacation Sensation	1989	$65.00
Barbie for President, seal	1992	$85.00
Radiant in Red	1992	$70.00
Astronaut	1994	$55.00
Sapphire Dream	1995	$100.00
WalMart		
Pink Jubilee	1987	$80.00
Lavender Looks	1989	$30.00
Ballroom Beauty	1991	$40.00
Wholesale Clubs		
Party Sensation	1990	$75.00
Fantastica	1992	$60.00
Peach Blossom	1992	$55.00
Season's Greetings	1994	$75.00
Woolworth		
Special Expressions, white	1989	$30.00
Sweet Lavender	1992	$30.00

Barbie Related Dolls, Friends and Family

First price indicates doll in good condition, no box; second price indicates mint-in-box.

Allan, 1964 – 1967		
Bendable legs	$175.00	$535.00
Straight legs	$30.00	$140.00
Bild Lilli, not Mattel		

German doll made prior to Barbie, clear plastic cylinder case

	$500.00	$600.00
Casey Twist 'N Turn		
1967	$70.00	$225.00
Chris, brunette		
1967 – 1970	$75.00	$230.00

Francie

Bendable leg	1966	$90.00	$365.00
Straight leg	1966	$115.00	$405.00
Twist 'N Turn	1967	$125.00	$425.00
Twist 'N Turn, black	1967	$550.00	$1,795.00
Malibu	1971	$20.00	$55.00
Julia, Talking	1969	$75.00	$215.00
Kelly, Quick Curl	1973	$30.00	$140.00
Yellowstone	1974	$85.00	$300.00

Ken, #1, straight leg, blue eyes, hard plastic hollow body, flocked hair, 12"
Mark: "Ken® MCMLX//by//Mattel//Inc."

	1961	$60.00	$220.00
Molded hair	1962	$45.00	$155.00
Bendable legs	1965	$100.00	$400.00
Midge, straight leg	1963	$70.00	$215.00
No freckles	1963	$150.00	$470.00
Bendable legs	1965	$175.00	$595.00

P.J.

Talking	1970	$60.00	$210.00
Live Action/Stage	1971	$90.00	$250.00
Ricky	1965	$40.00	$160.00

Skipper

Straight leg, blonde	1964	$50.00	$195.00
Bendable leg	1965	$70.00	$325.00
Skooter, straight leg	1965	$40.00	$180.00
Bendable leg	1966	$75.00	$395.00
Stacy, talking	1968	$95.00	$335.00
Twist 'N Turn	1968	$100.00	$320.00
Todd	1966	$60.00	$190.00
Tutti	1967	$45.00	$170.00
Twiggy	1967	$90.00	$350.00

Barbie Accessories

Animals

Blinking Beauty (horse)	1988	$25.00
Dallas (horse)	1981	$40.00
Dancer (horse)	1971	$100.00
Prance (horse)	1988	$35.00
Mitzi Meow (cat)	1994	$10.00
Prince (French poodle)	1985	$35.00
Sachi (dog)	1992	$10.00
Snowball (dog)	1990	$35.00
Tag-along Wags	1992	$15.00

Cases

Barbie & Midge Case, red, European

	1964	$95.00
Black four-doll case	1961	$25.00
Fashion Queen	1964	$150.00
Miss Barbie black	1964	$160.00

11½" vinyl Mattel bendable leg Midge #1080, out of box, circa 1965, $275.00. Courtesy McMasters Doll Auctions.

Miss Barbie Carrying Case

	1964	$160.00

Clothing

Name of outfit, stock number; price for mint in package, much less for loose.

Aboard Ship	1631	$475.00
Arabian Knights	874	$410.00
Ballerina	989	$140.00
Barbie Baby Sits	953	$260.00
Barbie in Holland	823	$255.00
Barbie in Mexico	820	$250.00
Barbie Learns to Cook	1634	$500.00
Benefit Performance	1667	$1,375.00
Bermuda Holidays	1810	$295.00
Coffee's On	1670	$180.00
Commuter Set	916	$1,300.00
Cruise Stripes	918	$140.00
Country Club Dance	1627	$450.00
Debutante Ball	1666	$1,185.00
Dinner at Eight	946	$240.00
Disco Date	1633	$280.00
Dreamy Blues	1456	$85.00
Easter Parade	971	$4,250.00
Evening Shade	961	$295.00
Fashion Editor	1635	$725.00
Floating Gardens	1696	$500.00
Friday Night Date	979	$285.00
Fraternity Dance	1638	$610.00
Garden Party	931	$175.00
Gay Parisienne	964	$4,200.00
Golden Girl	911	$180.00
Golden Evening	1610	$250.00
Goldswinger	1494	$245.00
Guinevere	873	$265.00
Here Comes the Bride	1665	$1,000.00
Holiday Dance	1639	$595.00
Ice Breaker	942	$130.00
Important Investment	1482	$95.00
Invitation to Tea	1632	$525.00
Junior Designer	1620	$325.00
Lunch on the Terrace	1649	$300.00
Lunchtime	1673	$285.00
Make Mine Midi	1861	$325.00
Matinee Fashion	1640	$495.00
Mood for Music	940	$200.00
Movie Date	933	$120.00
Mink Coat	1699	$4,000.00
Modern Art	1625	$515.00

Music Center Matinee	1663	$600.00
Orange Blossom	985	$200.00
Outdoor Art Show	1650	$500.00
Pan American Stewardess	1678	$4,500.00
Photo Fashion	1648	$445.00
Party Date	958	$275.00
Plantation Belle	966	$565.00
Pink Moonbeams	1694	$350.00
Poodle Parade	1643	$850.00
Pretty as a Picture	1652	$450.00
Registered Nurse	991	$260.00
Red Flare	939	$165.00
Red Riding Hood & Wolf	880	$585.00
Riding in the Park	1668	$595.00
Roman Holiday	968	$4,500.00
Senior Prom	951	$225.00
Silken Flame	977	$200.00
Skater's Waltz	1629	$395.00
Ski Queen	1948	$220.00
Slumber Party	1642	$260.00
Solo in the Spotlight	982	$350.00
Sophisticated Lady	993	$395.00
Sweater Girl	976	$175.00
Sweet Dreams, pink	973	$420.00
Student Teacher	1622	$400.00
Sunflower	1683	$295.00
Tennis Anyone	941	$120.00
Theatre Date	959	$175.00
The Yellow Go	1816	$825.00
White Magic	1607	$300.00
Wedding Day	972	$410.00
Winter Holiday	975	$270.00
Zokko	1820	$195.00
Furniture, Suzy Goose		
Canopy Bed, cardboard box	1960s	$125.00
Piano & Bench, Music Box	1960s	$550.00
Vanity & Bench	1960s	$125.00
Wardrobe	1960s	$150.00
Vehicles		
Austin Healy, orange	1962	$275.00
'57 Chevy	1989	$90.00
Country Camper	1971	$45.00
Dune Buggy	1970	$300.00
Hot Rod, blue	1963	$295.00
Sport Plane	1964	$3,000.00
Snow Princess Sled	1981	$300.00

11¾" vinyl Mattel Mod Hair Ken, circa 1973, mint in box, $90.00. Courtesy McMasters Doll Auctions.

First price is for doll in good condition, but with flaws; second price is for doll in excellent condition with original outfit.

14" vinyl American Character Betsy McCall with hard-to-find trunk and three outfits, all original, circa 1961+, $525.00. Courtesy June Algeier.

29" vinyl Horsman Betsy McCall with hard plastic body, jointed wrists, $295.00. Courtesy Christine McWilliams.

AMERICAN CHARACTER

1957+, 8", hard plastic, seven-piece body with jointed knees, not marked on body

Ballerina	$75.00	$275.00
Cowgirl	$75.00	$275.00
Riding Habit	$75.00	$250.00
School Days	$400.00*	
Street Dress	$75.00	$250.00
Sunsuit/boxed	$350.00* with	*Story of Betsy McCall* book
Original shoes and socks		$25.00

1961, vinyl, rooted hair, medium high heels, round sleep eyes

Mark: "McCall 1958"

14"	$75.00	$300.00
School Days outfit	$125.00	$400.00

Vinyl, rooted hair, slender limbs (more for flirty eyes)

22"	$75.00	$300.00

All vinyl, rooted hair

29 – 30"	$125.00	$475.00
36"	$175.00	$625.00

HORSMAN

1975, vinyl

Mark: "Horsman Dolls, Inc. 1967"

13"	$25.00	$85.00

1971

Mark: "B.M.C. Horsman, 1971"

29"	$75.00	$325.00

IDEAL DOLL COMPANY, 1952 – 1953

Designed by Bernard Lipfert, from *McCall* magazine's paper doll, vinyl head, hard plastic (Toni) body, saran wig

Mark: "McCall Corp.®" on head; "IDEAL DOLL//P 90" on back

14"	$90.00	$250.00

Vinyl/plastic with extra joints

22"	$100.00	$275.00

Mark: "McCall, 1959

36"	$225.00	$550.00

Sandy McCall

Mark: "McCall 1959"

36"	$300.00	$650.00

UNEEDA

Ca. 1964, vinyl and hard plastic, brown or blue sleep eyes, reddish rooted hair, no marks

11½"	$35.00	$125.00

Buddy Lee

Ca. 1920 – 1963. Trademark doll of H.D. Lee Co., Inc., first made of composition; ca. 1948 made in hard plastic, unmarked. Engineer had Lee label on hat and overalls; cowboy hatband printed, *"Ride 'Em in Lee Rider Overalls."*

First price for played-with, incomplete outfit; second price for mint doll.

Coca-Cola uniform
White with green stripe
	$125.00	$625.00

Tan with green stripe
	$135.00	$650.00

Cowboy
	$90.00	$400.00

Engineer
	$95.00	$400.00

Gas station attendant
	$65.00	$285.00+

Hard Plastic
	$250.00	$425.00

13" hard plastic Buddy Lee gas station attendant, with MM labeled shirt and hat, possibly Minute Man service station, circa 1950s, $325.00. Courtesy Louise Williams.

Bucherer

1921 – 1930+, Armiswil, Switzerland. Made metal bodied dolls with composition head, hands, and feet, some with changeable heads — Charlie Chaplin, Mutt and Jeff, regional costumes, and others.

6½" – 7½
Regional	$100.00	$285.00
Mutt and Jeff, ea.	$175.00	$600.00+

Cabbage Patch Kids

1978+, Babyland General Hospital, Cleveland, GA. cloth, needle sculpture

"A" blue edition	1978	$1,500.00+
"B" red edition	1978	$1,200.00+
"C" burgundy edition	1979	$900.00+
"D" purple edition	1979	$800.00+
"X" Christmas edition	1979	$1,200.00+
"E" bronze edition	1980	$1,200.00+
Preemie edition	1980	$650.00+
Celebrity edition	1980	$600.00+
Christmas edition	1980	$600.00+
Grand edition	1980	$750.00+
New Ears edition	1981	$125.00+
Ears edition	1982	$150.00+
Green edition	1983	$400.00+
"KP" dark green edition	1983	$550.00+
"KPR" red edition	1983	$550.00+

23" cloth Xavier Roberts Little People Yonah all original with yarn hair, needle sculpture features, marked 1B0794-1000, circa 1983, $850.00. Courtesy Joanne Morgan.

"KPB," burgundy edition	1983	$200.00
Oriental edition	1983	$850.00
Indian edition	1983	$850.00
Hispanic edition	1983	$750.00
"KPZ" edition	1983 – 1984	$175.00
Champagne edition		
	1983 – 1984	$900.00
"KPP," purple edition	1984	$250.00
Sweetheart edition	1984	$250.00
Bavarian edition	1984	$250.00
World Class edition	1984	$175.00

"KPF," "KPG," "KPH," "KPI," "KPJ" editions

	1984 – 1985	$100.00 – 150.00+

Emerald edition

	1985	$100.00+

Coleco Cabbage Patch Kids

1983, have powder scent and black signature stamp

Boys and Girls	$95.00
Bald babies	$100.00
With pacifiers	$50.00 – $75.00
With freckles	$100.00
Black boys or girls	
With freckles	$175.00
Without freckles	$75.00
Red Hair boys, fuzzy hair	$175.00

1984 – 1985, green signature stamp in 1984; blue signature stamp in 1985. Most dolls are only worth retail price, exceptions are

Single tooth, brunette with ponytail	
	$165.00+
Popcorn hairdos, rare	$200.00
Gray-eyed girls	$165.00
Freckled girl, gold hair	$95.00

OTHER

Baldies, popcorn curl with pacifier, red popcorn curls, single tooth, freckled girls, and gold braided hair are valued at retail to $65.00. Still easily obtainable for collectors are a host of other Cabbage Patch Kids, including ringmaster, clown, baseball player, astronaut, travelers, twins, babies, Splash Kid, Cornsilk Kid, valued at $30.00 – $50.00.

Talking, 1987, MIB $140.00*

Cameo Doll Co.

1922 – 1930+, New York City, Port Allegheny, PA. Joseph L. Kallus's company made composition dolls, some with wood segmented bodies and cloth bodies. First price for played-with dolls; second price for mint dolls.

---

* at auction

BISQUE

Baby Bo Kaye, 1925

Bisque head, made in Germany, molded hair, open mouth, glass eyes, cloth body, composition limbs, good condition. *Mark: "J.L. Kallus: Copr. Germany// 1394/30"*

17"	$1,875.00	$2,500.00
20"	$2,100.00	$2,800.00

All-bisque, molded hair, glass sleep eyes, open mouth, two teeth, swivel neck, jointed arms, legs, molded pink or blue shoes, socks, unmarked, some may retain original round sticker on body

5"	$700.00	$1,500.00
6"	$900.00	$1,800.00

CELLULOID

Baby Bo Kaye

Celluloid head, made in Germany, molded hair, open mouth, glass eyes, cloth body

12"	$200.00	$400.00
15"	$350.00	$750.00

22" composition Cameo Scootles, original red and white checked romper, circa 1925+, $1,500.00. Courtesy Janet Hill.

COMPOSITION

Annie Rooney, 1926

Jack Collins, designer, all-composition, yarn wig, legs painted black, molded shoes

12"	$125.00	$475.00+
17"	$175.00	$700.00+

Baby Blossom, 1927, "DES, J.L.Kallus"

Composition upper torso, cloth lower body, legs, molded hair, open mouth

19"	$300.00	$1,100.00

Baby Bo Kaye

Composition head, molded hair, open mouth, glass eyes, light crazing

14"	$350.00	$675.00

Bandy, 1929

Composition head, wood segmented body, marked on hat *"General Electric/ Radio"* designed by J. Kallus

18½"	$1,000.00*

Betty Boop, 1932

Composition head character, wood segmented body, molded hair, painted features, label on torso

11"	$200.00	$650.00
13½"	$200.00	$950.00

12" composition Betty Boop, copyright by Fleischer Studios on red heart label on dress, character head, painted eyes, molded hair, composition and wood segmented body, molded dress and high heels, circa 1932, $500.00. Courtesy McMasters Doll Auctions.

Champ, 1942

Composition with freckles

16"	$175.00	$585.00

10" composition Cameo Margie with wood segmented body, molded hair, side-glancing painted eyes, circa 1929, $250.00. Courtesy Odis Gregg.

Giggles, 1946, "Giggles Doll, A Cameo Doll"
Composition with molded loop for ribbon

12"	$90.00	$350.00
14"	$150.00	$600.00

Ho-Ho, 1940, painted plaster, laughing mouth

5½"	$50.00	$200.00

Joy, 1932
Composition head character, wood segmented body, molded hair, painted features, label on torso

10"	$75.00	$300.00
15"	$125.00	$475.00

Margie, 1929
Composition head character, wood segmented body, molded hair, painted features, label on torso

9½"	$75.00	$285.00

All-composition, 1935

6"	$50.00	$190.00
10"	$75.00	$285.00

Pete the Pup, 1930 – 1935
Composition head character, wood segmented body, molded hair, painted features, label on torso

9"	$70.00	$265.00

Pinkie, 1930 – 1935
Composition head character, wood segmented body, molded hair, painted features, label on torso

10"	$100.00	$375.00

Composition body

10"	$75.00	$285.00

Pop-Eye, 1935
Composition head character, wood segmented body, molded hair, painted features, label on torso

	$75.00	$300.00

Pretty Bettsie
Composition head, molded hair, painted side-glancing eyes, open/closed mouth, composition one-piece body and limbs, wooden neck joint, molded and painted dress with ruffles, shoes, and socks, triangular red tag on chest marked *"Pretty Bettsie//Copyright J. Kallus"*

18"	$125.00	$500.00

Scootles, 1925+
Rose O'Neill design, all-composition, no marks, painted side-glancing eyes, paper wrist tag

8"	$200.00	$975.00* all original with hang tag
13"	$225.00	$925.00
15"	$185.00	$650.00
22"	$375.00	$1,500.00

Composition, sleep eyes

15"	$175.00	$700.00

Black composition

15"	$200.00	$725.00

* at auction

"The Selling Fool," 1926

Wood segmented body, hat represents radio tube, composition advertising doll for RCA Radiotrons

16"	$200.00	$800.00

HARD PLASTIC AND VINYL

Baby Mine, 1962 – 1964

Vinyl and cloth, sleep eyes

16"	$25.00	$100.00
19"	$35.00	$125.00

On Miss Peep hinged body

16"	$35.00	$135.00

HO HO, "Rose O'Neill," laughing

mouth, squeaker, tag

White, 7"	$35.00	$125.00
Black, 7"	$65.00	$275.00

18" vinyl Cameo Miss Peep pin jointed arms and legs, played with, circa late 1960s, $45.00; if mint in box, $60.00. Private collection.

Miss Peep, 1957 – 1970s+

Pin jointed shoulders and hips, vinyl

15"	$20.00	$45.00
18"	$25.00	$60.00

Black

18"	$40.00	$75.00

1970s+, ball-jointed shoulders, hips

17"	$12.50	$50.00
21"	$25.00	$70.00

Miss Peep, Newborn, 1962, vinyl head and rigid plastic body

18"	$10.00	$40.00

Pinkie, 1950s

10 – 11"	$75.00	$150.00

Scootles, 1964, vinyl

14"	$50.00	$195.00
19"	$90.00	$350.00
27"	$135.00	$535.00

Composition

AMERICAN, unknown maker, or little known manufacturer.

First price is for poorer quality, worn doll; second price is for excellent doll original or appropriately dressed. More for exceptional dolls with elaborate costume or accessories.

Baby, 1910+

Wigged or molded hair, painted or sleep eyes, composition or cloth body with bent legs

12"	$65.00	$225.00
18"	$75.00	$300.00
24"	$110.00	$425.00

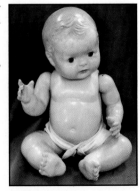

15" composition by unknown maker, unmarked, painted eyes, painted molded hair, jointed bent-leg composition body, came dressed in diaper, circa 1930, $150.00. Courtesy Jean Thompson.

12" composition Regal Bobbie Anne a Kiddie Pal Dolly, in suitcase trunk with four extra original outfits, hang tag, painted eyes, molded hair, bent arms, $400.00. Courtesy Elizabeth Surber.

12½" composition Maxine Mitzi, a Patsy-type with painted eyes, bent arm, original clothing, left foot touch-up, circa 1929, $365.00. Courtesy Debbie Crume.

Dionne Quint types, ca. 1934+, all-composition, jointed five-piece baby or toddler body, molded hair or wig, with painted or sleep eyes, closed or open mouth

7 – 8"	$35.00	$140.00
13"	$65.00	$250.00
18"	$90.00	$350.00

CHILD

Costumed in ethnic or theme outfit, all composition, sleep or painted eyes, mohair wig, closed mouth, original costume

Lesser quality

9 – 11"	$15.00	$75.00

Better quality

9 – 11"	$45.00	$185.00

Early child, ca. 1910 – 1920, unmarked, cork-stuffed cloth body, painted features, may have molded hair

12"	$35.00	$145.00
18"	$50.00	$200.00

Early Child, character face, ca. 1910 – 1920

12"	$50.00	$200.00
18"	$75.00	$300.00
24"	$115.00	$450.00

MaMa doll, ca. 1922+, wigged or painted hair, sleep or painted eyes, cloth body, with crier and swing legs, lower composition legs and arms

16"	$70.00	$250.00
20"	$90.00	$350.00
24"	$115.00	$450.00

Patsy-type girl, 1928+, molded, painted bobbed hair, sleep or painted eyes, closed pouty mouth, composition or hard stuffed cloth body

10"	$45.00	$175.00
14"	$70.00	$250.00
19"	$80.00	$300.00

With molded hair loop

15"	$50.00	$200.00

Shirley Temple-type girl, 1934+, all-composition, five-piece jointed body, blonde curly wig, sleep eyes, open mouth, teeth, dimples

16"	$100.00	$400.00
19"	$125.00	$450.00

OTHERS

Animal head doll, ca. 1930s, all-composition on Patsy-type five-piece body, could be wolf, rabbit, cat, monkey

9½"	$55.00	$210.00

Denny Dimwitt, Toycraft Inc, ca. 1948, all-composition, nodder, painted clothing

      11½" $65.00 $225.00

Jackie Robinson, complete in box

      13" $300.00 $1,000.00

Kewty, 1930, made by Domec of Canada, all-composition Patsy-type, molded bobbed hair, closed mouth, sleep eyes, bent left arm

      13½" $80.00 $350.00

Lone Ranger, *"TLR Co, Inc.//Doll Craft Novelty Co. NYC,"* cloth body, hat marked

      20" $1,400.00* in original box

Louis Vuitton, 1955, ceramic, type composition with labeled case and wardrobe

      19" $2,200.00*

Maiden America, "1915, Kate Silverman," all-composition, patriotic ribbon

      8½" $45.00 $185.00

Miss Curity, composition, eye shadow, in nurse's uniform

      18" $150.00 $500.00

Monica Studios, See that category.

Pinocchio, composition and wood character

      16½" $125.00 $425.00

Puzzy, 1948, "H of P"

      15" $100.00 $400.00

24" American composition Stein-feld Bros. Baby Roslee, tin sleep eyes, open mouth, two teeth, original mohair wig, cloth body, composition arms, legs, original white dress, boxed, circa 1920, $175.00. Courtesy McMasters Doll Auctions.

Raleigh-McCutcheon, Jessie, 1916 – 1920, Chicago, IL. All composition, painted or sleep eyes, painted and molded hair or wigged, cloth or composition bodies, some with metal spring joints, unmarked

Baby

      11½" $100.00 $400.00

      13½" $125.00 $500.00

Child

      11½" $115.00 $450.00

      16½" $165.00 $650.00

      18½" $235.00 $950.00

      19" $1,050.00*

Refugee, Madame Louise Doll Co. ca. 1945, represents victims of WWII

      20" $550.00* MIB

Santa Claus, composition molded head, composition body, original suit, sack

      19" $150.00 $500.00

Sizzy, 1948, "H of P"

      14" $75.00 $300.00

Uncle Sam, various makers

All original, cloth body

      13" $900.00*

Ca. 1918, straw-filled

      30" $450.00*

* at auction

Thumbs-Up, to raise money for ambulances during WWII, see photo '97 edition

8"	$50.00	$175.00

Whistler, composition head, cotton body, composition arms, open mouth

14½"	$125.00	$225.00

GERMAN

Composition head, composition or cloth body, wig or painted molded hair, closed or open mouth with teeth, dressed. May be Amusco, Sonneberger Porzellanfabrik, or others.

Character Baby

Cloth body

18"	$95.00	$350.00

Composition baby body, bent limbs

16"	$125.00	$425.00

Child

Composition shoulder head, cloth body, composition arms

20"	$150.00	$300.00

Socket head, all-composition body

13"	$75.00	$275.00
19"	$125.00	$425.00
21"	$175.00	$500.00

Dora Petazold, character child, ca. 1920, cloth body

19"	$175.00	$575.00

Neapolitan

Adult, finely modeled character face, stick or wire bodies, elaborately dressed

13 – 14"	$1,300.00	$1,800.00
16"	$1,700.00	$2,000.00

Cosmopolitan

Ginger, ca. 1955, hard plastic, bent knees

7½"	$40.00	$150.00

Straight leg

7½"	$50.00	$175.00

10½" Cosmopolitan Miss Ginger, rigid vinyl body, soft vinyl head, rooted hair, and an extra outfit in an original box, circa 1957 $150.00. Courtesy Cathie Clark.

Little Miss Ginger, ca. 1957, vinyl, rooted hair, sleep eyes, teen doll, tagged clothes

10½"	$50.00	$190.00

Pam, hard plastic, sleep eyes, synthetic wig, closed mouth

8"	$20.00	$65.00

Deluxe Reading

Deluxe Topper, Deluxe Premium, also uses names Topper Toys and Topper Corp. Made mechanical dolls, battery operated, ca. 1960 – 1970s. These play dolls are collectible because so few survived intact.

First price is for played-with doll, second price is for complete doll, in excellent-to-mint condition.

HARD PLASTIC OR VINYL

Baby

21" vinyl Deluxe Premium Sweet Judy with jointed body at neck, arms, legs and torso, rooted saran hair, sleep eyes, blue dress with lace trim, blue hat, circa 1950s, $100.00. Courtesy Diana Jenness.

Baby Boo, 1965, battery operated

21"	$12.00	$45.00

Baby Catch A Ball, 1969, battery operated

18"	$15.00	$55.00

Baby Magic, 1966, blue sleep eyes, rooted saran hair, magic wand has magnet that opens/closes eyes

18"	$15.00	$50.00

Baby Peek 'N Play, 1969, battery operated

18"	$12.00	$45.00

Baby Tickle Tears

14"	$9.00	$35.00

Suzy Cute, move arm and face changes expressions

7"	$7.00	$28.00

Child or Adult

Betty Bride, 1957, also called Sweet Rosemary, Sweet Judy, Sweet Amy, one-piece vinyl body and limbs, more if many accessories

30"	$25.00	$90.00

Candy Fashion, 1958, made by Deluxe Premium, a division of Deluxe Reading, sold in grocery stores, came with three dress forms, extra outfit

21"	$23.00	$85.00

Dawn Series, circa 1969 – 1970s, all vinyl doll with additional friends, Angie, Daphne, Denise, Glori, Jessica, Kip, Long Locks, Majorette, Maureen, black versions of Van and Dale. Accessories available, included Apartment, Fashion Show, outfits.

Dawn

6"	$7.50	$30.00

Dawn Model Agency, boxed

6"	$30.00	$45.00

Dawn & others outfits

Loose, but complete	$10.00+
NRFP	$25.00+

Fashion Show Stage in box

	$50.00	$75.00

Go Gos

Private Ida, 1965, one of the Go Gos

6"	$6.00	$45.00

Tom Boy, 1965, one of the Go Gos

6"	$12.00	$45.00

Little Miss Fussy, battery operated

18"	$6.00	$35.00

Little Red Riding Hood, 1955, vinyl, synthetic hair, rubber body, book, basket

23"	$50.00	$125.00

Party Time, 1967, battery operated

18"	$10.00	$45.00

Penny Brite, circa 1963+, all vinyl, rooted blonde hair, painted eyes, bendable and straight legs, extra outfits, case, furniture available
Marks: A – 9/B150 (or B65) DELUXE READING CORP.//c. 1963.

8"	$20.00	$35.00
Outfit, NRFP	$25.00 – $35.00	
Kitchen set	$50.00	

Smarty Pants and other mechanicals, 1971, battery operated

19"	$6.00	$35.00

Suzy Homemaker, 1964, hard plastic and vinyl, jointed knees
Mark: *"Deluxe Reading Co."*

21"	$12.00	$45.00

Sweet Amy, ca. 1957 vinyl, Deluxe Toy Creations, one-piece body

17"	$25.00	$100.00
25"	$35.00	$125.00

Eegee

1917+. Brooklyn, NY. E.G. Goldberger made composition and cloth dolls, imported bisque heads from Armand Marseille, made character head composition, mama dolls, babies, carnival dolls, and later the company made hard plastic and vinyl dolls.

First price for played-with doll, second price for completely original excellent condition doll.

> *Marks:*
> *Trademark, EEGEE,*
> *or circle with the words,*
> *"TRADEMARK*
> *//EEGEE//Dolls//MADE*
> *IN USA"*
> *Later changed to just*
> *initials, E.G.*

COMPOSITION

Add more for exceptional doll, tagged, extra outfits, or accessories.

Baby, cloth body, bent limbs

16"	$25.00	$100.00

Child, open mouth, sleep eyes

14"	$40.00	$160.00
18"	$55.00	$210.00

MaMa Doll, ca. 1920s – 1930s, composition head, sleep or painted eyes, wigged or molded hair, cloth body with crier, swing legs, composition lower arms and legs

16"	$75.00	$250.00
20"	$100.00	$350.00

Miss Charming, 1936, all-composition, Shirley Temple look-alike

19"	$125.00	$450.00

Miss Charming, pin-back button $50.00

HARD PLASTIC AND VINYL

Andy, 1963, vinyl, teen-type, molded painted hair, painted eyes, closed mouth

12"	$9.00	$35.00

Annette, 1963, vinyl, teen-type fashion, rooted hair, painted eyes

11½"	$15.00	$55.00

Child, 1966, marked *"20/25 M/13"*

19"	$10.00	$50.00

16" hard plastic Eegee baby with rooted hair, sleep eyes, cloth body, pouty mouth, vinyl arms, circa 1950s, $38.00. Courtesy Marcie Montgomery.

Child, walker, all-vinyl rooted long blonde hair, or short curly wig, blue sleep eyes, closed mouth

25"	$15.00	$50.00
28"	$20.00	$65.00
36"	$25.00	$85.00

Babette, 1970, vinyl head, stuffed limbs, cloth body, painted or sleep eyes, rooted hair

15"	$10.00	$40.00
25"	$18.00	$65.00

Baby Care, 1969, vinyl, molded or rooted hair, sleep or set glassine eyes, drink and wet doll, with complete nursery set

18"	$12.00	$45.00

Baby Carrie, 1970, rooted or molded hair, sleep or set glassine eyes with plastic carriage or carry seat

14"	$10.00	$40.00
18"	$10.00	$45.00
24"	$15.00	$60.00

Baby Luv, 1973, vinyl head, rooted hair, painted eyes, open/closed mouth, marked *"B.T. Eegee,"* cloth body, pants are part of body

14"	$10.00	$35.00

Baby Susan, 1958, marked *"Baby Susan"* on head

8½"	$4.00	$20.00

Baby Tandy Talks, 1963, pull string activates talking mechanism, vinyl head, rooted hair, sleep eyes, cotton and foam-stuffed body and limbs

14"	$10.00	$35.00
20"	$20.00	$65.00

Ballerina, 1964, vinyl head and hard plastic body

31"	$25.00	$100.00

1967, vinyl head, foam-filled body

18"	$8.00	$30.00

Barbara Cartland, painted features, adult

15"	$15.00	$52.00

Beverly Hillbillies, Clampett family from 1960s TV sitcom

Car	$80.00	$350.00

Granny Clampett, gray rooted hair

14"	$20.00	$65.00

Fields, W. C., 1980, vinyl ventriloquist doll by Juro, division of Goldberger

30"	$65.00	$210.00

Flowerkins, 1963
Marked "F-2" on head; seven dolls in series.

Boxed	16"	$15.00	$60.00

Gemmette, 1963, rooted hair, sleep eyes, jointed vinyl, dressed in gem colored dressed, includes child's jeweled ring, Misses Amethyst, Diamond, Emerald, Ruby, Sapphire, and Topaz

15½"	$15.00	$50.00

Georgie, Georgette, 1971, vinyl head, cloth bodies, redheaded twins

22"	$12.00	$50.00

Gigi Perreau, 1951, early vinyl head, hard plastic body, open/closed smiling mouth

17"	$175.00	$700.00

Karena Ballerina, 1958, vinyl head, rooted hair, sleep eyes, closed mouth, hard plastic body, jointed knees, ankles, neck, shoulders, and hips, head turns when walks

21"	$12.00	$45.00

Little Debutantes, 1958, vinyl head, rooted hair, sleep eyes, closed mouth, hard plastic body, swivel waists, high-heeled feet

18"	$15.00	$50.00
20"	$20.00	$75.00

My Fair Lady, 1958, all-vinyl, fashion type, swivel waist, fully jointed

20"	$15.00	$75.00

Parton, Dolly, 1978

11½"	$5.00	$25.00
18"	$12.00	$45.00

Posi Playmate, 1969, vinyl head, foam-filled vinyl body, bendable arms and legs, painted or rooted hair, sleep or painted eyes

12"	$5.00	$20.00

Puppetrina, 1963+, vinyl head, cloth body, rooted hair, sleep eyes, pocket in back for child to insert hand to manipulate doll's head and arms

22"	$8.00	$35.00

Shelly, 1964, Tammy-type, grow hair

12"	$5.00	$18.00

Sniffles, 1963, vinyl head, rooted hair, sleep eyes, open/closed mouth, marked *"13/14 AA-EEGEE"*

12"	$5.00	$20.00

Susan Stroller, ca. 1955, vinyl head, hard plastic walker body, rooted hair, closed mouth

20"	$12.00	$45.00
23"	$15.00	$60.00
26"	$20.00	$80.00

Tandy Talks, 1961, vinyl head, hard plastic body, freckles, pull string talker

20"	$15.00	$50.00

Effanbee

Effanbee Doll Company, 1910+, New York, NY. Bernard E. Fleischaker and Hugo Baum founders. Trademark *"EFFANBEE DOLLS//THEY WALK//THEY TALK//THEY SLEEP"* registered in 1918. Made dolls in composition and later hard plastic and vinyl. Currently, the company is owned by Stanley and Irene Wahlberg, who are reintroducing limited edition collectible dolls such as Patsy Joan, Skippy, Wee Patsy, and others.

First price indicates played-with doll in good condition, but with flaws; second price indicates doll in excellent condition with appropriate or original clothes. More for exceptional doll with wardrobe or accessories.

BISQUE

Mary Jane, ca. 1920

Some with bisque heads, others all-composition; bisque head, manufactured by Lenox Potteries, NJ, for Effanbee, sleep eyes, composition body, wooden arms and legs, wears Bluebird pin

20"	$525.00	$700.00

EARLY COMPOSITION

Babies

Baby Bud, 1918+

All-composition, painted features, molded hair, open/closed mouth, jointed arms, legs molded to body. One finger goes into mouth.

6"	$50.00	$195.00
Black	$65.00	$225.00

Baby Dainty, 1912+

Name given to a variety of dolls, with composition heads, cloth bodies, some toddler types, some mama-types with crier

12 – 14"	$80.00	$245.00
16"	$100.00	$285.00
Vinyl		
10"	$10.00	$40.00

15" black composition Effanbee Grumpykins, painted side-glancing eyes, cloth body, crier, original outfit, some paint flaking, circa 1927+, $350.00. Courtesy Janet Hill.

Baby Effanbee, ca. 1925

Composition head, cloth body

12 – 13"	$45.00	$165.00

Baby Evelyn, ca. 1925

Composition head, cloth body

17"	$75.00	$275.00

Baby Grumpy, 1915+, also later variations

Composition character, heavily molded painted hair, frowning eyebrows, painted intaglio eyes, pin-jointed limbs, cork-stuffed cloth body, gauntlet arms, pouty mouth

Mold #172, 174, 176

11½"	$85.00	$325.00
14½"	$125.00	$425.00

Baby Grumpy Gladys, 1923, composition shoulder head, cloth body
Marked in oval, "Effanbee//Baby Grumpy// copr. 1923"

15"	$85.00	$350.00

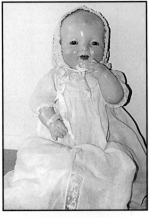

19" composition Effanbee Bubbles, tin sleep eyes, open mouth with finger held up to insert into mouth, cloth body, circa 1924+, $250.00. Private collection.

Grumpy Aunt Dinah, black, cloth body, striped stocking legs

14½"	$110.00	$425.00

Grumpykins, 1927, composition head, cloth body, composition arms, some with cloth legs, others with composition legs

12"	$75.00	$300.00
Black	$85.00	$375.00

Grumpykins, Pennsylvania Dutch Dolls, ca. 1936, dressed by Marie Pollack in Mennonite, River Brethren and Amish costumes

12"	$85.00	$300.00

Bubbles, ca. 1924+

Composition shoulder head, open/closed mouth, painted teeth, painted molded hair, sleep eyes, cloth body, bent-cloth legs, some with composition toddler legs, composition arms, finger of left hand fits into mouth, wore heart necklace

Various marks including: "Effanbee//Bubbles//Copr. 1924//Made in U.S.A."

16"	$100.00	$375.00
22"	$125.00	$525.00
25"	$200.00	$750.00

Lamkins, ca. 1930+

Composition molded head, sleep eyes, open mouth, cloth body, with crier, chubby composition legs, with feet turned in, fingers curled, molded gold ring on middle finger

16"	$150.00	$475.00

Pat-o-pat, 1925+

Composition head, painted eyes, cloth body with mechanism which, when pressed causes hands to clap

13"	$50.00	$150.00
15"	$80.00	$200.00

Characters, 1912+

Composition, heavily molded hair, painted eyes, pin-jointed cloth body, composition arms, cloth or composition legs

Some marked "Deco"

Cliquot Eskimo, ca. 1920

Painted eyes, molded hair, felt hands, mohair suit

18"	$150.00	$525.00

Coquette, Naughty Marietta, ca. 1915+

Composition girl, molded bow in hair, side-glancing eyes, cloth body

12"	$100.00	$400.00

Harmonica Joe, 1923

Cloth body, with rubber ball when squeezed, provides air to open mouth with harmonica

15"	$85.00	$350.00

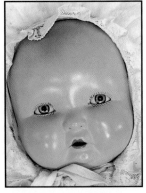

16" composition Effanbee Lamkins character baby with flange neck, sleep eyes, cloth body, molded ring on finger, realistically shaped feet, redressed, circa 1931, $350.00. Private collection.

Irish Mail Kid, 1915, or Dixie Flyer
Composition head, cloth body, arms sewn to steering handle of wooden wagon
    10" $125.00 $350.00

Johnny Tu-face, 1912
Composition head with face on front and back, painted features, open/closed crying mouth, closed smiling mouth, painted molded hair, cloth body, red striped legs, cloth feet, dressed in knitted romper and hat
    16" $150.00 $325.00

Pouting Bess, 1915
Composition head with heavily molded curls, painted eyes, closed mouth, cloth cork stuffed body, pin jointed
Mark: "166" on back of head
    15" $85.00 $350.00

Whistling Jim, 1916
Composition head, with heavily molded hair, painted intaglio eyes, perforated mouth, cork stuffed cloth body, black sewn-on cloth shoes, wears red striped shirt, blue overalls
Mark, label: "Effanbee//Whistling Jim//Trade Mark"
    15" $85.00 $350.00

20" composition Effanbee Mama Doll with sleep eyes, composition limbs, mohair wig, original clothes, cloth body, some cracks, flaking on body, circa 1930s, $95.00. Courtesy Dolores Jesurun.

LATE COMPOSITION

American Children, 1936 – 1939
All-composition, designed by Dewees Cochran, open mouth, separated fingers can wear gloves
Marks: heads may be unmarked, "Effanbee//Anne Shirley" on body
    Barbara Joan
    15" $350.00 $700.00
    Barbara Ann
    17" $1,400.00* MIB
    Barbara Lou
    21" $450.00 $900.00
Closed mouth, separated fingers, sleep or painted eyes
Marks: "Effanbee//American//Children" on head; "Effanbee//Anne Shirley" on body
    Boy
    17" $400.00 $1,600.00
Gloria Ann, paper purse tag reads *"Gloria Ann"*
18½" $400.00 $1,600.00
Peggy Lou, paper purse tag, holds gloves, reads, *"Peggy Lou"*
20½" $500.00 $1,800.00

20" composition Effanbee Sweetie Pie also called Baby Bright Eyes and Tommy Tucker, sleep eyes, cloth body, crier, original outfit lacks shoes, circa 1939 – 1940s, $275.00. Courtesy Nancy Rich.

8" composition Effanbee Butin-nose, dressed in original ethnic costume, possibly Turkey, circa 1936, $225.00. Courtesy Janet Hill.

Anne Shirley, 1936 – 1940
All-composition, more grown-up body style
Mark: "EFFANBEE//ANNE SHIRLEY"

14"	$75.00	$300.00
18"	$95.00	$325.00
21"	$125.00	$425.00
27"	$150.00	$550.00

Movie Anne Shirley, 1935 – 1940
1934 RKO movie character, Anne Shirley from *Anne of Green Gables* movie. All-composition, marked *"Patsy"* or other Effanbee doll, red braids, wearing Anne Shirley movie costume and gold paper hang tag stating *"I am Anne Shirley."* The Anne Shirley costume changes the identity of these dolls.

Mary Lee/Anne Shirley, open mouth, head marked *"©Mary Lee,"* on marked *"Patsy Joan"* body

16"	$250.00	$500.00

Patsyette/Anne Shirley, body marked *"Effanbee// Patsyette// Doll"*

9½"	$150.00	$325.00

Patricia/Anne Shirley, body marked *"Patricia"*

15"	$200.00	$550.00

Patricia-kin/Anne Shirley, head marked *"Patricia-kin,"* body marked *"Effanbee//Patsy Jr.,"* hang tag reads *"Anne Shirley"*

11½"	$175.00	$375.00

Brother or Sister, 1943
Composition head, hands, cloth body, legs, yarn hair, painted eyes.

Brother

6"	$60.00	$235.00

Sister,

12"	$45.00	$175.00

Butin-nose: See Patsy family, and vinyl.

Candy Kid, 1946+
All-composition, sleep eyes, toddler body, molded painted hair, closed mouth

13½"	$75.00	$300.00

Black

13½"	$150.00	$600.00

Charlie McCarthy, 1937
Composition head, hands, feet, painted features, mouth opens, cloth body, legs
Marked: "Edgar Bergen's Charlie McCarthy//An Effanbee Product"

15"	$125.00	$550.00
17 – 19"	$175.00	$775.00
19"	$2,000.00* in box, top hat, tails	

20" composition Effanbee Charlie McCarthy, all original with black tuxedo, Effanbee pinback button, painted brown eyes, hinged ventriloquist mouth, circa 1937, $525.00. Courtesy Odis Gregg.

* at auction

Happy Birthday Doll, ca. 1940
Music box in body, heart bracelet
17" $1,050.00*

Historical Dolls, 1939+
All-composition, jointed body, human hair wigs, painted eyes, made only three sets of 30 dolls depicting history of apparel, 1492 – 1939, very fancy original costumes, metal heart bracelet
Head marked "Effanbee//American//Children," on body, "Effanbee//Anne Shirley."
21" $650.00 $1,500.00+
Too few in database for reliable range.

Historical Replicas, 1939+
All-composition, jointed body, copies of sets above, but smaller, human hair wigs, painted eyes, original costumes
14" $250.00 $600.00

14" Effanbee composition historical replica Unity of a Nation 1896, original costume, metal heart bracelet, circa 1939, $550.00. Courtesy Bev Mitchell.

Howdy-Doody, 1947 – 1949
Composition head, brown sleep eyes, open/closed mouth, painted molded teeth, cloth body, plaid shirt, personalized neck scarf, *"HOWDY DOODY,"* jeans and boots, cowboy hat
Effanbee gold heart paper hang tag reads *"I AM AN//EFFANBEE //DURABLE DOLL//THE DOLL//SATIN-SMOOTH//SKIN."*
20" $65.00 $275.00
23" $75.00 $300.00
1950s, hard plastic head, cloth body
18" $50.00 $200.00

Honey, ca. 1947 – 1948
All-composition jointed body, human hair wig, sleep eyes, closed mouth
18" $80.00 $300.00
21" $100.00 $400.00
All hard plastic, ca. 1949 – 1955, see Vinyl and Hard Plastic later in this category.

Ice Queen, 1937+
Composition, open mouth, skater outfit
17" $200.00 $850.00

14" Effanbee composition historical replica Colonial Prosperity 1711, original costume, metal heart bracelet, circa 1939, $550.00. Courtesy Bev Mitchell.

Little Lady, 1939+
All-composition, wigged, sleep eyes, more grown-up body, separated fingers, gold paper hang tag. Many in formals, as brides, or fancy gowns with matching parasol. During war years yarn hair was used; may have gold hang tag with name, like Gaye or Carole.
15" $365.00* box
18" $95.00 $325.00
21" $125.00 $425.00
27" $150.00 $625.00

* at auction

11" composition Effanbee Patsy Baby with metal heart bracelet, green sleep eyes, all-composition, circa 1931, $275.00. Courtesy McMasters Doll Auctions.

11" composition Effanbee Patsy Baby contained in original labeled box, brown sleep eyes, closed mouth, tousle skin wig, circa 1931, $475.00. Courtesy McMasters Doll Auctions.

Lovums, ca. 1928

Composition swivel head, shoulder plate, and limbs, cloth body, sleep eyes, painted molded hair or wigged, can have bent baby legs or toddler legs

16"	$100.00	$400.00
20"	$125.00	$450.00

Mae Starr, ca. 1928

Talking doll, composition shoulder head, cloth body, open mouth, four teeth, with cylinder records
Marked: "Mae//Starr// Doll"

29"	$200.00	$750.00

MaMa Dolls, ca. 1921+

Composition shoulder head, painted or sleep eyes, molded hair or wigged, cloth body, swing legs, crier, with composition arms, and lower legs

18"	$75.00	$350.00
24"	$125.00	$400.00

Marionettes, 1937+

Puppets designed by Virginia Austin, composition, painted eyes
Clippo, clown

15"	$85.00	$300.00

Emily Ann

14"	$825.00	$300.00

Lucifer, black

15"	$525.00* mint-in-box	

Merrilee, ca. 1924

Mama doll, with composition shoulder head, sleep eyes, open mouth, cloth body, crier, swing legs
Marked on shoulder plate: "Effanbee// Merrilee// Copyr.// Doll" in oval

24"	$150.00	$550.00
27"	$175.00	$600.00

Portrait Dolls, ca. 1940

All-composition, Bo-Peep, Ballerina, Bride, Groom, Gibson Girl, Colonial Maid, etc.

12"	$65.00	$250.00

Rosemary, 1926

Marks: "EFFANBEE//ROSEMARY//WALK/ TALK//SLEEP" in oval "MADE IN US"

18"	$100.00	$350.00
24"	$150.00	$425.00

Suzanne, ca. 1940

All-composition, jointed body, sleep eyes, wigged, closed mouth, may have magnets in hands to hold accessories. More for additional accessories or wardrobe.

14"	$100.00	$325.00

Suzette, ca. 1939

All-composition, fully jointed, painted side-glancing eyes, closed mouth, wigged

11"	$75.00	$265.00

Sweetie Pie, 1939+

Also called Baby Bright Eyes, Tommy Tucker, Mickey, composition bent limbs, sleep eyes, caracul wig, cloth body, crier. Issued again in 1952+ in hard plastic, cloth body, and vinyl limbs, painted hair or synthetic wigs. Wore same pink rayon taffeta dress with black and white trim as Noma doll.

16"	$75.00	$300.00
20"	$85.00	$350.00
24"	$100.00	$400.00

W. C. Fields, 1929+

Composition shoulder head, painted features, hinged mouth, painted teeth. In 1980 made in vinyl. See Legend Series.

Marked: "W.C. Fields//An Effanbee Product"

17½"	$250.00	$950.00

Patsy Family, 1928+

Composition through 1947, later issued in vinyl and porcelain. Many had gold paper hang tag and metal bracelet that read *"Effanbee Durable Dolls."* More for black, special editions, costumes or with added accessories.

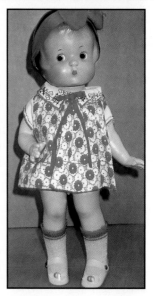

14" composition Effanbee Patsy marked "EFFAN-BEE//PATSY//PAT. PEND.//DOLL," all original tagged dress with box, circa 1928+, $600.00. Courtesy Irene Grundtvig.

Babies

Patsy Baby, 1931

Painted or sleep eyes, wigged or molded hair, composition baby body, advertised as Babykin, came also with cloth body, in pair, layettes, trunks

Marks: on head, "Effanbee//Patsy Baby"; on body, "Effanbee //Patsy// Baby"

10 – 11"	$125.00	$350.00
11"	$475.00* boxed	

Patsy Babyette, 1932

Sleep eyes

Marked on head "Effanbee"; on body, "Effanbee//Patsy //Babyette"

9"	$100.00	$325.00

Patsy Baby Tinyette, 1934

Painted eyes, bent-leg composition body

Marked on head, "Effanbee"; on body, "Effanbee//Baby/ /Tinyette"

6½"	$90.00	$300.00

Quints, 1935

Set of five Patsy Baby Tinyettes in original box, from FAO Schwarz with organdy christening gowns and milk glass bottles, all in excellent condition.

Set of five

6½"	$450.00	$1,750.00

* at auction

26" all-composition Effanbee Patricia Ruth, marked "Patsy Ruth," brown sleep eyes, closed rosebud mouth, human hair wig, dressed in original pink silk dress, leatherette T-strap shoes, circa 1934, $3,600.00. Courtesy McMasters Doll Auctions.

15" composition Effanbee Patsy, molded and painted eyes, hair, head turns and tilts, arms and legs jointed, dressed in pink checked cotton with embroidered organdy ruffle at shoulders, matching bonnet, circa 1928, $350.00. Courtesy Iva Mae Jones.

Children

Patsy, ca. 1924, cloth body, composition legs, open mouth, upper teeth, sleep eyes, painted or human hair wig, with composition legs to hips

Marked in half oval on back shoulder plate, "Effanbee//Patsy"

15"	$100.00	$300.00

Patsy, ca. 1926, mama doll, open mouth, upper teeth, sleep eyes, human hair wig, cloth body with crier and swing legs, composition arms and lower legs

Marked on shoulder plate in oval: "Effanbee//Patsy//Copr.// Doll"

22"	$100.00	$400.00
29"	$150.00	$550.00

Patsy, 1928, all-composition jointed body, painted or sleep eyes, molded headband on red molded bobbed hair, or wigged, bent right arm, with gold paper hang tag, metal heart bracelet

Marked on body: "Effanbee//Patsy//Pat. Pend.//Doll"

14"	$225.00	$550.00

Patsy, Oriental with black painted hair, painted eyes, in fancy silk pajamas and matching shoes

14"	$350.00	$750.00

Patsy, 1946, all-composition jointed body, bright facial coloring, painted or sleep eyes, wears pink or blue checked pinafore

14"	$200.00	$450.00

Patsy Alice, ca. 1933, advertised in Effanbee's *Patsytown News* for two years

24"	$400.00	$1,200.00

No doll with this name has been positively identified.

Patsy Ann, 1929, all-composition, closed mouth, sleep eyes, molded hair, or wigged

Marked on body: "Effanbee//'Patsy-Ann'//©//Pat. #1283558"

19"	$275.00	$600.00
19"	$875.00* boxed, tagged	

Patsy Ann, 1959, all-vinyl, full jointed, rooted saran hair, sleep eyes, freckles across nose

Head marked "Effanbee// Patsy Ann//©1959"; body marked "Effanbee//Official Girl Scout"

15"	$75.00	$250.00

Patsy Ann, 1959, limited edition, vinyl, sleep eyes, white organdy dress, with pink hair ribbon

Marked "Effanbee//Patsy Ann//©1959" on head; "Effanbee" on body

15"	$100.00	$285.00

* at auction

Patsyette, 1931, composition

9½" $150.00 $425.00

Black, Dutch, Hawaiian

9½" $200.00 $650.00+

Patsy Fluff, 1932

All-cloth, with painted features, pink checked rompers and bonnet

16" $500.00 $1,000.00

Too few examples in database for reliable range.

Patsy Joan, 1931, composition

16" $225.00 $550.00

Patsy Joan, 1946

Marked, *"Effandbee"* on body, with extra "d" added

17" $200.00 $500.00

17" composition Effanbee Patsy Joan with side-parted hair, original outfit, circa 1946, $400.00. Courtesy Jane Foster.

Patsy Jr., 1931

All-composition, advertised as Patsykins

Marks: "Effanbee//Patsy Jr.//Doll"

11½" $150.00 $400.00

Patsy Lou, 1930

All-composition, molded red hair, or wigged

Marks: "Effanbee//Patsy Lou" on body

22" $275.00 $625.00

Patsy Mae, 1934

Shoulder head, sleep eyes, cloth body, crier, swing legs

Marks: "Effanbee//Patsy Mae" on head; "Effanbee//Lovums//c//Pat. No. 1283558" on shoulder plate

29" $700.00 $1,400.00

Patsy Ruth, 1934

Shoulder head, sleep eyes, cloth body, crier, swing legs

Marks: "Effanbee//Patsy Ruth" on head; "Effanbee//Lovums//©//Pat. No. 1283558" on shoulder plate

26" $650.00 $1,300.00+

Patsy Tinyette Toddler, ca. 1935

Painted eyes

Marks: "Effanbee" on head; "Effanbee// Baby/ /Tinyette" on body

7¾" $100.00 $325.00+

Tinyette Toddler, tagged "Kit & Kat"

In Dutch costume $800.00 for pair

Wee Patsy, 1935

Head molded to body, molded painted shoes and socks, jointed arms and hips, advertised only as "Fairy Princess," pinback button

Marks on body: "Effanbee//Wee Patsy"

5¾" $150.00 $475.00

In trousseau box $250.00 $650.00+

Related items

Metal heart bracelet, reads *"Effanbee Durable Dolls,"* $25.00 (original bracelets can still be ordered from Shirley's Doll House)

Metal personalized name bracelet for Patsy family, $65.00

15" composition Effanbee Patricia as Martha Washington, green eyes, all original, $500.00. Private collection.

Patsy Ann, Her Happy Times, c. 1935, book by Mona Reed King, $75.00

Patsy For Keeps, c 1932, book by Ester Marian Ames, $125.00

Patricia Series, 1935, all sizes advertised in *Patsytown News*

All-composition slimmer bodies, sleep eyes, wigged, later WWII-era Patricias had yarn hair and cloth bodies

Patricia, wig, sleep eyes, marked, *"Effanbee Patricia"* body

15"	$225.00	$525.00

Patricia Ann, wig, marks unknown

19"	$375.00	$750.00

Too few in database for reliable range.

Patricia Joan, wig, marks unknown, slimmer legs

16"	$325.00	$650.00

Too few in database for reliable range.

Patricia-Kin, wig

Mark: "Patricia-Kin" head; "Effanbee //Patsy Jr." body

11½"	$275.00	$450.00

Patricia Lou, wig, marks unknown

22"	$300.00	$600.00

Too few in database for reliable range.

Patricia Ruth

Head marked: "Effanbee//Patsy Ruth," no marks on slimmer composition body

27"	$700.00	$1,350.00
27"	$3,600.00*	

Patsy Related dolls and variants

Betty Bee, tousel head, 1932

All-composition, short tousel wig, sleep eyes

Marked on body: "Effanbee//Patsy Lou"

22"	$250.00	$400.00

Betty Bounce, tousel head, 1932+

All-composition, sleep eyes, used Lovums head on body, *marked: "Effanbee//'Patsy Ann'//©//Pat. #1283558"*

19"	$200.00	$350.00

Betty Brite, 1932

All-composition, short tousel wig, sleep eyes, *some marked: "Effanbee//Betty Brite"* on body and others marked on head "© Mary-Lee"; on body, "Effanbee Patsy Joan"

Gold hang tag reads *"This is Betty Brite, The lovable Imp with tiltable head and movable limb, an Effanbee doll."*

16"	$175.00	$300.00

19" composition Effanbee Patsyette White Horse Inn Tyrolean girl and boy, wears a new metal heart bracelet, dressed in original costume, circa 1936, $425.00. Courtesy McMasters Doll Auctions.

4" composition Effanbee Suzanne in original pink and white dress, sleep eyes, human hair wig, metal heart bracelet, lovely coloring, circa 1940, $325.00. Courtesy Joanne Morgan.

18" composition Effanbee Little Lady purchased as all original, blue sleep eyes, rosebud mouth, brown human hair wig, fully jointed body, circa 1939 – 1942, $200.00. Courtesy Iva Mae Jones.

Butin-nose, ca. 1936+

All composition, molded painted hair, features, distinct feature is small nose, usually has regional or special costume; name "button" misspelled to "Butin"

8"	$85.00	$275.00

Cowboy outfit

8"	$95.00	$325.00

Dutch pair, with gold paper hang tags reading: *"Kit and Kat"*

8"	$250.00	$525.00

Oriental, with layette

8"	$250.00	$525.00

Mary Ann, 1932+

Composition, sleep eyes, wigged, open mouth

Marked: "Mary Ann" on head; "Effanbee//'Patsy Ann'//©//Pat. #1283558" on body

19"	$200.00	$350.00

Mary Lee, 1932

Composition, sleep eyes, wigged, open mouth

Marked: "©//Mary Lee" on head; "Effanbee//'Patsy Joan" on body

16½"	$225.00	$325.00

MiMi, 1927

All-composition, blue painted eyes, prototype of 1928 Patsy, but name change indicates a very short production run

Marked on body: "Effanbee//MiMi//Pat.Pend//Doll"

14"	$250.00	$600.00

Patsy/Patricia, 1940

Used a marked Patsy head on a marked Patricia body, all-composition, painted eyes, molded hair, may have magnets in hands to hold accessories

Marked on body: "Effanbee//'Patricia'"

15"	$300.00	$600.00

Skippy, 1929

Advertised as Patsy's boyfriend, composition head, painted eyes, painted molded blond hair, composition or cloth body, with composition molded shoes and legs

Marked on head: "Effanbee//Skippy//©//P. L. Crosby"; on body, "Effanbee//Patsy//Pat. Pend// Doll"

14"	$275.00	$600.00

White Horse Inn, with pin

$1,400.00*

RUBBER

Dy-Dee, 1934+

Hard rubber head, sleep eyes, jointed rubber bent-leg body, drink/wet mechanism, molded painted hair.

14" composition Effanbee black Skippy Soldier, painted brown eyes to side, closed mouth, molded and painted hair, cloth body, composition arms and legs, original army uniform, replaced tie and belt, circa 1940, $1,350.00. Courtesy McMasters Doll Auctions.

11" composition Effanbee Portrait in pink and black southern belle type costume, packaged in original picture frame display type box, others included Bo Peep, Bride and Groom, majorette, and more, all original, 1952, $250.00. Courtesy Jill Sanders.

Early dolls had molded ears, after 1940 had applied rubber ears, nostrils, and tear ducts. Later made in hard plastic and vinyl.

Marked: "Effanbee//Dy-Dee Baby" with four patent numbers

Dy-Dee Wee

9"	$75.00	$300.00

Dy-Dee-ette, Dy-Dee Ellen

11"	$50.00	$200.00

Dy-Dee Kin

13"	$65.00	$225.00

Dy-Dee Baby, Dy-Dee Jane

15"	$100.00	$400.00

Dy-Dee Lou, Dy-Dee Louise

20"	$125.00	$450.00

Dy-Dee in layette trunk, with accessories

15"	$150.00	$475.00

Dy-Dee Accessories

Dy-Dee marked bottle

	$7.50	$15.00

Dy-Dee pattern pajamas

	$8.00	$25.00

Dy-Dee book, *Dy-Dee Doll's Days*, c 1937, by Peggy Vandegriff, with black and white pictures

5½" x 6¾"	$25.00	$55.00

VINYL AND HARD PLASTIC

Alyssa, ca. 1960 – 1961

Vinyl head, hard plastic jointed body, walker, including elbows, rooted saran hair, sleep eyes

23"	$90.00	$225.00

Armstrong, Louis, 1984 – 1985, vinyl

15½"	$25.00	$85.00

Baby Lisa, 1980

Vinyl, designed by Astry Campbell, represents a 3-month-old baby, in wicker basket with accessories

11"	$50.00	$150.00

Baby Lisa Grows Up, 1983

Vinyl, toddler body, in trunk with wardrobe

	$50.00	$150.00

Button Nose, 1968 – 1971

Vinyl head, cloth body

18"	$9.00	$35.00

Champagne Lady, 1959

Vinyl head and arms, rooted hair, blue sleep eyes, lashes, hard plastic body, from Lawrence Welk's TV show, Miss Revlon-type

21"	$75.00	$275.00
23"	$85.00	$300.00

Churchill, Sir Winston, 1984, vinyl
$20.00 $75.00
Currier & Ives, vinyl and hard plastic
12" $12.00 $45.00
Disney dolls, 1977 – 1978
Snow White, Cinderella, Alice in Wonderland, and Sleeping Beauty
14" $45.00 $185.00
16½" $85.00 $325.00
Fluffy, 1954+, all-vinyl
10" $10.00 $35.00
Black $12.00 $45.00
Girl Scout $15.00 $75.00
Gumdrop, 1962+
Vinyl, jointed toddler, sleep eyes, rooted hair
16" $9.00 $35.00
Hagara, Jan
Designer, all-vinyl, jointed, rooted hair, painted eyes
Christina, 1984
15" $50.00 $200.00
Larry, 1985 $25.00 $95.00
Laurel, 1984
15" $40.00 $150.00
Lesley, 1985 $20.00 $85.00
Half Pint, 1966 – 1983
All-vinyl, rooted hair, sleep eyes, lashes
11" $8.00 $30.00
Happy Boy, 1960
Vinyl, molded hair, tooth, freckles, painted eyes
11" $10.00 $45.00
Hibel, Edna
Designer, 1984 only, all-vinyl
Flower Girl
11" $40.00 $165.00
Contessa $50.00 $185.00

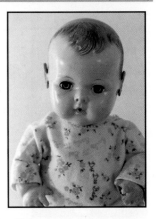

15" hard rubber Effanbee Dy-Dee Baby, with applied ears, sleep eyes, painted molded hair, open mouth for bottle, original name print pajamas, good condition, circa 1940s, $225.00. Private collection.

Honey, 1949 – 1958
Hard plastic (see also composition), saran wig, sleep eyes, closed mouth
Marked on head and back, "Effanbee," had gold paper hang tag that read: "I am// Honey//An//Effanbee//Sweet//Child"
Honey, ca. 1949 – 1955, all hard plastic, closed mouth, sleep eyes
14" $250.00 $500.00
17" $300.00 $600.00
Honey Walker, 1952+
All hard plastic with walking mechanism; Honey Walker Junior Miss, 1956 – 1957, hard plastic, extra joints at knees and ankles permit her to wear flat or high-heeled shoes. Add $50.00 for jointed knees, ankles.
14" $65.00 $350.00
19" $175.00 $425.00

16" hard plastic Effanbee Tintair — Effanbee's competitor to Ideal's Toni — used a Honey doll with white Dynel wig that could be colored, original dress, circa 1951, $300.00. Courtesy Micki Beston.

15½" composition Effanbee Anne Shirley, mohair wig, sleep eyes, lovely color, magnet hands can hold metal heart Effanbee Durable Dolls bracelet or metal accessories, circa 1940, $295.00. Courtesy Lee Ann Beaumont.

Humpty Dumpty, 1985 $25.00 $75.00

Katie, 1957, molded hair

8½"	$15.00	$50.00

Legend Series, vinyl

1980, W.C. Fields,	$70.00	$265.00
1981, John Wayne, cowboy	$50.00	$300.00
1982, John Wayne, cavalry	$50.00	$350.00
1982, Mae West	$25.00	$100.00
1983, Groucho Marx	$20.00	$95.00
1984, Judy Garland, Dorothy		
	$20.00	$90.00
1985, Lucille Ball	$17.50	$85.00
1986, Liberace	$17.50	$95.00
1987, James Cagney	$15.00	$70.00

Lil Sweetie, 1967

Nurser with no lashes or brow

16"	$25.00	$45.00

Limited Edition Club, vinyl

1975, Precious Baby	$115.00	$350.00
1976, Patsy Ann	$85.00	$300.00
1977, Dewees Cochran	$40.00	$135.00
1978, Crowning Glory	$35.00	$105.00
1979, Skippy	$75.00	$265.00
1980, Susan B. Anthony	$35.00	$100.00
1981, Girl with Watering Can		
	$25.00	$90.00
1982, Princess Diana	$25.00	$100.00
1983, Sherlock Holmes	$40.00	$150.00
1984, Bubbles	$25.00	$100.00
1985, Red Boy	$25.00	$85.00
1986, China head	$17.50	$60.00
1987 – 1988, Porcelain Grumpy (2,500)		
		$125.00
Vinyl Grumpy		$50.00

Martha and George Washington, 1976 – 1977

All-vinyl, fully jointed, rooted hair, blue eyes, molded lashes

11" pair	$40.00	$155.00

Mickey, 1956 – 1972

All-vinyl, fully jointed, some with molded hat, painted eyes

10"	$20.00	$75.00

Miss Chips, 1966 – 1981

All-vinyl, fully jointed, side-glancing sleep eyes, rooted hair

17"	$9.00	$35.00
Black 17"	$12.00	$45.00

Noma, The Electronic Doll, ca. 1950

Hard plastic, cloth body, vinyl limbs, battery-operated talking doll wore pink rayon taffeta dress with black and white check trim

27"	$125.00	$375.00

Polka Dottie, 1954
Vinyl head, with molded pigtails on fabric body, or with hard plastic body

21"	$60.00	$165.00

Latex body

11"	$30.00	$120.00

Presidents, 1984+
Lincoln

18"	$15.00	$75.00

Washington

16"	$15.00	$65.00

Teddy Roosevelt

17"	$17.50	$75.00

F. D. Roosevelt, 1985

	$15.00	$75.00

Prince Charming or Cinderella, Honey
All-hard plastic

16"	$165.00	$425.00

Pun'kin, 1966 – 1983
All-vinyl, fully jointed toddler, sleep eyes, rooted hair

11"	$15.00	$30.00

Rootie Kazootie, 1954
Vinyl head, cloth or hard plastic body, smaller size has latex body

11"	$30.00	$120.00
21"	$60.00	$165.00

Roosevelt, Eleanor, 1985, vinyl

14½"	$15.00	$70.00

Santa Claus, 1982+, designed by Faith Wick
"Old Fashioned Nast Santa," No. 7201, vinyl head, hands, stuffed cloth body, molded painted features, *marked "Effanbee//7201 c//Faith Wick"*

18"	$25.00	$75.00

Suzie Sunshine, 1961 – 1979
Designed by Eugenia Dukas, all-vinyl, fully jointed, rooted hair, sleep eyes, lashes, freckles on nose. Add $25.00 more for black.

18"	$15.00	$50.00

Sweetie Pie, 1952, hard plastic

27"	$65.00	$325.00

Tintair, hard plastic, hair color set, to compete with Ideal's Toni

15"	$250.00	$400.00

Twain, Mark, 1984, all-vinyl, molded features

16"	$20.00	$70.00

18" Effanbee hard plastic Honey in tagged Schiaparelli outfit, circa 1950s, $425.00. Courtesy McMasters Doll Auctions.

14" vinyl Effanbee Skippy limited edition, with original outfit, pin, circa 1979, $250.00. Courtesy Millie Carol.

Effanbee (cont.)

Wicket Witch, 1981 – 1982, designed by Faith Wick

No. 7110, vinyl head, blonde rooted hair, painted features, cloth stuffed body, dressed in black, with apple and basket

Head marked: "Effanbee//Faith Wick//7110 19cc81"

18"	$25.00	$75.00

Ethnic

11½" composition Skookum Squaw with papoose, wooden feet, blanket, circa 1930s – 1940s, $125.00. Private collection.

This category describes dolls costumed in regional dress to show different nationalities, facial characteristics or cultural background. Examples are dolls in regional costumes that are commonly sold as souvenirs to tourists. A well-made beautiful doll with accessories or wardrobe may be more.

Cloth

8"	$50.00	$175.00
13"	$65.00	$200.00

Native American Indian

8"	$65.00	$225.00
13"	$75.00	$300.00
23"	$85.00	$350.00

Skookum, 1915+ designed by Mary McAboy, painted features, with side-glancing eyes, mohair wigs, cloth figure wrapped in Indian blanket, with folds representing arms, wooden feet, later plastic, label on bottom of foot. Box marked Skookum *"Bully Good."*

First price indicates incomplete, but still very good; second price is excellent to mint with box.

6"	$25.00	$65.00
10 – 12"	$100.00	$125.00
16 – 18"	$150.00	$250.00
33"	$950.00	$1,500.00+

Hard Plastic, unmarked or unknown maker

7"	$5.00	$15.00
12"	$7.50	$30.00

Baitz, Austria, 1970s, painted hard plastic, painted side-glancing eyes, open "o" mouth, excellent quality, tagged and dressed in regional dress

8"	$40.00	$75.00

Freundlich

Ralph A. Freundlich, 1923+, New York City. Formerly Jeanette Doll Co, then Ralph Freundlich, Inc. Made composition dolls, some with molded caps in military uniform.

Baby Sandy, ca. 1939 – 1942, all-composition, jointed toddler body, molded hair, painted or sleep eyes, smiling mouth

8"	$75.00	$300.00
12"	$100.00	$400.00
15"	$125.00	$500.00

Dummy Dan, ventriloquist doll, Charlie McCarthy look-alike

15"	$40.00	$150.00
21"	$90.00	$350.00

General Douglas MacArthur, ca. 1942, all-composition, jointed body, bent arm salutes, painted features, molded hat, jointed, in khaki uniform, with paper tag

18"	$85.00	$350.00

18" composition Freundlich General MacArthur, painted eyes, closed mouth, painted molded hat with military insignia, jointed composition body, right arm bent to salute, original military uniform, circa 1940s, $155.00. Courtesy McMasters Doll Auctions.

Military dolls, ca. 1942+, all-composition, molded hats, painted features, original clothes, with paper tag

Soldier, Sailor, WAAC, or WAVE

15"	$65.00	$275.00

Orphan Annie and her dog, Sandy

12"	$85.00	$325.00

Pinocchio, composition and cloth, with molded hair, painted features, brightly colored cheeks, large eyes, open/closed mouth

Tagged: "Original as portrayed by C. Collodi"

16"	$125.00	$500.00

Red Riding Hood, Wolf, Grandma, 1930s, composition, set of three, in schoolhouse box, original clothes

9½"	$250.00	$750.00

Trixie, 1930s, all-composition, painted features, unmarked body, in original box

11½"	$75.00	$150.00

Gabriel

THE LONE RANGER SERIES

Vinyl action figures with horses, separate accessory sets available.

Dan Reed on Banjo, blond hair, figure on palomino horse

9"	$15.00	$50.00

Butch Cavendish on Smoke, black hair, mustache, on black horse

9"	$20.00	$80.00

Lone Ranger on Silver, masked figure on white horse

9"	$25.00	$100.00

Little Bear, Indian boy

6"	$25.00	$100.00

Red Sleeves, vinyl Indian figure, black hair, wears shirt with red sleeves

9"	$25.00	$100.00

Tonto on Scout, Indian on brown and white horse

9"	$20.00	$80.00

Gene

1996. Designed by Mel Odom marketed through Ashton Drake.

Premiere	$69.95	$600.00
Red Venus	$69.95	$125.00
Monaco	$69.95	$100.00
Sparkling Seduction '97		
	$79.95	$90.00
Blue Goddess	$69.95	$90.00
Pin Up	$69.95	$90.00
Gene Specials		
FAO Schwarz On the Avenue		$175.00+
Hollywood Convention package		$500.00+
Middendorf "Downtown Excursion"		
		$225.00
NALED Midnight Romance		$155.00+

17" vinyl Ashton Drake Gene, designed by Mel Odom, as White Hyacinth, white street coat and hat ensemble, circa 1998, $150.00. Courtesy Mia Tognacci.

Gibbs, Ruth

Ca. 1940s+, Flemington, NJ. Made dolls with china and porcelain heads and limbs, pink cloth bodies. Dolls designed by Herbert Johnson.

> *Marks: RG on back shoulder blade Box labeled: "GODEY LITTLE LADY DOLLS," Dolls designed by Herbert Johnson.*

Godey's Lady Book Dolls
　　Pink-tint shoulder head, cloth body
　　Boxed

7"	$75.00	$210.00

Caracul wig, original outfit

9½"	$200.00	$295.00

Hard plastic, mint-in-box, with identification

11"	$200.00

9½" glazed porcelain Ruth Gibbs Godey Little Lady with caracul wig, painted features, original costume, circa late 1940s – 1950s, $295.00. Courtesy Chantal Jeschien.

Gilbert Toys

Honey West, 1965, vinyl, vinyl arms, hard plastic torso and legs, rooted blonde hair, painted eyes, painted beauty spot near mouth, head marked *"K73"* with leopard

11½"	$60.00	$125.00

The Man From U.N.C.L.E. characters from TV show of the 1960s. Other outfits available.

Ilya Kuryakin (David McCallum)

12¼"	$25.00	$100.00

12½" vinyl Gilbert The Man from U.N.C.L.E. action figures, Ilya Kuryakin, and Napoleon Solo, painted hair and features; 11¾" Honey West, rooted blonde hair, painted eyes, circa 1965, $100.00 each. Courtesy McMasters Doll Auctions.

Napoleon Solo (Robert Vaughn)
| 12¼" | $25.00 | $100.00 |

James Bond, Secret Agent 007, character from James Bond movies
| 12¼" | $20.00 | $75.00 |
| 12¼" | $430.00* | |

Girl Scout Dolls

1920+, listed chronologically.

First price for played-with doll missing accessories; second price is for mint doll.

1920s Girl Scout doll in Camp Uniform

Pictured in Girls Scout 1920 handbook, all-cloth, mask face, painted features, wigged, gray green uniform

| 13" | $250.00 | $600.00+ |

Too few in database for reliable range.

Grace Corry, 1929

Composition shoulder head, cloth body with crier, molded hair, painted features, original uniform

Mark on shoulder plate: "by Grace Corry"; body stamped "Madame Hendren Doll//Made in USA"

| 13" | $350.00 | $700.00+ |

Too few in database for reliable range.

Averill Mfg. Co, ca. 1936

Believed to be designed by Maud Tousey Fangel, all-cloth, printed and painted features

| 16" | $100.00 | $400.00+ |

Too few in database for reliable range.

13" vinyl Avon Girl Scout, designed by Kathy Jeffers, circa 1995, $20.00. Courtesy Fran Fabian.

Georgene Novelties, ca. 1940

All-cloth, flat-faced painted features, yellow yarn curls, wears original silver green uniform, with red triangle tie

Hang tag reads: "Genuine Georgene Doll//A product of Georgene Novelties, Inc., NY//Made in U.S.A."

| 15" | $100.00 | $400.00 |

Georgene Novelties, ca. 1949 – 1954

All-cloth, mask face, painted features and string hair

| 13½" | $75.00 | $250.00 |

1954 – 1958
Same as previous listing, but now has a plastic mask face
13½"	$35.00	$100.00

Terri Lee, 1949 – 1958
Hard plastic, Brownie and Intermediate Scout had felt hats and oilcloth saddle shoes
16"	$125.00	$450.00

Tiny Terri Lee, 1956 – 1958
Hard plastic, walker, sleep eyes, wig, plastic shoes
10"	$65.00	$225.00

Ginger, ca. 1956 – 1958, made by Cosmopolitan for Terri Lee, hard plastic, straight-leg walker, synthetic wig
7½" – 8"	$100.00	$225.00
7½"	$385.00*	

Vogue, 1956 – 1957+
Ginny, hard plastic, straight-legged walker with sleep eyes and painted eyelashes; in 1957 had bending leg and felt hat
8"	$225.00	$325.00

Girl Scout uniform, boxed to fit Ginny
$105.00*	

Uneeda, 1959 – 1961
Ginny look-alike, vinyl head, hard plastic body, straight-leg walker, Dynel wig, *marked "U" on head*
8"	$50.00	$150.00

Effanbee, Patsy Ann, 1959+
All-vinyl jointed body, saran hair, with sleep eyes, freckles on nose, Brownie or Girl Scout
15"	$95.00	$350.00

Effanbee Suzette, ca. 1960
Jointed vinyl body, sleep eyes, saran hair, thin body, long legs
15"	$95.00	$350.00

Effanbee Fluffy, 1964 – 1972
Vinyl dolls, sleep eyes, curly rooted hair, Brownie had blonde wig; Junior was brunette. Box had clear acetate lid, printed with Girl Scout trademark, and catalog number.
8"	$65.00	$175.00

Effanbee Fluffy Cadette, 1965
11"	$75.00	$300.00

Effanbee Pun'kin Jr., 1974 – 1979+
All-vinyl, sleep eyes, long straight rooted hair Brownie and Junior uniforms
11½"	$25.00	$75.00

Hallmark, 1979
All cloth, Juliette Low, from 1916 handbook, wearing printed 1923 uniform
6½"	$25.00	$65.00

Jesco, ca. 1985, Katie
All-vinyl, sleep eyes, long straight rooted hair, look-alike Girl Scout, dressed as Brownie, and Junior
9"	$25.00	$75.00

---

* at auction

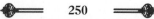

Madame Alexander, 1992

Vinyl, unofficial Girl Scout, sleep eyes

8"	$15.00	$60.00

Hard Plastic

Numerous companies made hard plastic dolls, ca. 1948 through the 1950s; dolls have all hard plastic jointed bodies, sleep eyes, lashes, synthetic wig, open or closed mouths. Marks: none, letters, little known, or other unidentified companies.

14"	$65.00	$250.00
18"	$75.00	$300.00
24"	$85.00	$325.00

DUCHESS DOLL CORPORATION

Ca. 1948 – 1950s. Made small hard plastic adult dolls, mohair wigs, painted or sleep eyes, jointed arms, stiff or jointed neck, painted molded shoes, about 7 – 7½" tall, costumes stapled on to body. Elaborate costumed, exceptional dolls may be more.

7"	$5.00	$15.00

13" hard plastic Furga Tilly in marked box, all original, excellent condition, circa 1950s – 1960s, $85.00. Courtesy Carol Bennett.

FURGA, ITALY

Child with sleep eyes, original simple outfit, more for elaborate dress

14"	$85.00	$175.00

IMPERIAL CROWN TOY COL (IMPCO)

Ca. 1950s, made hard plastc or vinyl dolls, rooted hair, synthetic wigs

Vinyl

16"	$35.00	$85.00

Hard Plastic

20"	$75.00	$200.00

KENDALL COMPANY

Miss Curity, ca. 1953

Hard plastic, jointed only at shoulders, blonde wigs, blue sleep eyes, molded-on shoes, painted stockings, uniform sheet vinyl, *"Miss Curity"* marked in blue on hat

7½"	$20.00	$75.00

RODDY OF ENGLAND, CA. 1950 – 1960s

Made by D.G. Todd & Co. Ltd., Southport, England. Hard plastic walker, sleep or set eyes. First price indicates played with doll; second price for mint-in-box.

Walking Princess, tagged

9"	$5.00	$20.00

ROSS PRODUCTS

Tina Cassini, designed by Oleg Cassini. Hard plastic, marked on back torso, *"TINA CASSINI"*; clothes tagged *"Made in British Crown Colony of Hong Kong."*

12"	$65.00	$250.00

7½" hard plastic Carlson Paul Revere with hang tag, sleep eyes, mohair wig, felt costume, circa 1950s, $25.00. Courtesy Joyce Peters.

1950s+. Made action figures and horses; many figures from Warner Brothers television productions.

TELEVISION OR MOVIE CHARACTERS, 8"

Annie Oakley, 1953 – 1956, by Gail Davis in *Annie Oakley*
    8" $200.00* with horse

Bret Maverick, ca. 1958, by James Garner in *Maverick*
    8" $510.00* with horse

Captain Chris Colt, 1957 – 1960, by Wade Preston in *Colt 45*
    8" $135.00 $250.00

Cheyenne Bodie, 1955 – 1963, by Clint Walker in *Cheyenne*
    8" $315.00* with horse

Clint Bonner, 1957 – 1959, by John Payne in *The Restless Gun*
    8" $135.00 $250.00

Colonel Ronald MacKenzie, ca. 1950s, by Richard Carlson, in *MacKenzies' Raiders*
    8" $810.00* with horse

Dale Evans, ca. 1958, #802, with horse, Buttermilk in *The Roy Rogers Show*
    8" $375.00* MIB

Gil Favor, ca. 1950s, in *Rawhide*
    8" $685.00* with horse

Jim Hardie, 1957 – 1963, by Dale Robertson in *Tales of Wells Fargo*
    8" $175.00

Josh Randall, ca. 1950s, by Steve McQueen in *Wanted Dead or Alive*
    8" $615.00* with horse

Major Seth Adams, 1957 – 1961, #824, by Ward Bond in *Wagon Train*
    8" $200.00* with horse

Paladin, 1957 – 1963, by Richard Boone in *Have Gun, Will Travel*
    8" $610.00* with horse

Roy Rogers, ca. 1955, and Trigger in *The Roy Rogers Show*
    8" $485.00* MIB with Trigger

Sgt. William Preston, ca. 1958, #804, by Richard Simmons in *Sgt. Preston of the Yukon*
    8" $700.00* with horse

Wyatt Earp, 1955 – 1961 by Hugh O'Brien in *Life and Legend of Wyatt Earp*
    8" $190.00* with horse

Other 8" Figures
    8" $380.00*

Brave Eagle, #812, and his horse, White Cloud
Buffalo Bill, #819, Pony Express Rider
Chief Thunderbird, and horse, Northwind
Cochise, #815, with pinto horse from *Broken Arrow*
Jim Bowie, #817, with horse, Blaze
General George Custer, #814, and horse, Bugler
General George Washington, #815 and horse, Ajax
General Robert E. Lee, #808, and horse, Traveler
Lone Ranger, #801, and horse, Silver
Tonto, #805, and horse, Scout
All others   8" $125.00 $225.00

* at auction

Baseball 8" Figures

Dick Groat with bat & hat	$1,000.00*
Duke Snider	$255.00*
Ernie Banks, #920	$430.00*
Hank Aaron, #912	$245.00*
Harvey Keunn	$325.00*
Rocky Colavita, no bat	$335.00*
Willie Mays	$245.00*
Yogi Berra, boxed	$280.00*

Hasbro

Ca. 1960s+. Hassenfeld Bros. Toy manufacturer, also makes plastic or plastic and vinyl dolls and action figures.

First price for doll in played with condition, or missing some accessories; second price for mint doll.

Adam, 1971, Boy for "World of Love" Series, all-vinyl, molded painted brown hair, painted blue eyes, red knit shirt, blue denim jeans
Mark: "Hasbro//U.S. Pat Pend//Made in//Hong Kong"

15½" vinyl Hasbro Little Miss No Name in original window-pane box, "The Doll with the Tear....I need someone to love me. I want to learn to play, please take me home with you and brush my tear away," circa 1965, $300.00. Courtesy Leslie Tannenbaum.

9"	$5.00	$18.00

Aimee, 1972, rooted hair, amber sleep eyes, jointed vinyl body, long dress, sandals, earrings

11½"	$25.00	$85.00

Dolly Darling, 1965

4½"	$10.00	$60.00

Flying Nun, 1965, plastic and vinyl

5"	$9.00	$35.00

G.I. Joe: See G.I. Joe section, following this category.

Jem: See Jem section, following this category.

Leggie, 1972

10"	$7.50	$30.00
Black	$10.00	$40.00

Little Miss No Name, 1965

15"	$35.00	$95.00

Mamas and Papas, 1967

	$12.00	$45.00

Show Biz Babies, 1967

	$12.00	$50.00
Mama Cass	$15.00	$50.00

Monkees, set of four

4"	$28.00	$110.00

Storybook, 1967, 3"

Goldilocks	$12.50	$50.00
Prince Charming	$15.00	$60.00
Rumpelstiltskin	$15.00	$55.00
Sleeping Beauty	$12.50	$50.00

*11½" hard plastic Hasbro G.I.
Joe mint in box with dog tags,
brochure, circa 1964 – 1979,
$300.00. Courtesy Jeff Jones.*

Snow White and Dwarfs

	$20.00	$75.00

Sweet Cookie, 1972, vinyl, with cooking accessories

18"	$35.00	$125.00

That Kid, 1967

21"	$22.50	$95.00

World of Love Dolls, 1971

White	9"	$5.00	$18.00
Black	9"	$5.00	$20.00

G.I. JOE

G.I. Joe Action Figures, 1964

Hard plastic head with facial scar, painted hair and no beard. First price indicates doll lacking accessories or nude; second price indicates mint doll in package. Add more for pristine package.

G.I. Joe Action Soldier, flocked hair, Army fatigues, brown jump boots, green plastic cap, training manual, metal dog tag, two sheets of stickers

11½"	$120.00	$450.00

Painted hair, red

	$140.00	$300.00

Black, painted hair

	$325.00	$1,300.00

Green Beret

Teal green fatigue jacket, four pockets, pants, Green Beret cap with red unit flashing, M-16 rifle, 45 automatic pistol with holster, tall brown boots, four grenades, camouflage scarf and field communication set

11"	$275.00	$1,500.00

G.I. Joe Action Marine

Camouflage shirt, pants, brown boots, green plastic cap, metal dog tag, insignia stickers, and training manual

11"	$80.00	$300.00

G.I. Joe Action Sailor

Blue chambray work shirt, blue denim work pants, black boots, white plastic sailor cap, dog tag, rank insignia stickers

	$75.00	$250.00

G.I. Joe Action Pilot

Orange flight suit, black boots, dog tag, stickers, blue cap, training manual

	$125.00	$300.00
Dolls only	$50.00	$95.00

G.I. Joe Action Soldier of the World, 1966
Figures in this set may have any hair and eye color combination, no scar on face, hard plastic heads

Australian Jungle Fighter

	$255.00	$1,050.00

British Commando, boxed

	$300.00	$1,150.00

French Resistance Fighter

	$150.00	$1,200.00

German Storm Trooper

	$400.00	$1,200.00

Japanese Imperial Soldier

	$175.00	$1,400.00

Russian Infantryman

Boxed	$350.00	$1,100.00
Doll, no box	$75.00	$250.00

Talking G.I. Joe, 1967 – 1969
Talking mechanism added, excluding Black figure, semi-hard vinyl head
Marks: "G.I. Joe®//Copyright 1964//By Hasbro®//Pat. No. 3,277,602//Made in U.S.A.

Talking G.I. Joe Action Soldier
Green fatigues, dog tag, brown boots, insignia, stripes, green plastic fatigue cap, comic book, insert with examples of figures speech

	$150.00	$300.00

Talking G.I. Joe Action Sailor
Denim pants, chambray sailor shirt, dog tag, black boots, white sailor cap, insignia stickers, Navy training manual, illustrated talking comic book, insert examples of figures speech

	$200.00	$1,000.00

Talking G.I. Joe Action Marine
Camouflage fatigues, metal dog tag, Marine training manual, insignia sheets, brown boots, green plastic cap, comic, and insert

	$60.00	$800.00

Talking G.I. Joe Action Pilot
Blue flight suit, black boots, dog tag, Air Force insignia, blue cap, training manual, comic book, insert

	$150.00	$1,000.00

G.I. Joe Action Nurse, 1967
Vinyl head, blonde rooted hair, jointed hard plastic body, nurse's uniform, cap, red cross armband, white shoes, medical bag, stethoscope, plasma bottle, two crutches, bandages, splints
Marks: "Patent Pending®//1967 Hasbro//Made in Hong Kong"

Boxed	$1,200.00	$1,850.00
Dressed	$200.00	$1,000.00
Nude	$40.00	$150.00

G.I. Joe, Man of Action, 1970 – 1975
Flocked hair, scar on face, dressed in fatigues with Adventure Team emblem on shirt, plastic cap
Marks: "G.I. Joe®//Copyright 1964//By Hasbro®// Pat. No. 3, 277, 602//Made in U.S. A."

	$15.00	$75.00
Talking	$45.00	$175.00

G.I. Joe, Adventure Team
Marks: "©1975 Hasbro ®//Pat. Pend. Pawt. R.I." Flocked hair and beard, six team members:

Air Adventurer, orange flight suit
$75.00 $285.00

Astronaut, talking, white flight suit, molded scar, dog tag pull string
$115.00 $450.00

Land Adventurer, black, tan fatigues, beard, flocked hair, scar
$90.00 $350.00

Land Adventurer, talking, camouflage fatigues
$115.00 $450.00

Sea Adventurer, light blue shirt, navy pants
$75.00 $300.00

Talking Adventure Team Commander, flocked hair, beard, green jacket, and pants
$115.00 $450.00

G.I. Joe Land Adventurer, flocked hair, beard, camouflage shirt, green pants
$70.00 150.00

G. I. Joe Negro Adventurer, flocked hair
$175.00 $750.00

G. I. Joe, "Mike Powers, Atomic Man"
$25.00 $55.00

G.I. Joe Eagle Eye Man of Action
$40.00 $125.00

G.I. Joe Secret Agent, unusual face, mustache
$115.00 $450.00

Sea Adventurer w/King Fu Grip
$80.00 $145.00

Bulletman, muscle body, silver arms, hands, helmet, red boots
$55.00 $125.00

Others

G.I. Joe Air Force Academy, Annapolis, or West Point Cadet
11" $125.00 $400.00

G.I. Joe Frogman, Underwater Demolition Set
11" $300.00*

G.I. Joe Secret Service Agent, limited edition of 200
11" $275.00*

Accessory Sets, mint, no doll included

Adventures of G.I. Joe

Adventure of the Perilous Rescue	$250.00
Eight Ropes of Danger Adventure	$200.00
Fantastic Free Fall Adventure	$275.00
Hidden Missile Discovery Adventure	$150.00
Mouth of Doom Adventure	$150.00
Adventure of the Shark's Surprise	$200.00
Adventure of the Perilous Rescue	$250.00

Accessory Packs or Boxed Uniforms and accessories
Air Force, Annapolis, West Point Cadet $200.00

Action Sailor	$350.00
Astronaut	$250.00
Crash Crew Fire Fighter	$275.00
Deep Freeze with Sled	$250.00
Deep Sea Diver	$250.00
Frogman Demolition Set	$375.00
Fighter Pilot, no package	$285.00*
Green Beret	$450.00
Landing Signal Officer	$250.00
Marine Jungle Fighter	$850.00
Marine Mine Detector	$275.00
Military Police	$325.00
Pilot Scramble Set	$275.00
Rescue Diver	$350.00
Secret Agent	$150.00
Shore Patrol	$300.00
Ski Patrol	$350.00

G.I. Joe Vehicles and Other Accessories, mint in package

Amphibious Duck, green plastic, Irwin	$600.00
Armored Car, green plastic, one figure	$150.00
Crash Crew Fire Truck, blue	$1,400.00
Desert Patrol Attack Jeep, tan, one figure	$1,400.00
Footlocker, with accessories	$400.00+
Iron Knight Tank, green plastic	$1,400.00
Jet Aeroplane, dark blue plastic	$550.00
Jet Helicopter, green, yellow blades	$350.00
Motorcycle and Side Car, by Irwin	$225.00
Personnel Carrier and Mine Sweeper	$700.00
Sea Sled and Frogman	$400.00
Space Capsule and Suit, gray plastic	$425.00
Staff Car, four figures, green plastic, Irwin	$900.00

JEM, 1986 – 1987

Jem dolls were patterned after characters in the animated television Jem series, ca. 1985 – 1988, and include a line of 27 dolls. All-vinyl fashion type with realistically proportioned body, jointed elbows, wrists, and knees, swivel waist, rooted hair, painted eyes, open or closed mouth and hole in bottom of each foot.

> Marks:
> On head:
> "HASBRO, INC."
> On back:
> "COPYRIGHT 1985
> (or 1986 or 1987)
> HASBRO, INC."
> followed by either
> "CHINA" or
> "MADE IN HONG
> KONG."
> Not all are marked on
> head.

All boxes say *"Jem"* and *"Truly Outrageous!"* Most came with cassette tape of music from Jem cartoon, plastic doll stand, poster, and hair pick. All 12½" tall, except Starlight Girls, 11".

First price is for excellent to near mint doll wearing complete original outfit; anything less is of lower value. Second price is for never removed from box doll (NRFB) which includes an excellent quality box. For an "Audition Contest" labeled box, add $10.00. A rule of thumb to calculate loose dolls which have been dressed in another outfit is the price of the mint/complete outfit plus the price of mint loose nude doll.

Left: 12" vinyl Hasbro Shana, On Stage Fashion Music is Magic, $25.00 mint/complete fashion; right: On Stage Fashion Love's Not Easy, mint/complete fashion $65.00; nude, $40.00. circa 1985 – 1986. *Courtesy Linda Holton.*

Left: 12" vinyl Hasbro Roxy wearing Smashin' Fashions Just Misbehavin, mint/complete fashion, $55.00; and right: There Ain't Nobody Better, mint/complete $40.00; doll nude $20.00; 1985 – 1986. *Courtesy Linda Holton.*

Jem and Rio	Stock No.	Mint	NRFB
Jem/Jerrica 1st issue	4000	$30.00	$40.00
Jem/Jerrica, star earrings	4000	$35.00	$45.00
Glitter 'n Gold Jem	4001	$60.00	$75.00
Rock 'n Curl Jem	4002	$20.00	$30.00
Flash 'n Sizzle Jem	4003	$30.00	$40.00
Rio, 1st issue	4015	$25.00	$35.00
Glitter 'n Gold Rio	4016	$25.00	$35.00
Glitter 'n Gold Rio, pale vinyl	4016	$125.00	$150.00
Holograms			
Synergy	4020	$45.00	$60.00
Aja, 1st issue	4201/4005	$45.00	$60.00
Aja, 2nd issue	4201/4005	$90.00	$125.00
Kimber, 1st issue	4202/4005	$40.00	$50.00
Kimber, 2nd issue	4202/4005	$75.00	$90.00
Shana, 1st issue	4203/4005	$125.00	$175.00
Shana, 2nd issue	4203/4005	$225.00	$275.00
Danse	4208	$45.00	$60.00
Video	4209	$25.00	$35.00
Raya	4210	$150.00	$175.00
Starlight Girls, 11", no wrist or elbow joints			
Ashley	4211/4025	$40.00	$55.00
Krissie	4212/4025	$35.00	$65.00
Banee	4213/4025	$25.00	$40.00
Misfits			
Pizzazz, 1st issue	4204/4010	$50.00	$65.00
Pizzazz, 2nd issue	4204/4010	$55.00	$75.00
Stormer, 1st issue	4205/4010	$50.00	$65.00
Stormer, 2nd issue	4205/4010	$60.00	$75.00
Roxy, 1st issue	4206/4010	$50.00	$65.00
Roxy, 2nd issue	4206/4010	$50.00	$65.00
Clash	4207/4010	$25.00	$35.00
Jetta	4214	$40.00	$55.00

Accesories

Glitter 'n Gold Roadster	$150.00	$250.00
Rock 'n Roadster	$65.00	$90.00
KJEM Guitar	$25.00	$40.00
New Wave Waterbed	$35.00	$50.00
Backstager	$25.00	$35.00
Star Stage	$30.00	$45.00
MTV jacket (promo)	$90.00	$125.00

Jem Fashions

Prices reflect NRFB (never removed from box or card), with excellent packaging. Damaged boxes or mint and complete, no packaging prices are approximately 25 percent less.

On Stage Fashions, 1st year, "artwork" on card

Award Night	4216/4040	$30.00
Music is Magic	4217/4040	$30.00
Dancin' the Night Away	4218/4040	$25.00
Permanent Wave	4219/4040	$25.00
Only the Beginning	4220/4040	$20.00
Command Performance	4221/4040	$35.00
Twilight in Paris	4222/4040	$25.00
Encore	4223/4040	$35.00

On Stage Fashions, 2nd year, "photo" on card

Award Night	4216/4040	$35.00
Music is Magic	4217/4040	$35.00
Permanent Wave	4219/4040	$30.00
Encore	4223/4040	$30.00
Friend or Stranger	4224/4040	$50.00
Come On In	4225/4040	$55.00
There's Melody Playing	4226/4040	$150.00
How You Play Game	4227/4040	$30.00
Love's Not Easy	4228/4040	$100.00
Set Your Sails	4229/4040	$35.00

Flip Side Fashions, 1st year "artwork" on box

Up & Rockin'	4232/4045	$20.00
Rock Country	4233/4045	$35.00
Gettin' Down to Business	4234/4045	$40.00
Let's Rock this Town	4235/4045	$30.00
Music in the Air	4236/4045	$35.00
Like a Dream	4237/4045	$30.00
Sophisticated Lady	4238/4045	$30.00
City Lights	3129/4045	$20.00

Flip Side Fashions, 2nd year "photo" on box

Gettin' Down to Business	4234/4045	$45.00
Let's Rock This Town	4235/4045	$35.00
Music in the Air	4236/4045	$40.00
Sophisticated Lady	4238/4045	$35.00
Putting it All Together	4240/4045	$75.00
Running Like the Wind	4241/4045	$125.00
We Can Change It	4242/4045	$125.00

Broadway Magic	4243/4045	$90.00
She Makes an Impression	4244/4045	$90.00
Lightnin' Strikes	4245/4045	$45.00

Smashin' Fashions, 1st year "artwork" on card (includes Rio fashions)

Rappin'	4248/4051	$40.00
On the Road with Jem	4249/4051	$25.00
Truly Outrageous	4250/4051	$125.00
Makin' Mischief	4251/4050	$30.00
Let the Music Play	4252/4050	$30.00
Outta My Way	4253/4050	$15.00
Just Misbehavin'	4254/4050	$65.00
Winning is Everything	4255/4050	$15.00

Smashin' Fashions, 2nd year, "photo" on card (Misfits fashions only)

Let the Music Play	4252/4050	$35.00
Just Misbehavin'	4254/4050	$75.00
Gimme, Gimme, Gimme	4256/4050	$25.00
You Can't Catch Me	4257/4050	$35.00
We're Off & Running	4258/4050	$35.00
You Gotta' Be Fast	4259/4050	$45.00
There Ain't Nobody Better	4260/4050	$50.00
Designing Woman	4261/4050	$35.00

Rio Fashion, 2nd year only, "photo" on card

Rappin'	4248/4051	$45.00
On the Road with Jem	4249/4051	$30.00
Truly Outrageous	4250/4051	$150.00
Time is Running Out	4271/4051	$25.00
Share a Little Bit	4272/4051	$125.00
Congratulations	4273/4051	$30.00
Universal Appeal	4274/4051	$25.00
It Takes a Lot	4275/4051	$25.00
It all Depends on Mood	4276/4051	$15.00

Glitter 'n Gold Fashions, 2nd year only, "photo" on boxes

Fire and Ice	4281/4055	$55.00
Purple Haze	4282/4055	$30.00
Midnight Magic	4283/4055	$30.00
Gold Rush	4284/4055	$60.00
Moroccan Magic	4285/4055	$75.00
Golden Days/Diamond Nights	4286/4055	$50.00

Music is Magic Fashion, 2nd year only, "photo" on boxes

Rock'n Roses	4296/4060	$35.00
Splashes of Sound	4297/4060	$25.00
24 Carat Sound	4298/4060	$35.00
Star Struck Guitar	4299/4060	$85.00
Electric Chords	4300/4060	$25.00
Rhythm & Flash	4301/4060	$35.00

Horsman, E.I.

1865 – 1980+, New York City. Founded by Edward Imeson Horsman, distributed, assembled, and made dolls, merged with Aetna Doll and Toy Co., and in 1909 obtained first copyright for a complete doll with his Billiken. Later made hard plastic and vinyl dolls.

COMPOSITION

First price is for played-with doll, or missing some clothing or accessories; second price is for doll in excellent condition, add more for exceptional doll.

Baby, 1930s – 1940s

15"	$50.00	$125.00

Baby Bumps, 1910 – 1917

Composition head, cloth cork stuffed body, blue and white cloth label on romper, copy of K*R #100 Baby mold

11"	$65.00	$250.00
Black	$75.00	$300.00

Billiken, 1909

Composition head, molded hair, slanted eyes, smiling closed mouth, on stuffed mohair or velvet body

Marks: Cloth label on body. "Billiken" on right foot.

12"	$100.00	$400.00

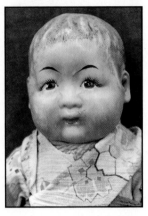

13½" composition Horsman Baby Butterfly with painted features, original tagged clothing: "Baby Butterfly//Horsman Co. New York//Produced Dec. 12 1913," some crazing, $650.00. Courtesy Nelda Shelton.

Baby Butterfly, ca. 1914

Oriental baby, composition head, hands, painted features

13"	$225.00	$650.00

Betty Ann, rubber arms and legs

19"	$100.00	$350.00

Betty Jane, all-composition

25"	$100.00	$300.00

Betty Jo, all-composition

16"	$65.00	$225.00

Body Twist, 1930, all-composition, with jointed waist

11"	$65.00	$225.00

Bright Star, 1937 – 1946, all-composition

19"	$75.00	$300.00

Campbell Kids, 1910+

By Helen Trowbridge, based on Grace Drayton's drawings, composition head, painted molded hair, side-glancing painted eyes, closed smiling mouth, composition arms, cloth body and feet.

Mark: EIH a 1910; cloth label on sleeve, "The Campbell Kids// Trademark by //Joseph Campbell// Mfg. by E.I. Horsman Co."

14"	$85.00	$325.00+

1930 – 1940s, all-composition

13"	$100.00	$350.00

25" composition Horsman Dimples, green tin sleep eyes, painted molded hair, beautiful coloring, circa 1927 – 1930, $450.00. Courtesy Barb Hilliker collection.

15" Horsman girl, all original including box labeled "Horsman Doll, Made in U.S.A. Genuine Horsman 'Art' doll," dressed in white winter outfit, circa late 1930s, $375.00. *Courtesy McMasters Doll Auctions.*

Three 12" composition Horsman Jo-Jo dolls, toddler body, marked "HORSMAN JO JO//C. 1937," original outfits, circa 1937, $250.00 each. Courtesy Gay Smedes.

Child, all-composition

14"	$65.00	$185.00

Cotton Joe, black

13"	$100.00	$400.00

Gene Carr Kids, 1915 – 1916

Composition head, molded, painted hair, painted eyes, open/closed smiling mouth with teeth, big ears, cloth body, composition hands, original outfit

Marks: Cloth tag reads: "MADE GENE CARR KIDS U.S.A.//FROM NEW YORK WORLD'S //LADY BOUNTIFUL COMIC SERIES//By E.I. HORSMAN CO. NY. 13½""

Blink	$90.00	$360.00
Carnival Kids	$75.00	$300.00
Lizzie	$90.00	$360.00
Mike	$90.00	$360.00
Skinney	$90.00	$360.00
Snowball, black	$135.00	$550.00
Polly Pru, 13"	$85.00	$325.00

Dimples, 1927 – 1930+

Composition head, arms, cloth body, or bent-leg body or bent-limb baby body, molded dimples, open mouth, sleep or painted eyes, *marked E.I. H.*

16 – 18"	$70.00	$250.00
20 – 22"	$90.00	$350.00

Laughing Dimples, open/closed mouth with painted teeth

22"	$185.00	$425.00

Dimples, toddler body

20"	$100.00	$385.00
24"	$150.00	$425.00

Dolly Rosebud, 1926 – 1930

Mama doll, composition head, limbs, dimples, sleep eyes

18"	$50.00	$175.00

Ella Cinders, 1928 – 1929

Based on a cartoon character, composition head, black painted hair or wig, round painted eyes, freckles under eyes, open/closed mouth, cloth body. Also came as all-cloth. *Mark: "1925//MNS"*

14"	$100.00	$400.00
18"	$175.00	$650.00

Gold Metal doll, 1930s, upper and lower teeth, cloth body

21"	$50.00	$200.00

HEeBee-SHEbees, 1925 – 1927

Based on drawings by Charles Twelvetrees, all-bisque or all-composition, painted features, molded undershirt and booties or various costumes

Marks: on all bisque, "Germany," and paper sticker on tummy, "COPYRIGHT BY//HEbee SHEbe//TRADE-MARK//CHAS. TWELVETREES"

Composition

10½"	$125.00	$500.00

16" hard plastic Horsman Roberta, all original with box, circa 1950s, $125.00. Courtesy Nancy Rich.

Jackie Coogan, "The Kid," 1921 – 1922

Composition head, hands, molded hair, painted eyes, cloth body, turtleneck sweater, long gray pants, checked cap

Button reads: "HORSMAN DOLL// JACKIE// COOGAN// KID// PATENTED"

13½"	$135.00	$465.00+
15½"	$160.00	$550.00+

Jeanie Horsman, 1937

Composition head and limbs, painted molded brown hair, sleep eyes, cloth body, *mark: "Jeanie© Horsman"*

14"	$65.00	$225.00

Jo Jo, 1937

All-composition, blue sleep eyes, wigged, over molded hair, toddler body

Mark: "HORSMAN JO JO//©1937"

13"	$75.00	$250.00

Mama Dolls, 1920+

Composition head, arms, and lower legs, cloth body with crier and stitched hip joints so lower legs will swing, painted or sleep eyes, mohair or molded hair

16" early vinyl Horsman boy with "Fairy Skin," an early unstable magic skin type plastic, all original, mint in box, circa late 1940s, $125.00. Courtesy Chantal Jeschien.

14 – 15"	$50.00	$185.00
19 – 21"	$75.00	$285.00
Rosebud	$75.00	$275.00
Peggy Ann	$85.00	$350.00

Naughty Sue, 1937, composition head, jointed body

16"	$100.00	$400.00

Peterkin, 1914 – 1930+

Cloth or composition body, character face, molded hair, painted or sleep eyes, closed smiling mouth, rectangular tag with name *"Peterkin"*

11"	$75.00	$300.00
13½"	$85.00	$350.00

Roberta, 1937, all-composition

16"	$115.00	$450.00

Sweetums, cloth body, drink and wet, box, accessories

15"	$75.00	$225.00

Tynie Baby, ca. 1924 – 1929

Bisque or composition head, sleep or painted eyes, cloth body, some all-bisque
Marks: *"a 1924//E.I. HORSMAN//CO. INC."* or *"E.I.H. Co. 1924"* on composition or *"a 1924 by//E I Horsman Co. Inc//Germany// 37"* incised on bisque head

All-bisque, with wardrobe, cradle

6"	$1,785.00*	
8"	$450.00	$1800.00

Bisque, head circumference

9"	$150.00	$600.00
12"	$200.00	$800.00

Composition

15"	$75.00	$300.00

HARD PLASTIC AND VINYL

First price is for doll in excellent condition, but with flaws; second price is for mint-in-box doll. Add more for accessories or wardrobe.

Angelove, 1974, plastic/vinyl made for Hallmark

12"	$10.00	$25.00

Answer Doll, 1966, button in back moves head

10"	$8.00	$15.00

Baby First Tooth, 1966

Vinyl head, limbs, cloth body, open/closed mouth with tongue and one tooth, molded tears on cheeks, rooted blonde hair, painted blue eyes
Mark: *"©Horsman Dolls Inc. //10141"*

16"	$20.00	$40.00

Baby Tweaks, ca. 1967

Vinyl head, cloth body, inset eyes, rooted saran hair
Mark: *"54//HORSMAN DOLLS INC.//Copyright 1967/67191"* on head

20"	$15.00	$30.00

Ballerina, 1957, vinyl, one-piece body and legs, jointed elbows

18"	$15.00	$50.00

Betty, 1951, all-vinyl, one-piece body and limbs

14"	$15.00	$60.00

Vinyl head, hard plastic body

16"	$15.00	$25.00

Betty Ann, vinyl head, hard plastic body

19"	$15.00	$60.00

Betty Jane, vinyl head, hard plastic body

25"	$20.00	$75.00

Betty Jo, vinyl head, hard plastic body

16"	$15.00	$30.00

---

* at auction

Bright Star, ca. 1952+, all hard plastic
    15" $125.00 $450.00

Bye-Lo Baby, 1972
Reissue, molded vinyl head, limbs, cloth body, white nylon organdy bonnet dress
    Mark: "3 (in square)//HORSMAN DOLLS INC.//©1972"
    14" $15.00 $55.00
1980 – 1990s
    14" $8.00 $25.00

Celeste, portrait doll, in frame, eyes painted to side
    12" $10.00 $35.00

Christopher Robin
    11" $10.00 $35.00

Cindy, 1950s, all hard plastic, *"170"*
    15" $50.00 $175.00+
    17" $65.00 $200.00+
1953, early vinyl
    18" $20.00 $60.00
1959, lady-type with jointed waist
    19" $25.00 $95.00
Walker
    16" $60.00 $225.00

Cindy Kay, 1950s+, all-vinyl child with long legs
    15" $25.00 $80.00
    20" $35.00 $125.00
    27" $60.00 $225.00

18" vinyl Horsman Poor Pitiful Pearl, rooted saran hair, watermelon mouth, original costume, circa 1959, $95.00. Courtesy Carol Bennett.

Cinderella, 1965, vinyl head, hard plastic body, painted eyes to side
    11½" $8.00 $30.00

Crawling Baby, 1967, vinyl, rooted hair
    14" $8.00 $25.00

Disney Exclusives, 1981
Cinderella, Snow White, Mary Poppins, Alice in Wonderland
    8" $10.00 $40.00

Elizabeth Taylor, 1976
    11½" $15.00 $45.00

Floppy, 1958, vinyl head, foam body and legs
    18" $8.00 $25.00

Flying Nun, 1965, TV character portrayed by Sally Field
    12" $50.00 $125.00

Gold Metal Doll, 1953, vinyl, molded hair
    26" $45.00 $185.00
1954, vinyl, boy
    15" $20.00 $75.00

Hansel & Gretel, 1963
Vinyl head, hard plastic body, rooted synthetic hair, closed mouth, sleep eyes
    Marks: "MADE IN USA" on body, on tag, "HORSMAN, Michael Meyerberg, Inc.," "Reproduction of the famous Kinemins in Michael Myerberg's marvelous Technicolor production of Hansel and Gretel"
    15" $50.00 $200.00

Jackie, 1961

Vinyl doll, rooted hair, blue sleep eyes, long lashes, closed mouth, high-heeled feet, small waist, nicely dressed. Designed by Irene Szor who says this doll named Jackie was not meant to portray Jackie Kennedy.

Mark: "HORSMAN//19a61//BC 18"

25"	$35.00	$125.00

Lullabye Baby, 1967 – 1968,

vinyl bent-leg body, rooted hair, inset station blue eyes, drink and wet feature, musical mechanism, Sears 1968 catalog, came on suedette pillow, in terry-cloth p.j.s

Mark: "2580//B144 8 //HORSMAN DOLLS INC//19©67"

12"	$4.00	$15.00

Mary Poppins, 1964

12"	$9.00	$35.00
16"	$20.00	$70.00
26", '66	$50.00	$200.00
36"	$90.00	$350.00

In box with Michael and Wendy

12" and 8"	$150.00

Police Woman, ca. 1976,

vinyl, plastic fully articulated body, rooted hair

9"	$10.00	$35.00

Poor Pitiful Pearl, 1959 – 1963,

vinyl, rooted saran hair

12"	$45.00	$85.00
18"	$50.00	$95.00

Tynie Baby, ca. 1950s,

vinyl, boxed

15"	$30.00	$110.00

Mary Hoyer Doll Mfg. Co.

Marks:
"THE MARY HOYER DOLL" or
"ORIGINAL MARY HOYER DOLL"

1937+, Reading, PA. Designed by Bernard Lipfert, all-composition, later hard plastic, then vinyl, swivel neck, jointed body, mohair or human hair wig, sleep eyes, closed mouth, original clothes, or knitted from Mary Hoyer patterns.

Composition

14"	$115.00	$450.00

Hard Plastic

14"	$125.00	$500.00

Gigi, circa 1950, with round Mary Hoyer mark found on 14" dolls, only 2,000 made by the Frisch Doll Company

18"	$1,000.00	$2,000.00

Vinyl, circa 1957+

Vicky, all-vinyl, high-heeled doll, body bends at waist, rooted saran hair, two larger sizes 12" and 14" were discontinued

10½"	$25.00	$100.00

14" hard plastic Mary Hoyer walker with red synthetic wig, beautiful color, re-dressed, circa mid to late 1940s, $200.00. Courtesy Joanne Morgan.

Margie, circa 1958, toddler, rooted hair, made by Unique Doll Co.

10"	$15.00	$75.00

Cathy, circa 1961, infant, made by Unique Doll Co.

10"	$10.00	$25.00

Janie, circa 1962, baby

8"	$10.00	$25.00

18" hard plastic Mary Hoyer Gigi, marked "Mary Hoyer," red mohair wig, green sleep eyes, in green knit costume with ice skates, circa 1950, $1,800.00+. Courtesy Barbara DeFeo.

Ideal Novelty and Toy Co.

1906 – 1980+, Brooklyn, NY. Produced their own composition dolls in early years.

CLOTH

Peanuts Gang, 1976 – 1978

All-cloth, stuffed printed dolls from Peanuts cartoon strip by Charles Schultz, Charlie Brown, Lucy, Linus, Peppermint Patty, and Snoopy

7"	$5.00	$20.00
14"	$8.00	$25.00

Snow White, 1938

Cloth body, mask face, painted eyes, black human hair wig, variation of red and white dress with small cape, Snow White and Seven Dwarfs printed on it. No other marks.

16"	$150.00	$550.00

Strawman, 1939

All-cloth, scarecrow character portrayed by Ray Bolger in *Wizard of Oz* movie. Yarn hair, all original, wearing dark jacket and hat, tan pants, round paper hang tag

17"	$200.00	$800.00
21"	$250.00	$1,000.00

COMPOSITION

Composition Baby Doll, 1913+

Composition head, molded hair or wigged, painted or sleep eyes, cloth or composition body. May have Ideal diamond mark or hang tag. Original clothes.

12"	$25.00	$100.00+
16"	$40.00	$150.00+
20"	$50.00	$200.00+
24"	$65.00	$250.00+

Marks:
Various including
"IDEAL" (in a diamond),
"US of A:
IDEAL NOVELTY," and
"TOY CO. BROOKLYN,
NEW YORK," and others.

17" composition Ideal Deanna Durbin, red taffeta plaid dress with umbrella, circa 1938 – 1941, $750.00+. Courtesy Gay Smedes.

16" composition Ideal Cinderella all original with hang tag, tagged costume, box, wig in original set, clear eyes, no crazing, circa 1938 – 1939, $1,250.00. Courtesy Leslie Tannenbaum.

13" composition Ideal Snow White using the Shirley Temple body, blue eyes, faint crazing, beautiful color, original red and white outfit, circa 1938+, $700.00. Courtesy Leslie Tannenbaum.

Composition Child or Toddler, 1915+

Composition head, molded hair, or wigged, painted or sleep eyes, cloth or composition body. May have Ideal diamond mark or hang tag. Original clothes.

13"	$35.00	$125.00+
15"	$40.00	$150.00+
18"	$50.00	$200.00+

Composition Mama Doll, 1921+

Composition head and arms, molded hair or wigged, painted or sleep eyes, cloth body with crier and stitched swing leg, lower part composition

16"	$50.00	$250.00+
20"	$75.00	$300.00+
24"	$85.00	$350.00+

Buster Brown, 1929

Composition head, hands, legs, cloth body, tin eyes, red outfit

Mark: "IDEAL" (in a diamond)

16"	$75.00	$300.00

Charlie McCarthy, 1938 – 1939

Hand puppet, composition head, felt hands, molded hat, molded features, wire monocle, cloth body, painted tuxedo

Mark: "Edgar Bergin's //©CHARLIE MCCARTHY //MADE IN U.S.A."

8"	$15.00	$60.00

Cinderella, 1938 – 1939

All-composition, brown, blonde, or red human hair wig, flirty brown sleep eyes, open mouth, six teeth, same head mold as Ginger, Snow White, Mary Jane with dimple in chin, some wore formal evening gowns of organdy and taffeta, velvet cape, had rhinestone tiara, silver snap shoes. Sears catalog version has Celanese rayon gown.

Marks: none on head; "SHIRLEY TEMPLE//13" on body

13"	$75.00	$300.00+
16"	$80.00	$325.00+
20"	$85.00	$350.00+
25"	$90.00	$375.00+
27"	$100.00	$400.00+

Cracker Jack Boy, 1917

Composition head, gauntlet hands, cloth body, molded boots, molded hair, wears blue or white sailor suit, cap, carries package of Cracker Jacks

14"	$100.00	$375.00

Deanna Durbin, 1938 – 1941

All composition, fully jointed, dark brown human hair wig, brown sleep eyes, open mouth, six teeth, felt tongue, original clothes, pin, reads: *"DEANNA DURBIN//A UNIVERSAL STAR."* More for fancy outfits.

Marks: *"DEANNA DURBIN//IDEAL DOLL"* on head; *"IDEAL DOLL//21"* on body

15"	$125.00	$500.00+
18"	$190.00	$750.00+
21"	$200.00	$800.00+
24"	$225.00	$925.00+
25"	$250.00	$1,000.00+

Flexies, 1938 – 1942

Composition head, gauntlet hands, wooden torso and feet, flexible wire tubing for arms and legs, original clothes, paper tag

Marks: *"IDEAL DOLL//Made in U.S. A."* or just *"IDEAL DOLL"* on head.

12" composition Ideal Fanny Bryce as Baby Snooks, wood torso and feet, flexy wire arms and legs, designed by Joseph Kallus, painted features, molded hair with loop, original costume, circa 1939, $295.00. Courtesy Odis Gregg.

Black Flexy, molded painted hair, painted eyes, closed smiling mouth, tweed patched pants, felt suspenders

13½"	$85.00	$325.00

Baby Snooks, based on a character by Fannie Brice, designed by Kallus, painted molded hair, painted eyes, open/closed mouth with teeth

13½"	$70.00	$275.00

Clown Flexy, looks like Mortimer Snerd, painted white as clown

13½"	$60.00	$225.00

Mortimer Snerd, Edgar Bergen's radio show dummy, molded painted blond hair, smiling closed mouth, showing two teeth

13½"	$70.00	$275.00

Soldier, closed smiling mouth, molded painted features, in khaki uniform

13½"	$65.00	$250.00

Sunny Sam and Sunny Sue, molded painted hair, girl bobbed hair, pouty mouth, boy as smiling mouth

13½"	$65.00	$250.00

Flossie Flirt, 1924 – 1931

Composition head, limbs, cloth body, crier, tin flirty eyes, open mouth, upper teeth, original outfit, dress, bonnet, combination, socks and shoes

Mark: *"IDEAL"* in diamond with *"U.S. of A"*

13" composition Ideal Sunny Sam, painted molded hair, flexible wire arms and legs, wooden torso and feet, felt suspenders, pants with patches, circa 1938+, $185.00. Courtesy Iva Mae Jones.

14"	$60.00	$225.00+
18"	$65.00	$250.00+
20"	$70.00	$275.00+
22"	$75.00	$300.00+
24"	$80.00	$350.00+
28"	$100.00	$400.00+

15" composition Ideal Judy Garland as Dorothy with the Cowardly Lion, circa 1940 – 1942, $2,800.00 for pair at auction. Courtesy McMasters Doll Auctions.

Jiminy Cricket, 1940

8½", composition head and wood segmented body, yellow suit, black coat, blue felt trim on hat, felt collar, ribbon necktie, carries a wooden umbrella

Marks: "JIMINY CRICKET//IDEAL" and "BY IDEAL NOVELTY & TOY CO." on foot

9"	$125.00	$500.00

Judy Garland, 1939 – 1940, as Dorothy from *The Wizard of Oz*

All-composition, jointed, wig with braids, brown sleep eyes, open mouth, six teeth, designed by Bernard Lipfert, blue or red checked rayon jumper, white blouse

Marks: "IDEAL" on head plus size number, and "USA" on body

13"	$250.00	$1,000.00+
15½"	$300.00	$1,200.00+
18"	$350.00	$1,400.00+

Judy Garland, 1940 – 1942

Teen, all-composition, wig, sleep eyes, open mouth, four teeth, original long dress

Hang tag reads: Judy Garland// A Metro Goldwyn Mayer//Star//in// "Little Nellie//Kelly." Original pin reads JUDY GARLAND METRO GOLDWYN MAYER STAR.

Marks: "IN U.S.A. on head," "IDEAL DOLLS," a backwards "21" on body

15"	$175.00	$700.00
21"	$250.00	$1,000.00

Pinocchio, 1939

Composition head, wood segmented body, painted features, clothes, yellow felt cap

Marks: "PINOCCHIO//Des. a by Walt Disney //Made by Ideal Novelty & Toy Co" on front, "© W.D.P./ /ideal doll//made in USA" on back

8"	$75.00	$300.00
11"	$115.00	$450.00
20"	$125.00	$550.00

Princess Beatrix, 1938 – 1943

Represents Princess Beatrix of the Netherlands, composition head, arms, legs, cloth body, flirty sleep eyes, fingers molded into fists, original organdy dress and bonnet

22" composition Ideal Princess Beatrix, cloth body, excellent color, with suitcase and layette, re-dressed, circa 1938 – 1943, $375.00+. Private collection.

14"	$40.00	$150.00
16"	$50.00	$185.00
22"	$55.00	$215.00
26"	$65.00	$250.00

Seven Dwarfs, 1938

Composition head and cloth body, or all-cloth, painted mask face, head turn, removable clothes, each dwarf has name on cap, pick and lantern

Cloth

12"	$50.00	$175.00

Composition

12"	$65.00	$250.00

Dopey, 1938

One of Seven Dwarfs, a ventriloquist doll, composition head and hands, cloth body, arms, and legs, hinged mouth with drawstring, molded tongue, painted eyes, large ears, long coat, cotton pants, felt shoes sewn to leg, felt cap with name, can stand alone

Mark: "IDEAL DOLL" on neck

20"	$200.00	$800.00

Snoozie, 1933+

Composition head, painted hair, hard rubber hands and feet, cloth body, open yawning mouth, molded tongue, sleep eyes, designed by Bernard Lipfert

18" composition Ideal Snoozie with cloth body, re-dressed, circa 1933, $200.00. Private collection.

Marks: "©B. Lipfert//Made for Ideal Doll & Toy Corp. 1933" or "©by B. Lipfert" or "IDEAL SNOOZIE//B. LIPFERT" on head

14"	$40.00	$150.00
16"	$65.00	$250.00
18"	$75.00	$300.00
20"	$90.00	$350.00

Snow White, 1938+

All-composition, jointed body, black mohair wig, flirty glass eyes, open mouth, four teeth, dimple in chin, used Shirley Temple body, red velvet bodice, rayon taffeta skirt pictures seven Dwarfs, velvet cape, some unmarked

Marks "Shirley Temple/18" or other size number on back

11½"	$125.00	$500.00
13 – 14"	$135.00	$550.00
19"	$150.00	$600.00
22"	$165.00	$650.00
27"	$175.00	$700.00

Snow White, 1938 – 1939, as above, but with painted molded bow and black hair, painted side-glancing eyes. Add 50 percent more for black version.

Mark: "IDEAL DOLL" on head

14½"	$50.00	$200.00
17½"	$100.00	$400.00
19½"	$150.00	$600.00

Soozie Smiles, 1923

Two-headed composition doll with smiling face, sleep or painted eyes, and crying face with tears, painted molded hair, cloth body and legs, composition arms, original clothes, tag, also in gingham check romper

15 – 17"	$75.00	$300.00

Tickletoes, 1928 – 1939

Composition head, rubber arms, legs, cloth body, squeaker in each leg,

Three 14" hard plastic Ideal Baby Coos with "Magic Skin" stuffed body, played with condition, but intact, circa 1948 – 1952, $50.00 each. Courtesy Millie Busch.

flirty sleep eyes, open mouth, two painted teeth, original organdy dress, bonnet, paper hang tag

Marks: "IDEAL" in diamond with "U.S. of A." on head

14"	$50.00	$275.00
17"	$75.00	$300.00
20"	$95.00	$325.00

Uneeda Kid, 1916

Advertising doll, carries package of Nabisco crackers, some have molded yellow hats, wears yellow rain coat, molded black boots

Painted eyes

11"	$75.00	$300.00

Sleep eyes

16"	$125.00	$475.00

ZuZu Kid, 1966 – 1967

Composition head, molded hair, composition hands, feet, cloth body, jointed hip, shoulders, girl in yellow with brown star clown costume, hat, hold small box ZuZu gingersnaps, licensed by National Biscuit Co.

15½"	$115.00	$450.00

HARD PLASTIC AND VINYL

April Showers, 1968

Vinyl, battery operated, splashes hands, head turns

14"	$8.00	$28.00

Baby Coos, 1948 – 1953, also Brother and Sister Coos

Designed by Bernard Lipfert, hard plastic head, stuffed magic skin body, jointed arms, sleep eyes, molded painted hair, closed mouth or cloth and vinyl body. Many magic skin bodies deteriorated or tuned dark.

Marks on head, "16 IDEAL DOLL// MADE IN U.S. A." or unmarked

14"	$25.00	$100.00
16"	$35.00	$125.00
18"	$40.00	$150.00
20"	$45.00	$175.00
22"	$50.00	$200.00
27"	$65.00	$260.00
30"	$75.00	$300.00

Baby Crissy, 1973 – 1976

All vinyl, jointed body, legs and arms foam filled, rooted auburn grow hair, two painted teeth, brown sleep eyes

Mark: "©1972//IDEAL TOY COPR.//2M 5511//B OR GHB-H-225" on back

White	24"	$15.00	$50.00
Black	24"	$20.00	$75.00

Baby Pebbles, 1963 – 1964

Character from the Flintstone cartoons, Hanna Barbera Productions, vinyl head, arms, legs, soft body, side-glancing blue painted eyes, rooted hair with topknot and bone, leopard print nightie and trim on flannel blanket. Also as an all-vinyl toddler, jointed body, outfit with leopard print.

11" Ideal Betsy Wetsy, toddler, all-vinyl with rooted saran hair, complete with a layette, circa 1959 – 1962, $175.00. Courtesy Cathie Clark.

Baby		
14"	$7.00	$25.00
Toddler		
16"	$10.00	$35.00

Tiny Pebbles, 1964 – 1966, smaller version, came with plastic log cradle in 1965.

Toddler	12"	$8.00	$30.00

Bamm-Bamm, 1964

Character from Flintstone TV cartoon, Hanna Barbera Productions, all-vinyl head, jointed body, rooted blond saran hair, painted blue side-glancing eyes, leopard skin suit, cap, club

	12"	$5.00	$20.00
	16"	$7.00	$25.00

Bat Girl

	11½"	$40.00	$150.00

Bat Man, 1966

Vinyl and cloth hand puppet, vinyl head, blue mask

		$40.00	$150.00

Action figure

	12"	$65.00	$250.00

Belly Button Babies, 1971

Me So Glad, Me So Silly, Me So Happy, vinyl head, rooted hair, painted eyes, press button in belly to move arms, head, and bent legs; both boy and girl versions

White	9½"	$5.00	$18.00
Black	9½"	$9.00	$25.00

Betsy McCall, 1952 – 1953: See that section.

Betsy Wetsy, 1937 – 1938

Hard rubber head, soft rubber body, sleep or painted eyes, molded hair, open mouth for bottle, drinks, wets, came with bottle, some in layettes

Marks: "IDEAL" on head, "IDEAL" on body

	11"	$25.00	$110.00
	15"	$35.00	$135.00
	19"	$40.00	$150.00

Big Jim Series

Vinyl action figures, many boxed accessory sets available

Big Jim, black hair, muscular torso

	9½"	$7.00	$25.00

13½" vinyl Ideal Cinnamon originally called Velvet's Little Sister, painted eyes, rooted auburn growing hair, orange polka dot outfit, also had other outfits available, 1972 – 1974, $40.00. Courtesy Penny Pittsley.

Big Josh, dark hair, beard

	9½"	$9.00	$35.00

Dr. Steele, bald head, silver tips on right hand

	9½"	$8.00	$32.00

Bizzie-Lizzie, 1971 – 1972

Vinyl head, jointed body, rooted blonde hair, sleep eyes, plugged into power pack, she irons, vacuums, used feather duster, two D-cell batteries

White	18"	$9.00	$35.00
Black	18"	$12.00	$45.00

Bonnie Braids, 1951 – 1953

Comic strip character, daughter of Dick Tracy and Tess Trueheart, vinyl head, jointed arms, "Magic Skin" rubber one-piece body, open mouth, one tooth, painted yellow hair, two yellow saran pigtails, painted blue eyes, coos when squeezed, long white gown, bed jacket, toothbrush, Ipana toothpaste

Mark: "©1951//Chi. Tribune//IDEAL DOLL//U.S.A." on neck

Baby

	11½"	$25.00	$100.00
	14"	$30.00	$135.00

Toddler, 1953, vinyl head, jointed hard plastic body, open/closed mouth with two painted teeth, walker

	11½"	$35.00	$140.00
	14"	$40.00	$160.00

Butterick Sew Easy Designing Set, 1953

Plastic mannequin of adult woman, molded blonde hair, came with Butterick patterns and sewing accessories

	14"	$15.00	$60.00

Captain Action® Superhero, 1966 – 1968

Represents a fictional character who changes disguises to become a new identity, vinyl articulated figure, dark hair and eyes

Captain Action 1967 Promo

	12"	$75.00	$300.00
Batman disguise			
		$65.00	$250.00
Capt. American disguise only		$250.00	
Capt. Flash Gordon accessories		$40.00	$150.00
Phantom disguise only		$50.00	$200.00
Steve Canyon disguise		$50.00	$200.00
Superman set w/dog		$45.00	$175.00
Lone Ranger outfit only		$50.00	$200.00
Spiderman disguise only		$65.00	$250.00
Tonto outfit only		$50.00	$200.00
Action Boy, 9"		$65.00	$250.00
Robin Accessories		$45.00	$175.00
Special Ed.		$75.00	$300.00

Dr. Evel	$50.00	$200.00
Dr. Evel's Accessories	$50.00	$250.00
Super Girl	$75.00	$300.00

Chelsea, 1967

Vinyl head, posable body, rooted straight hair, mod fashions, earrings, strap shoes

| 24" | $15.00 | $50.00 |

Cinnamon, Velvet's Little Sister, 1972 – 1974

Vinyl head, painted eyes, rooted auburn growing hair, orange polka dotted outfit, additional outfits sold separately

Marks: "©1971//IDEAL TOY CORP.//G-H-12-H18//HONG KONG//IDEAL 1069-4 b" head "©1972//IDEAL TOY CORP.//U.S. PAT-3-162-976//OTHER PAT. PEND.//HONG KONG" on back

18" vinyl Ideal Crissy, with vinyl body, swivel waist, growing hair, with box, original turquoise outfit, circa 1969, $50.00. Courtesy Angie Gonzales.

White

| 13½" | $12.00 | $45.00 |

Black

| 13½" | $15.00 | $60.00 |

Clarabell, 1954, clown from *Howdy Doody* TV show

Mask face, cloth body, dressed in satin Clarabelle outfit with noise box and horn

| 16" | $20.00 | $80.00 |
| 20" | $25.00 | $100.00 |

Crissy®, Beautiful Crissy, 1969 – 1974

All-vinyl, dark brown eyes, long hair, turn knob in back to make hair grow, some with swivel waist (1971), pull string to turn head (1972), pull string to talk (1971). Reissued ca. 1982 – 1983. First year hair grew to floor length. More for black version.

1969, white

| 17½" | $25.00 | $100.00 |

1969, black

| 17½" | $40.00 | $150.00 |

Dina, Crissy's friend

| 17½" | $40.00 | $100.00 |

Daddy's Girl, 1961

Vinyl head and arms, plastic body, swivel waist, jointed ankles, rooted saran hair, blue sleep eyes, closed smiling mouth, preteen girl, label on dress reads *"Daddy's Girl"*

Marks: "IDEAL TOY CORP.//g-42-1" on head, "IDEAL TOY CORP.//G-42" on body

| 38" | $300.00 | $1,200.00 |
| 42" | $350.00 | $1,400.00 |

Davy Crockett and his horse, 1955 – 1956

All-plastic, can be removed from horse, fur cap, buckskin clothes

| 4½" | $13.00 | $50.00 |

Dennis, the Menace, 1976

All-cloth, printed doll, comic strip character by Hank Ketcham, blond hair, freckles, wearing overalls, striped shirt

7"	$5.00	$20.00
14"	$7.50	$30.00

Diana Ross, 1969

From the Supremes (singing group), all-vinyl, rooted black bouffant hair-do, gold sheath, feathers, gold shoes, or chartreuse mini-dress, print scarf and black shoes

17½"	$45.00	$165.00

Dorothy Hamill, 1978

Olympic skating star, vinyl head, plastic posable body, rooted short brown hair, comes on ice rink stand with skates; also extra outfits available

11½"	$8.00	$30.00

Evel Knievel, 1974 – 1977

All-plastic stunt figure, helmet, more with stuntcycle

7"	$7.50	$25.00

14" vinyl Ideal Harriet Hubbard Ayer, blue sleep eyes, closed mouth, synthetic hair in original set, hard plastic body, vinyl arms, all original in box with make-up kit, circa 1953, $380.00. Courtesy McMasters Doll Auctions.

Harriet Hubbard Ayer, 1953, Cosmetic doll

Vinyl stuffed head, hard plastic (Toni) body, wigged or rooted hair, came with eight-piece H. H. Ayer cosmetic kit, beauty table and booklet

Marks: "MK 16//IDEAL DOLL" on head "IDEAL DOLL//P-91" on body

14"	$50.00	$200.00
16"	$60.00	$225.00
19"	$65.00	$250.00
21"	$75.00	$300.00

Hopalong Cassidy, 1949 – 1950

Vinyl stuffed head, vinyl hands, molded painted gray hair, painted blue eyes, one piece body, dressed in black cowboy outfit, leatherette boots, guns, holster, black felt hat

Marked: "Hopalong Cassidy" on buckle

18"	$20.00	$80.00
21"	$22.50	$85.00
23"	$25.00	$100.00
25"	$35.00	$125.00
27"	$40.00	$150.00

Plastic, with horse, Topper

4½"	$10.00	$40.00

Howdy Doody, 1950 – 1953

Television personality, hard plastic head, red painted molded hair, freckles, ventriloquist doll, mouth operated by pull string, cloth body and limbs, dressed in cowboy outfit, scarf reads "*HOWDY DOODY*"

Mark: "IDEAL" on head

19"	$25.00	$100.00
24"	$40.00	$150.00

1954, with vinyl hands, wears boots, jeans

18"	$50.00	$200.00
20"	$65.00	$250.00
25"	$75.00	$300.00

Judy Splinters, 1949 – 1950

Vinylite TV character

18"	$50.00	$200.00

Kissy, 1961 – 1964

Vinyl head, rigid vinyl toddler body, rooted saran hair, sleep eyes, jointed wrists, press hands together and mouth puckers, makes kissing sound, original dress, panties, t-strap sandals

Marks: "©IDEAL CORP.//K-21-L" on head "IDEAL TOY CORP.// K22//PAT. PEND." on body

White

22½"	$20.00	$75.00

Black

	$35.00	$150.00

Kissy Baby, 1963 – 1964, all-vinyl, bent legs

22"	$15.00	$55.00

Tiny Kissy, 1963 – 1968, smaller toddler, red outfit, white pinafore with hearts

Marks: "IDEAL CORP.//K-16-1" on head "IDEAL TOY CORP./K-16-2" on body

White

16"	$12.00	$45.00

Black

	$20.00	$80.00

Loni Anderson, 1981, star of TV sitcom, *WKRP in Cincinnati*

Vinyl, posable fashion doll packaged with picture of Loni Anderson. This doll was featured in Ideal's 1981 catalog in a red dress, white high heels, blonde wig, unsure how many produced

11½"	$10.00	$50.00

Lori Martin, 1961, character from National Velvet TV show

All-vinyl, swivel waist, jointed body, including ankles, blue sleep eyes, rooted dark hair, individual fingers, dressed shirt, jeans, black vinyl boots, felt hat

19" hard plastic Ideal Howdy Doody marked "Ideal//Doll" with movable jaw, sleep eyes, vinyl hands, cloth body and limbs, all original, except replaced boots, shown with 1951 Rice Krispies ad, $200.00. Courtesy Ursula Mertz.

16" hard plastic Ideal Mary Hartline in rare green dress, circa 1952, $450.00. Courtesy Iva Mae Jones.

20" vinyl Ideal Miss Revlon in Cherries a la Mode red and white dress, $250.00. Courtesy June Algeier.

10½" vinyl Ideal Little Miss Revlon, swivel waist, high-heeled feet, rooted hair, sleep eyes, pierced ears, all original, with rosy cheeks, circa 1958 – 1960, $125.00. Courtesy Chantal Jeschien.

Marks: "Metro Goldwyn Mayer Inc.//Mfg. by//IDEAL TOY CORP//38" on head, "©IDEAL TOY CORP.//38" on back

36"	$175.00	$750.00
38"	$200.00	$800.00

Magic Skin Baby, 1940, 1946 – 1949

Hard plastic head, one-piece molded latex body and legs, jointed arms, sleep eyes, molded painted hair, some with fancy layettes or trunks, latex usually darkened

13 – 14"	$25.00	$50.00
15 – 16"	$20.00	$75.00
17 – 18"	$25.00	$100.00
20"	$35.00	$125.00

Marama, 1940: See Shirley Temple section.

Mary Hartline, 1952, from TV personality on *Super Circus* show

Hard plastic, fully jointed, blonde nylon wig, blue sleep eyes, lashes, black eyeshadow over and under eye, red, white, or green drum majorette costume and baton, red heart paper hangdog, with original box

Marks: "P-91//IDEAL DOLL//MADE IN U.S.A." on head, "IDEAL DOLL//P-91 or IDEAL//16" on body

7½"	$35.00	$125.00
16"	$300.00	$650.00
23"	$350.00	$750.00

Miss Clairol, Glamour Misty, 1965 – 1966

Vinyl head arms, rigid plastic legs, body, rooted platinum blonde saran hair, side-glancing eyes. Teen doll had cosmetics to change her hair, high-heeled feet. All original.

Marks: "©1965//IDEAL TOY CORP//W-12-3" on neck, "©1965 IDEAL" in oval on lower rear torso

12"	$10.00	$40.00

Miss Curity, 1953

Hard plastic, saran wig, sleep eyes, black eyeshadow, nurse's outfit, navy cape, white cap, Bauer & Black first aid kit and book, curlers, uses Toni body

Mark: "P-90 IDEAL DOLL, MADE IN U.S.A." on head

14½"	$300.00	$650.00
22"	$400.00	$750.00

Miss Ideal, 1961

All vinyl, rooted nylon hair, jointed ankles, wrists, waist, arms, legs, closed smiling mouth, sleep eyes, original dress, with beauty kit and comb

Marks: "©IDEAL TOY CORP.//SP-30-S"
head; "©IDEAL TOY CORP.//G-30-S" back

25"	$100.00	$375.00
30"	$125.00	$475.00

Miss Revlon, 1956 – 1959

Vinyl, hard plastic teenage body, jointed shoulders, waist, hips, and knees, high-heeled feet, rooted saran hair, sleep eyes, lashes, pierced ears, hang tag, original dress. Some came with trunks.

Mark: "VT 20//IDEAL DOLL"

15"	$100.00	$350.00
18"	$150.00	$500.00
20"	$200.00	$600.00
23"	$225.00	$700.00

1957

26"	$75.00	$300.00

36" vinyl Ideal Patty Playpal, vinyl body, jointed wrists, sleep eyes, saran rooted wig, closed mouth, bright cheek color, circa 1959, $200.00. Courtesy Kathy & Roy Smith.

Little Miss Revlon, 1958 – 1960

Vinyl head and strung body, jointed head, arms, legs, swivel waist, high-heeled feet, rooted hair, sleep eyes, pierced ears with earrings, original clothes, with box, many extra boxed outfits available

10½"	$85.00	$145.00

Mysterious Yokum, Li'l Honest Abe, 1953

Son of comic strip character, Li'l Abner, hard plastic head, body, "Magic Skin" arms and legs, painted eyes, molded hair, forelock, wears overalls, one suspender, knit cap and sock

$15.00	$55.00

Palooka, Joan, 1953

Daughter of comic strip character, Joe Palooka, vinyl, head, "Magic Skin" body, jointed arms and legs, yellow molded hair, topknot of yellow saran, blue painted eyes, open/closed mouth, smells like baby powder, original pink dress with blue ribbons, came with Johnson's baby powder and soap

Mark: "©1952//HAM FISHER//IDEAL DOLL" on head

14"	$20.00	$75.00

Patti Playpal and related dolls, 1959 – 1962

All-vinyl, jointed wrists, sleep eyes, curly or straight saran hair, bangs, closed mouth, blue or red and white check dress with pinafore, three-year-old size, reissued in 1981 and 82 from old molds

Mark: "IDEAL TOY CORP.//G 35 OR B-19-1" on head

White	35"	$50.00	$275.00
Black	35"	$75.00	$325.00

Pattite, 1960

All-vinyl, rooted saran hair, sleep eyes, red and white check dress, white pinafore with her name on it, looks like Patti Playpal

18"	$65.00	$250.00

Pattitie, 1960, walker

18"	$70.00	$270.00

38" vinyl Ideal Peter Playpal, all original, blue sleep eyes, freckles, pug nose, closed smiling mouth, rooted hair, five-piece body, circa 1960 – 1961, $500.00. Courtesy McMasters Doll Auctions.

22" hard plastic Ideal Saucy Walker with flirty eyes, head turns from side to side when walking, open/closed mouth, teeth, saran wig, original dress, circa 1951 – 1955, $400.00. Courtesy Mary Evelyn Graf.

Bonnie Play Pal, 1959

Patti's three-month-old sister, made only one year, vinyl, rooted blonde hair, blue sleep eyes, blue and white check outfit, white shoes and socks

24"	$65.00	$250.00

Penny Play Pal, 1959

Vinyl jointed body, rooted blonde or brown curly hair, blue sleep eyes, wears organdy dress, vinyl shoes, socks, Patti's two-year-old sister, made only one year

Marks: "IDEAL DOLL//32-E-L" or "B-32-B PAT. PEND." on head, "IDEAL" on back

32"	$75.00	$300.00

Johnny Play Pal, 1959

Vinyl, blue sleep eyes, molded hair, Patti's three-month-old brother

24"	$65.00	$250.00

Peter Playpal, 1960 – 1961

Vinyl, gold sleep eyes, freckles, pug nose, rooted blond, brunet hair, original clothes, black plastic shoes

Marks: "©DEAL TOY CORP.// BE-35-38" on head, "©IDEAL TOY CORP.//W-38//PAT. PEND." on body

38"	$225.00	$850.00

Walker

38"	$225.00	$850.00

Suzy Play Pal, 1959

Vinyl, jointed body, rooted curly short blonde saran hair, blue sleep eyes, wears purple dotted dress, Patti's one-year-old sister

28"	$75.00	$300.00

Plassie, 1942

Hard plastic head, painted molded hair, composition shoulder plate, composition limbs, stuffed pink oilcloth body, blue sleep eyes, original dress, bonnet

Mark: "IDEAL DOLL//MADE IN USA//PAT.NO. 225 2077" on head

17"	$25.00	$100.00
19"	$35.00	$125.00
24"	$45.00	$175.00

Samantha, 1965 – 1966, from TV show, *Bewitched*

Vinyl head, body, rooted saran hair, posable arms and legs, wearing red witch's costume, with broom, painted side-glancing eyes, other costume included negligee

Mark: "IDEAL DOLL//M-12-E-2" on head

12"	$35.00	$135.00

Tabitha, 1966, baby from TV show, *Bewitched*, vinyl head, body, rooted platinum hair, painted blue side-glancing eyes, closed mouth, came in pajamas

Mark: "©1965//Screen Gems, Inc.//Ideal Toy Corp.//T.A. 18-6//H-25" on head

14"	$20.00	$75.00

20" vinyl Ideal Snoozie, all original in box, blonde rooted saran hair, sleep eyes, turn knob, she squirms, opens and closes her eyes and cries, cloth body with vinyl arms and legs, circa 1964, $55.00. Courtesy Iva Mae Jones.

Saucy Walker, 1951 – 1955

All hard plastic, walks, turns head from side to side, flirty blue eyes, crier, open/closed mouth, teeth, holes in body for crier, saran wig, plastic curlers, came as toddler, boy, and "Big Sister"

16"	$35.00	$125.00
22"	$50.00	$200.00
Black		
16"	$50.00	$200.00
Big Sister, 1954		
25"	$40.00	$150.00

1960 – 1961

All-vinyl, rooted saran hair, blue sleep eyes, closed smiling mouth, walker, original print dress, pinafore, box

Marks: "©IDEAL TOY CORP.//T28X-60" or "IDEAL TOY CO.//BYE S 285 B" on head "IDEAL TOY CORP.//T-28 Pat. Pend." on body

28"	$50.00	$200.00
32"	$65.00	$250.00

Smokey, the Bear, 1953+

Bakelite vinyl face and paws, rayon plush stuffed body, vinyl forest ranger hat, badge, shovel, symbol of USA National Forest Service, wears Smokey marked belt, twill trousers, came with Junior Forest Ranger kit. Issued on 50th anniversary of Ideal's original teddy bear.

18"	$15.00	$50.00
25"	$20.00	$75.00
1957, Talking		
	$25.00	$100.00

Snoozie, 1949

1933 doll reissued in vinyl, cloth body with Swiss music box

11"	$20.00	$75.00
16"	$25.00	$100.00
20"	$40.00	$150.00

1958 – 1965

All-vinyl, rooted saran hair, blue sleep eyes, open/closed mouth, cry voice, knob makes doll wiggle, close eyes, crier, in flannel pajamas

14"	$6.00	$27.50

1964 – 1965

Vinyl head, arms, legs, soft body, rooted saran hair, sleep eyes, turn knob, she squirms, opens and closes eyes, and cries

Marks: "©1965//IDEAL TOY CORP//YTT-14-E" on head, "IDEAL TOY CORP//U.S. PAT. NO. 3,029,552" on knob on back

20"	$12.00	$45.00

12" vinyl Ideal Tammy family, including Tammy, Ted, and little sister 9" Pepper, all boxed, circa 1962, $50.00 each. Courtesy McMasters Doll Auctions.

Sparkle Plenty, 1947 – 1950

Hard plastic head, "Magic Skin" body may be dark, yarn hair, character from Dick Tracy comics

14"	$50.00	$200.00

Tammy and Her Family

Tammy, 1962+, vinyl head, arms, plastic legs and torso, head joined at neck base

Marks: "©IDEAL TOY CORP.//BS12" on head, "©IDEAL TOY CORP.//BS-12//1" on back

	12"	$15.00	$50.00
Black	12"	$40.00	$80.00
Pos'n	12"	$25.00	$50.00
Dad	12"	$20.00	$50.00
Mom	12"	$20.00	$50.00
Ted	12"	$30.00	$50.00
Pepper	9"	$20.00	$45.00
Clothing on cards		$8.00	$20.00

Thumbelina, 1961 – 1962

Vinyl head and limbs, soft cloth body, painted eyes, rooted saran hair, open/closed mouth, wind knob on back moves body, crier in 1962

16"	$9.00	$35.00
20"	$12.00	$45.00

1982 – 1983

All-vinyl one-piece body, rooted hair, comes in quilted carrier, also black

7"	$5.00	$15.00

1982, 1985

Reissue from 1960s mold, vinyl head, arms, legs, cloth body, painted eyes, crier, open mouth, molded or rooted hair, original with box

18"	$8.00	$30.00

18" Ideal vinyl Thumbelina, cloth body, all original with tag, 1983 – 1985, $45.00. Courtesy Marie Rodgers.

14" hard plastic Ideal Toni marked "P-90," mint in box, with beautiful color, original outfit, play wave accessories, circa 1949, $600.00+. Courtesy Rae Klenke.

19" Ideal Tiffany Taylor, all-vinyl with rooted hair, the top of her heads turns, so blonde hair changes to dark hair, painted eyes, long eyelashes, circa 1974 – 1976, $65.00. Courtesy Cathie Clark.

Thumbelina, Ltd. Production Collector's Doll, 1983 – 1985

Porcelain, painted eyes, molded painted hair, beige crocheted outfit with pillow booties, limited edition 1,000

18"	$20.00	$75.00
24"	$25.00	$100.00

Tiny Thumbelina, 1962 – 1968

Vinyl head, limbs, cloth body, painted eyes, rooted saran hair, wind key in back makes body head move, original tagged clothes

Marks: "IDEAL TOY CORP.//OTT 14" on head, "U.S. PAT. #3029552" on body

14"	$7.50	$30.00

Tiffany Taylor, 1974 – 1976

All-vinyl, rooted hair, top of head turns to change color, painted eyes, teenage body, high-heeled, extra outfits available

19"	$12.00	$45.00
Black	$15.00	$50.00

Toni, 1949, designed by Bernard Lipfert

All hard plastic, joined body, Dupont nylon wig, usually blue eyes, rosy cheeks, closed mouth, came with Toni wave set and curlers in original dress, with hang tag

Marks: "IDEAL DOLL//MADE IN U.S.A." on head, "IDEAL DOLL" and P-series number on body

P-90	14"	$150.00	$575.00
P-91	16"	$175.00	$625.00
P-92	18"	$185.00	$675.00
P-93	21"	$200.00	$750.00
P-94	23"	$225.00	$800.00

Velvet, 1971 – 1973

Crissy's cousin, vinyl head, body, grow hair, talker, pull string

Marks: "©1969//IDEAL TOY CORP.//GH-15-H-157" on head, "© 1971//IDEAL TOY CORP.//TV 15//US PAT 3162973//OTHER PATENTS PEND." on back

15"	$12.00	$45.00

Ideal (cont.)

Velvet, 1974, non-talker, other accessories, grow hair
15"	$9.00	$35.00

Mia, 1971, vinyl, grow hair, Velvet's friend
15"	$10.00	$35.00

Tressy, 1970, vinyl , grow hair
17½"	$40.00	$100.00

Wizard of Oz Series, 1984 – 1985
Tin Man, Lion, Scarecrow, Dorothy, and Toto, all-vinyl, six-piece posable bodies
9"	$7.00	$25.00

Wonder Woman, 1967 – 1968
All-vinyl, posable body, rooted hair, painted side-glancing eyes, dressed in costume
11½"	$35.00	$125.00

Kenner

11½" Ideal Blythe, all-vinyl with a pull string that changes dolls eye color, circa 1974, $75.00. Courtesy Cathie Clark.

First price indicates played with or missing accessories doll; second price is for mint condition doll.

Baby Bundles
White	16"	$4.00	$20.00
Black	16"	$6.00	$25.00

Baby Yawnie, 1974
Vinyl head, cloth body
15"	$5.00	$20.00

Bob Scout, 1974
9"	$80.00* black, MIB

Blythe, 1974
Pull string to change color of eyes, "mod" clothes
11½"	$25.00	$75.00

Butch Cassidy or Sundance Kid
4"	$4.00	$15.00

Charlie Chaplin, 1973
All-cloth, walking mechanism
14"	$25.00	$90.00

Cover Girls, 1978
Posable elbows and knees, jointed hands
Dana, black	12½"	$30.00	$60.00
Darci, blonde	12½"	$20.00	$55.00
Darci, brunette	12½"	$20.00	$55.00
Darci, redhead	12½"	$20.00	$55.00
Erica, redhead	12½"	$45.00	$100.00

Crumpet 1970, vinyl and plastic
8"	$8.00	$30.00

Dusty, 1974, vinyl teenage doll
11"	$10.00	$20.00

Gabbigale, 1972
White	18"	$10.00	$35.00

Black	18"	$12.00	$45.00

Garden Gals, 1972, hand bent to hold watering can

	6½"	$3.00	$10.00

Hardy Boys, 1978,   Shaun Cassidy, Parker Stevenson

	12"	$5.00	$27.50

Indiana Jones, 1981

	12"	$50.00	$150.00

International Velvet, 1976, Tatum O'Neill

	11½"	$8.00	$25.00

Jenny Jones and baby, 1973, all-vinyl
Jenny, 9", Baby, 2½"

	set	$8.00	$25.00

Rose Petal, 1984, scented

	7"	$10.00	$20.00

Six Million Dollar Man Figures, 1975 – 1977

TV show starring Lee Majors
Bionic Man, Big Foot

	13"	$7.00	$25.00

Bionic Man, Masketron Robot

	13"	$8.00	$30.00

Bionic Woman, Robot

	13"	$5.00	$20.00

Jaime Sommers, Bionic Woman

	13"	$20.00	$75.00

Oscar Goldman, 1975 – 1977, with exploding briefcase

	13"	$15.00	$50.00

Skye, black, teenage friend of Dusty

	11"	$8.00	$25.00

Steve Austin, The Bionic Man, with equipment and accessories

	13"	$8.00	$29.00

Steve Austin, Bionic Grip, 1977

	13"	$25.00	$95.00

Star Wars Figures, 1974 – 1978

Large size action figures

First price indicates doll played with or missing accessories; second price is for mint-in-box/package doll. Complete doll in excellent condition would be somewhere in between. Never-removed-from-box would bring greater prices.

Ben-Obi-Wan Kenobi

	12"	$25.00	$95.00

Boba Fett

	13"	$55.00	$175.00

C-3PO

	12"	$35.00	$135.00

12½" vinyl Kenner Darci auburn rooted hair, long turquoise gown, on plastic stand, jointed hands, poseable elbows and knees, circa 1978, $20.00. Private collection.

13" vinyl Kenner Jaime Sommers Bionic Woman, all original in box, blonde rooted hair, painted features, open mouth with teeth, circa 1976, $75.00. Courtesy Penny Pittsley.

Chewbacca
12" $40.00 $145.00

Darth Vader
12" $50.00 $200.00

Han Solo
12" $125.00 $475.00

IG-88
15" $150.00 $600.00

Jawa
8½" $25.00 $100.00

Leia Organa
11½" $65.00 $275.00

Luke Skywalker
12" $65.00 $275.00

R2-D2, robot
7½" $45.00 $175.00

Stormtrooper
12" $50.00 $200.00

Strawberry Shortcake, ca. 1980 – 1986
5" $6.00 $25.00
14" $7.50 $35.00
18" $10.00 $50.00

Steve Scout, 1974
9" $5.00 $20.00

Sweet Cookie, 1972
18" $8.00 $30.00

Terminator, Arnold Schwarzenneger, 1991, talks
13½" $15.00 $30.00

Kewpie

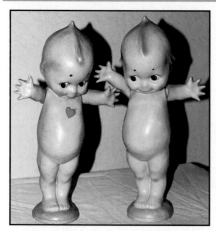

12" composition Rose O'Neill Kewpies, jointed arms, stiff legs, circa 1930s – 1940s, $275.00 each. Courtesy Amanda Hash.

BISQUE KEWPIES: See also Antique Kewpie section.

ALL-CLOTH

All-cloth, made by Kreuger, all one piece, including clothing
8" $50.00 $225.00
12" $825.00* satin body, silk screen face
20" $150.00 $600.00

Kewpie Baby, 1960s, hinged joints
15" $45.00 $185.00
18" $75.00 $300.00

Kewpie Baby, one-piece stuffed body and limbs
15", 18" $75.00 $300.00

* at auction

CELLULOID

2"	$9.00	$35.00
5"	$20.00	$85.00
12"	$75.00	$350.00
Black		
5"	$40.00	$170.00

COMPOSITION

All-composition, jointed arms only

9"	$40.00	$165.00
12"	$60.00	$250.00

Jointed neck, shoulders, hips

9"	$60.00	$225.00
13"	$770.00* boxed 1946 Cameo original	

Black, ca. 1946, jointed arms only

11"	$150.00	$575.00

Composition flange head, half arms, cloth body, tagged floral dress

11"	$880.00*	

Talcum shaker, original box, composition

6½"	$75.00	$250.00

HARD PLASTIC, 1950s

One-piece body and head

8"	$60.00	$120.00
12"	$95.00	$185.00

Jointed five-piece body, at shoulders, neck, hips

8½"	$200.00	$385.00
13"	$300.00	$435.00

VINYL

Vinyl head, limbs, cloth body

16"	$50.00	$185.00

Hinge jointed (Miss Peep's body)

16"	$55.00	$225.00

Jointed shoulder only

9"	$10.00	$40.00
12"	$18.00	$60.00

Jointed neck, shoulder, hips

9"	$20.00	$75.00
14"	$50.00	$170.00
27"	$90.00	$275.00

Molded one-piece, no joints

9"	$7.00	$25.00
14"	$15.00	$55.00

Black

10"	$17.00	$50.00
12"	$20.00	$70.00

Bean Bag type body, 1970s

10"	$10.00	$35.00

Plush, 1960s, usual red body with vinyl face mask, made by Knickerbocker

10" vinyl Cameo black Kewpie, painted side-glancing eyes, watermelon mouth, hang tag, mint in box, circa 1984, $50.00. Courtesy Carol Fairchild.

6"	$5.00	$35.00
10"	$15.00	$55.00

Ragsy, 1964, vinyl, one-piece, molded-on clothes with heart on chest

8"	$10.00	$40.00

No heart, 1971

8"	$4.00	$15.00

Thinker, 1971, one-piece vinyl, sitting down

4"	$5.00	$20.00

Ward's Anniversary, 1972

8"	$15.00	$55.00

Klumpe

Caricature figures made of felt over wire armature with painted mask faces, produced in Barcelona, Spain, from about 1952 to the mid-1970s. Figures represent professionals, hobbyists, Spanish dancers, historical characters, and contemporary males and females performing a wide variety of tasks. Of the 200 or more different figures, the most common are Spanish dancers, bull fighters, and doctors. Some Klumpes were imported by Effanbee in the early 1950s. Originally the figures had two sewn-on identifying cardboard tags.

10" felt Sawbones with Roldan paper tag, circa 1960s, $125.00. Courtesy Sharon Kolibaba.

10½" unmarked cloth Klumpe-type cowboy, circa 1950s – 1960s, $78.00. Courtesy Christine McWilliams.

Average figure

10½"	$25.00	$95.00+

Elaborate figure, MIB with accessories

10½"	$225.00

Knickerbocker

CLOTH

Clown

17"	$5.00	$25.00

Disney characters

Donald Duck, Mickey Mouse, etc., all-cloth

10½"	$125.00	$425.00

Mickey Mouse, ca. 1930s, oil cloth eyes

15"	$3,100.00*

Pinocchio, cloth and plush

13"	$65.00	$250.00

Seven Dwarfs, 1939+
      14" $65.00 $260.00
Snow White, all-cloth
      16" $95.00 $365.00

COMPOSITION

Child, 1938+
      15" $55.00 $285.00
"Dagwood" comic strip characters
Composition, painted features, hair
Alexander
      9" $100.00 $375.00
Dagwood
      14" $175.00 $650.00
Mickey Mouse, 1930s – 1940s
Composition, cloth body
      18" $300.00 $1,100.00
Jiminy Cricket, all-composition
      10" $125.00 $495.00
Pinocchio, all-composition
      13" $125.00 $400.00
      14" $1,500.00* in original labeled box
Seven Dwarfs, 1939+
      9" each $75.00 $275.00
Sleeping Beauty, 1939+, bent right arm
      15" $100.00 $425.00
      18" $130.00 $495.00
Snow White, 1937+, all-composition, bent right arm, black wig
      15" $110.00 $435.00
      20" $125.00 $475.00
Molded hair and ribbon
Mark: "WALT DISNEY//1937//KNICKERBOCKER"
      13" $75.00 $360.00
Set of seven Dwarfs, Snow White, mohair wigs, beards
      9 – 11" $1,300.00*

HARD PLASTIC AND VINYL

Bozo Clown
      14" $7.00 $25.00
      24" $17.00 $60.00
Cinderella
Two faces, one sad; one with tiara
      16" $5.00 $20.00
Flintstone characters
      6" $3.00 $10.00
      17" $9.00 $43.00
Kewpies: See Modern Kewpie section.
Little House on the Prairie, 1978
      12" $6.00 $22.00
"Little Orphan Annie" comic strip characters, 1982
Little Orphan Annie, vinyl
      6" $5.00 $17.50

15" cloth Knickerbocker Mickey Mouse Clown, oil-cloth pie eyes, circa 1930s, $3,100.00. Courtesy McMasters Doll Auctions.

* at auction

Daddy Warbucks

	7"	$5.00	$17.50

Punjab

	7"	$4.00	$18.00

Miss Hannigan

	7"	$4.00	$18.00

Molly

	5½"	$4.00	$12.00

Soupy Sales, 1966
Vinyl and cloth, non-removable clothes

	13"	$35.00	$135.00

Two-faced dolls, 1960s
Vinyl face masks, one crying, one smiling

	12"	$5.00	$18.00

Lawton Doll Co.

Wendy Lawton, 1979+, Turlock, CA.

Price indicates complete mint-in-box doll; dolls missing accessories or with flaws would be priced less.

14" porcelain Wendy Lawton The Little Drummer Boy, boxed, with 9" all-porcelain jointed baby Jesus in a handmade wooden manger, limited edition of 500 marked pieces, circa 1993, $500.00. Courtesy Iva Mae Jones.

Childhood Classics

Alice in Wonderland	1983		$3,000.00+
Anne of Green Gables	1986	14"	$1,600.00+
Hans Brinker	1985	14"	$850.00
Heidi	1984	14"	$850.00
Laura Ingalls	1986		$600.00
Little Eva	1988		$750.00
Lil' Princess	1989	14"	$850.00
Pollyanna	1986	14"	$800.00

Disney World Specials

1st Main Street		$450.00
2nd Liberty Square (250)		$400.00
3rd Tish		$400.00
4th Karen (50)		$800.00
5th Goofy Kid (100)		$800.00
6th Melissa & Her Mickey		$750.00
7th Christopher, Robin, Pooh	12"	$750.00

Guild Dolls

Ba Ba Black Sheep	1989	$750.00
Lavender Blue	1990	$450.00
To Market, To Market	1991	$550.00

Special Editions

Marcella & Raggedy Ann		
	1988	$795.00
Flora McFlimsey	1993	$1,000.00

Other Specials

Josephine, souvenir doll of Modesto, CA, UFDC Region 2 Conference outfits, book, duck, suitcase

	12"	$1,200.00+

Britta, Marta, Toy Village, Lansing, MI			$595.00
Morgan, Toy Village, Lansing MI			$695.00
Kitty, The Toy Store, Toledo, OH			$400.00
Little Colonel, Dolly Dears, Birmingham, AL			$425.00
1st WL Convention, Lotta Crabtree			$1,300.00+
2nd WL Convention, Through the Looking Glass, 1995			
		16"	$1,100.00+

Timeless Ballads

Annabel Lee	1987	18"	$500.00
Highland Mary	1987	18"	$700.00
She Walks In Beauty	1988	18"	$500.00
Young Charlotte	1987	18"	$500.00

Marx

9" vinyl Marx Veronica, Betty, and Jughead comic characters; Jughead has molded hair, Betty and Veronica are wigged, painted features, MIB, circa 1975, $30.00 each. Courtesy McMasters Doll Auctions.

ARCHIE AND FRIENDS

Characters from comics, vinyl, molded hair or wigged, painted eyes, in package

Archie	8½"	$10.00	$30.00
Betty	8½"	$10.00	$30.00
Jughead	8½"	$10.00	$30.00
Veronica	8½"	$10.00	$30.00

JOHNNY APOLLO DOUBLE AGENT, vinyl, trench coat, circa 1970s

12"	$25.00	$50.00

MISS SEVENTEEN, 1961

Hard plastic, high heeled, fashion-type doll, modeled like the German Bild Lilli, Barbie doll's predecessor, came in black swimsuit, black box, fashion brochure pictures 12 costumes, she was advertised as "A Beauty Queen."

18"	$175.00	$300.00

Too few in database for reliable range.

MISS MARLENE

Hard plastic, high heeled, Barbie-type, ca. 1960s, blonde rooted wig

7"	$170.00* original box, costume

MISS TODDLER

Also know as Miss Marx, vinyl, molded hair, ribbons, battery operated walker, molded clothing

18"	$75.00	$155.00

11½" rigid vinyl artic-ulated Marx Quick Draw Johnny West, molded blue clothing and lever on back, out of box, some acces-sories, circa 1970s, $75.00. Courtesy Chad Moyer.

11½" rigid vinyl articulated Marx Princess Wildflower with papoose in vinyl cradle, 22-piece vinyl accessories, from Johnny West Best of the West series, circa 1965 – 1976, $150.00. Courtesy Chad Moyer.

Sindy, vinyl

11"	$5.00	$35.00

Gayle, Sindy's friend, black vinyl

11"	$25.00	$75.00

JOHNNY WEST FAMILY OF ACTION FIGURES, 1965 – 1976

Adventure or Best of the West Series, rigid vinyl, articulated figures, molded clothes, came in box with vinyl accessories and extra clothes. Had horses, dogs, and other accessories available. First price indicates played with, missing some accessories; second price for complete in box; more if never-removed-from-box or special sets.

Bill Buck, brown molded-on clothing, 13 pieces, coonskin cap

11½"	$35.00	$125.00

Captain Tom Maddox, blue molded-on clothing, brown hair, 23 pieces

11½"	$25.00	$90.00

Chief Cherokee, tan or light color molded-on cloth-ing, 37 pieces

11½"	$25.00	$100.00

Daniel Boone, tan molded-on clothing, coonskin cap

11½"	$30.00	$115.00

Fighting Eagle, tan molded-on clothes, with Mohawk hair, 37 pieces

11½"	$45.00	$135.00

General Custer, dark blue molded-on clothing, yel-low hair, 23 pieces

11½"	$25.00	$85.00

Geronimo, light color molded-on clothing

11½"	$25.00	$95.00

Orange body

11½"	$50.00	$125.00

Jamie West, dark hair, molded-on tan cloth-ing, 13 accessories

9"	$20.00	$45.00

Jane West, blonde hair, turquoise molded on clothing, 37 pieces

11½"	$20.00	$50.00
Orange body	$25.00	$45.00

Janice West, dark hair, turquoise molded-on clothing, 14 pieces

9"	$20.00	$45.00

Jay West, blond hair, tan molded-on clothing, 13 accessories, later brighter body colors

9"	$20.00	$45.00

Jeb Gibson, c. 1973, black figure, molded-on green clothing

12"	$100.00	$200.00

Johnny West, brown hair, molded-on brown clothing, 25 pieces

12"	$25.00	$90.00

Johnny West, with quick draw arm, blue clothing

12"	$20.00	$55.00

Josie West, blonde, turquoise molded-on clothing, later with bright green body

9"	$20.00	$45.00

Princess Wildflower, off-white molded-on clothing, with papoose in vinyl cradle, 22 pieces of accessories

11½"	$50.00	$130.00

Sam Cobra, outlaw, with 26 accessories

11½"	$25.00	$100.00

Sam Cobra, quick draw version

	$35.00	$125.00

9" rigid vinyl articulated Marx Janice West of the Johnny West Series, molded-on clothing, 14 pieces of vinyl clothing and accessories, box, circa 1965 – 1976, $75.00. Courtesy Chad Moyer.

Sheriff Pat Garrett (Sheriff Goode in Canada), molded-on blue clothing, 25 pieces of accessories

11½"	$35.00	$125.00

Zeb Zachary, dark hair, blue molded-on clothing, 23 pieces

11½"	$30.00	$110.00

KNIGHT AND VIKING SERIES, CA. 1960s

Action figures with accessories

Gordon, the Gold Knight, molded-on gold clothing, brown hair, beard, mustache

11½"	$35.00	$125.00

Sir Stuart, Silver Knight, molded-on silver clothing, black hair, mustache, goatee

11½"	$35.00	$125.00

Brave Erik, Viking with horse, ca. 1967, molded-on green clothing, blond hair, blue eyes

11½"	$50.00	$150.00

Odin, the Viking, ca. 1967, brown molded-on clothing, brown eyes, brown hair, beard

11½"	$50.00	$150.00

SINDY

A 1970s fashion-type doll, rooted hair, painted eyes, wires in limbs allow her to pose. Originated in England by Pedigree, also made in US and New Zealand.

11"	$10.00	$35.00

SOLDIERS, CA. 1960s

Articulated action figures with accessories

Buddy Charlie, Montgomery Wards, exclusive, a buddy for GI Joe, molded-on military uniform, brown hair

11½"	$35.00	$100.00

Stony "Stonewall" Smith, molded-on Army fatigues, blond hair, 36-piece accessories

11½"	$25.00	$100.00

Matchbox

Freddy Krueger, 1989, vinyl, pull string talker horror movie *Nightmare on Elm Street* character played by Robert England

18"	$30.00	$60.00

PeeWee Herman, 1987 TV character, vinyl and cloth, ventriloquist doll in gray suit, red bow tie

26"	$20.00	$65.00

PeeWee Herman, pull string talker

18"	$10.00	$36.00

Mattel

Baby Beans, 1971 – 1975
Vinyl head, bean bag dolls, terry cloth or tricot bodies filled with plastic and foam

12"	$5.00	$20.00

Talking

12"	$7.00	$25.00

Baby First Step, 1965 – 1967
Battery operated walker, rooted hair, sleep eyes, pink dress

18"	$7.00	$22.00

Talking

18"	$8.00	$27.00

Baby Go Bye-Bye and Her Bumpety Buggy, 1970
Doll sits in car, battery operated, 12 maneuvers

11"	$4.00	$12.00

Baby's Hungry, 1967 – 1968
Battery operated, eyes move and lips chew when magic bottle or spoon is put to mouth, wets, plastic bib

17"	$8.00	$22.00

Baby Love Light
Battery operated

16"	$5.00	$18.00

Baby Pattaburp, 1964 – 1966
Vinyl, drinks milk, burps when patted, pink jacket, lace trim

16"	$7.00	$22.00

Baby Play-A-Lot, 1972 – 1973
Posable arms, fingers can hold things, comes with 20 toys, moves arm to brush teeth, moves head, no batteries, has pull string and switch

16"	$5.00	$22.00

Baby Say 'N See, 1967 – 1968
Eyes and lips move while talking, white dress, pink yoke

17"	$10.00	$35.00

17" vinyl Mattel Baby Secret, original outfit with name on bib, blue eyes, red rooted hair, stuffed body, played with, circa 1966 – 1967, $35.00. Private collection.

Baby Secret, 1966 – 1967
Vinyl face and hands, stuffed body, limbs, red hair, blue eyes, whispers 11 phrases, moves lips

18"	$10.00	$35.00

Baby Small Talk, 1968 – 1969
Says eight phrases, infant voice, addition outfits available

10¾"	$10.00	$20.00

Black

10¾"	$15.00	$25.00

Baby Tender Love, 1970 – 1973
Baby doll, realistic skin, wets, can be bathed
Newborn

13"	$4.00	$12.00

Talking

16"	$5.00	$18.00

Living, 1970

20"	$8.00	$27.00

Molded hairpiece, 1972

11½"	$9.00	$33.00

Brother, sexed

11½"	$10.00	$38.00

Baby Teenie Talk, 1965

17"	$7.00	$22.00

Baby Walk 'n Play, 1968

11"	$4.00	$12.00

Baby Walk 'n See

18"	$5.00	$18.00

Barbie: See that section.
Bozo

18"	$8.00	$28.00

Buffy and Mrs. Beasley, 1967 & 1974
Characters from TV sitcom, *Family Affair.*
Buffy, vinyl, rooted hair, painted features, holds small Mrs. Beasley, vinyl head, on cloth body

6½"	$75.00	$185.00

Talking Buffy, vinyl, 1969 – 1971, holds tiny 6" rag Mrs. Beasley

10¾"	$50.00	$200.00

Mrs. Beasley, 1967 – 1974, talking vinyl head, cloth body, square glasses, blue polka-dot dress

22"	$50.00	$175.00

Mrs. Beasley, 1973, non-talker

15½"	$15.00	$55.00

Captain Kangaroo, 1967
Sears only, talking character, host for TV kids program

19"	$20.00	$75.00

Captain Laser, 1967
Vinyl, painted features, blue uniform, silver accessories, batteries operate laser gun, light-up eyes

12"	$70.00	$265.00

15½" vinyl Mattel Drowsy pull string talker, cloth body, rooted hair, painted eyes with molded drooping lids, circa 1965 – 1974, played with condition, $8.00. Courtesy Marie Rodgers.

6½" vinyl Mattel Buffy holding Mrs. Beasley with the black hard to keep glasses, tagged, circa 1967+, $150.00. Courtesy Bonnie Baskins.

19" vinyl Mattel Chatty Cathy hard plastic body, pull string talker, blue sleep eyes, rooted hair, freckles, open, closed mouth with two teeth, original sundress not complete, does not talk, circa 1962 – 1964, $75.00. Courtesy Darleen Foote.

24" vinyl Mattel Charming Chatty, lacks glasses, played with condition, extra clothes, circa 1963 – 1964, $75.00. Courtesy Christine McWilliams.

Casper, the Ghost, ca. 1964

	16"	$7.00	$28.00
1971	5"	$3.00	$10.00

Chatty Cathy Series

Chatty Cathy, 1960 – 1963, vinyl head, hard platic body, pull string activates voice, dressed in pink and white checked or blue party dresses, 1963 – 1965, says 18 new phrases, red velvet and white lace dress, extra outfits available

Blonde

20"	$35.00	$175.00

Brunette, brown eyes

20"	$85.00	$335.00

Black, 1961 – 1963

20"	$100.00	$400.00

Chatty Baby, 1962 – 1964, red pinafore over rompers

18"	$15.00	$60.00

Charmin' Chatty, 1963 – 1964

Talking doll, soft vinyl head, closed smiling mouth, hard vinyl body, long rooted hair, long legs, five records placed in left side slot, one-piece navy skirt, white middy blouse, with red sailor collar, red socks and saddle shoes, glasses, five disks; extra outfits and 14 more disks available

24"	$55.00	$200.00

Tiny Chatty Baby, 1963 – 1964

Smaller version of Chatty Baby, blue rompers, blue, white striped panties, bib with name, talks, other outfits available

15½"	$7.00	$30.00

Black

5½"	$10.00	$40.00

Tiny Chatty Brother, 1963 – 1964

Boy version of Tiny Chatty Baby, blue and white suit and cap, hair parted on side

15½"	$8.00	$35.00

Cheerful Tearful, 1966 – 1967

Vinyl, blonde hair, face changes from smile to pout as arm is lowered, feed her bottle, wets and cries real tears

7"	$5.00	$25.00

Dancerina, 1969 – 1971

Battery operated, posable arms, legs, turns, dances with control knob on head, pink ballet outfit

24"	$20.00	$85.00

Baby Dancerina, 1970

Smaller version, no batteries, turn-knob on head, white ballet outfit

16"	$15.00	$55.00

Black
16" $20.00 $65.00
Teeny Dancerina
12" $8.00 $30.00
Debbie Boone, 1978
11½" $12.00 $40.00
Dick Van Dyke, 1969
As Mr. Potts in movie, *Chitty Chitty Bang Bang,* all-cloth, flat features, talks in actor's voice
Mark: "© Mattel 1969" on cloth tag
24" $18.00 $85.00
Drowsy, 1965 – 1974
Vinyl head, stuffed body, sleepers, pull-string talker
15½" $15.00 $125.00
Dr. Dolittle, 1968
Character patterned after Rex Harrison in movie version, talker, vinyl with cloth body
24" $18.00 $55.00
All vinyl
6" $6.00 $22.00

6" vinyl Mattel Baby Tearful Cheerful drink and wet doll, press tummy, frowns, circa 1967, $16.50. Courtesy Angie Gonzales.

Gramma Doll, 1970 – 1973
Sears only, cloth, painted face, gray yarn hair, says ten phrases, talker, foam-filled cotton
11" $4.00 $15.00
Grizzly Adams, 1971
10" $10.00 $40.00
Guardian Goddesses, 1979
11½" $40.00 $165.00
Herman Munster, 1965
Cloth doll, talking TV character, *The Munsters*
21" $8.00 $28.00
Julia, 1969, TV character nurse, from *Julia*
One-piece uniform
11½" $35.00 $125.00
Two-piece uniform
11½" $45.00 $175.00
Talking
11½" $40.00 $135.00
Liddle Kiddles, 1966+
Small dolls of vinyl over wire frame, posable, painted features, rooted hair and came with bright costumes and accessories, packaged on 8½" x 9½" cards.
Mark: "1965// Mattel Inc.// Japan" on back
First price is for complete doll and accessories, excellent condition; second price (or one price only) is for mint complete doll and accessories. Add more for mint in package (or card) and never-removed-from-package. Less for worn dolls with missing accessories.

1966, First Series

3501 Bunson Bernie	3"	$45.00	$55.00
3502 Howard "Biff" Boodle	3½"	$55.00	$75.00
3503 Liddle Diddle	2¾"	$45.00	$55.00
3505 Babe Biddle	3½"	$45.00	$55.00
3506 Calamity Jiddle	3"	$45.00	$55.00
3507 Florence Niddle	2¾"	$45.00	$55.00
3508 Greta Griddle	3"	$45.00	$55.00
3509 Millie Middle	2¾"	$45.00	$55.00
3510 Beat A Diddle	3½"	$155.00	$180.00

1967, Second Series

3513 Sizzly Friddle	3"	$50.00	$60.00
3514 Windy Fiddle	2¾"	$50.00	$60.00
3515 Trikey Triddle	2¾"	$40.00	$55.00
3516 Freezy Sliddle	3½"	$40.00	$50.00
3517 Surfy Skiddle	3"	$50.00	$60.00
3518 Soapy Siddle	3½"	$55.00	$75.00
3519 Rolly Twiddle	3½"	$125.00	$150.00
3548 Beddy Bye Biddle (with robe)		$60.00	$70.00
3549 Pretty Priddle	3½"	$50.00	$65.00

1968, Third Series

3587 Baby Liddle	2¾"	$175.00	$200.00
3551 Telly Viddle	3½"	$50.00	$65.00
3552 Lemons Stiddle	3½"	$50.00	$65.00
3553 Kampy Kiddle	3½"	$50.00	$65.00
3554 Slipsy Sliddle	3½"	$50.00	$60.00
Storybook Kiddles, 1967 – 1968		$60.00 – $100.00	
Skediddle Kiddles, 1968 – 1970	4"	$25.00+	
Playhouse Kiddles, 1970	3½"	$95.00	
Kiddles 'N Kars, 1969 – 1970	2¾"	$55.00	
Tea Party Kiddles, 1970 – 1971	3½"	$100.00	
Lucky Locket Kiddles, 1967 – 1970	2"	$25.00+	
Kiddle Kolognes, 1968 – 1970	2"	$25.00+	
Kola Kiddles, 1968 – 1969	2"	$35.00	
Sweet Treat Kiddles, 1969 – 1970	2"	$65.00	
Liddle Kiddle Playhouses, 1966 – 1968		$40.00+	

Osmond Family

Donny or Marie Osmond, 1978

	12"	$12.00	$40.00

Jimmy Osmond, 1979

	10"	$15.00	$65.00

Scooba Doo, 1964

Vinyl head, rooted hair, cloth body, talks in Beatnik phrases, blonde or black hair, striped dress

	23"	$25.00	$100.00

Shogun Warrior

All plastic, battery operated

	23½"	$65.00	$250.00

Shrinkin' Violette, 1964 – 1965
Cloth, yarn hair, pull-string talker, eyes close, mouth moves

16"	$25.00	$125.00

Sister Belle, 1961 – 1963
Vinyl, pull string talker, cloth body

16"	$45.00	$100.00

Small Talk Baby, 1968 – 1969
Pull-string talker, extra costumes available

White	10¾"	$15.00	$45.00
Black	10¾"	$20.00	$50.00

Small Talk Sister, 1968 – 1969, little girl, will stand alone, talker, mini dress, white boots, additional costumes available

	10¾"	$7.00	$25.00

Star Spangled dolls
Uses Sunshine Family adults, *marked "1973"*
Regina/Richard Stanton

	$12.00	$45.00

Southern Belle

	$12.00	$45.00

New England Girl

	$12.00	$45.00

Pioneer Daughter

	$12.00	$45.00

23" vinyl Mattel Scooba Doo pull string talker, beatnik type, rooted hair, sleep eyes with dark eyeshadow at corners, cloth body, long legs, re-dressed, circa 1965, $25.00. Courtesy Teddy Callens.

Sunshine Family, The
Vinyl, posable, come with Idea Book, Father, Mother, Baby

Steve

	9"	$6.00	$30.00

Stephie

	7½"	$6.00	$30.00

Sweets

	3½"	$4.00	$20.00

Tatters, 1965 – 1967
Talking cloth doll, wears rag clothes

19"	$10.00	$38.00

Teachy Keen, 1966 – 1970
Sears only, vinyl head, cloth body, ponytail, talker, tells child to use accessories included, buttons, zippers, comb

16"	$9.00	$32.00

Tinkerbelle

19"	$7.00	$22.00

Tippee Toes, 1968 – 1970
Battery operated, legs move, rides accessory horse, tricycle, knit sweater, pants

17"	$5.00	$18.00
Tricycle/horse	$5.00	$18.00

16" vinyl Mattel Talking Sister Belle, cloth body, yarn hair, TV character, pull string talker, says 11 different phrases, #0730, circa 1961 – 1963, $175.00. Courtesy Marie Emmerson.

Welcome Back Kotter, 1973, characters from TV sitcom
Freddie "Boom Boom" Washington

	9"	$4.00	$15.00

Arnold Horshack

	9"	$5.00	$20.00

Gabe Kotter

	9"	$8.00	$30.00

Zython, 1977
Has glow-in-the-dark head. Enemy in *Space 1999* series.

		$25.00	$100.00

Mego

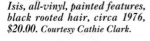

Action Jackson, 1971 – 1972
Vinyl head, plastic body, molded hair, painted black eyes, action figure, many accessory outfits

Mark: "©Mego Corp//Reg. U.S. Pat. Off.//Pat. Pend.//Hong Kong//MCMLXXI"

	8"	$8.00	$30.00

Black

	8"	$20.00	$75.00

Dinah-mite, Black

		$5.00	$20.00

Batman, 1974

	8"	$4.00	$15.00

Arch enemy

	8"	$4.00	$15.00

Captain and Tennille
Daryl Dragon and Toni Tennille, 1977, recording and TV personalities, Toni Tennille doll has no molded ears

	12½"	$10.00	$40.00

8" Mego Joanna Cameron as Isis, all-vinyl, painted features, black rooted hair, circa 1976, $20.00. Courtesy Cathie Clark.

Cher, 1976
TV and recording personality and husband Sonny Bono, all-vinyl, fully jointed, rooted long black hair, also as grow-hair doll

	12"	$12.00	$45.00

Cher, in Indian outfit

	12"	$17.00	$65.00

Sonny Bono

	12"	$12.00	$45.00

CHiP's 1977
California Highway Patrol TV show, Jon Baker, Francis "Ponch" Poncherello

	8"	$4.00	$10.00

Diana Ross, 1977
Recording and movie personality, all-vinyl, fully jointed, rooted black hair, long lashes

	12½"	$45.00	$125.00

Farrah Fawcett, 1977

Model, movie, and television personality, starred as Jill in *Charlie's Angels,* vinyl head, rooted blonde hair, painted green eyes

    12½" $20.00 $45.00

Flash Gordon Series, ca. 1977+

Vinyl head, hard plastic articulated body

Dale Arden

    9" $25.00 $100.00

Dr. Zarkov

    9½" $25.00 $100.00

Flash Gordon

    9½" $25.00 $100.00

Ming, the Merciless

    9½" $25.00 $100.00

Mego David Soul as Hutch and Paul Michael Glaser as Starsky, all-vinyl, fully jointed including waists, both 7½", circa 1976, $25.00 each. Courtesy Cathie Clark.

Happy Days Series, 1976

Characters from *Happy Days* TV sitcom, Henry Winkler starred as Fonzie, Ronnie Howard as Richie, Anson Williams as Potsie, and Donny Most as Ralph Malph

Fonzie

    8" $5.00 $20.00

Richie, Potsie, Ralph

    $4.00 $15.00

Jaclyn Smith, 1977

Vinyl

    12½ $50.00 $100.00

Joe Namath, 1970

Football player, actor, soft vinyl head, rigid vinyl body, painted hair and features

    12" $15.00 $55.00

12½" vinyl Mego KISS rock group, with Gene Simmons, Ace Frehley, Peter Cris, and Paul Stanley, all-vinyl, fully jointed, rooted hair, painted features and makeup, circa 1978, $150.00 each. Courtesy McMasters Doll Auctions.

KISS, 1978
Rock group, with Gene Simmons, Ace Frehley, Peter Cris, and Paul
Stanley, all-vinyl, fully jointed, rooted hair, painted features and makeup

12½"	$50.00	$150.00+

Laverne and Shirley, 1977
TV sitcom; Penny Marshall, played Laverne, Cindy Williams, Shirley,
also, from the same show, David Lander as Squiggy, and Michael McKean as
Lenny, all-vinyl, rooted hair, painted eyes

11½"	$25.00	$50.00

Our Gang, 1975
From *Our Gang* movie shorts, that replayed on TV, included characters
Alfalpha, Buckwheat, Darla, Mickey, Porky, and Spanky

6"	$5.00	$20.00

Planet of the Apes Movie Series, ca. 1970s

Astronaut	8"	$30.00	$120.00
Ape Soldier	8"	$25.00	$100.00
Cornelius	8"	$35.00	$140.00
Dr. Zaius	8"	$40.00	$150.00
Zira	8"	$35.00	$140.00

Planet of the Apes TV Series, ca. 1974

Alan Verdon	8"	$40.00	$150.00
Galen	8"	$25.00	$100.00
General Urko	8"	$40.00	$150.00
General Ursus	8"	$25.00	$100.00
Peter Burke	8"	$40.00	$150.00

Star Trek TV Series, ca. 1973 – 1975

Captain Kirk	8"	$15.00	$60.00
Dr. McCoy	8"	$20.00	$75.00
Klingon	8"	$25.00	$100.00
Lt. Uhura	8"	$15.00	$60.00
Mr. Scott	8"	$20.00	$75.00
Mr. Spock	8"	$15.00	$60.00

Star Trek Movie Series, ca. 1979

Acturian	12½"	$25.00	$100.00
Captain Kirk	12½"	$15.00	$60.00
Ilia	12½"	$15.00	$60.00
Mr. Spock	12½"	$25.00	$100.00

Star Trek Aliens, ca. 1975 – 1976

Andorian	8"	$80.00	$325.00
Cheron	8"	$35.00	$130.00
Mugato	8"	$75.00	$300.00
Talos	8"	$65.00	$250.00
The Gorn	8"	$50.00	$200.00
The Romulan	8"	$150.00	$600.00

Starsky and Hutch, 1976
Police TV series, Paul Michael Glaser as Starsky, David Soul as Hutch,
Bernie Hamilton as Captain Dobey, Antonio Fargas as Huggy Bear, also includ-
ed a villain, Chopper, all-vinyl, jointed waists

7½"	$6.00	$25.00

Suzanne Somers, 1978

Actress, TV personality, starred as Chrissy in *Three's Company,* all-vinyl, fully jointed, rooted blonde hair, painted blue eyes, long lashes

12½"	$7.00	$28.00

Waltons, The, 1975

From TV drama series, set of two 8" dolls per package, all-vinyl

Johnboy and Ellen	$10.00	$35.00
Mom and Pop	$10.00	$35.00
Grandma and Grandpa	$10.00	$35.00

Wonder Woman Series, ca. 1976 – 1977

Vinyl head, rooted black hair, painted eyes, plastic body

Lt. Diane Prince	12½"	$40.00	$150.00
Nubia	12½"	$25.00	$100.00
Nurse	12½"	$10.00	$40.00
Queen Hippolyte	12½"	$25.00	$100.00
Steve Trevor	12½"	$25.00	$100.00
Wonder Woman	12½"	$40.00	$150.00

Molly'es

Mollye Goldman, 1920+, International Doll Co., Philadelphia, PA. Designed and created clothes for dolls of cloth, composition, hard plastic, and vinyl. Name marked only on vinyls; others may have had paper hang tags. She used dolls made by other companies. Also designed clothes for other makers.

First price is for doll in good condition, but with flaws; second price is for doll in excellent condition original clothes. More for exceptional doll with fancy wardrobe or accessories.

CLOTH

Child

15"	$40.00	$150.00
18"	$45.00	$165.00
24"	$65.00	$215.00
29"	$85.00	$325.00

Internationals

13"	$27.00	$95.00
15"	$45.00	$155.00
27"	$75.00	$300.00

Girl/Lady

16"	$50.00	$195.00
21"	$75.00	$300.00

COMPOSITION

Baby

15"	$40.00	$175.00
21"	$60.00	$250.00

Cloth body

18"	$25.00	$100.00

14" cloth Molly'es Jane and American Nurse, with hang tag marked Made by Molly'es, painted blue eyes, blonde mohair wig, cloth body, all original, circa 1920s+, $300.00. Courtesy Dee Cermak.

Toddler

15"	$50.00	$235.00
21"	$75.00	$295.00

Child

15"	$50.00	$185.00
18"	$70.00	$265.00

Girl/Lady, add more for ball gown

16"	$90.00	$365.00
21"	$130.00	$525.00

HARD PLASTIC

Baby

14"	$25.00	$95.00
20"	$40.00	$150.00

Cloth body

17"	$25.00	$90.00
23"	$35.00	$140.00

Child

14"	$50.00	$200.00+
18"	$75.00	$300.00+
23"	$100.00	$400.00+

Girl/Lady

17"	$75.00	$315.00
20"	$80.00	$415.00
25"	$110.00	$465.00

VINYL

Baby

8½"	$6.00	$22.00
12"	$5.00	$27.00
15"	$9.00	$43.00

Child

8"	$7.00	$25.00
10"	$9.00	$35.00
15"	$15.00	$60.00

Girl/Lady

Little Women

9"	$9.00	$40.00

Monica Dolls

Ca. 1941 – 1951. Monica Dolls from Hollywood, designed by Hansi Share, made composition and later hard plastic with long face and painted or sleep eyes, eyeshadow, unique feature is very durable rooted human hair. Did not have high-heeled feet and unmarked, but wore paper wrist tag reading *"Monica Doll, Hollywood."* Composition dolls had pronounced widow's peak in center of forehead.

Composition, 1941 – 1949

Painted eyes, Veronica, Jean, and Rosalind were names of 17" dolls produced in 1942.

11"	$75.00	$295.00
15"	$150.00	$525.00
17"	$175.00	$750.00
20 – 21"	$250.00	$950.00
24"	$300.00	$1,200.00

Hard plastic, 1949 – 1951, sleep eyes, Elizabeth, Marion, or Linda

| 14" | $150.00 | $600.00 |
| 18" | $200.00 | $800.00 |

20" composition Monica from Monica Studios has rooted human hair, blue painted eyes, rosy cheeks, original long dress, circa 1940s, $375.00. Courtesy Odis Gregg.

Nancy Ann Storybook

1936+, San Francisco, CA. Started by Rowena Haskin (Nancy Ann Abbott). Painted bisque, mohair wig, painted eyes, head molded to torso, jointed limbs, either sticker on outfit or hang tag, in box, later made in hard plastic.

First price for played-with or missing accessories doll; second price for mint or mint-in-box. Add 30 percent or more for black dolls. Selected auction prices reflect once-only extreme high prices and should be noted accordingly. Painted bisque baby prices vary with outfits.

BABY ONLY, 1936+

Pink/blue mottled or sunburst box with gold label, gold foil sticker on clothes *"Nancy Ann Dressed Dolls," marked "87," "88," or "93," "Made in Japan,"* no brochure

| Baby | 3½" – 4½" | $100.00 | $400.00 |

BABY OR CHILD

1937

Child marked "Made in Japan," "1146," "1148," or "Japan" sunburst box with gold label, gold foil sticker on clothes read *"Nancy Ann Dressed Dolls,"* no brochure

| Baby | 3½" – 4½" | $275.00 | $700.00 |
| Child | 5" | $500.00 | $1,200.00 |

Two early Nancy Ann babies 4½" open fist babies were called Little Miss Pattycake and closed fist babies were called Rock-a-Bye Baby, circa 1941, $100.00 each. Courtesy Cathie Clark.

5" painted bisque Nancy Ann Storybook in white box with blue dots, To Market, To Market, #120, silver label, excellent condition, plaid dress, brochure, bracelet, circa 1941 – 1942, $75.00. Courtesy Arthur Mock.

5" painted bisque Nancy Ann Storybook in blue box with white dots, jointed legs, painted molded socks and shoes, booklet, missing bracelet, circa 1940, $150.00. Courtesy Arthur Mock.

1938

Marked *"America"* (baby *marked "87," "88," or "93" "Made in Japan"*), colored box, sunburst pattern with gold label, gold foil sticker on clothes: *"Judy Ann,"* no brochure

Baby	3½" – 4½"	$200.00	$325.00
Child	5"	$200.00	$500.00

1938

Marked *"Judy Ann USA"* and *"Story Book USA"* (baby *marked "Made in USA"* and *"88, 89, and 93 Made in Japan"*), colored box, sunburst pattern with gold or silver label, gold foil sticker on clothes: *"Storybook Dolls,"* no brochure

3½"– 4½"	$225.00	$325.00
5"	$200.00	$300.00

Complete with teddy bear, dress tagged *"Judy Ann"* blue box, silver dots, marked *"Japan 1146"*

5"	$160.00	$650.00
Judy Ann mold	$100.00	$500.00
Storybook mold	$100.00	$350.00
Jointed bisque		

Pussy Cat, Pussy Cat, complete with pet

5"	$100.00	$300.00

1939

Child, molded socks and molded bangs (baby has star-shaped hands), colored box with small silver dots, silver label, gold foil sticker on clothes, *"Storybook Dolls,"* no brochure

Baby	3½" – 4½"	$75.00	$150.00
Child	5"	$125.00	$225.00

1940

Child has molded socks only (baby has star-shaped bisque hands), colored box with white polka dots, silver label, gold foil sticker on clothes, *"Storybook Dolls,"* has brochure

Baby	3½" – 4½"	$60.00	$135.00
Child	5"	$50.00	$200.00

1941 – 1942

Child has pudgy tummy or slim tummy; baby has star-shaped hands or fist, white box with colored polka dots, with silver label, gold foil bracelet with name of doll and brochure

Baby	3½" – 4½"	$65.00	$125.00
Child	5"	$20.00	$75.00

1943 – 1947

Child has one-piece head, body, and legs, baby has fist hands, white box with colored polka dots, silver label, ribbon tie or pin fastener, gold foil bracelet with name of doll and brochure

5" painted bisque Nancy Ann Storybook in white box, pink dots, Thursdays Child Has Far to Go, #183, circa 1943 – 1947, silver label brochure, no bracelet, $75.00. Courtesy Arthur Mock.

8" hard plastic Nancy Ann Muffie all hard plastic, turning head walker, mint in her box, marked "Playtime Dolls by Nancy Ann, San Francisco, California," circa 1954, $200.00. Courtesy Cathie Clark.

Baby	3½" – 4½"	$60.00	$125.00
Child	5"	$25.00	$65.00

1947 – 1949

Child has hard plastic body, painted eyes, baby has bisque body, plastic arms and legs, white box with colored polka dots with *"Nancy Ann Storybook Dolls"* between dots, silver label, brass snap, gold foil bracelet with name of doll and brochure. More for special outfit.

Baby	3½" – 4½"	$45.00	$90.00

Ca. 1949

Hard plastic, both have black sleep eyes, white box with colored polka dots and *"Nancy Ann Storybook Dolls"* between dots, silver label, brass or painted snaps, gold foil bracelet with name of doll and brochure

Baby	3½" – 4½"	$40.00	$75.00
Child	5"	$15.00	$50.00

Ca. 1953

Hard plastic, child has blue sleep eyes, except for 4½" girls; baby has black sleep eyes, white box with colored polka dots, some with clear lids, silver label, gripper snap, gold foil bracelet with name of doll and brochure

Baby	3½" – 4½"	$40.00	$75.00* comes only in christening dress
Child	5"	$12.00	$35.00

SPECIAL DOLLS

Judy Ann, marked *"Japan 1146"* or America mold

	5"	$200.00	$800.00

Mammy and Baby, marked *"Japan 1146"* or America mold

	5"	$150.00	$1,200.00

Storybook USA

	5"	$125.00	$500.00

Topsy, bisque black doll, jointed leg

All-bisque		$75.00	$400.00
Plastic arms		$50.00	$150.00

10" Nancy Ann Storybook hard plastic unmarked Debbie in original outfit, with synthetic wig, sleep eyes, circa 1950s, $65.00. Courtesy Bev Mitchell.

Nancy Ann 5" Bride, mint in her original box, all painted bisque, blonde wig, painted features, circa 1939+, $75.00. Courtesy Cathie Clark.

Topsy, all plastic, painted or sleep eye

Topsy, all plastic, painted or sleep eye	$30.00	$100.00

White boots, bisque jointed leg dolls

5"	Add $50.00	

SERIES DOLLS, DEPENDING ON MOLD MARK
All-Bisque

    Around the World Series

Chinese	$300.00	$1,200.00
English Flower Girl	$150.00	$400.00
Portuguese	$200.00	$450.00
Poland	$200.00	$450.00
Russia	$200.00	$1,200.00
Other Countries	$100.00	$400.00

    Masquerade Series

Ballet Dancer	$200.00	$800.00
Cowboy	$200.00	$800.00
Pirate	$200.00	$800.00

    Sports Series

	$300.00	$1,200.00

    Flower Series (bisque)

	$175.00	$400.00

    Margie Ann Series

Margie Ann	$60.00	$175.00
Margie Ann in other outfits	$125.00	$350.00
Powder & Crinoline Series	$60.00	$175.00

Bisque or Plastic

Operetta or Hit Parade Series	$60.00	$175.00

Hard Plastic

    Big and Little Sister Series, or Commencement Series (except baby)

	$30.00	$100.00

    Bridal, Dolls of the Day, Dolls of the Month, Fairytale, Mother Goose, Nursery Rhyme, Religious, and Seasons Series, painted or sleep eye

	$20.00	$75.00

OTHER DOLLS

Audrey Ann, toddler, marked *"Nancy Ann Storybook 12"*

6"	$250.00	$975.00

Nancy Ann Style Show

Hard plastic, sleep eyes, long dress, unmarked

18"	$300.00	$600.00

MIB, hang tag

18"	$800.00	$1,000.00

Vinyl head, plastic body, all original, complete

18"	$300.00	$500.00

Muffie, 1953 – 1956

1953, hard plastic, wig, sleep eyes, strung straight leg, non-walker, painted lashes

8"	$75.00	$350.00

18" hard plastic Nancy Ann Style Show Dash of Spice, all original, no marks on doll, with box, circa 1950s, $600.00. Courtesy Dee Cermak.

1954, hard plastic walker, molded eyelashes, brows

8"	$65.00	$185.00

1955 – 1956, vinyl head, molded or painted upper lashes, rooted saran wig, walker or bent-knee walker

8"	$60.00	$165.00

Davy Crockett, 1955, walker, molded painted lashes, all original

8"	$175.00*

Muffie, 1968+, reissued, hard plastic

8"	$45.00	$105.00

Lori Ann

Vinyl

17½"	$45.00	$165.00

Debbie

Hard plastic in school dress, name on wrist-tag/box

10"	$45.00	$170.00

Vinyl head, hard plastic body

10"	$25.00	$110.00

Hard plastic walker

10½"	$40.00	$160.00

Vinyl head, hard plastic walker

10½"	$23.00	$90.00

Little Miss Nancy Ann, 1959

Nude

8½"	$25.00	$100.00 MIB
Day dress	$25.00	$50.00 MIB
Other outfits	$30.00	$75.00 MIB

Miss Nancy Ann, 1959, marked *"Nancy Ann,"* vinyl head, rooted hair, rigid vinyl body, high-heeled feet

Nude

10½"	$25.00	$85.00 MIB
Day dress	$25.00	$50.00 MIB

Other outfits	$30.00	$75.00 MIB
Baby Sue Sue, 1960s, vinyl		
Doll only	$25.00	$150.00 MIB
Outfit	$50.00	$75.00 MIB

Old Cottage Dolls

10" English composition Old Cottage Toys Twee-dle Dee and Tweedle Dum, circa 1968, all original, $625.00 pair. Courtesy Dorothy Bohlin.

7½" composition Old Cottage Doll Pearlie girl with felt body, so-called because of the pearl buttons and sequins on her black dress, 1948+, $135.00. Courtesy Dorothy Bohlin.

Late 1940s on, England.

Mrs. M.E. Fleischmann made dolls with hard composition type heads, felt body, some with wire armature, oval hang tag has trademark "Old Cottage Dolls," special characters may be more.

8"	$35.00	$100.00
10"	$50.00	$150.00

Tweedle Dee or Tweedle Dum, circa 1968

8"	$200.00	$350.00

Pleasant Company

1986+, Pleasant Rowland, Middleton, WI. Vinyl dolls, sleep eyes, cloth body, vinyl limbs. Each doll has own identity, time era, with many accessories for that time period. First price is for played with doll; second price is retail.

Felicity and book, 1774		
18"	$55.00	$82.00
Kirsten and book, 1854		
18"	$55.00	$82.00
Addy (black) and book, 1864		
18"	$65.00	$82.00
Samantha and book, 1904		
18"	$55.00	$82.00
Molly and book, 1944		
18"	$55.00	$82.00

18" vinyl Pleasant Company American Girl Josephina sleep eyes, open/closed mouth with two teeth, black synthetic wig, cloth body, vinyl limbs, Christmas dress with her doll and chicken and chilies, 1997, basic doll with book, $82.00. Private collection.

1915+. Designed by Johnny Gruelle in 1915, made by various companies. Ann wears dress with apron; Andy, shirt and pants with matching hat.

P.J. VOLLAND, 1920 – 1934

Early dolls marked *"Patented Sept. 7, 1915."* All-cloth, tin or wooden button eyes, painted features. Some have sewn knee or arm joints, sparse brown or auburn yarn hair, oversize hands, feet turned outward.

Raggedy Ann and Andy

15 – 16"	$400.00	$1,700.00

Beloved Belindy

15"	$600.00	$2,300.00

15½" cloth Georgene Novelties Raggedy Andy and 15" Raggedy Ann, some fading, soil, circa 1930s – 1960s, $375.00 for pair. Courtesy Debbie Crume.

MOLLYE GOODMAN, 1935 – 1938

Marked on chest *"Raggedy Ann and Andy Dolls Manufactured by Mollye's Doll Outfitters."* Nose outlined in black, red heart on chest, reddish-orange hair, multicolored legs, blue feet, some have oilcloth faces.

15"	$225.00	$900.00
17"	$250.00	$1,000.00
21"	$275.00	$1,100.00

Did not make Beloved Belindy

GEORGENE NOVELTIES, 1938 – 1962

Ann has orange hair and a top knot, six different mouth styles; early ones had tin eyes, later ones had plastic, six different noses, seams in middle of legs and arms to represent knees and elbows. Feet turn forward, red and white striped legs. All have hearts that say *"I love you"* printed on chest. Tag sewn to left side seam, several variations, all say *"Georgene Novelties, Inc."*

Raggedy Ann or Andy, 1930s – 1960s

1930s	15"	$90.00	$350.00
	18"	$165.00	$625.00
1940s	13"	$1,000.00* pair	
	18"	$85.00	$325.00
	21"	$100.00	$400.00
1950s	18"	$50.00	$300.00
	44"	$1,200.00* excellent condition	
1960 – 1963			
	15"	$25.00	$110.00
	18"	$35.00	$150.00

17½" cloth Volland Raggedy Andy and 16½" Volland Raggedy Ann, played with condition, circa 1920 – 1934, $2,000.00 for pair. Courtesy Debbie Crume.

Awake/Asleep, pair

1940s	12"	$175.00	$650.00

Beloved Belindy

1950s	15"	$125.00	$750.00

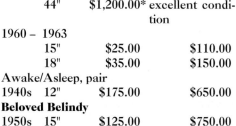

Raggedy Ann & Andy (cont.)

KNICKERBOCKER, 1962 – 1982

Printed features, hair color change from orange to red; there were five mouth and five eyelash variations, tags were located on clothing back or pants seam.

Raggedy Ann or Andy, 1960s

15"	$75.00	$300.00
30 – 36"	$125.00	$500.00

Raggedy Ann Talking, 1960s

	$70.00	$265.00

Beloved Belindy, ca. 1965

15"	$200.00	$750.00

Raggedy Ann, 1970s

12"	$12.00	$45.00
15"	$15.00	$80.00
24"	$25.00	$135.00
30 – 36"	$50.00	$300.00

Talking, 1974

12"	$25.00	$100.00

Raggedy Ann, 1980s

16"	$7.00	$25.00
24"	$15.00	$55.00
30 – 36"	$35.00	$110.00

Camel with Wrinkled Knees

	$45.00	$175.00

APPLAUSE TOY COMPANY, 1981 – 1983, HASBRO (PLAYSKOOL), 1983+

8"	$2.00	$15.00
12"	$4.00	$30.00
17"	$5.00	$50.00
25"	$9.00	$65.00
36"	$15.00	$150.00
48"	$25.00	$175.00

NASCO/BOBBS-MERRILL, 1972

Cloth head, hard plastic doll body, printed features, apron marked *"Raggedy Ann"*

24"	$45.00	$150.00

BOBBS-MERRILL CO., 1974

Ventriloquist dummy, hard plastic head, hands, foam body, printed face.

30"	$50.00	$175.00

Ravca, Bernard

Ca. 1924 – 1935+, Paris and New York. Stitched stockinette characters, label reads *"Original Ravca//Fabrication Francaise"* or hang tag reads *"Original Ravca."* Some all cloth or gesso/papier-mache.

CLOTH — STOCKINETTE

Celebrities, Occupations, or Literary characters

7"	$38.00	$135.00
9½"	$40.00	$155.00
12"	$55.00	$210.00
17"	$75.00	$365.00

Queen Elizabeth

36"	$850.00*	Ravca cloth label on wrist

Military figures, such as Hitler, Mussolini

17"	$250.00	$1,300.00
20"	$450.00	$2,600.00
27"	$1,000.00	$5,000.00+

Peasants/Old People

7"	$23.00	$100.00
9"	$25.00	$135.00
12"	$35.00	$165.00
15"	$50.00	$235.00
23"	$75.00	$275.00

GESSO — PAPIER-MACHE

12"	$100.00	$435.00
15"	$150.00	$625.00
17"	$250.00	$1,000.00
20"	$375.00	$1,525.00

Cloth Ravca man and woman, sculptured stockinette faces, painted blue eyes, wrinkle lines painted on, white mohair wigs, padded wire armature bodies, peasant-type clothing, circa 1930s, $265.00 pair.
Courtesy McMasters Doll Auctions.

Remco Industries

Vinyl Remco Littlechap family, Dr. John 14½", 55.00; Lisa 13½", $60.00; Judy 12", $60.00; Libby 10½", $55.00, all mint with boxes, with brochures, circa 1963.
Courtesy McMasters Doll Auctions.

Ca. 1960 – 1974. One of the first companies to market with television ads. First price is for played-with doll; second price is for mint-in-box.

Addams Family

5½"	$5.00	$20.00

Baby Crawlalong, 1967

20"	$5.00	$20.00

Baby Grow a Tooth, 1968

Vinyl and hard plastic, rooted hair, blue sleep eyes, open/closed mouth, one tooth, grows her own tooth, battery operated

15"	$7.00	$25.00

Black

14"	$8.00	$30.00

Baby Know It All, 1969

17"	$4.00	$20.00

Baby Laugh A Lot, 1970

Rooted long hair, painted eyes, open/closed mouth, teeth, vinyl head, hands, plush body, push button, she laughs, battery operated

	16"	$5.00	$20.00
Black	16"	$8.00	$30.00

Baby Glad 'N Sad, 1967

Vinyl and hard plastic, rooted blonde hair, painted blue eyes

14"	$5.00	$20.00

Baby Stroll A Long, 1966

15"	$4.00	$15.00

Beatles, 1964

Vinyl and plastic, English singing group, Paul McCartney, Ringo Starr, George Harrison, and John Lennon. Paul 4⅞", all others 4½" with guitars bearing their names.

Set of 4	$100.00	$400.00
Paul	$40.00	$105.00

Dave Clark Five, 1964

Set of five musical group, vinyl heads, rigid plastic bodies

Set		$50.00	
Dave Clark	5"	$8.00	$15.00

Other band members have name attached to leg

3"	$4.00	$10.00

Heidi and friends, 1967, in plastic case

Rooted hair, painted side-glancing eyes, open/closed mouth, all-vinyl, press button and dolls wave

Heidi	5½"	$10.00	$40.00
Herby	4½"	$3.00	$12.00

Jan, Oriental

5½"	$10.00	$40.00

Little Sister Hildi

5½"	$65.00*

Winking Heidi, 1968	$2.50	$13.00

Jeannie, I Dream of

6"	$5.00	$18.00

Jumpsy, 1970, vinyl and hard plastic, jumps rope, rooted blonde hair, painted blue eyes, closed mouth, molded-on shoes and socks

	14"	$5.00	$20.00
Black	14"	$7.00	$25.00

Laurie Partridge, 1973

19"	$22.00	$85.00

L.B.J., 1964

	5½"	$9.00	$45.00

Littlechap Family, 1963+

Vinyl head, arms, jointed hips, shoulders, neck, black molded painted hair, black eyes

Set of four		$125.00	$400.00
Dr. John Littlechap	14½"	$25.00	$95.00
Judy Littlechap	12"	$20.00	$55.00
Libby Littlechap	10½"	$20.00	$50.00
Lisa Littlechap	13½"	$20.00	$55.00
Littlechap Accessories			
Dr. John's Office		$75.00	$325.00
Bedroom		$25.00	$110.00
Family room		$25.00	$110.00
Dr. John Littlechap's outfits			
Golf outfit		$30.00	
Medical		$65.00	
Suit		$50.00	
Tuxedo		$70.00	
Lisa's outfits			
Evening dress		$90.00	
Coat, fur trim		$50.00	
Libby's, Judy's outfits			
Jeans/sweater		$30.00	
Dance dress		$45.00	

Mimi, 1973

Vinyl and hard plastic, battery operated singer, rooted long blonde hair, painted blue eyes, open/closed mouth, record player in body, sings *I'd Like to Teach the World to Sing.* Song used for Coca-Cola® commercial; sings in different languages.

	19"	$15.00	$50.00
Black	19"	$20.00	$60.00

Grandpa Munster, #1821, 1964, vinyl head, one-piece plastic body

4¾"	$65.00	$110.00	

Orphan Annie, 1967

	15"	$9.00	$45.00

Sweet April, 1971

Vinyl	5½"	$2.50	$10.00
Black	5½"	$4.00	$15.00

Tippy Tumbles, 1968

Vinyl, rooted red hair, stationary blue eyes, does somersaults, batteries in pocketbook

	16"	$5.00	$20.00

Tumbling Tomboy, 1969

Rooted blonde braids, closed smiling mouth, vinyl and hard plastic, battery operated

	17"	$5.00	$20.00

8" hard plastic Richwood Toys Inc. Sandra Sue, flat foot walker, #41, taffeta rooster-tail dress, replaced hat, circa 1954, $225.00. Courtesy Peggy Millhouse.

Sandra Sue, ca. 1940s, 1950s. Hard plastic, walker, head does not turn, slim body, saran wigs, sleep eyes. Some with high-heeled feet, only marks are number under arm or leg. All prices reflect outfits with original socks, shoes, panties, and accessories.

First price is for played with doll, incomplete costume; second price is for complete mint-in-box doll.

Sandra Sue, 8"

Flat feet, in camisole, slip, panties, shoes, and socks

	$55.00	$175.00
In school dress	$65.00	$200.00+
In party/Sunday dress	$95.00	$250.00

Special coat, hat, and dress, limited editions, Brides, Heidi, Little Women, Majorette

	$85.00+	$250.00
Sport or play clothes	$45.00	$175.00
MIB Twin Sandra Sues		$395.00

Too few in database for reliable range.

High-heeled feet, camisole, slip, panties, shoes, socks

	$40.00	$150.00
In school dress	$40.00	$175.00+
In party/Sunday dress	$75.00	$200.00+

Special coat, hat and dress, limited editions, Brides, Heidi, Little Women, Majorette

	$75.00	$200.00+
Sport or play clothes		
	$40.00	$150.00
MIB Twin Sandra Sues		$350.00

Too few in database for reliable range.

Sandra Sue Outfits: mint, including all accessories

School dress	$5.00	$15.00
Party dress	$15.00	$25.00
Specials	$35.00	$50.00
Sport sets	$15.00	$25.00

Cindy Lou, 14"

Hard plastic, jointed dolls were purchased in bulk from New York distributor, fitted with double-stitched wigs by Richwood.

All prices include shoes, socks, panties, slips, and accessories.

In camisole, slip, panties, shoes, and socks

	$45.00	$165.00+
In school dress		
	$75.00	$175.00+

8" hard plastic Richwood Sandra Sue Bride, sleep eyes, painted lashes, saran wig, circa 1940s – 1950s, $275.00. Courtesy Peggy Millhouse.

In party dress	$95.00	$225.00
In special outfits	$85.00+	$250.00
In sports outfits	$65.00	$175.00

Cindy Lou Outfits: mint, including all accessories

School dress	$35.00
Party dress	$45.00
Special outfit	$50.00
Sports clothes	$35.00

Roldan

Roldan Characters are similar to Klumpe figures in many respects. They were made in Barcelona, Spain, from the early 1960s until the mid-1970s. They are made of felt over a wire armature with painted mask faces. Like Klumpe, Roldan figures represent professionals, hobbyists, dancers, historical characters, and contemporary males and females performing a wide variety of tasks.

Some, but not all Roldans, were imported by Rosenfeld Imports and Leora Dolores of Hollywood. Figures originally came with two sewn-on identifying cardboard tags. Roldan characters most commonly found are doctors, Spanish dancers, and bull fighters. Roldan characters tend to have somewhat smaller heads, longer necks, and more defined facial features than Klumpe.

8" cloth Roldan Artist in original costume holds artist's palette and brush, circa 1960, $85.00. Courtesy Sondra Gast.

Common figures	$30.00	$100.00+
Elaborate figure, MIB with accessories		$225.00

Sasha

1965 – 1986+. Sasha dolls were created by Swiss artist, Sasha Morgenthaler, who handcrafted 20" children and 13" babies in Zurich, Switzerland, from the 1940s until her death in 1975. Her handmade studio dolls had cloth or molded bodies, five different head molds and were hand painted by Sasha Morgenthaler. To make her dolls affordable as children's playthings, she licensed Gotz Puppenfabric (1964 – 1970) in Germany and Frido Trendon Ltd. (1965 – 1986) in England to manufacture 16" Sasha dolls in series. The manufactured dolls were made of rigid vinyl with painted features. Gotz Dolls, Inc. was granted a new license in 1994 and is currently producing them in Germany.

Price range reflects rarity, condition, and completeness of doll, outfit, and packaging, and varies with geographic location. First price is for doll without original clothing and/or in less than perfect condition; second price is for mint-in-box (or tube).

16" vinyl Sasha No. 1 by Trendon Ltd. to commemorate 20th anniversary of the production of Sasha in England, it is based on the first Sasha manufactured in England Sasha blonde Blue Cord #4101, MIB, $350.00. Courtesy Dorisanne Osborn.

20" molded vinyl studio original Sasha made by Sasha Morgen-thaler 1968, type C III (Type C molded body; Type III face), Recently, Sasha Morgenthaler's studio originals sold for $10,000.00 – $14,000.00 at auction and private sales. Courtesy Dorisanne Osborn.

ORIGINAL STUDIO SASHA DOLL, CA. 1940S – 1974
Made by Sasha Morganthaler in Switzerland. Some are signed on soles of feet, have wrist tags or wear labeled clothing.

20"	$2,000.00	$9,000.00 – $14,000.00

GOTZ SASHA DOLL, 1964 – 1970, GERMANY
Girls or boys, two face molds. Marked *"Sasha Series"* in circle on neck and in three-circle logo on back. Three different boxes were used. Identified by wrist tag and/or booklet.

16"	$300.00	$1,500.00

FRIDO-TRENDON LTD., 1964 – 1970, ENGLAND
Unmarked on body, wore wrist tags and current catalogs were packed with doll.

Child, 1965 – 1968, packaged in wide box

16"	$100.00	$1,000.00

Child, 1969 – 1972, packaged in crayon tubes

16"	$100.00	$600.00

Sexed Baby, 1970 – 1978, styrofoam cradles package or straw box and box
White or black

	$100.00	$300.00

Unsexed Baby, 1978 – 1986, packaged in styrofoam wide or narrow cradles or straw basket and box

	$100.00	$300.00

Child, 1973 – 1975, packaged in shoe box style box

16"	$100.00	$400.00

Child, 1975 – 1980, black, white, shoe box style box

16"	$100.00	$300.00

Child, 1980 – 1986, black, white, packaged in photo box with flaps

	$100.00	$250.00

#1 Sasha Anniversary doll

16"	$175.00	$300.00

117S, Sasha "Sari" 1986, black hair *estimated only 400 produced before English factory closed January 1986

　　16"　　　　$450.00　　　　$700.00

130E Sasha "Wintersport" 1986, blonde hair

　　16"　　　　$400.00　　　　$600.00

330E Gregor Sandy (hair) "Hiker"

　　16"　　　　$450.00　　　　$750.00

Limited Editions

Made by Trendon Sasha Ltd. in England, packaged in box with outer sleeve picturing individual doll. Limited edition Sasha dolls marked on neck with date and number. Number on certificate matches number on doll's neck.

1981 "Velvet," girl, light brown wig, production number planned, 5,000

　　　　　　$300.00　　　　$450.00

1982 "Pintucks" girl, blonde wig, production number planned, 6,000

　　　　　　$300.00　　　　$450.00

20" molded vinyl Sasha made by Sasha Morgenthaler in 1965, representing the Baurunkinder or farm children of Switzerland, C I, (Type C molded 5-piece body, Type I face) $10,000.00 to $14,000.00 at auction. Courtesy Dorisanne Osborn.

1983 "Kiltie" girl, red wig, production number planned, 4,000

　　　　　　$350.00　　　　$500.00

1984 "Harlequin" girl, rooted blonde hair, production number planned 4,000

　　　　　　$200.00　　　　$350.00

1985 "Prince Gregor" boy, light brown wig, production number planned, 4,000

　　　　　　$250.00　　　　$400.00

1986 "Princess Sasha" girl, blonde wig, production number planned, 3,500, but only 350 were made.

　　　　　　$1,000.00　　　　$1,500.00

GOTZ DOLLS INC., 1995 +, GERMANY

They received the license in September 1994; dolls introduced in 1995.

Child, 1995 – 1996

Marked *"Gotz Sasha"* on neck and *"Sasha Series"* in three circle logo on back. About 1,500 of the dolls produced in 1995 did not have mold mark on back. Earliest dolls packaged in generic Gotz box, currently in tube, wear wrist tag, Gotz tag, and have mini-catalog.

　　16½"　　　　$300.00 retail

Baby, 1996

Baby, unmarked on neck, marked *"Sasha Series"* in three circle logo on back. First babies were packaged in generic Gotz box or large tube, currently packaged in small "Baby" tube. Wears Sasha wrist tag, Gotz booklet and current catalog.

　　12"　　　　$150.00 retail

16" vinyl Sasha by Gotz Puppenfabrik 1998 Alberto, new Swiss farm child, based on original by Sasha Morgenthaler In Puppenmuseum Sasha Morgenthaler in Zurich, Switzerland, after paintings of Albert Anker, $300.00. Courtesy Dorisanne Osborn.

21" composition Ideal Baby Shirley Temple, molded hair, open mouth with teeth, flirty sleep eyes, original dress and pin, circa 1935, $1,750.00. Courtesy Iva Mae Jones.

1934+, Ideal Novelty Toy Corp., New York. Designed by Bernard Lipfert, 1934 – 1940s. Composition head and jointed body, dimples in cheeks, green sleep eyes, open mouth, teeth, mohair wig, tagged original dress, center-snap shoes. Prototype dolls may have paper sticker inside head and bias trimmed wig.

First price is for incomplete or played-with doll. Second price is for doll in excellent to mint condition, all original. Add more for exceptional dolls or special outfits like Ranger or Wee Willie Winkie.

> Marks:
> SHIRLEY TEM-
> PLE//IDEAL NOV. &
> TOY on back of head
> and SHIRLEY TEM-
> PLE on body. Some
> marked only on head
> and with a size.

COMPOSITION

Shirley Temple

11"	$400.00	$950.00
11"	$5,880.00* mint, in Ranger costume, trunk	
13"	$350.00	$725.00
16"	$400.00	$800.00
17"	$200.00	$875.00
18"	$250.00	$950.00
20"	$275.00	$1,100.00
22"	$325.00	$1,250.00
25"	$350.00	$1,400.00
25"	$3,885.00* in Wee Willie Winkie costume	
27"	$400.00	$1,750.00

Baby Shirley

18"	$400.00	$1,200.00
21"	$500.00	$1,500.00

Hawaiian, "Marama," Ideal used the composition Shirley Temple mold for this doll representing a character from the movie *Hurricane*, black yarn hair, wears grass skirt, Hawaiian costume

18"	$400.00	$950.00

Shirley at the Organ, special display stand with composition Shirley Temple at non-functioning organ, music provided by record. $3,500.00+

*Too few in database for reliable range.

Accessories:

Button, three types	$125.00
Buggy, wood	$650.00
Buggy, wicker	$500.00
Dress, tagged	$125.00 – $175.00
Trunk	$175.00 – $225.00

11" composition Ideal Shirley Temple Rangerette, tin eyes, mohair wig, original hat, gun and pin, faint crazing, circa 1936, $2,000.00. Courtesy Leslie Tannenbaum.

VARIANTS

Japanese, unlicensed Shirleys
All-bisque

6"	$65.00	$250.00

Celluloid

5"	$45.00	$185.00
8"	$65.00	$245.00

Celluloid, Dutch Shirley Temple, ca. 1937+
All-celluloid, open crown, metal pate, sleep eyes, dimples in cheeks. Marked: *"Shirley Temple"* on head, may have additional marks, dressed in Dutch costume.

13"	$90.00	$350.00
15"	$100.00	$400.00

Composition Japanese, heavily molded brown curls, painted eyes, open/closed mouth with teeth, body stamped *"Japan"*

7½"	$75.00	$300.00

VINYL

First price indicates doll in excellent condition with flaws; second price is for excellent condition doll original clothes, accessories. The newer the doll the more perfect it must be to command higher prices.

1957
All-vinyl, sleep eyes, synthetic rooted wig, open/closed mouth, teeth, came in two-piece slip and undies, tagged Shirley Temple, came with gold plastic script pin reading *"Shirley Temple,"* marked on back of head: *"ST//12"*

12"	$115.00	$250.00

1958 – 1961
Marked on back of head: *"S.T.//15," "S.T.//17"* or *"S.T.//19,"* some had flirty ("Twinkle") eyes; add more for flirty eyes or 1961 Cinderella, Bo Peep, Heidi, and Red Riding Hood

15"	$100.00	$375.00
17"	$115.00	$450.00
19"	$125.00	$500.00

1960, Jointed wrists, marked *"ST-35-38-2"*

35 – 36"	$550.00	$2,000.00

1972, Montgomery Wards reissue, plain box

17"	$50.00	$225.00

1973, red dot "Stand Up and Cheer" outfit, box with Shirley pictures, extra outfits available

16"	$45.00	$165.00

1982 – 1983

8"	$8.00	$30.00
12"	$9.00	$35.00

19" vinyl Ideal Shirley Temple, all original, sleep eyes, unusual tagged dress of flowered sharkskin taffeta, circa 1958 – 1961, $400.00. Courtesy Iva Mae Jones.

19" vinyl Ideal Shirley Temple in original box, with curlers, two hang tags, one for Twinkle eyes marked purse, brochure, circa 1958 – 1961, $600.00. Courtesy Leslie Tannenbaum.

1984, by Hank Garfinkle
Marked "Doll Dreams & Love"

| | 36" | $75.00 | $300.00 |

1994+, Shirley Temple Dress-Up Doll, Danbury Mint, similar to 1987 doll; no charge for doll, get two outfits bimonthly

| | 16" | $30.00 | $60.00 |

1996 Danbury Mint, Little Colonel, Rebecca/Sunnybrook Farm, and Heidi

| | 16" | $25.00, retail at Target stores |

PORCELAIN

1987+, Danbury Mint

| | 16" | $65.00 | $90.00 |

1990+, Danbury Mint, designed by Elke Hutchens, in costumes from *The Little Princess, Bright Eyes, Curly Top, Dimples,* and others. Marked on neck: *"Shirley Temple//1990."*

| | 20" | $150.00 | $240.00 |

1997 Toddler, Danbury Mint, designed by Elke Hutchens, porcelain head, arms, legs, cloth body, pink dress, more dolls in the toddler series include Flower Girl and others

| | 20" | $129.00 retail |

Sun Rubber

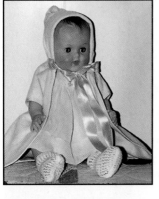

Ca. 1930s+, Barberton, OH.

Betty Bows, 1953

Molded hair with loop for ribbon, drink and wet baby, jointed body

| | 11" | $12.00 | $45.00 |

Psyllium, 1937

Molded painted hard rubber, moving head, blue pants, white suspenders, black shoes and hat

| | 10" | $3.00 | $15.00 |

Sun Babe, ca. 1940s – 1950s, all-rubber, painted eyes, drink-wet type

| | 10" | $10.00 | $40.00 |

18" vinyl Sun Rubber Bannister Baby in original pink flannel hooded robe, nylon dress, and accessories, circa 1954, $95.00. Courtesy Marian Pettygrove.

Terri Lee

1946 – 1962, Lincoln, NE and Apple Valley, CA. First dolls composition, then hard plastic and vinyl. Closed pouty mouth, painted eyes, wigged, jointed body.

First price indicates played-with doll or missing accessories; second price is mint-in-box. More for fancy costume, additional wardrobe.

Terri Lee

Composition, 1946 – 1947
16" $80.00 $375.00
Painted hard plastic, 1947 – 1950
16" $125.00 $500.00
Hard plastic, 1951 – 1962
16" $150.00 $400.00
Terri Lee Bride
16" $2,000.00* NRFB
Vinyl, less if sticky
16" $80.00 $250.00
Talking
16" $135.00 $400.00

Benji, painted plastic, brown, 1947 – 1958, black lambs wool wig
16" $150.00 $600.00

Connie Lynn, 1955, hard plastic, sleep eyes, caracul wig, bent-limb baby body
19" $125.00 $400.00

Gene Autry, 1949 – 1950, painted plastic
16" $450.00 $1,800.00

Jerry Lee, hard plastic, caracul wig
16" $125.00 $500.00

Linda Lee, 1950 – 1951, vinyl
12" $20.00 $75.00
1952 – 1958, vinyl baby
10" $45.00 $145.00

Mary Jane, Terri Lee look-alike, hard plastic walker
16" $50.00 $265.00

Patty Jo, Bonnie Lou, black
16" $150.00 $600.00

Tiny Terri Lee, 1955 – 1958
10" $50.00 $175.00

Accessories

Terri Lee Outfits:
  Ball gown $100.00
  Brownie uniform $45.00
  Girl Scout uniform $45.00
  Riding habit $150.00
  School dress $40.00
  Skater $100.00
Jerri Lee Outfits:
  Two-piece pant suit $100.00
  Short pant suit $100.00
  Western shirt/jeans $70.00

> **Marks:**
> On torso,
> "TERRI LEE" and
> early dolls,
> "PAT. PENDING."

10" vinyl Tiny Terri Lee, painted molded features, long white christening dress, circa 1955 – 1958, $150.00. Courtesy Catherine Shupe.

16" hard plastic Terri Lee in Hawaiian outfit, $300.00. Courtesy Maxine Jackson.

Trolls

Trolls portray supernatural beings from Scandinavian folklore. They have been manufactured by various companies including Helena and Martii Kuuslkoski who made Fauni Trolls, ca. 1952+ (sawdust filled cloth dolls); Thomas Dam, 1960+; and Scandia House, later Norfin®; Uneeda Doll and Toy Wishniks®; Russ Berrie; Ace Novelty; Treasure Trolls; Applause Toys; Magical Trolls; and many other companies who made lesser quality vinyl look-alikes, mostly unmarked, to take advantage of the fad. Most are all-vinyl or vinyl with stuffed cloth bodies.

Troll Figures

2½"	$3.00	$15.00
5"	$7.00	$25.00
7"	$10.00	$40.00
10"	$15.00	$55.00
12"	$17.00	$65.00
15"	$22.00	$85.00

Troll Animals

Cow, unmarked

6"	$50.00	$125.00

Donkey, Dam, 1964

9"	$40.00	$150.00

Giraffe, Thomas Dam

11½"	$35.00	$125.00

Monkey, Thomas Dam

7"	$75.00	$300.00

Pig, Norfin, Thomas Dam

6½"	$20.00	$75.00

Uneeda

19" vinyl Uneeda Dollikins, has hard plastic multi-jointed body including joints at upper arm, elbows, wrists, and ankles, original costume lacks shoes, circa 1957 – 1960, $125.00. Courtesy Nancy Rich.

1917+, New York City. Made composition head dolls, including Mama dolls and made the transition to plastics and vinyl.

COMPOSITION

Rita Hayworth, as "Carmen," ca. 1948

From *The Loves of Carmen* movie, all-composition, red mohair wig, unmarked, cardboard tag

14"	$135.00	$565.00

Uneeda Kid, Biscuit Boy, ca. 1914 – 1919

Painted features, cloth body, composition arms, molded black boots, white romper, yellow rain slicker, hat, carries box of Uneeda Biscuit. 11½" size has molded yellow hat.

11½"	$225.00	$325.00
16"	$275.00	$500.00

HARD PLASTIC AND VINYL

Baby Dollikins, 1960

Vinyl head, hard plastic jointed body with jointed elbows, wrists, and knees

21"	$12.00	$45.00

Baby Trix, 1965
  19" $8.00 $30.00

Bareskin Baby, 1968
  12½" $5.00 $20.00

Blabby, 1962+
  14" $7.00 $28.00

Coquette, 1963+
  16" $7.00 $28.00
Black 16" $9.00 $36.00

Dollikin, 1960s, multi-joints
  20" $35.00 $125.00

Fairy Princess, 1961
  32" $40.00 $110.00

Freckles, 1960, vinyl head, rigid plastic body, marked *"22"* on head
  32" $25.00 $100.00

Freckles, 1973
Ventriloquist doll, vinyl head, hands, rooted hair, cotton stuffed cloth body
  30" $17.00 $70.00

Jennifer, 1973
Rooted side-parted hair, painted features, teen body, mod clothing
  18" $7.00 $25.00

Magic Meg, w/Hair That Grows
Vinyl and plastic, rooted hair, sleep eyes
  16" $7.00 $25.00

Pir-thilla, 1958
Blows up balloons, vinyl, rooted hair, sleep eyes
  12½" $4.00 $12.00

Purty, 1973
Long rooted hair, vinyl and plastic, painted features
  11" $7.00 $25.00

Pollyanna, 1960, for Disney
  11" $9.00 $35.00
  17" $130.00* MIB
  31" $40.00 $150.00

Seranade, 1962
Vinyl head, hard plastic body, rooted blonde hair, blue sleep eyes, red and white dress, speaker in tummy, phonograph and records came with doll, used battery
  21" $15.00 $55.00

Suzette (Carol Brent)
  12" $13.00 $65.00

Tiny Teen, 1957 – 1959
Vinyl head, rooted hair, pierced ears, six-piece hard plastic body, high-heeled feet to compete with Little Miss Revlon, wrist tag
  10½" $40.00 $135.00

15" vinyl Uneeda Granny and Me has painted on glasses, circa 1990s, $25.00. Courtesy Lori Rose.

29" vinyl Annette Himstead Friederika all original, circa 1988, $2,200.00. Courtesy Elizabeth Surber.

18" vinyl Magic Attic Doll, Megan designed by Robert Tonner, circa 1996, $60.00. Courtesy Millie Busch.

Ca. 1950s+. By the mid-1950s, vinyl (polyvinylchloride) was being used for dolls. Material that was soft to the touch and processing that allowed hair to be rooted were positive attractions. Vinyl became a desirable material and the market was soon deluged with dolls manufactured from this product. Many dolls of this period are of little known manufacturers, unmarked, or marked only with a number. With little history behind them, these dolls need to be mint-in-box and totally complete to warrant top prices. With special accessories or wardrobe values may be more.

23" vinyl Worlds of Wonder Julie, a sophisticated talking doll with computer chip, tape recorder in cloth body, mouth moves when talking, rooted blonde hair, accessories available including this blue and white tagged dress, 1987, $150.00. Courtesy Fran Fabian.

UNKNOWN MAKER

Baby

Vinyl head, painted or sleep eyes, molded hair or wig, bent legs, cloth or vinyl body

12"	$2.50	$10.00
16"	$3.00	$12.00
20"	$5.00	$20.00

Child

Vinyl head, jointed body, painted or sleep eyes, molded hair or wig, straight legs

14"	$5.00	$14.00
22"	$6.00	$25.00

Adult

Vinyl head, painted or sleep eyes, jointed body, molded hair or wig, smaller waist with male or female modeling for torso

8"	$5.00	$25.00
18"	$20.00	$75.00

KNOWN MAKER

Baby Berry

Alfred E. Newman

20"	$50.00	$200.00

Captain Kangaroo

19"	$40.00	$150.00
24"	$64.00	$245.00

Christopher Robin
18" $60.00 $175.00
Daisy Mae
14" $55.00 $190.00
Emmett Kelly (Willie the Clown)
15" $45.00 $185.00
21" $100.00 $325.00
Lil Abner
14" $50.00 $200.00
21" $70.00 $265.00
Mammy Yokum, 1957
Molded hair
14" $45.00 $175.00
21" $70.00 $275.00
Yarn hair
14" $50.00 $200.00
21" $75.00 $300.00
Nose lights up
23" $85.00 $325.00
Pappy Yokum, 1957
14" $35.00 $135.00
21" $65.00 $260.00
Nose lights up
23" $85.00 $325.00

DEE & CEE, Canada
Marylee, 1967+, rigid vinyl, rooted hair, sleep eyes
17" $75.00 $300.00

Himstedt, Annette, 1986+
Distributed by Timeless Creations, a division of Mattel, Inc. Swivel rigid vinyl head with shoulder plate, cloth body, vinyl limbs, inset eyes, real lashes, molded eyelids, holes in nostrils, human hair wig, bare feet, original in box.
Barefoot Children, 1986, 26"
Bastian $200.00 $800.00
Beckus $400.00 $1,500.00
Ellen $200.00 $900.00
Fatou $275.00 $1,100.00
Kathe $200.00 $800.00
Lisa $200.00 $800.00
Paula $175.00 $800.00
Blessed are the Children, 1988, 31"
Friederike $550.00 $2,200.00
Kasimir $500.00 $2,000.00
Makimura $350.00 $1,400.00
Malin $350.00 $1,600.00
Michiko $400.00 $1,500.00

20" vinyl Worlds of Wonder Pamela talking doll, rooted hair, inset eyes, played with, circa 1986 – 1987, original tagged outfit, $50.00. Courtesy Marie Rodgers.

11" vinyl Paris Doll Corp. Jaci, closed mouth, turquoise plastic sleep eyes, jointed vinyl body, designed by 12-year-old Jaci Barrett, brochure shows Parents magazine approval seal, original skating dress and cap 1956, $15.00. Courtesy Penny Hustler.

18" vinyl Valentine high-heeled girl with sleep eyes, rooted synthetic wig, rigid vinyl body, original strapless net formal with marked Valentine box, circa 1950s, $95.00. Courtesy Penny Pittsley.

Reflections of Youth, 1989 – 1990, 26"

Adrienne	$200.00	$900.00
Ayoka	$550.00	$1,100.00
Janka	$200.00	$900.00
Kai	$215.00	$900.00

Playmates, 1985+

Made animated talking dolls using a tape player in torso powered by batteries. Extra costumes, tapes, and accessories available. More for black versions.

Cricket, circa 1986+		
25"	$50.00	$125.00
Corky, circa 1987+		
25"	$50.00	$125.00

World of Wonder, circa 1985 – 1987+

Fremont, CA. Made talking dolls and Teddy Ruxpin powered by batteries, had extra accessories, voice cards.

Pamela, The Living Doll, 1986+		
21"	$45.00	$125.00
Julie, 1987+		
24"	$50.00	$150.00
Extra costume	$5.00	$25.00

Teddy Ruxpin, 1985+ animated talking bear

20"	$15.00	$50.00

Vogue

8" composition Vogue Toddles, unmarked (used R& B doll), in original dress and pinafore as American Girl, circa 1942, $300.00. Courtesy Betty Jane Fronefield.

1930s+, Medford, MA. Jennie Graves started the company and dressed "Just Me" dolls in early years, also used dolls from Arranbee, had Bernard Lipfert design Ginny. After several changes of ownership, Vogue dolls was recently purchased, in 1995, by the Lawton Doll Company.

GINNY FAMILY

Toddles

Composition, 1937 – 1948, name stamped in ink on bottom of shoe. Some early dolls which have been identified as "Toodles" (spelled with two o's) are blank dolls from various companies used by Vogue. Painted eyes, mohair wig, jointed body; some had gold foil labels reading "*Vogue.*"

First price indicates doll in good condition, but with flaws; second price indicates doll in excellent condition with original clothes. More for fancy outfits such as Red Riding Hood or Cowboy/Cowgirl or with accessories.

8"	$125.00	$425.00

Ginny, painted hard plastic, 1948 – 1950

Marked *"Vogue"* on head, *"Vogue Doll"* on body, painted eyes, molded hair with mohair wig. Clothing tagged *"Vogue Dolls"* or *"Vogue Dolls, Inc. Medford Mass.,"* inkspot tag on white with blue letters.

8"	$100.00	$375.00

With poodle cut wig

8"	$125.00	$400.00

Outfit only $65.00 – $90.00+

Ginny, 8", hard plastic walkers, 1950 – 1953

Transitional to walkers, sleep eyes, painted lashes, strung, Dynel wigs, new mark on back torso: *"GINNY//VOGUE DOLLS//INC. //PAT PEND.//MADE IN U.S.A."* Coronation Queen, 1953, has elaborate braid on her costume, silver wrist tags.

8" hard plastic Vogue Ginny transitional strung roller skater, #1800 series, circa 1951, $300.00. Courtesy Peggy Millhouse.

Common dress

8"	$95.00	$350.00
Ballerina	$150.00	$600.00

Beryl, Cheryl

$1,000.00* each

Queen	$250.00	$1,350.00
Skater	$150.00	$600.00

Square Dancer

$900.00*

Black Ginny, 1953 – 1954

8"	$150.00	$600.00+
8"	$1,900.00* mint	

Ginny, hard plastic, 1954 – 1956, seven-piece body, molded lash walkers, sleep eyes, Dynel or saran wigs

Marked: "VOGUE" on head, *"GINNY//VOGUE DOLLS//INC.//PAT. NO. 2687594//MADE IN U.S.A."* on back of torso

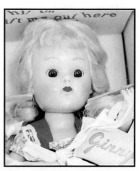

8" hard plastic Vogue Ginny, sleep eyes, painted lash, wig, all original in pink and white outfit, with pink vinyl Ginny purse, pink necklace, circa 1950s, $325.00. Courtesy Sally DeSmet.

8"	$55.00	$200.00
Outfit only		$40.00+

Davy Crockett, coonskin cap, brown jacket, pants, toy rifle, in box

8"	$935.00*	

Crib Crowd, 1950

Baby with curved legs, sleep eyes, poodle cut (caracul) wig

8"	$175.00	$650.00+

Easter Bunny

8"	$350.00	$1,400.00

* at auction

8" hard plastic Vogue Ginny Dutch pair, painted eyes, round foil Vogue tag on clothing, circa 1948 – 1950, $750.00+ for pair. Courtesy Gay Smedes.

8" hard plastic Vogue Ginny, molded lash walker, sleep eyes, trunk, hang tag, five extra outfits plus accessories, circa 1955 – 1956, $600.00. Courtesy Rae Klenke.

Ginny, hard plastic, 1957
Bent-knee (jointed) walker, molded lashes, sleep eyes, Dynel or saran wigs

8"	$45.00	$175.00
Outfit only	$40.00+	

Ginny, 1960, big walker carried 8" doll dressed just like her

36"	$350.00

Too few in database for reliable range.

Ginny, 1963+
Soft vinyl head, hard plastic walker body, rooted hair

8"	$13.00	$50.00

Ginny, 1965
All-vinyl, straight legs, non-walker

8"	$10.00	$40.00

Ginny, 1972
Painted eyes, made in Hong Kong by Tonka

8"	$10.00	$40.00

Ginny, 1977 – 1981
Made in Hong Kong by Lesney, thinner body, painted or sleep eyes, vinyl

8"	$9.00	$35.00

Sasson Ginny, 1978 – 1979

8"	$9.00	$35.00

8" vinyl Vogue Ginnette, open mouth, painted eyes, jointed body, white nylon party dress with tie, petticoat, red polka dot flannelette diaper and bonnet, wood Dolly Tender, white wood top folds down, circa 1955+, $150.00. Courtesy Iva Mae Jones.

Two Ginny dolls made by the Lesney Co, circa 1980, in special gift packs, dressed to play sports with two extra outfits, $35.00 each. Courtesy Cathie Clark.

Ginny, 1984 – 1986
Some porcelain and also vinyl by Meritus, made in Hong Kong

Porcelain

8"	$15.00	$50.00

Ginny, 1986+, vinyl, by Dakin

8"	$5.00	$20.00

Ginny Baby

12"	$10.00	$40.00
18"	$13.00	$50.00

Ginnette, 1955+, all-vinyl baby

8"	$100.00	$350.00

Jill, 1957 – 1962, seven-piece hard plastic teenage body, high heeled doll, big sister to Ginny (made in vinyl in 1965), extra wardrobe

10½"	$85.00	$275.00
Street dress	$15.00	$25.00
Fancy dress	$30.00	$50.00

8" Vogue hard plastic, painted lash, straight leg walker, Kinder Crowd dress, circa 1954, $300.00. Courtesy Cathie Clark.

Jan, 1958 – 1962, Jill's girlfriend, vinyl head, six-piece rigid vinyl body, swivel waist

10½"	$40.00	$150.00

Jeff, 1958 – 1962, vinyl head, five-piece rigid vinyl body, molded painted hair

10¾"	$25.00	$100.00

Jimmy, 1958, vinyl, little brother to Ginnette

8"	$15.00	$60.00

Miss Ginny, 1972

16"	$15.00	$45.00

Tiny Miss Ginny, 1951 – 1954, hard plastic, five-piece toddler body, wrist tag, Dynel wig

8"	$200.00	$575.00

GINNY EXCLUSIVES
Enchanted Doll House

1988	$35.00	$135.00

Little Friends, 1991, Alaska

	$15.00	$60.00

11" all-vinyl, Vogue Jeff, blue sleep eyes, molded lash and black painted hair, wears his Cabana outfit, circa 1960. $100.00. Two 8" Vogue hard plastic, painted lash Ginny dolls in beach attire, circa 1954 – 1955, $200.00 each. Courtesy Cathie Clark.

16" vinyl Vogue Baby Dear with cloth body, original, circa 1961+, $165.00. Courtesy Debbie Crume.

Meyer's Collectibles
1985, Gigi's Favorite
$20.00 $80.00
1986, Fairy Godmother
$45.00 $155.00
1987, Cinderella and Prince Charming
$45.00 $190.00
1988, Clown
$20.00 $90.00
1989, Cowgirl
$20.00 $90.00
1992, Storytime Ginny, limited
$25.00 $100.00
1993, Sweet Violet Ginny, limited
$40.00 $125.00
1994, Remember Jackie
$30.00 $110.00

Modern Doll Convention
1986, Rose Queen
$65.00 $275.00
1987, Ginny at Seashore
$22.00 $100.00
1988, Ginny's Claim
$20.00 $90.00
1989, Ginny in Nashville
$35.00 $135.00
1990, Ginny in Orlando
$20.00 $90.00

Shirley's Doll House
1985, Ginny Goes Country
$23.00 $90.00
1986, Ginny Goes to County Fair
$23.00 $90.00
1987, black Ginny in swimsuit
$25.00 $95.00
1988, Santa & Mrs. Claus
$20.00 $80.00
1989, Sunday Best, black boy or girl
$15.00 $60.00

Toy Village, Lansing, MI
Ashley Rose $15.00 $70.00

U.F.D.C. (United Federation of Doll Clubs)
1987 Miss Unity $45.00 $155.00
1988 Ginny Luncheon Souvenir
$35.00 $140.00

Vogue Doll Club
1990, Member Special
$25.00 $95.00

Vogue Review Luncheon

1989	$35.00	$170.00
1990	$25.00	$100.00
1991	$18.00	$85.00

Ginny Accessories

First price is played with; second price is mint-in-box or package

Book: Ginny's First Secret

	$35.00	$125.00

Furniture: chair, bed, dresser, wardrobe, dress, rocking chair

each	$15.00	$55.00
Ginny Gym	$115.00	$450.00
Ginny Name Pin	$12.00	$50.00
Ginny Pup, Steiff	$45.00	$165.00+
Ginny's House	$250.00	$1,000.00
Luggage set	$25.00	$100.00
Parasol	$4.00	$15.00
School bag	$20.00	$75.00
Shoes/shoe bag	$10.00	$40.00

16" vinyl Vogue platinum Brikette, rigid vinyl body and legs, ball-jointed twist and turn body, circa 1960, freckles, green sleep eyes, played with, $15.00. Courtesy Jane Horst.

COMPOSITION

Jennie, sleep eyes, open mouth, mohair wig, five-piece composition body

13"	$175.00	$700.00

Cynthia, sleep eyes, open mouth, mohair wig, five-piece composition body

13"	$75.00	$325.00

HARD PLASTIC & VINYL

Baby Dear, 1959 – 1964, designed by Eloise Wilkin, painted eyes, vinyl head, limbs, cloth body, topknot or rooted hair, white tag on body, *"Vogue Dolls, Inc.";* left leg stamped *"1960/E.Wilkins"* on 12", *"E.Wilkins/1960"* on 18"

12"	$60.00	$225.00
18"	$125.00	$325.00

Baby Dear One, 1962, a one-year-old toddler version of Baby Dear, sleep eyes, two teeth

Marked *"C//1961//E.Wilkins//Vogue Dolls//Inc."* on neck, tag on body, mark on right leg

25"	$40.00	$300.00

Baby Dear Musical, 1962 – 1963, 12" metal, 18" wooden shaft winds, plays tune, doll wiggles

12"	$15.00	$60.00
18"	$25.00	$85.00

8" Vogue all hard plastic Wee Imp, fully jointed, including bend knees, sleep eyes, orange saran wig, circa 1960, $175.00. Courtesy Cathie Clark.

Baby Dear (Two), 1965, two-year-old toddler of Baby Dear, all-vinyl, open mouth, two teeth

17"	$20.00	$80.00
23"	$45.00	$100.00

Brikette, 1959

Swivel waist joint, green flirty eyes in 22" size only, freckles, rooted straight yellow or orange hair, paper hang tag reads *"I'm //Brikette//the//red headed//imp"*

	22"	$18.00	$65.00
1960	16"	$10.00	$40.00

1978, no swivel waist, curly hair

	16"	$5.00	$20.00

Li'l Imp

	10½"	$18.00	$65.00

Littlest Angel, 1961 – 1963, vinyl head, hard plastic, bent knee walker, sleep eyes, same doll as Arranbee Littlest Angel, rooted hair

	10½"	$25.00	$85.00

1967 – 1980, all-vinyl, jointed limbs, rooted red, blonde or brunette hair, looks older

	11"	$25.00	$55.00
	15"	$25.00	$50.00

Love Me Linda (Pretty as a Picture), 1965 – 1968

	15"	$7.00	$23.00

Wee Imp, 1960

Hard plastic body, red wig, green eyes, freckles

	8"	$90.00	$375.00

Welcome Home Baby, ca. 1977 – 1980, designed by Eloise Wilkin, marked *"Vogue"*

	18"	$15.00	$65.00

Welcome Home Baby Turns Two, toddler, mark: *"42260 Lesney Prod. Corp.//1979//Vogue Doll"*

	22"	$40.00	$150.00

Robin Woods

13" vinyl Robin Wood's Let's Play Dolls Alice Darling Alice with hang tag, by Alexander Doll Co., mint in box, circa 1992, $120.00. Courtesy Millie Carol.

Ca. 1980s+. Creative designer for various companies, including Le Petit Ami, Robin Woods Company, Madame Alexander (Alice Darling), Horsman, and Playtime Productions.

Price indicates mint complete doll; anything else would bring a lesser price.

EARLY CLOTH DOLLS

Price depends on how well painted and quality of clothing and construction. The quality varies greatly in these early cloth dolls.

Children, very rare

Betsy Bluebonnet	$350.00
Enchanted Baby	$450.00
Jane	$450.00
Jessica	$350.00
Laura	$350.00

Children, rare

Mollie	$300.00
Rachel	$300.00
Rueben	$350.00
Stevie	$350.00

Children, common

City Child	$100.00
Elizabeth	$100.00
Mary Margaret	$100.00
How Do I Love Thee	$300.00

Clowns, very rare

Aladdin	$500.00
Sinbad	$500.00
Wynter	$400.00
Yankee Doodle	$500.00

Clowns, rare

Cinamette	$350.00+
Happy Holiday, 1984 – 1986	$300.00+
Kubla	$300.00+

Clowns, common

Bon Bon	$200.00
Frolic	$200.00
Happy Birthday	$200.00
Little Star	$200.00

14" vinyl Robin Woods Bonnie, made for Carol & Co., dressed in blue and white checked outfit for the Modern Doll Convention Bluebonnet Luncheon, marked 1994, $130.00. Private collection.

1987

Catherine	14"	$200.00+
Christmas dolls, Nicholas & Noel, pair		
	14"	$300.00+

1988

Dickens	14"	$200.00
Kristina Kringle	14"	$200.00
Merry Carol	14"	$200.00

1989

Elizabeth St. John	14"	$100.00
Heidi, red, white, blue	14"	$200.00
Heidi, brown outfit	14"	$100.00
Hope	14"	$125.00
Lorna Doone	14"	$100.00
Mary of Secret Garden	14"	$135.00
Scarlett Christmas	14"	$200.00+
William Noel	14"	$100.00

1990 Camelot Castle Collection

Bobbi	16"	$75.00
Kyleigh Christmas	14"	$100.00
Lady Linet	14"	$75.00
Lady of the Lake	14"	$125.00
Marjorie	14"	$75.00
Meaghan (special)	14"	$200.00+
Melanie, Phebe	14"	$75.00

Tessa at the Circus	14"	$100.00
Tess of the D'urbervilles		
	14"	$200.00

1991 Shades of Day collection
5,000 pieces each, Dawn, Glory, Stormy, Joy, Sunny, Veil, Serenity

Each	14"	$125.00

Others

Alena	14"	$100.00
Bette Jack	14"	$100.00
Bouquet, Lily	14"	$100.00
Delores	14"	$150.00
Eliza Doolittle	14"	$100.00
Mistress Mary	8"	$85.00
Miss Muffet	14"	$100.00
Pumpkin Eaters	8"	$75.00
Rose, Violet	14"	$100.00
Rosemary	14"	$75.00
Sleeping Beauty Set	8"	$200.00
Tennison	14"	$100.00
Victoria	14"	$100.00

ROBIN WOODS LIMITED EDITIONS

Merri, 1991 Doll Convention Disney World, Christmas Tree doll, doll becomes the tree   14" $200.00

Mindy, Made for Disney's Robin Wood's Day, limited to 300

	14"	$150.00

Rainey, 1991 Robin Woods Club

	14"	$150.00

J.C. Penney Limited Editions
Angelina, 1990 Christmas angel

	14"	$200.00

Noelle, Christmas angel

	14"	$200.00

Julianna, 1991, little girl holiday shopper

	14"	$175.00

Robin Woods Exclusives
Gina, The Earthquake Doll, The Doll Place, Ann Parsons of Burlingame, CA   14" $200.00

Bibliography

Anderson, Johana Gast. *Twentieth Century Dolls*. Wallace Homestead, 1971.

———. *More Twentieth Century Dolls*. Wallace Homestead, 1974.

———. *Cloth Dolls*. Wallace Homestead., 1984.

Axe, John. *Effanbee, A Collector's Encyclopedia 1949 – 1983*. Hobby House Press, 1983.

———. *The Encyclopedia of Celebrity Dolls*. Hobby House Press, 1983.

———. *Tammy and Her Family of Dolls*. Hobby House Press, 1995.

Blitman, Joe. *Francie and Her Mod, Mod, Mod, Mod World of Fashion*. Hobby House Press, 1996.

Casper, Peggy Wiedman. *Fashionable Terri Lee Dolls*. Hobby House Press, 1988.

Clark, Debra. *Troll Identification & Price Guide*. Collector Books, 1993.

Coleman, Dorothy S., Elizabeth Ann, and Evelyn Jane. *The Collector's Book of Dolls' Clothes*. Crown Publishers, 1975.

———. *The Collector's Encyclopedia of Dolls, Vol. I & II*. Crown Publishers, 1968, 1986.

Crowsey, Linda. *Madame Alexander, Collector's Dolls Price Guide #22*. Collector Books, 1997.

DeWein, Sibyl and Ashabraner, Joan. *The Collector's Encyclopedia of Barbie Dolls and Collectibles*, Collector Books, 1977.

Garrison, Susan Ann. *The Raggedy Ann & Andy Family Album*. Schiffer Publishing, 1989.

Hedrick Susan, and Matchette, Vilma. *World Colors, Dolls & Dress*. Hobby House Press, 1997.

Hoyer, Mary. *Mary Hoyer and Her Dolls*. Hobby House Press, 1982.

Izen, Judith. *A Collector's Guide to Ideal Dolls*. Collector Books, 1994.

Izen, Judith and Stover, Carol. *Collector's Encyclopedia of Vogue Dolls*. Collector Books, 1997.

Judd, Polly and Pam. *African and Asian Costumed Dolls*. Hobby House Press, 1995.

———. *Cloth Dolls, Identification and Price Guide*. Hobby House Press, 1990.

———. *Compo Dolls,Vol I & II*. Hobby House Press, 1991, 1994.

———. *European Costumed Dolls, Identification and Price Guide*. Hobby House Press, 1994.

———. *Hard Plastic Dolls, I & II*. Hobby House Press, 1987, 1994.

———. *Glamour Dolls of the 1950s & 1960s*. Hobby House Press, 1988.

———. *Santa Dolls & Figurines*. Hobby House Press, 1992.

Langford, Paris. *Liddle Kiddles*. Collector Books, 1996.

Lewis, Kathy and Don. *Chatty Cathy Dolls*. Collector Books, 1994.

Mandeville, A. Glenn. *Ginny, An American Toddler Doll*. Hobby House Press, 1994.

Mansell, Collette. *The Collector's Guide to British Dolls Since 1920*. Robert Hale, 1983.

Morris, Thomas. *The Carnival Chalk Prize, I & II*. Prize Publishers, 1985, 1994.

Moyer, Patsy. *Doll Values*. Collector Books, 1997.

———. *Modern Collectible Dolls*. Collector Books, 1997.

Niswonger, Jeanne D. *That Doll Ginny*. Cody Publishing, 1978.

———. *The Ginny Doll Family*. 1996.

Olds, Patrick C. *The Barbie Doll Years*. Collector Books, 1996.

Outwater, Myra Yellin. *Advertising Dolls*. Schiffer, 1998.

Pardella, Edward R. *Shirley Temple Dolls and Fashions*. Schiffer Publishing, 1992.

Perkins, Myla. *Black Dolls*. Collector Books, 1993.

———. *Black Dolls Book II*. Collector Books, 1995.

Robison, Joleen Ashman and Sellers, Kay. *Advertising Dolls*. Collector Books, 1992.

Schoonmaker, Patricia N. *Effanbee Dolls: The Formative Years, 1910 – 1929*. Hobby House Press, 1984.

———. *Patsy Doll Family Encyclopedia Vol. 1 & II*. Hobby House Press, 1992, 1998.

Smith, Patricia R. *Madame Alexander Collector Dolls*. Collector Books, 1978.

———. *Modern Collector's Dolls*. Series 1 – 8, Collector Books.

It is recommended that when contacting the references below and requesting information that you enclose a SASE (self-addressed stamped envelope) if you wish to receive a reply.

ALEXANDER DOLL COMPANY
The Review
PO Box 330
Mundelein, IL 60060-0330
847-949-9200
fax: 847-949-9201
e-mail: http://www.madc.org
Official publication of the
Madame Alexander Doll Club,
quarterly, plus two "Shoppers,"
$20.00 per year.

AMERICAN CHARACTER
Debby Davis, Collector/Dealer
3905 N. 15th St.
Milwaukee, WI 53206

ANTIQUE DOLLS
Matrix
PO Box 1410
New York, NY 10023
Can research your wants

ANTIQUE AND MODERN DOLLS
Rosalie Whyel Museum of Doll Art
1116 108th Avenue N.E.
Bellevue, WA 98004
206-455-1116
fax: 206-455-4793

AUCTION HOUSES
Call or write for a list of upcoming
auctions, or if you need information
about selling a collection.
McMasters Doll Auctions
James and Shari McMasters
PO Box 1755
Cambridge, OH 43725
800-842-3526 or
614-432-4419
fax: 614-432-3191

BARBIE DOLLS, MATTEL
Miller's Fashion Doll
PO Box 8488
Spokane, WA 99203-0488
509-747-0139
fax: 509-455-6115
Credit card subscription
800-874-5201
Six issues, $29.95

Dream Dolls Galleries & More,
Collector/Dealer
5700 Okeechobee Blvd. #20
West Palm Beach, FL 33417
888-839-3655
e-mail: dollnmore@aol.com

Jaci Jueden, Collector/Dealer
575 Galice Rd.
Merlin, OR 97532
e-mail: fudd@cdsnet.net

Steven Pim, Collector/Dealer
3535 17th St.
San Francisco, CA 94110

BETSY MCCALL
Betsy's Fan Club
Marci Van Ausdall, Editor
PO Box 946
Quincy, CA 95971

Quarterly, $15.50 per year
CELEBRITY DOLLS
Celebrity Doll Journal
Loraine Burdick, Editor
413 10th Ave. Ct. NE
Puyallup, WA 98372
Quarterly, $10.00 per year

CHATTY CATHY, MATTEL
Chatty Cathy Collector's Club
Lisa Eisenstein, Editor
PO Box 140
Readington, NJ 08870-0140
Quarterly newsletter, $28.00
e-mail: Chatty@eclipse.net

COMPOSITION AND TRAVEL DOLLS
Effanbee's Patsy Family
Patsy & Friends Newsletter
PO Box 311
Deming, NM 88031
e-mail: Patsyandfriends@zianet.com
Bi-monthly, $20.00 per year

COSTUMING
Doll Costumer's Guild
Helen Boothe, Editor
7112 W. Grovers Ave
Glendale, AZ 85308
$16.00 per year, bimonthly

French Fashion Gazette
Adele Leurquin, Editor
1862 Sequoia SE
Port Orchard, WA 98366

DIONNE QUINTUPLETS
Quint News
Jimmy and Fay Rodolfos,
Editors
PO Box 2527
Woburn, MA 01888

Connie Lee Martin
Collector/Dealer
4018 East 17th St.
Tucson, AZ, 85711

DOLL REPAIRS
Fresno Doll Hospital
1512 N. College
Fresno, CA 93728
209-266-1108

Kandyland Dolls
PO Box 146
Grande Ronde, OR 97347
503-879-5153

Life's Little Treasures
PO Box 585
Winston OR 97496
541-679-3472

Oleta's Doll Hospital
1413 Seville Way
Modesto, CA 95355
209-523-6669

GENE — ASHTON DRAKE GALLERIES
9200 N. Maryland Ave.
Niles, IL 60714-9853
888-For-Gene

GIRL SCOUTS
Girl Scout Doll Collector's Patch
Pidd Miller
PO Box 631092
Houston, TX, 77263

Diane Miller, Collector
13151 Roberta Place
Garden Grove, CA 92643

Ann Sutton, Collector/Dealer
2555 Prine Road
Lakeland, FL 33810-5703
E-Mail: Sydneys@aol.com

HASBRO — JEM DOLLS
Linda E. Holton, Collector/Dealer
P.O. Box 6753
San Rafael, CA 94903

HITTY
Friends of Hitty Newsletter
Virginia Ann Heyerdahl, Editor
2704 Belleview Ave
Cheverly, MD 20785
Quarterly, $12.00 per year

IDEAL
Ideal Collectors' Newsletter
Judith Izen, Editor
PO Box 623
Lexington, MA 02173
e-mail: Jizen@aol.com
Quarterly, $20.00 per year

INTERNET
Ebay auction site
http://cayman.ebay2

Internet Lists & Chat Rooms
AG Collector
For American Girl, Heidi Ott,
and other 18" play dolls, no selling, just talk. e-mail: ag_
collector-request@lists.best.com

Barbie chat
E-Mail: Fashion-ga.unc.edu

Doll Chat List
Friendly collectors talk dolls, no
flaming permitted, a great group.
E-mail is forwarded to your
address from host, no fees.
To subscribe:
e-mail: DollChat-Request@nbi.com
then type subscribe

Sasha
E-mail: sasha-1-Subscribe@make-
list.com

Shirley Temple
e-mail: shirleycollect-sub-
scribe@makelist.com

KLUMPE DOLLS
Sondra Gast, Collector/Dealer
PO Box 252
Spring Valley, CA 91976
fax: 619-444-4215

LAWTON, WENDY
Lawton Collectors Guild
PO Box 969
Turlock, CA 95381

Toni Winder, Collector/Dealer
1484 N. Vagedes
Fresno CA 93728
e-mail: TTUK77B@prodigy.com

LIDDLE KIDDLES
For a signed copy of her book,
Liddle Kiddles, $22.95 post pd.
Write: *Paris Langford*
415 Dodge Ave
Jefferson, LA 70127
504-733-0676

MODERN DOLL CONVENTION
Cathie Clark, Chairman
2018 Kenton St
Springfield, OH 45505
513-322-3780

MUSEUMS
Arizona Doll & Toy Museum
(Stevens House in Heritage
Square)
602 E. Adams St.
Phoenix, AZ 85004
602-253-9337
Tues. – Sun., adm. $2.50, closed
Aug.

Enchanted World Doll Museum
"The castle across from the Corn
Palace"
615 North Main
Mitchell, SD 57301
606-996-9896
fax: 606-996-0210

Land of Enchantment Doll Museum
5201 Constitution Ave.
Albuquerque, NM 87110-5813
505-821-8558
fax: 505-255-1259

*Margaret Woodbury Strong
Museum*
1 Manhattan Square
Rochester, NY 14607
716-263-2700

Rosalie Whyel Museum of Doll Art
1116 108th Avenue N.E.
Bellevue, WA 98004
206-455-1116

fax: 206-455-4793
www.dollart.com

NANCY ANN STORYBOOK
Elaine Pardee, Collector/Dealer
PO Box 6108
Santa Rosa, CA 95406
707-585-3655

ORIENTAL DOLLS
Ninsyo Journal — Jade
Japanese American Dolls Enthu-
siasts
406 Koser Ave
Iowa City, IA 52246
e-mail:
Vickyd@jadejapandolls.com

RAGGEDY ANN
Rags Newsletter
Barbara Barth, Editor
PO Box 823
Atlanta, GA 30301
Quarterly $16.00

ROBERT TONNER DOLL CLUB
Robert Tonner Doll Company
PO Box 1187
Kingston, NY 12402
fax: 914-339-1259
Credit card: 914-339-9537
Dues: $19.95

ROLDAN DOLLS
Sondra Gast, Collector/Dealer
PO Box 252
Spring Valley, CA 91976
fax: 619-444-4215

**SANDRA SUE DOLLS, RICHWOOD
TOYS INC.**
Peggy Millhouse, Collector/Dealer
510 Green Hill Road
Conestoga, PA 17516
e-mail: peggyin717@aol.com

SASHA DOLLS
Friends of Sasha
Quarterly Newsletter
Dorisanne Osborn, Editor
Box 187
Keuka Park, NY 14478

SHIRLEY TEMPLE
*Australian Shirley Temple Collec-
tors News*
Quarterly Newsletter

Victoria Horne, Editor
39 How Ave.
North Dandenong
Victoria, 3175, Australia
$25.00 U.S.

Lollipop News
Shirley Temple Collectors by the Sea
PO Box 6203
Oxnard, CA 93031
Membership dues: $14.00 year

Shirley Temple Collectors News
Rita Dubas, Editor
881 Colonial Road
Brooklyn NY 11209
Quarterly, $20.00 year
http://www.ritadubasdesign.com/
shirley/
e-mail: bukowski@wazoo.com

TERRI LEE
Daisy Chain Newsletter
Terry Bukowski, Editor
3010 Sunland Dr.
Alamogordo, NM 88310
$20.00 per year, quarterly

Ann Sutton, Collector/Dealer
2555 Prine Road
Lakeland, FL 33810-5703
e-mail: Sydneys@aol.com

Betty J. Woten, Collector
12 Big Bend Cut Off
Cloudcroft, NM 88317-9411

VOGUE
Ginny Doll Club
PO Box 338
Oakdale, CA 95361-0338
800-554-1447

**UNITED FEDERATION OF DOLL
CLUBS**
10920 N. Ambassador Dr.,
Suite 130
Kansas City, MO 64153
816-891-7040
fax: 816-891-8360
http://www.ufdc.org/

WOODS, ROBIN
Toni Winder, Collector/Dealer
1484 N. Vagedes
Fresno, CA 93728

Mold Index

Symbol Index

Anchor with AM	Armand Marseille
Anvil	Franz Schmidt
AT	Thuiller, A.
Bee/Crown	Goebel
Bell	Kling
Circle dot	Bru
Circle with American Character	
inside	American Character
Circle with K and mirror K	Kruse, Kathe
Circle with Lenci	Lenci
Circle with sun rays	Kuhnlenz, Gebruder
Clover	Adolf Wislizenus
Clover	Limbach
Coat of arms	Otto Gans, Recknagel
Crossed Bones	Knoch, Gebruder
Crossed Hammers	Recknagel
Crossed Swords	Bahr & Proschild

Crown	Kestner
Crown/Cloverleaf	Limbach
Diamond (Ideal)	Ideal Novelty and Toy Co.
Diamond with SNF	Societe Nobel Francaise
Dragon	Neuman & Marx
Eagle	Peticolin
Eiffel Tower	Danel & Cie
Elephant on button in ear,	Steiff,
other button in ear	Margarete
Heart with Kewpie	Kewpie
Heart with BP	Bahr & Proschild
Heart with BSW	Schmidt, Bruno
Helmet	Buschow & Beck
Horseshoe	Heubach, Ernst
HS entertwined mark	Steiner, Hermann
K (star) R	Kammer & Reinhardt
Ladybug	Hermsdorfer Celluloidwarenfabrik
Mermaid	Schoberl & Becker

Mold Index (cont.)

Mold	Numbers	Maker	Mold	Numbers	Maker
750	130	A. Marseille	1123	20	Alt, Beck & Gottschalck
758	161	Simon & Halbig	1127	20	Alt, Beck & Gottschalck
759	161	Simon & Halbig	1129	137	Simon & Halbig
769	161	Simon & Halbig	1142	20, 21, 34	Alt, Beck & Gottschalck
784	20, 21	Alt, Beck & Gottschalck	1144	21	Alt, Beck & Gottschalck
786	21	Alt, Beck & Gottschalck	1148	164	Simon & Halbig
790	13, 130	A. Marseille	1159	24, 137, 164	Simon & Halbig
800	133	A. Marseille	1160	166	Simon & Halbig
830	11		1170	162	Simon & Halbig
833	11		1199	137	Simon & Halbig
852	165	Simon & Halbig	1200	53	Catterfelder Puppenfabrik
870	20	Alt, Beck & Gottschalck	1210	20, 21	Alt, Beck & Gottschalck
880	12, 21	Alt, Beck & Gottschalck, Borgfeldt	1214	20, 21	Alt, Beck & Gottschalck
881	14		1234	20	Alt, Beck & Gottschalck
882	21	Alt, Beck & Gottschalck	1235	20	Alt, Beck & Gottschalck
886	14, 165	Simon & Halbig	1246	164	Simon & Halbig
890	14, 20, 34	Alt, Beck & Gottschalck,	1248	43, 162	Simon & Halbig
		Simon & Halbig	1249	162	Simon & Halbig
900	130	A. Marseille	1250	162	Simon & Halbig
905	161	Simon & Halbig	1254	20	Alt, Beck & Gottschalck
908	161	Simon & Halbig	1256	34	Alt, Beck & Gottschalck
911	20	Alt, Beck & Gottschalck	1260	162	Simon & Halbig
912	20	Alt, Beck & Gottschalck	1262	150	Schmidt, Franz
915	20	Alt, Beck & Gottschalck	1263	150	Schmidt, Franz
916	20	Alt, Beck & Gottschalck	1267	150	Schmidt, Franz
919	163	Simon & Halbig	1269	163	Simon & Halbig
927	130	A. Marseille	1270	150	Schmidt, Franz
929	163	Simon & Halbig	1271	150	Schmidt, Franz
930	43, 163, 165	Simon & Halbig	1272	150	Schmidt, Franz
940	164	Simon & Halbig	1279	163	Simon & Halbig
949	43, 163, 164	Simon & Halbig	1288	34	Alt, Beck & Gottschalck
950	87, 164, 165	Pozellanfabrik Mengersgereuth	1294	160	Simon & Halbig
969	164	Simon & Halbig	1295	150	Schmidt, Franz
970	42, 130	A. Marseille	1296	150	Schmidt, Franz
971	42, 130, 131	A. Marseille	1297	150	Schmidt, Franz
972	21	Amberg, Louis & Sons	1299	164	Simon & Halbig
973	21	Amberg, Louis & Sons	1302	43	Simon & Halbig
975	130	A. Marseille	1303	43	Simon & Halbig
979	161	Simon & Halbig	1303	165	Simon & Halbig
980	130	A. Marseille	1304	20, 164	Alt, Beck & Gottschalck,
982	21	Amberg, Louis & Sons			Simon & Halbig
983	21	Amberg, Louis & Sons	1305	165	Simon & Halbig
984	130	A. Marseille	1308	165	Simon & Halbig
985	130	A. Marseille	1310	150	Schmidt, Franz
990	20, 130	Alt, Beck & Gottschalck, A. Marseille	1322	19, 20, 138	Alt, Beck & Gottschalck
991	130	A. Marseille	1329	137, 138	Simon & halbig
992	42, 130	A. Marseille	1339	43	Simon & Halbig
995	42, 130	A. Marseille	1342	19, 20	Alt, Beck & Gottschalck
996	130	A. Marseille	1346	19	Alt, Beck & Gottschalck
1000	20, 21, 34, 161	Alt, Beck & Gottschalck,	1348	76	Cuno & Otto Dressel
		Simon & Halbig	1349	76	Cuno & Otto Dressel
1003	21	Alt, Beck & Gottschalck	1352	19, 20	Alt, Beck & Gottschalck
1006	136	Amusco	1357	20, 53	Alt, Beck & Gottschalck,
1008	20	Alt, Beck & Gottschalck			Catterfelder Puppenfabrik
1009	43, 162	Simon & Halbig	1358	20, 43	Alt, Beck & Gottschalck,
1010	162	Simon & Halbig			Simon & Halbig
1019	164	Simon & Halbig	1361	19, 20	Alt, Beck & Gottschalck
1020	141	Muller & Strasburger	1362	20	Alt, Beck & Gottschalck
1028	20, 21, 34	Alt, Beck & Gottschalck	1367	20	Alt, Beck & Gottschalck
1029	162	Simon & Halbig	1368	20, 25, 43	Alt, Beck & Gottschalck, Averill,
1032	20	Alt, Beck & Gottschalck			Georgene, Simon & Halbig
1039	8, 43, 162, 163, 165	Simon & Halbig	1376	158	Schuetzmeister & Quendt
1040	162	Simon & Halbig	1388	165	Simon & Halbig
1044	20	Alt, Beck & Gottschalck	1394	11	Borgfeldt
1046	20, 21	Alt, Beck & Gottschalck	1394	47	Borgfeldt
1049	162	Simon & Halbig	1402	25	Averill, Georgene
1059	162	Simon & Halbig	1410	82	Borgfeldt
1064	20, 34	Alt, Beck & Gottschalck	1428	160	Simon & Halbig
1069	162	Simon & Halbig	1448	164	Simon & Halbig
1070	109, 120,	Kestner, Koenig & Wernicke	1469	76, 164	Cuno & Otto Dressel, Simon & Halbig
1071	150	Schmidt, Franz	1478	165	Simon & Halbig
1078	162, 165, 166	Simon & Halbig	1488	161, 165	Simon & Halbig
1079	43, 166, 162	Simon & Halbig	1489	161	Simon & Halbig
1080	162	Simon & Halbig	1498	161	Simon & Halbig
1099	137	Simon & Halbig	1890	131	A. Marseille
1100	53	Catterfelder Puppenfabrik	1892	131	A. Marseille
1109	162	Simon & Halbig	1893	131	A. Marseille
1112	21	Alt, Beck & Gottschalck	1894	42, 131, 132	A. Marseille

Name Index

Name Index (cont.)

Name Index (cont.)

Name Index (cont.)